TEST BANK II

TEST BANK II

JOHN BRINK
Calvin College

to accompany

David G. Myers

Psychology
Sixth Edition

WORTH PUBLISHERS

Test Bank II
by John Brink
to accompany
Myers: **Psychology**, Sixth Edition

Printed in the United States of America

ISBN: 1-57259-996-0
        1-57259-961-8 (Test Banks I and II package)

Printing: 5 4 3 2 1

Year: 04 03 02 01

Cover art by John Collier

Worth Publishers
41 Madison Avenue
New York, NY 10010
www.worthpublishers.com

Contents

Preface

Test Bank II to accompany *Psychology*, Sixth Edition, by David G. Myers includes almost 2000 carefully crafted multiple-choice questions, covering each of the eighteen textbook chapters. With our two test banks, instructors can now choose from more than 4000 test questions, many of which have been newly created for this latest edition of *Psychology*. This test bank also contains questions on the PsychSim computer simulations, the PsychQuest CD-ROM modules, and *The Brain*, Second Edition, and *The Mind*, Second Edition, modules.

Preceding each multiple-choice question, the following information is provided to help you to select questions.

1. Chapter topic: Taken from the textbook headings and subheadings, this identification tag allows you to scan the questions and select the appropriate balance of questions from the topics you wish to cover.

2. Textbook page number: This provides you with a reference should students question the basis for an answer. Some instructors may wish to provide students who answered incorrectly with this page number so that they can see the correct answer in context.

3. Difficulty level: Each item is rated "easy," "medium," or "difficult." You can select those that challenge your students to the extent appropriate for your course. About half the questions are in the "medium" range, one quarter "easy," and one quarter "difficult." As new items are added to the Test Bank, we continue to assess item difficulty so that about half the questions are in the "medium" range, one-quarter "easy," and one-quarter "difficult."

4. Type of question: Either factual/definitional or conceptual.

   Factual/definitional questions test students' knowledge of information that is explicitly presented in the textbook. Specifically, they test knowledge of methods and theories, research discoveries, important people and events, and the language of psychology. Approximately 60 percent of the questions are factual/definitional.

   Conceptual questions test students' ability to analyze, synthesize, or apply information presented in the textbook. Conceptual questions may require deduction from general principles or the application of psychological facts or concepts to everyday life. Approximately 40 percent of the questions are conceptual.

5. Learning objectives: Each question is keyed to one of the learning objectives listed on the first page of each chapter of this Test Bank, and also in the Instructor's Resources.

These Test Bank questions are the database for a test-generation program available on a single CD-ROM in both Windows and Macintosh formats. Instructors who adopt Psychology, 6/e, may obtain the electronic version of the Test Bank and test-generating software from Worth Publishers. The computerized version of the Test Bank allows instructors to select questions either manually or randomly, to edit questions, and to print multiple versions of an exam. The computerized Test Bank also includes Internet testing functionality. This will give the instructor the option of posting the test on the Internet, in addition to the standard option of creating a print or network-administered exam.

I wish to express special appreciation to Janet Sheeres for her word-processing efficiency and to Betty Shapiro Probert of The Special Projects Group for her valuable editorial help with this Test Bank. The Test Bank has also benefitted from validation information and other feedback from its users, and I welcome such information and feedback from you, plus any suggestions you may have for making the testing package more effective.

John Brink
June 2000

TEST BANK II

Introduction

Learning Objectives

Psychology's Roots (pp. 2-4)

1. Define *psychology* and trace its historical development.

Psychology's Big Issues (pp. 4-6)

2. Describe psychology's concerns regarding stability and change, rationality and irrationality, nature and nurture.

Psychology's Perspectives (pp. 6-7)

3. Briefly describe the different perspectives from which psychologists examine behavior and mental processes and explain their complementarity.

Psychology's Subfields (pp. 7-9)

4. Identify some of the basic and applied research subfields of psychology.

5. Describe the mental health professions of clinical psychology and psychiatry.

Studying Psychology (pp. 10-11)

6. Discuss several principles for effective learning and explain the PRTR study method.

Psychology's roots, p. 2
Difficult, Factual/Definitional, Objective 1, Ans: b

1. Wilhelm Wundt, who founded the first psychology laboratory, was both a:
    a. psychoanalyst and psychiatrist.
    b. physiologist and philosopher.
    c. sociologist and psychiatrist.
    d. theologian and philosopher.

Psychology's roots, p. 2
Medium, Factual/Definitional, Objective 1, Ans: a
2.   Ivan Pavlov pioneered the study of:
      a. learning.
      b. perception.
      c. personality.
      d. mental illness.

Psychology's roots, p. 4
Medium, Factual/Definitional, Objective 1, Ans: b
3.   Wilhelm Wundt was concerned primarily with the study of:
      a. maladaptive behaviors.
      b. mental processes.
      c. inherited traits.
      d. social relationships.

Psychology's roots, p. 4
Difficult, Conceptual, Objective 1, Ans: e
4.   In a study of human visual experience, research participants are asked to carefully monitor and describe their own immediate and ongoing visual sensations. The participants are employing a research technique known as:
      a. PRTR.
      b. clinical intuition.
      c. psychoanalysis.
      d. natural selection.
      e. introspection.

Psychology's roots, p. 4
Difficult, Conceptual, Objective 1, Ans: a
5.   The study of inner thoughts and feelings is to the study of observable behavior as _____ is to _____.
      a. Wundt; Watson
      b. Aristotle; Plato
      c. Watson; Freud
      d. Freud; Wundt

Psychology's roots, p. 4
Difficult, Conceptual, Objective 1, Ans: c
6.   Behavior is to mental processes as _____ is to _____.
      a. nature; nurture
      b. sensation; memory
      c. talking; understanding
      d. stability; change

Psychology's roots, p. 4
Easy, Factual/Definitional, Objective 1, Ans: d
7.   In order to evaluate various theories of human behavior, contemporary psychologists rely most heavily on the process of:
      a. introspection.
      b. psychoanalysis.
      c. natural selection.
      d. scientific observation.

Psychology's big issues, p. 4
Medium, Conceptual, Objective 2, Ans: d
8. Mr. Firkin wonders whether his quiet and introverted 15-year-old son will ever become a more extraverted and talkative adult. Mr. Firkin is primarily concerned with the issue of:
   a. behavior versus mental processes.
   b. nature versus nurture.
   c. rationality versus irrationality.
   d. stability versus change.

Psychology's big issues, p. 5
Medium, Conceptual, Objective 2, Ans: c
9. Gloria was surprised to discover the extent to which her own ethnic and sexual stereotypes biased her perceptions of others. Gloria's reaction most directly highlights the issue of:
   a. nature versus nurture.
   b. stability versus change.
   c. rationality versus irrationality.
   d. behavior versus mental processes.

Psychology's big issues, p. 5
Easy, Conceptual, Objective 2, Ans: c
10. Angie wonders whether her calm and relaxed personality style was learned or inherited. Angie's concern is most directly relevant to the issue of:
    a. stability versus change.
    b. behavior versus mental processes.
    c. nature versus nurture.
    d. rationality versus irrationality.

Psychology's big issues, p. 5
Medium, Conceptual, Objective 2, Ans: d
11. Experience is to genes as _____ is to _____.
    a. chromosome; DNA
    b. heredity; environment
    c. Wundt; Pavlov
    d. nurture; nature
    e. Plato; Aristotle

Psychology's big issues, p. 5
Difficult, Factual/Definitional, Objective 2, Ans: d
12. Which philosopher emphasized that certain ideas were inborn and NOT dependent upon sensory experience?
    a. Aristotle
    b. David Hume
    c. John Locke
    d. Plato

Psychology's big issues, p. 5
Difficult, Factual/Definitional, Objective 2, Ans: a
13. John Locke emphasized that human knowledge is a product of:
    a. sensory experience.
    b. natural selection.
    c. brain chemistry.
    d. unconscious forces.

Psychology's big issues, p. 5
Medium, Factual/Definitional, Objective 2, Ans: b
14.   Plato and Aristotle disagreed about the relative importance of:
       a. basic and applied research.
       b. nature and nurture.
       c. behavior and mental processes.
       d. psychology and psychiatry.

Psychology's big issues, p. 5
Difficult, Conceptual, Objective 2, Ans: b
15.   Nature is to nurture as _____ is to _____.
       a. behavioral perspective; evolutionary perspective
       b. Descartes; Locke
       c. social-cultural perspective; neuroscience perspective
       d. Aristotle; Plato

Psychology's big issues, p. 5
Difficult, Conceptual, Objective 2, Ans: d
16.   Plato and Descartes would have been most likely to agree that:
       a. the mind is like a blank table at birth.
       b. mind and brain are really the same thing.
       c. psychologists should focus on the study of observable behavior.
       d. psychologists can obtain valuable knowledge without the use of scientific observation.

Psychology's big issues, p. 5
Easy, Factual/Definitional, Objective 2, Ans: b
17.   Charles Darwin suggested that the evolution of living organisms is guided by:
       a. rational thought.
       b. natural selection.
       c. introspection.
       d. unconscious motives.

Psychology's big issues, p. 5
Difficult, Factual/Definitional, Objective 2, Ans: c
18.   The inheritance of behavioral characteristics was emphasized by:
       a. John Locke.
       b. John Watson.
       c. Charles Darwin.
       d. all the above.

Psychology's perspectives, p. 6
Easy, Factual/Definitional, Objective 3, Ans: e
19.   Which perspective is most directly concerned with how the brain influences behaviors and
       mental states?
       a. cognitive
       b. social-cultural
       c. psychodynamic
       d. behavioral
       e. neuroscience

Psychology's perspectives, p. 6
Medium, Conceptual, Objective 3, Ans: d

20. Which perspective is most relevant to understanding the impact of strokes and brain diseases on memory?
     a. evolutionary
     b. behavioral
     c. psychodynamic
     d. neuroscience
     e. behavior genetics

Psychology's perspectives, p. 6
Medium, Conceptual, Objective 3, Ans: c

21. In a class lecture, Professor Hampton emphasized the extent to which abnormal body chemistry can contribute to psychological disorders. The professor's lecture highlighted a _____ perspective on psychological disorders.
     a. psychodynamic
     b. behavior genetics
     c. neuroscience
     d. social-cultural
     e. cognitive

Psychology's perspectives, p. 6
Easy, Factual/Definitional, Objective 3, Ans: b

22. The evolutionary perspective emphasizes the impact of _____ on human traits.
     a. introspection
     b. natural selection
     c. unconscious motives
     d. rational thought

Psychology's perspectives, p. 6
Medium, Factual/Definitional, Objective 3, Ans: a

23. Which perspective highlights the reproductive advantages of specific behavioral traits?
     a. evolutionary
     b. cognitive
     c. behavioral
     d. social-cultural
     e. behavior genetics

Psychology's perspectives, p. 6
Medium, Conceptual, Objective 3, Ans: c

24. Mark believes that people's dislike of bitter-tasting foods is an inherited trait because it has enhanced human survival. His belief best illustrates the _____ perspective.
     a. psychodynamic
     b. social-cultural
     c. evolutionary
     d. behavioral
     e. cognitive

Psychology's perspectives, p. 6
Easy, Factual/Definitional, Objective 3, Ans: e
25.   Which perspective is most directly concerned with understanding the relative impact of heredity and experience on personality development?
       a. cognitive
       b. behavioral
       c. psychodynamic
       d. neuroscience
       e. behavior genetics

Psychology's perspectives, p. 6
Medium, Conceptual, Objective 3, Ans: c
26.   The behavior genetics perspective would be most directly concerned with the issue of:
       a. stability or change.
       b. rationality or irrationality.
       c. nature or nurture.
       d. behavior or mental processes.
       e. basic research or applied research.

Psychology's perspectives, p. 6
Difficult, Conceptual, Objective 3, Ans: b
27.   Professor Reed estimates that most of the variation in people's susceptibility to depression can be attributed to hereditary differences. The professor's assessment would be most directly relevant to the _____ perspective.
       a. psychodynamic
       b. behavior genetics
       c. neuroscience
       d. cognitive
       e. evolutionary

Psychology's perspectives, p. 6
Easy, Factual/Definitional, Objective 3, Ans: b
28.   A clinical psychologist who explains behavior in terms of unconscious drives and conflicts is employing a(n) _____ perspective.
       a. evolutionary
       b. psychodynamic
       c. behavioral
       d. social-cultural

Psychology's perspectives, p. 6
Medium, Conceptual, Objective 3, Ans: c
29.   The high school counselor has suggested that Skylar's romantic feelings for her physics teacher reflect her unconscious longings for affection from her father. The counselor's assessment reflects a(n) _____ perspective.
       a. behavioral
       b. evolutionary
       c. psychodynamic
       d. social-cultural

Psychology's perspectives, p. 6
Medium, Factual/Definitional, Objective 3, Ans: a

30. The behavioral perspective emphasizes the influence of _____ on behavior.
    a. environmental circumstances
    b. unconscious motives
    c. brain chemistry
    d. heredity

Psychology's perspectives, p. 6
Medium, Factual/Definitional, Objective 3, Ans: a

31. The behavioral perspective is most likely to emphasize the importance of:
    a. learning.
    b. introspection.
    c. natural selection.
    d. self-esteem.

Psychology's perspectives, p. 6
Difficult, Conceptual, Objective 3, Ans: a

32. Natassia believes that boys learn to be more aggressive than girls primarily because they are more likely than girls to be encouraged by adults to fight. Natassia's belief most directly exemplifies the _____ perspective.
    a. behavioral
    b. evolutionary
    c. cognitive
    d. behavior genetics
    e. neuroscience

Psychology's perspectives, p. 6
Difficult, Conceptual, Objective 3, Ans: b

33. The evolutionary perspective is to _____ as the behavioral perspective is to _____.
    a. observation; introspection
    b. nature; nurture
    c. basic research; applied research
    d. rationality; irrationality

Psychology's perspectives, p. 6
Easy, Factual/Definitional, Objective 3, Ans: a

34. Which psychological perspective highlights the manner in which people encode, process, store, and retrieve information?
    a. cognitive
    b. psychodynamic
    c. behavioral
    d. behavior genetics
    e. evolutionary

Psychology's perspectives, p. 6
Medium, Conceptual, Objective 3, Ans: d

35. The study of human problem-solving strategies is most likely to be a central focus of the _____ perspective.
    a. behavioral
    b. evolutionary
    c. social-cultural
    d. cognitive
    e. behavior genetics

Psychology's perspectives, p. 6
Medium, Conceptual, Objective 3, Ans: b

36. Dr. MacPherson believes that the way students attend to, organize, and think about the information in their textbooks will strongly influence their ability to later remember and use what they have studied. Dr. MacPherson's ideas most directly exemplify the _____ perspective.
    a. social-cultural
    b. cognitive
    c. psychodynamic
    d. behavioral
    e. neuroscience

Psychology's perspectives, p. 6
Easy, Factual/Definitional, Objective 3, Ans: d

37. Which psychological perspective is most likely to examine how group membership influences individual attitudes and behaviors?
    a. neuroscience
    b. cognitive
    c. evolutionary
    d. social-cultural

Psychology's perspectives, p. 6
Medium, Conceptual, Objective 3, Ans: e

38. Dr. Kozak has concluded that the unusually low incidence of alcoholism among citizens of a small African country can be attributed to strong fundamentalistic religious influences in that region. This belief best illustrates a(n) _____ perspective.
    a. behavior genetics
    b. cognitive
    c. psychodynamic
    d. neuroscience
    e. social-cultural

Psychology's perspectives, p. 6
Medium, Conceptual, Objective 3, Ans: a

39. Karen insists that intellectual skills are inherited, whereas Claire argues that intelligence is developed through educational experiences. Karen and Claire have differing perspectives on intelligence that:
    a. may complement one another.
    b. are impossible to test scientifically.
    c. illustrate the distinction between behavior and mental processes.
    d. illustrate the conflict between psychology and psychiatry.

Psychology's perspectives, p. 7
Medium, Factual/Definitional, Objective 3, Ans: a

40. A theoretical perspective in psychology can be like a two-dimensional view of a three-dimensional object because each perspective is:
    a. limited in its scope.
    b. likely to contradict other perspectives.
    c. of little value for applied research.
    d. impossible to test scientifically.

Psychology's subfields, p. 8
Easy, Conceptual, Objective 4, Ans: b

41. Dr. Tiao conducts basic research on the effects of head injuries on people's problem-solving and abstract-reasoning skills. Which psychological specialty does her research best represent?
    a. developmental psychology
    b. biological psychology
    c. industrial/organizational psychology
    d. personality psychology

Psychology's subfields, p. 8
Medium, Conceptual, Objective 4, Ans: c

42. Dr. Winkle conducts basic research on the systematic changes in intelligence associated with aging. It is most likely that Dr. Winkle is a(n) _____ psychologist.
    a. clinical
    b. social
    c. developmental
    d. industrial/organizational

Psychology's subfields, p. 8
Difficult, Conceptual, Objective 4, Ans: e

43. Dr. Howard conducts basic research on the relative effectiveness of massed practice and spaced practice on a person's ability to remember information. Dr. Howard is most likely a _____ psychologist.
    a. social
    b. developmental
    c. personality
    d. biological
    e. cognitive

Psychology's subfields, p. 8
Medium, Conceptual, Objective 4, Ans: d

44. Dr. Wilcox conducts basic research on the behavioral differences between introverted and extraverted people. Dr. Wilcox is most likely a(n) _____ psychologist.
    a. biological
    b. clinical
    c. industrial/organizational
    d. personality

Psychology's subfields, p. 8
Medium, Conceptual, Objective 4, Ans: c

45.   Dr. Veenstra conducts basic research on the impact of racial stereotypes on prejudicial behaviors. Dr. Veenstra is most likely a(n) _____ psychologist.
   a. developmental
   b. clinical
   c. social
   d. biological
   e. industrial/organizational

Psychology's subfields, p. 8
Medium, Conceptual, Objective 4, Ans: b

46.   Dr. Ochoa develops tests to accurately identify the most qualified job applicants in a large manufacturing firm. Which psychological specialty does Dr. Ochoa's work best represent?
   a. developmental psychology
   b. industrial/organizational psychology
   c. biological psychology
   d. clinical psychology
   e. psychiatry

Psychology's subfields, p. 8
Easy, Factual/Definitional, Objective 5, Ans: c

47.   Which professional specialty focuses on the diagnosis and treatment of people with psychological disorders?
   a. personality psychology
   b. biological psychology
   c. clinical psychology
   d. developmental psychology

Psychology's subfields, p. 8
Medium, Conceptual, Objective 5, Ans: c

48.   Working in a community mental health center, Dr. Thatcher treats adults who suffer from severe depression. Dr. Thatcher is most likely a(n) _____ psychologist.
   a. personality
   b. industrial/organizational
   c. clinical
   d. developmental

Psychology's subfields, p. 8
Easy, Factual/Definitional, Objective 5, Ans: d

49.   The specialist who is most likely to prescribe a drug for the treatment of a psychological disorder is a:
   a. developmental psychologist.
   b. clinical psychologist.
   c. personality psychologist.
   d. psychiatrist.

Studying psychology, p. 10
Medium, Conceptual, Objective 6, Ans: c

50. The PRTR method encourages students to:
    a. read each text chapter quickly in order to minimize boredom.
    b. read each text chapter without any preconceptions about what they might learn.
    c. preview a text chapter's organization before actually reading the chapter itself.
    d. read entire text chapters at one sitting in order to maximize comprehension.
    e. do all the above.

Studying psychology, p. 11
Easy, Factual/Definitional, Objective 6, Ans: a

51. For effective mastery of course material, the text emphasizes the value of:
    a. spaced practice and overlearning.
    b. speed reading and massed practice.
    c. introspection and psychoanalysis.
    d. all the above.

SPECIAL NOTE TO TEST BANK USERS

Multiple-choice test questions covering *PsychSim* computer simulations, *PsychQuest* modules, *The Brain* 2nd Ed. video modules, and *The Mind* 2nd Ed. video modules are located in this test bank after Chapter 18.

CHAPTER 1

Thinking Critically With Psychological Science

Learning Objectives

The Need for Psychological Science (pp. 13-20)

1. Describe the hindsight bias and explain how it often leads us to perceive psychological research as merely common sense.

2. Discuss how overconfidence contaminates our everyday judgments.

3. Explain how the scientific attitude encourages critical thinking.

4. Describe the relationship between psychological theories and scientific research.

Description (pp. 20-24)

5. Compare and contrast case studies, surveys, and naturalistic observation, and explain the importance of proper sampling.

Correlation (pp. 24-30)

6. Describe both positive and negative correlations, and explain how correlational measures can aid the process of prediction.

7. Explain why correlational research fails to provide evidence of cause-effect relationships.

8. Discuss how people form illusory correlations and perceive order in random sequences.

Experimentation (pp. 31-34)

9. Identify the basic elements of an experiment, and discuss how experimental control contributes to causal explanation.

Statistical Reasoning (pp. 34-38)

10. Explain how bar graphs can be designed to make a small difference appear to be large.

11. Describe the three measures of central tendency and the two measures of variation.

12.   Discuss three important principles in making generalizations from samples, and describe how psychologists make inferences about differences between groups.

Frequently Asked Questions About Psychology (pp. 39-44)

13.   Explain the value of artificially simplified laboratory conditions in learning about principles of behavior, and discuss the generalizability of psychological research in terms of culture and gender.

14.   Explain why psychologists study animals, and discuss the ethics of experimentation with both animals and humans.

15.   Describe how personal values can influence psychologists' research and its application, and discuss the possibility for misuse of research findings.

Did we know it all along?, p. 14
Medium, Factual/Definitional, Objective 1, Ans: c
1.   The hindsight bias most directly contributes to the perception that:
      a. psychological theories are simply reflections of researchers' personal values.
      b. psychological experiments are artificial.
      c. psychological theories and observations are merely common sense.
      d. psychology is potentially dangerous.

Did we know it all along?, pp. 14-15
Easy, Factual/Definitional, Objective 1, Ans: e
2.   The hindsight bias leads people to perceive research findings as:
      a. invalid.
      b. unpredictable.
      c. inexplicable.
      d. unreplicable.
      e. unsurprising.

Did we know it all along?, pp. 14-15
Medium, Conceptual, Objective 1, Ans: c
3.   Whether informed that research has supported the value of cosmetic surgery for boosting self-esteem or informed that the esteem-enhancing value of cosmetic surgery has been refuted by research, most people would consider the findings to be common sense. This best illustrates the power of:
      a. random sampling.
      b. the false consensus effect.
      c. the hindsight bias.
      d. illusory correlation.
      e. the double-blind procedure.

Did we know it all along?, pp. 14-15
Medium, Conceptual, Objective 1, Ans: d

4.   If psychologists were to find that we are especially attracted to people whose traits are different from our own, this discovery would likely seem obvious and unsurprising to college students because:

    a. most students have had many personal experiences in which they were attracted to people quite different from themselves.

    b. this finding is consistent with common sense.

    c. college students are themselves very eager to interact with those who are different from themselves.

    d. students, like everyone else, have a tendency to exaggerate their ability to have foreseen the outcome of past discoveries.

Did we know it all along?, pp. 14-15
Medium, Conceptual, Objective 1, Ans: a

5.   According to Emily's grandfather, Adolf Hitler's obvious emotional instability made it clear that Germany would inevitably lose World War II. The grandfather's claim best illustrates:

    a. the hindsight bias.

    b. illusory correlation.

    c. the false consensus effect.

    d. an illusion of control.

    e. random sampling.

Did we know it all along? pp. 14-15
Medium, Factual/Definitional, Objective 1, Ans: d

6.   If falsely informed that they had correctly identified a homicide suspect, research participants subsequently recalled being highly confident at the time they made their identification. This best illustrates the dangers of:

    a. the false consensus effect.

    b. illusory correlation.

    c. an illusion of control.

    d. the hindsight bias.

Did we know it all along?, pp. 14-15
Difficult, Conceptual, Objective 1, Ans: b

7.   Dr. Donelian wants to reduce his students' perception that psychological experiments merely document the obvious. His best strategy would be to ask the students to:

    a. describe how experimental hypotheses were derived from basic psychological principles.

    b. predict the outcomes of experiments before they are told the actual results.

    c. explain the outcomes of experiments after they are told the actual results.

    d. conduct their own experiments.

    e. develop their own theories.

Overconfidence, p. 15
Easy, Factual/Definitional, Objective 2, Ans: c

8.   Our estimates of the accuracy of our own everyday judgments best demonstrate:

    a. the placebo effect.

    b. illusory correlation.

    c. overconfidence.

    d. the false consensus effect.

Overconfidence, pp. 15-16
Medium, Factual/Definitional, Objective 2, Ans: e

9. When provided with the unscrambled solution to anagrams, people underestimate the difficulty
    of solving the anagrams by themselves. This best illustrates:
    a. illusory correlation.
    b. the false consensus effect.
    c. random assignment.
    d. wording effects.
    e. overconfidence.

Overconfidence, pp. 15-16
Easy, Conceptual, Objective 2, Ans: a

10. As people prepare for a test, they often believe that they understand the course material better
    than they actually do. This best illustrates:
    a. overconfidence.
    b. illusory correlation.
    c. the false consensus effect.
    d. critical thinking.

Overconfidence, pp. 15-16
Medium, Conceptual, Objective 2, Ans: a

11. Thinking that she had outperformed most of her classmates, Glenda was surprised to receive
    just an average grade on her psychology test. Glenda's experience best illustrates:
    a. overconfidence.
    b. the hindsight bias.
    c. the false consensus effect.
    d. negative correlation.
    e. illusory correlation.

The scientific attitude, p. 16
Medium, Factual/Definitional, Objective 3, Ans: a

12. When Moses encouraged the testing of whether a prophet's predictions actually proved true, he
    best illustrated the appropriateness of:
    a. skeptical inquiry.
    b. overconfidence.
    c. the placebo effect.
    d. the false consensus effect.
    e. random sampling.

The scientific attitude, p. 17
Difficult, Factual/Definitional, Objective 3, Ans: c

13. As scientists, psychologists adopt an attitude of skepticism because they believe that:
    a. people are unlikely to reveal what they are really thinking.
    b. most common sense ideas about human behavior are wrong.
    c. ideas about human behavior need to be objectively tested.
    d. all the above are true.

The scientific attitude, p. 17
Easy, Conceptual, Objective 3, Ans: c

14. Those who approach the study of psychology with an attitude of curious skepticism are especially likely to:
    a. perceive illusory correlations.
    b. ignore disconfirming evidence.
    c. question the validity of research findings.
    d. demonstrate overconfidence.
    e. dismiss the value of replication.

The scientific attitude, p. 17
Medium, Factual/Definitional, Objective 3, Ans: a

15. When psychologists insist that "the rat is always right," they are emphasizing the scientific attitude of:
    a. humility.
    b. respect for animals.
    c. ecological sensitivity.
    d. enthusiasm for animal research studies.

The scientific attitude, p. 17
Easy, Factual/Definitional, Objective 3, Ans: a

16. Critical thinkers can best be described as:
    a. questioning.
    b. cynical.
    c. overconfident.
    d. pessimistic.
    e. impatient.

The scientific attitude, p. 17
Medium, Conceptual, Objective 3, Ans: b

17. A willingness to question others' assumptions is to _____ as a willingness to question our own preconceptions is to _____.
    a. the survey; naturalistic observation
    b. skepticism; humility
    c. overconfidence; hindsight bias
    d. experimentation; replication

The scientific method, p. 18
Easy, Factual/Definitional, Objective 4, Ans: c

18. An explanation using an integrated set of principles that organizes and predicts observations is called a(n):
    a. experiment.
    b. hypothesis.
    c. theory.
    d. survey.

The scientific method, p. 18
Medium, Conceptual, Objective 4, Ans: e

19.   According to Professor Fayad, we like people who like us because their affection for us boosts our own self-esteem. His idea is an example of:
      a. naturalistic observation.
      b. illusory correlation.
      c. hindsight bias.
      d. the false consensus effect.
      e. a theory.

The scientific method, pp. 18-19
Difficult, Conceptual, Objective 4, Ans: c

20.   Compared to nonscientific theories, the unique feature of scientific theories is that they:
      a. provide explanations.
      b. guide observations.
      c. generate testable hypotheses.
      d. are never disconfirmed.

The scientific method, p. 19
Medium, Factual/Definitional, Objective 4, Ans: e

21.   Hypotheses are best described as:
      a. assumptions.
      b. replications.
      c. explanations.
      d. confirmations.
      e. predictions.

The scientific method, p. 19
Easy, Conceptual, Objective 4, Ans: c

22.   A specification of how a researcher manipulates an independent variable is known as a(n):
      a. control condition.
      b. replication.
      c. operational definition.
      d. hypothesis.

The scientific method, p. 19
Medium, Conceptual, Objective 4, Ans: d

23.   In reporting the impact of alcohol consumption on self-consciousness, psychological researchers would specify exactly how they measured self-consciousness. They are thereby providing a(n):
      a. experimental hypothesis.
      b. standard deviation.
      c. double-blind procedure.
      d. operational definition.

The scientific method, p. 19
Medium, Conceptual, Objective 4, Ans: a

24.   Operational definitions are most likely to facilitate:
      a. replication.
      b. illusory correlation.
      c. hindsight bias.
      d. the false consensus effect.

The scientific method, p. 19
Easy, Factual/Definitional, Objective 4, Ans: c

25. Replication involves:
    a. the selection of random samples.
    b. perceiving order in random events.
    c. repeating an earlier research study.
    d. rejecting ideas that cannot be scientifically tested.
    e. overestimating the extent to which others share our views.

The scientific method, p. 19
Medium, Factual/Definitional, Objective 4, Ans: c

26. In order to verify a new scientific discovery, psychological researchers are most likely to engage in the process of:
    a. naturalistic observation.
    b. random sampling.
    c. replication.
    d. positive correlation.
    e. hypothesis generation.

The scientific method, p. 19
Difficult, Conceptual, Objective 4, Ans: a

27. On the basis of his own research, Professor Bolden claims that eating an apple every day helps improve children's reading skills. How might he best offer further support for this claim?
    a. replication
    b. naturalistic observation
    c. random sampling
    d. correlational research

The case study, p. 20
Medium, Conceptual, Objective 5, Ans: c

28. In order to gain further understanding of how brain malfunctions influence behavior, Dr. Mosher extensively and carefully observed and questioned two stroke victims. Which research method did Dr. Mosher employ?
    a. random sampling
    b. the survey
    c. the case study
    d. experimentation

The case study, p. 20
Difficult, Factual/Definitional, Objective 5, Ans: c

29. Which research method did Sigmund Freud use extensively in the process of developing his well-known theory of personality?
    a. the survey
    b. naturalistic observation
    c. the case study
    d. experimentation

The case study, p. 21
Medium, Factual/Definitional, Objective 5, Ans: d

30. Those who rely on the case-study method need to be especially alert to the dangers of:
    a. hindsight bias.
    b. the false consensus effect.
    c. random assignment.
    d. false generalization.

The case study, p. 21
Difficult, Conceptual, Objective 5, Ans: b

31. After helping two psychotherapy clients deal with the loss of their jobs, Dr. Price began to grossly overestimate the national rate of unemployment. In this instance, Dr. Price should be warned of the limits of:
    a. surveys.
    b. case studies.
    c. correlational evidence.
    d. the hindsight bias.

The survey, p. 21
Easy, Factual/Definitional, Objective 5, Ans: b

32. The survey is a research method in which:
    a. individuals are carefully observed in their natural environments.
    b. a representative sample of individuals are questioned regarding their opinions or behaviors.
    c. an individual is studied in great detail.
    d. an investigator determines the extent to which two variables influence each other.

The survey, p. 21
Medium, Conceptual, Objective 5, Ans: a

33. Which of the following techniques would be the most effective way of investigating the relationship between the political preferences and the economic status of North Americans?
    a. the survey
    b. naturalistic observation
    c. experimentation
    d. the case study

The survey, p. 21
Easy, Conceptual, Objective 5, Ans: e

34. A majority of respondents in a national survey agreed that "classroom prayer should not be allowed in public schools." Only 33 percent of respondents in a similar survey agreed that "classroom prayer in public schools should be banned." These divergent findings best illustrate the importance of:
    a. an illusion of control.
    b. the hindsight bias.
    c. the false consensus effect.
    d. sampling errors.
    e. wording effects.

The survey, p. 22
Easy, Factual/Definitional, Objective 5, Ans: d
35.   The false consensus effect refers to the tendency to:
      a. perceive a relationship where none exists.
      b. generalize from extreme cases.
      c. reject ideas that can't be scientifically tested.
      d. exaggerate the extent to which others agree with us.
      e. ignore disconfirming evidence.

The survey, p. 22
Medium, Conceptual, Objective 5, Ans: a
36.   Because Julie thinks very highly of herself, she assumes that she is well regarded by most of
      her acquaintances. This conclusion best illustrates:
      a. the false consensus effect.
      b. the hindsight bias.
      c. the placebo effect.
      d. an illusion of control.

The survey, p. 22
Difficult, Conceptual, Objective 5, Ans: a
37.   Christine, who is opposed to capital punishment, was extremely surprised to learn that the
      results of a survey indicated that the vast majority of the population approved of capital
      punishment. Christine's surprise best illustrates the power of:
      a. the false consensus effect.
      b. the placebo effect.
      c. random assignment.
      d. the double-blind procedure.
      e. the hindsight bias.

The survey, p. 22
Easy, Factual/Definitional, Objective 5, Ans: b
38.   The complete set of cases from which samples may be drawn is called a(n):
      a. control condition.
      b. population.
      c. case study.
      d. independent variable.
      e. survey.

The survey, p. 22
Medium, Conceptual, Objective 5, Ans: e
39.   In order to learn about the political attitudes of all students enrolled at Arizona State
      University, Professor Marlow randomly selected 800 of these students to complete an attitude
      questionnaire. In this instance, all the students enrolled at Arizona State University are
      considered to be a(n):
      a. independent variable.
      b. representative sample.
      c. control condition.
      d. dependent variable.
      e. population.

The survey, p. 22
Medium, Factual/Definitional, Objective 5, Ans: b
40. A random sample of a large group is one in which:
    a. the number of people included in the sample is determined by chance.
    b. every member in the group has an equal chance of being included.
    c. personality differences among research participants are practically nonexistent.
    d. all the above are true.

The survey, p. 22
Medium, Factual/Definitional, Objective 5, Ans: e
41. Which procedure helps to ensure that the participants in a survey are representative of a larger population?
    a. random assignment
    b. replication
    c. correlation
    d. naturalistic observation
    e. random sampling

The survey, p. 22
Easy, Factual/Definitional, Objective 5, Ans: d
42. In order to generalize accurately, it is important to observe a _____ sample of cases.
    a. diverse
    b. homogeneous
    c. self-selected
    d. representative
    e. memorable

The survey, p. 22
Medium, Conceptual, Objective 5, Ans: a
43. After she was painfully deceived by her boyfriend, Mary concluded that men just can't be trusted. In this instance, Mary ought to remind herself that reasonable generalizations depend on:
    a. observing representative samples.
    b. recognizing that others may not share our opinions.
    c. distinguishing causation from mere correlation.
    d. realizing that random events may not look random.

The survey, p. 22
Difficult, Conceptual, Objective 5, Ans: b
44. Mrs. Blair concludes that boys do not read as well as girls because the vast majority of students in her remedial reading classes are boys. Mrs. Blair's conclusion best illustrates the danger of:
    a. the hindsight bias.
    b. generalizing from select cases.
    c. confusing correlation with causation.
    d. the false consensus effect.

The survey, p. 23
Difficult, Factual/Definitional, Objective 5, Ans: a
45. According to Shere Hite's highly publicized research, 70 percent of women married five years or more reported having extramarital affairs. Her survey results were misleading because she failed to use a technique known as:
a. random sampling.
b. replication.
c. the double-blind procedure.
d. naturalistic observation.
e. statistical inference.

Naturalistic observation, p. 23
Difficult, Conceptual, Objective 5, Ans: a
46. In order to study the development of relationships, Dr. Rubin carefully observed and recorded patterns of verbal and nonverbal behaviors among men and women in singles bars. Which research method did Dr. Rubin employ?
a. naturalistic observation
b. replication
c. the survey
d. the case study
e. experimentation

Naturalistic observation, p. 23
Easy, Factual/Definitional, Objective 5, Ans: a
47. Naturalistic observation is most useful for:
a. describing behaviors.
b. predicting attitudes.
c. explaining complex behavior patterns.
d. uncovering cause-effect relationships.

Naturalistic observation, p. 24
Easy, Conceptual, Objective 5, Ans: b
48. Which research method would be most effective for identifying the mating rituals of North American deer?
a. survey research
b. naturalistic observation
c. experimentation
d. the double-blind procedure

Correlation, p. 24
Easy, Factual/Definitional, Objective 6, Ans: d
49. A statistical measure that indicates how well one factor predicts a second factor is called a(n):
a. dependent variable.
b. independent variable.
c. survey.
d. correlation coefficient.
e. replication.

Correlation, p. 24
Easy, Conceptual, Objective 6, Ans: d

50.   Which of the following statistical measures is most helpful for indicating the extent to which
      level of physical attractiveness can be used to predict frequency of dating?
      a. standard deviation
      b. mean
      c. medium
      d. correlation coefficient
      e. range

Correlation, p. 24
Difficult, Conceptual, Objective 6, Ans: b

51.   In order to assess the extent to which mortality rates increase as people age, researchers would
      be likely to employ:
      a. case study research.
      b. correlational research.
      c. experimental research.
      d. all the above.

Correlation, p. 24
Easy, Factual/Definitional, Objective 6, Ans: d

52.   A scatterplot graphically depicts the:
      a. standard deviation of a distribution of scores.
      b. arithmetic average of a distribution of scores.
      c. total population from which samples may be drawn.
      d. degree of relationship between two variables.

Correlation, pp. 24-25
Difficult, Factual/Definitional, Objective 6, Ans: b

53.   A researcher would be most likely to discover a negative correlation between:
      a. body height and body weight.
      b. self-esteem and depression.
      c. education and personal wealth.
      d. intelligence and academic success.

Correlation, pp. 24-25
Medium, Factual/Definitional, Objective 6, Ans: b

54.   If the points on a scatterplot are clustered in a pattern that extends from lower left to upper
      right, this would suggest that the two variables depicted are:
      a. normally distributed.
      b. positively correlated.
      c. negatively correlated.
      d. not correlated.

Correlation, pp. 24-25
Medium, Conceptual, Objective 6, Ans: b

55.   If college graduates typically earn more money than high school graduates, this would indicate
      that level of education and income are:
      a. causally related.
      b. positively correlated.
      c. independent variables.
      d. dependent variables.
      e. negatively correlated.

Correlation, pp. 24-25
Easy, Factual/Definitional, Objective 6, Ans: c

56.   A correlation coefficient is a measure of the:
    a.   difference between the highest and lowest scores in a distribution.
    b.   average squared deviation of scores from a sample mean.
    c.   direction and strength of the relationship between two variables.
    d.   statistical significance of a difference between two sample means.
    e.   frequency of scores at each level of some measure.

Correlation, p. 25
Easy, Factual/Definitional, Objective 6, Ans: d

57.   A correlation coefficient can range in value from:
    a.   0 to 100.
    b.   0 to 1.00.
    c.   1 to 99.
    d.   −1.00 to +1.00.

Correlation, p. 25
Difficult, Conceptual, Objective 6, Ans: b

58.   A correlation between self-esteem and annual income of −.75 would indicate that:
    a.   lower levels of self-esteem are associated with lower levels of annual income.
    b.   higher levels of annual income are associated with lower levels of self-esteem.
    c.   it is impossible to predict annual income levels from knowledge of self-esteem levels.
    d.   self-esteem has no causal influence on annual income.

Correlation, p. 25
Medium, Conceptual, Objective 6, Ans: d

59.   Which of the following correlations between annual income and education level would best enable you to predict annual income on the basis of level of education?
    a.   +.05
    b.   −.01
    c.   +.10
    d.   +.50
    e.   −.001

Correlation, p. 25
Medium, Conceptual, Objective 6, Ans: b

60.   Which of the following correlation coefficients expresses the strongest degree of relationship between two variables?
    a.   +.10
    b.   −.67
    c.   .00
    d.   −.10
    e.   +.59

Correlation and causation, p. 26
Easy, Factual/Definitional, Objective 7, Ans: c

61.   If those with low self-esteem are also particularly likely to suffer from depression, this would not necessarily indicate that low self-esteem triggers negative emotions because:
    a.   sampling extreme cases leads to false generalizations.
    b.   events often seem more probable in hindsight.
    c.   correlation does not prove causation.
    d.   random sequences often don't look random.

Correlation and causation, p. 26
Medium, Conceptual, Objective 7, Ans: d

62. Mr. Brown has gathered evidence showing that the weight of grade school students correlates positively with reading skill. Before he uses this evidence to conclude that body weight enhances reading ability, Mr. Brown should first be reminded that:
a. events often seem more probable in hindsight.
b. random sequences of events often don't look random.
c. sampling extreme cases leads to false generalizations.
d. correlation does not prove causation.
e. the tendency to seek confirming information promotes illusory correlations.

Correlation and causation, p. 26
Difficult, Conceptual, Objective 7, Ans: c

63. If psychologists discovered that people who live at the poverty level have more aggressive children than do wealthy people, this would indicate that:
a. poverty has a negative influence on children's behavior.
b. some of the same factors that lead to poverty also contribute to aggressiveness.
c. people's economic status and the aggressiveness of their children are negatively correlated.
d. all the above are true.

Correlation and causation, p. 26
Difficult, Conceptual, Objective 7, Ans: c

64. A positive correlation between self-esteem and academic success would indicate that:
a. a positive self-concept contributes to academic success.
b. academic success contributes to a favorable self-image.
c. those with high self-esteem are more academically successful than those with low self-esteem.
d. all the above are true.

Illusory correlations, p. 26
Easy, Factual/Definitional, Objective 8, Ans: d

65. The perception of a relationship between two variables that does not actually exist is called:
a. the hindsight bias.
b. the false consensus effect.
c. an illusion of control.
d. illusory correlation.
e. confirmation bias.

Illusory correlations, p. 26
Medium, Factual/Definitional, Objective 8, Ans: a

66. The belief that weather conditions signal the onset of arthritis pain best illustrates:
a. an illusory correlation.
b. an illusion of control.
c. the hindsight bias.
d. the false consensus effect.
e. random sampling.

Illusory correlations, p. 26
Difficult, Factual/Definitional, Objective 8, Ans: d

67. The sequential occurrence of two highly unusual events is most likely to contribute to:
     a. the false consensus effect.
     b. the hindsight bias.
     c. the placebo effect.
     d. an illusory correlation.

Illusory correlations, p. 26
Medium, Conceptual, Objective 8, Ans: b

68. Because she had a serious traffic accident on Friday the 13th of last month, Sheryl is convinced that all Friday the 13ths will bring bad luck. Sheryl's belief best illustrates:
     a. the illusion of control.
     b. illusory correlation.
     c. the hindsight bias.
     d. the false consensus effect.
     e. random sampling.

Perceiving order in random events, p. 28
Difficult, Factual/Definitional, Objective 8, Ans: d

69. If someone were to flip a coin six times, which of the following sequences of heads (H) and tails (T) would be most likely?
     a. H H H T T T
     b. H T T H T H
     c. H H H H H H
     d. All the above would be equally likely.

Perceiving order in random events, pp. 28-29
Medium, Conceptual, Objective 8, Ans: c

70. Daniel and Donald are identical twins who were separated at birth and raised in different countries. When they were finally reunited for the first time as adults, the men were amazed to discover that they were both plumbers, both avid tennis players, and both addicted to chocolates. The men would be best advised to recognize the danger of:
     a. randomly sampling their life experiences.
     b. attributing their similarities to chance.
     c. perceiving order in random events.
     d. assuming that most people share their attitudes and interests.

Perceiving order in random events, pp. 28-29
Difficult, Conceptual, Objective 8, Ans: e

71. The King James Version of the Bible was completed when William Shakespeare was forty-six years old. In Psalm 46 of this translation, the forty-sixth word is "shake," and the forty-sixth word from the end is "spear." Before concluding that the biblical translators were trying to be humorous with these specific word placements, you would be best advised to recognize the danger of:
     a. explaining events in hindsight.
     b. randomly sampling biblical passages.
     c. generalizing from extreme examples.
     d. assuming that most people share your opinions.
     e. perceiving order in coincidental events.

Perceiving order in random events, p. 29
Difficult, Factual/Definitional, Objective 8, Ans: a
72.   The fact that the very same individual won the New Jersey lottery on two separate occasions best illustrates:
      a. the laws of statistical probability.
      b. an illusion of control.
      c. the false consensus effect.
      d. illusory correlation.

Thinking critically about hot and cold streaks (Box), p. 30
Medium, Factual/Definitional, Objective 8, Ans: d
73.   People tend to _____ the extent to which professional basketball players' successful shots are made in succession.
      a. radically underestimate
      b. slightly underestimate
      c. accurately estimate
      d. overestimate

Thinking critically about hot and cold streaks (Box), p. 30
Difficult, Factual/Definitional, Objective 8, Ans: d
74.   Mutual fund investors who are tempted to move their assets to the top-performing funds of the previous year should be reminded of the dangers of:
      a. naturalistic observation.
      b. random sampling.
      c. the false consensus effect.
      d. illusory correlation.

Experimentation, p. 31
Easy, Factual/Definitional, Objective 9, Ans: a
75.   Incorrectly interpreting correlation as evidence of causation is best avoided by making use of:
      a. the experiment.
      b. survey research.
      c. the case study.
      d. naturalistic observation.

Experimentation, p. 31
Medium, Conceptual, Objective 9, Ans: a
76.   Which of the following research strategies would provide the most effective way of demonstrating that the observation of violence on television causes children to act aggressively?
      a. the experiment
      b. naturalistic observation
      c. the survey
      d. the case study

Experimentation, p. 31
Difficult, Conceptual, Objective 9, Ans: c

77.   Experimentation is more useful than correlational measures for testing the claim that:
    a. children who view a great deal of television violence are also likely to be unusually aggressive.
    b. people who exercise frequently are less likely to suffer from depression than infrequent exercisers.
    c. people's friendliness and feelings of happiness are increased by consumption of alcohol.
    d. people who consume excessive amounts of coffee experience higher than normal levels of anxiety.

Experimentation, pp. 24, 31
Medium, Conceptual, Objective 9, Ans: b

78.   Correlation is to _____ as experimentation is to _____.
    a. cause; effect
    b. prediction; explanation
    c. the hindsight bias; false consensus
    d. random assignment; random sampling
    e. dependent variable; independent variable

Experimentation, p. 31
Medium, Factual/Definitional, Objective 9, Ans: b

79.   Unlike correlational studies, experiments involve:
    a. randomly selecting participants.
    b. manipulating the factors of interest.
    c. studying observable behaviors.
    d. all the above.

Experimentation, p. 31
Medium, Factual/Definitional, Objective 9, Ans: c

80.   The experiment is a research method in which:
    a. a random sample of individuals are questioned regarding their opinions and behaviors.
    b. individuals are carefully observed in their natural environment.
    c. an investigator manipulates one or more variables that might affect behavior.
    d. an individual is studied in great detail.

Experimentation, p. 31
Medium, Conceptual, Objective 9, Ans: b

81.   In order to test the potential effect of hunger on taste sensitivity, groups of research participants are deprived of food for differing lengths of time before they engage in a taste-sensitivity test. This research is an example of:
    a. correlational research.
    b. an experiment.
    c. survey research.
    d. a case study.
    e. naturalistic observation.

Experimentation, pp. 31-32
Easy, Factual/Definitional, Objective 9, Ans: e

82.   In a drug treatment study, participants given a pill containing no actual drug are receiving a:
      a. random sample.
      b. case study.
      c. false consensus.
      d. replication.
      e. placebo.

Experimentation, p. 32
Difficult, Factual/Definitional, Objective 9, Ans: b

83.   In order to minimize the placebo effect, researchers are likely to make use of:
      a. a scatterplot.
      b. the double-blind procedure.
      c. random sampling.
      d. standard deviations.

Experimentation, p. 32
Easy, Factual/Definitional, Objective 9, Ans: d

84.   The double-blind procedure is most likely to be utilized in _____ research.
      a. survey
      b. case study
      c. correlational
      d. experimental

Experimentation, p. 32
Difficult, Conceptual, Objective 9, Ans: c

85.   Ali has volunteered to participate in an experiment evaluating the effectiveness of aspirin. Neither he nor the experimenters know whether or not the pills he takes during the experiment contain aspirin or are merely placebos. The investigators are apparently making use of:
      a. naturalistic observation.
      b. random sampling.
      c. the double-blind procedure.
      d. replication.
      e. the false consensus effect.

Experimentation, p. 32
Difficult, Conceptual, Objective 9, Ans: e

86.   In an experiment designed to study the effectiveness of a new drug, subjects who receive a placebo are participating in the _____ condition.
      a. dependent variable
      b. correlational
      c. experimental
      d. naturalistic observation
      e. control

Experimentation, p. 32
Medium, Factual/Definitional, Objective 9, Ans: d

87. In order to provide a baseline against which they can evaluate the effects of a specific treatment, experimenters make use of a(n):
   a. dependent variable.
   b. random sample.
   c. independent variable.
   d. control condition.
   e. experimental condition.

Experimentation, p. 32
Medium, Conceptual, Objective 9, Ans: d

88. Research participants consumed either caffeinated or decaffeinated beverages in a study of the effects of caffeine on anxiety levels. Those who received the decaffeinated drinks were exposed to the _____ condition.
   a. survey
   b. experimental
   c. correlational
   d. control

Experimentation, p. 32
Medium, Conceptual, Objective 9, Ans: d

89. In a test of the effects of cigarette smoking on physical health and development, groups of monkeys were raised in either a smoke-free or smoke-infested environment. Monkeys in the smoke-infested environment were exposed to the _____ condition.
   a. correlational
   b. survey
   c. control
   d. experimental

Experimentation, p. 32
Easy, Factual/Definitional, Objective 9, Ans: d

90. Random assignment is most likely to be utilized in _____ research.
   a. survey
   b. case study
   c. correlational
   d. experimental

Experimentation, p. 32
Medium, Factual/Definitional, Objective 9, Ans: a

91. In order to minimize any preexisting differences between participants who are in different conditions of an experiment, psychologists make use of:
   a. random assignment.
   b. replication.
   c. random sampling.
   d. correlation.

Experimentation, p. 32
Difficult, Conceptual, Objective 9, Ans: e

92.   In order to study the effects of noise on worker productivity, researchers have one group of
       subjects work in a noisy room and a second group work in a quiet room. To ensure that any
       differences in the productivity of the two groups actually result from the different noise levels
       to which the groups are exposed, the researchers would use:
       a. the case study.
       b. correlational measurement.
       c. naturalistic observation.
       d. replication.
       e. random assignment.

Experimentation, pp. 22, 32
Difficult, Conceptual, Objective 9, Ans: b

93.   Random sampling is to _____ as random assignment is to _____.
       a. correlational studies; case studies
       b. surveys; experiments
       c. illusory correlation; false consensus
       d. replication; correlation
       e. description; prediction

Experimentation, p. 32
Easy, Factual/Definitional, Objective 9, Ans: c

94.   In a psychological experiment, researchers are interested in studying the potential effects of the
       _____ variable.
       a. dependent
       b. control
       c. independent
       d. behavioral

Experimentation, p. 32
Medium, Conceptual, Objective 9, Ans: e

95.   Knowing the difference between an experimental condition and a control condition is most
       relevant to understanding the nature of:
       a. correlations.
       b. random sampling.
       c. replication.
       d. external validity.
       e. independent variables.

Experimentation, p. 32
Medium, Conceptual, Objective 9, Ans: c

96.   In order to study some effects of alcohol consumption, Dr. Chu tested the physical coordination
       skills of 21-year-old men who were first assigned to drink a beverage with either 4, 2, or 0
       ounces of alcohol in the laboratory. In this study, the independent variable consisted of:
       a. the age of the research participants.
       b. the physical coordination skills of the research participants.
       c. the amount of alcohol consumed.
       d. the effects of alcohol consumption.
       e. all the above.

Experimentation, p. 32
Medium, Factual/Definitional, Objective 9, Ans: b
97.   The dependent variable in an experiment is the factor:
  a. that is directly manipulated by the investigator.
  b. that may be influenced by the experimental treatment.
  c. whose effect is being studied.
  d. that causes the behavior being studied.

Experimentation, p. 32
Medium, Conceptual, Objective 9, Ans: d
98.   In an experimental study of the effects of sleep deprivation on memory, memory would be the:
  a. control condition.
  b. independent variable.
  c. experimental condition.
  d. dependent variable.

Experimentation, p. 33
Difficult, Factual/Definitional, Objective 9, Ans: d
99.   Some participants in a subliminal persuasion experiment thought that they were receiving
      subliminal affirmations of their self-esteem when in reality they were receiving subliminal
      memory-enhancement instructions. These individuals subsequently demonstrated:
  a. an actual improvement in their memory.
  b. an erroneous belief that their memory had improved.
  c. an actual enhancement in self-esteem.
  d. an erroneous belief that their self-esteem had improved.

Describing data, p. 35
Medium, Conceptual, Objective 10, Ans: b
100. The percentage of college students whose grade point averages fall into various performance
      categories could be represented in a:
  a. standard deviation.
  b. bar graph.
  c. scatterplot.
  d. correlation coefficient.

Measures of central tendency, p. 35
Easy, Factual/Definitional, Objective 11, Ans: a
101. The mode, median, and mean are measures of:
  a. central tendency.
  b. variation.
  c. correlation.
  d. statistical significance.

Measures of central tendency, p. 35
Medium, Factual/Definitional, Objective 11, Ans: b
102. The mode of a distribution of scores is the:
  a. score exceeded by 50 percent of all the scores.
  b. most frequently occurring score.
  c. arithmetic average of all the scores.
  d. difference between the highest and lowest scores.

Measures of central tendency, p. 35
Medium, Conceptual, Objective 11, Ans: e

103. Six different high school students spent $10, $13, $2, $12, $13, and $4, respectively, on entertainment. The mode of this group's entertainment expenditures is:
      a. $9.
      b. $10.
      c. $11.
      d. $12.
      e. $13.

Measures of central tendency, p. 35
Easy, Factual/Definitional, Objective 11, Ans: d

104. The arithmetic average of a distribution of scores is the:
      a. mode.
      b. median.
      c. standard deviation.
      d. mean.
      e. range.

Measures of central tendency, p. 35
Medium, Factual/Definitional, Objective 11, Ans: b

105. The most commonly reported measure of central tendency is the:
      a. mode.
      b. mean.
      c. normal distribution.
      d. median.
      e. standard deviation.

Measures of central tendency, p. 35
Medium, Conceptual, Objective 11, Ans: c

 106. During the past month, Henri and Sylvia each ate 10 candy bars, while Jerry ate 8, Tricia ate 6, and Tahli ate only 1. The mean number of candy bars eaten by these individuals was:
      a. 1.
      b. 5.
      c. 7.
      d. 8.
      e. 10.

Measures of central tendency, p. 35
Medium, Factual/Definitional, Objective 11, Ans: c

 107. In any distribution of scores, an equal number of scores are both greater than and less than:
      a. the mode.
      b. the mean.
      c. the median.
      d. all the above.

Measures of central tendency, p. 35
Medium, Conceptual, Objective 11, Ans: c
108. Mr. and Mrs. Berry have five children aged 2, 3, 7, 9, and 9. The median age of the Berry children is:
    a. 3.
    b. 6.
    c. 7.
    d. 8.
    e. 9.

Measures of central tendency, p. 35
Medium, Conceptual, Objective 11, Ans: e
109. In a distribution of test scores, which measure of central tendency would likely be the most affected by a couple of extremely high scores?
    a. median
    b. range
    c. mode
    d. standard deviation
    e. mean

Measures of central tendency, pp. 35-36
Difficult, Factual/Definitional, Objective 11, Ans: a
110. The mode, median, and mean are most likely to have different values when they:
    a. describe a skewed distribution.
    b. are derived from a limited range of scores.
    c. represent the central tendency of a random sample.
    d. represent the central tendency of an entire population.

Measures of central tendency, p. 36
Easy, Factual/Definitional, Objective 11, Ans: e
111. In order to understand the British newspaper headline "Income for 62% Is Below Average," it is necessary to appreciate the distinction between the _____ and the mean.
    a. range
    b. standard deviation
    c. mode
    d. normal distribution
    e. median

Measures of central tendency, p. 36
Difficult, Conceptual, Objective 11, Ans: e
112. Seven members of a girls' club reported the following individual earnings from their sale of raffle tickets: $5, $9, $4, $11, $6, $4, and $3. In this distribution of individual earnings, the median is _____ the mean and _____ the mode.
    a. greater than; greater than
    b. less than; less than
    c. equal to; equal to
    d. greater than; less than
    e. less than; greater than

Measures of central tendency, p. 36
Difficult, Conceptual, Objective 11, Ans: b

113. Seven members of a 4H club reported the following individual earnings from their sale of cakes: $7, $13, $3, $5, $2, $9, and $3. In this distribution of individual earnings, the mean is _____ the mode and _____ the median.
    a. equal to; equal to
    b. greater than; greater than
    c. equal to; less than
    d. greater than; equal to
    e. less than; less than

Measures of central tendency, p. 36
Difficult, Conceptual, Objective 11, Ans: d

114. For which of the following distributions of scores would the median most clearly be a more appropriate measure of central tendency than the mean?
    a. 16, 28, 4, 8, 24
    b. 9, 6, 9, 12, 9
    c. 8, 9, 12, 10, 16
    d. 6, 18, 4, 5, 2
    e. 3, 4, 3, 4, 2

Central tendency and variation, pp. 35, 36
Medium, Conceptual, Objective 11, Ans: a

115. Variation is to central tendency as _____ is to _____.
    a. range; median
    b. frequency distribution; percentile rank
    c. mode; mean
    d. scatterplot; bar graph
    e. correlation; scatterplot

Central tendency and variation, pp. 35, 36
Medium, Conceptual, Objective 11, Ans: b

116. Standard deviation is to mean as _____ is to _____.
    a. median; mode
    b. variation; central tendency
    c. scatterplot; bar graph
    d. correlation; scatterplot
    e. normal distribution; percentile rank

Measures of variation, p. 36
Easy, Factual/Definitional, Objective 11, Ans: c

117. Which of the following provides a rough indication of the degree of variation among a set of scores?
    a. correlation coefficient
    b. scatterplot
    c. range
    d. median
    e. percentile rank

Measures of variation, p. 36

Medium, Factual/Definitional, Objective 11, Ans: b

118. The range is:
    a. a total population from which samples may be drawn.
    b. the difference between the highest and lowest scores in a distribution.
    c. the most commonly used measure of variation.
    d. the average deviation of scores from the mean.
    e. the most frequently occurring score in a distribution of scores.

Measures of variation, p. 36
Easy, Conceptual, Objective 11, Ans: c

119. The IQ scores of the five members of the Duluth family are 100, 82, 104, 96, and 118. For this distribution of scores, the range is:
    a. 6.
    b. 14.
    c. 36.
    d. 48.
    e. 100.

Measures of variation, p. 36
Medium, Conceptual, Objective 11, Ans: e

120. Two students in an art class are at least 20 years older than the others. Which measure of variation of class members' ages is most affected by the ages of these two students?
    a. mean
    b. standard deviation
    c. mode
    d. median
    e. range

Measures of variation, p. 36
Easy, Factual/Definitional, Objective 11, Ans: b

121. The standard deviation is a measure of:
    a. central tendency.
    b. variation.
    c. statistical significance.
    d. correlation.

Measures of variation, p. 36
Difficult, Conceptual, Objective 11, Ans: e

122. Professor Woo noticed that the distribution of students' scores on her last biology test had an extremely small standard deviation. This indicates that the:
    a. test was given to a very small class of students.
    b. test was a poor measure of the students' knowledge.
    c. mean test score was lower than the median score.
    d. students generally performed very well on the test.
    e. students' scores tended to be very similar to one another.

Measures of variation, p. 36
Medium, Conceptual, Objective 11, Ans: a
123. In order to calculate the value of the standard deviation, it would be most reasonable to first compute the value of the:
   a. mean.
   b. range.
   c. correlation coefficient.
   d. median.

Making inferences, p. 37
Medium, Conceptual, Objective 12, Ans: c
124. After his property was vandalized by a small group of teenagers, Mr. Mahmood concluded that most teenagers are irresponsible and delinquent. Mr. Mahmood ought to be reminded that accurate generalizations depend on:
   a. a realization that random events may not look random.
   b. an awareness of the false consensus effect.
   c. the observation of representative samples.
   d. the selection of samples from a normally distributed population.

Making inferences, p. 37
Medium, Factual/Definitional, Objective 12, Ans: a
125. One can most accurately estimate a population mean if a sample is _____ in size and _____ in variability.
   a. large; low
   b. small; high
   c. large; high
   d. small; low

Making inferences, p. 37
Medium, Conceptual, Objective 12, Ans: a
126. Faustin, a member of his college's golf team, has an opportunity to play against a nationally acclaimed professional golfer. How many holes of golf should Faustin choose to play with the professional in order to maximize his own slim chances of winning?
   a. 9
   b. 18
   c. 27
   d. 36
   e. 72

Making inferences, p. 37
Difficult, Conceptual, Objective 12, Ans: a
127. If half the students at Quincy College have blue eyes, which of the following events is most probable?
   a. In a Quincy College class consisting of 15 students, 12 or more have blue eyes.
   b. In a Quincy College class consisting of 30 students, 24 or more have blue eyes.
   c. In a Quincy College class consisting of 45 students, 36 or more have blue eyes.
   d. All the above are equally probable.

Making inferences, p. 37
Difficult, Conceptual, Objective 12, Ans: b

128.   As the size of a sample _____, the size of the standard deviation is most likely to
_____.
    a. increases; increase
    b. increases; decrease
    c. decreases; remain the same
    d. increases or decreases; remain the same

Making inferences, p. 37
Medium, Conceptual, Objective 12, Ans: d

129.   A random sample of females was observed to exhibit a lower average level of self-esteem than
    a random sample of males. In order to assess the likelihood that this observed difference
    reflects a real difference in the average self-esteem of the total population of males and
    females, it is necessary to:
    a. construct a scatterplot.
    b. calculate a correlation coefficient.
    c. plot the distribution of self-esteem levels among all males and females.
    d. conduct a test of statistical significance.
    e. do all the above.

Making inferences, p. 37
Difficult, Factual/Definitional, Objective 12, Ans: c

130.   An observed difference between two sample groups is more likely to be statistically significant
    if:
    a. the observed difference is small.
    b. the sample groups are small.
    c. the standard deviations of the sample groups are small.
    d. any of the above are true.

Can laboratory experiments illuminate everyday life?, p. 39
Medium, Factual/Definitional, Objective 13, Ans: a

131.   Psychology experiments are typically designed to:
    a. test and evaluate theoretical principles.
    b. observe behaviors that are unobservable outside the laboratory.
    c. re-create the naturally occurring conditions that influence people's daily behaviors.
    d. do all the above.

Does behavior depend on one's culture?, p. 40
Medium, Conceptual, Objective 13, Ans: b

132.   Slender women are considered especially beautiful in one country; in another country, stout
    women are seen as particularly attractive. In both countries, however, women perceived as very
    beautiful receive preferential treatment. This best illustrates that _____ often underlie
    cultural differences.
    a. negative correlations
    b. common psychological processes
    c. gender differences
    d. unconscious preferences
    e. genetic dissimilarities

Does behavior vary with gender?, p. 40
Medium, Factual/Definitional, Objective 13, Ans: d
133. Psychologists report that there are gender differences in our risk of:
    a. alcoholism.
    b. depression.
    c. eating disorders.
    d. all the above.

Why do psychologists study animals?, pp. 40-41
Medium, Factual/Definitional, Objective 14, Ans: d
134. Psychologists study animals because:
    a. animal behavior is easier to control than human behavior.
    b. animal physiology is often simpler and easier to understand than human physiology is.
    c. it is ethically more acceptable to conduct certain types of research with animals than with humans.
    d. all of the above are true.

Is it ethical to experiment on animals?, pp. 41-42
Medium, Factual/Definitional, Objective 14, Ans: a
135. Scientists who defend the use of animals in experimental research typically claim that:
    a. the well-being of humans should be placed above the well-being of animals.
    b. competent scientists have no justifiable reason to inflict pain on animals.
    c. animals should be used only in research that directly benefits the animals involved.
    d. allegations that pain is sometimes inflicted on animals are simply untrue.

Is it ethical to experiment on people?, pp. 42-43
Easy, Factual/Definitional, Objective 14, Ans: d
136. Psychologists occasionally deceive research participants about the true purpose of an experiment in order to prevent them from:
    a. worrying about the potential harm or discomfort they may experience.
    b. realizing that their privacy is being violated.
    c. deciding that they really don't want to take part in the experiment.
    d. trying to confirm the experimenters' predictions.

Is it ethical to experiment on people?, p. 43
Difficult, Factual/Definitional, Objective 14, Ans: c
137. Ethical principles developed by the American Psychological Association and the British Psychological Society urge psychological investigators to:
    a. forewarn potential research participants of the exact hypothesis they will be helping the psychologist to test.
    b. avoid the use of laboratory experiments when the behaviors of interest can be directly observed in natural settings.
    c. ensure that research participants give informed consent to participating in the research.
    d. do all the above.

Is psychology free of value judgments?, p. 43
Easy, Factual/Definitional, Objective 15, Ans: d

138.   The personal values of psychologists are likely to influence their choice of:
       a. topics of investigation.
       b. research methods.
       c. explanatory theories.
       d. all the above.

Thinking critically about the death penalty (Box), p. 44
Medium, Factual/Definitional, Objective 15, Ans: a

139.   Postmodernism is most likely to emphasize that human knowledge is:
       a. socially constructed.
       b. scientifically objective.
       c. biologically determined.
       d. psychologically meaningless.

Thinking critically about the death penalty (Box), p. 44
Difficult, Factual/Definitional, Objective 15, Ans: d

140.   Postmodernism is most likely to question the possibility of:
       a. naturalistic observation.
       b. social consensus.
       c. critical thinking.
       d. scientific objectivity.

Thinking critically about the death penalty (Box), p. 44
Medium, Factual/Definitional, Objective 15, Ans: d

141.   The most accurate indicator of public attitudes toward capital punishment in the United States
       is provided by:
       a. the number of states that have passed legislation in support of capital punishment.
       b. the actual decisions made by jurors in capital punishment cases.
       c. newspaper editorial responses to capital punishment issues.
       d. public opinion survey findings.

CHAPTER 2

Neuroscience and Behavior

Learning Objectives

1. Explain why psychologists are concerned with human biology.

Neural Communication (pp. 48-54)

2. Describe the structure of a neuron, and explain how neural impulses are generated.

3. Describe how nerve cells communicate, and discuss the impact of neurotransmitters and drugs on human behavior.

The Nervous System (pp. 54-57)

4. Identify the major divisions of the nervous system and describe their functions, noting the three types of neurons that transmit information through the system.

5. Contrast the simplicity of the neural pathways involved in reflexes with the complexity of neural networks.

The Brain (pp. 58-80)

6. Identify and describe several techniques for studying the brain.

7. Describe the functions of the brainstem, thalamus, cerebellum, and limbic system.

8. Identify the four lobes of the cerebral cortex, and describe the sensory and motor functions of the cortex.

9. Discuss the importance of the association areas, and describe how damage to several different cortical areas can impair language functioning.

10. Discuss the capacity of the brain to reorganize following injury or illness.

11. Describe research on the split brain, and discuss what it reveals regarding normal brain functioning.

12.   Discuss the relationships among brain organization, right- and left-handedness, and physical health.

The Endocrine System (pp. 80-81)

13.   Describe the nature and functions of the endocrine system and its interaction with the nervous system.

Introduction, p. 47
Medium, Factual/Definitional, Objective 1, Ans: c
1.   Aristotle believed that the mind was most intimately connected with the:
a.   head.
b.   stomach.
c.   heart.
d.   liver.

Introduction, p. 47
Medium, Factual/Definitional, Objective 1, Ans: e
2.   The nineteenth-century theory that bumps on the skull reveal a person's abilities and traits is called:
a.   evolutionary psychology.
b.   behavior genetics.
c.   molecular biology.
d.   biological psychology.
e.   phrenology.

Introduction, p. 47
Medium, Factual/Definitional, Objective 1, Ans: d
3.   Who first suggested that different regions of the brain control different aspects of behavior?
a.   Aristotle
b.   Hippocrates
c.   John Locke
d.   Franz Gall

Introduction, p. 48
Medium, Conceptual, Objective 1, Ans: b
4.   Professor Samuels conducts research on the relationship between the limbic system and sexual motivation. Her research interests best represent the psychological specialty known as:
a.   clinical psychology.
b.   biological psychology.
c.   psychoanalysis.
d.   psychiatry.
e.   behavior genetics.

Neurons, p. 48
Easy, Factual/Definitional, Objective 2, Ans: a
5.   The cells that serve as the basic building blocks of the body's information processing system are called:
a.   neurons.
b.   neurotransmitters.
c.   vesicles.
d.   glial cells.

Neurons, p. 48
Easy, Factual/Definitional, Objective 2, Ans: d
6. The branching extensions of nerve cells that receive incoming signals from sensory receptors or from other neurons are called the:
    a. axons.
    b. synapses.
    c. cell bodies.
    d. dendrites.
    e. neurotransmitters.

Neurons, p. 48
Easy, Factual/Definitional, Objective 2, Ans: d
7. The part of a neuron that transmits neural messages to other neurons or to muscles or glands is called the:
    a. dendrite.
    b. synapse.
    c. association area.
    d. axon.
    e. cell body.

Neurons, p. 48
Medium, Factual/Definitional, Objective 2, Ans: a
8. Which part of a neuron is often encased by the myelin sheath?
    a. axon
    b. glial cell
    c. cell body
    d. dendrite

Neurons, p. 48
Difficult, Conceptual, Objective 2, Ans: b
9. Signal reception is to _____ as signal transmission is to _____.
    a. interneuron; neural network
    b. dendrite; axon
    c. neurotransmitter; hormone
    d. sympathetic nervous system; parasympathetic nervous system

Neurons, p. 48
Easy, Factual/Definitional, Objective 2, Ans: d
10. The myelin sheath helps to increase the _____ of neural impulses.
    a. frequency
    b. intensity
    c. threshold
    d. speed

Neurons, p. 48
Medium, Factual/Definitional, Objective 2, Ans: d
11. The slowdown of neural communication in multiple sclerosis involves a degeneration of the:
    a. dendrites.
    b. blood cells.
    c. corpus callosum.
    d. myelin sheath.
    e. pituitary gland.

Neurons, p. 49
Easy, Factual/Definitional, Objective 2, Ans: a
12.   An action potential refers to a:
       a. neural impulse.
       b. synaptic gap.
       c. neurotransmitter.
       d. reflex.

Neurons, p. 49
Medium, Factual/Definitional, Objective 2, Ans: c
13.   The movement of positively charged ions across the membrane of a neuron produces a(n):
       a. neural network.
       b. synapse.
       c. action potential.
       d. myelin sheath.
       e. interneuron.

Neurons, p. 49
Medium, Factual/Definitional, Objective 2, Ans: c
14.   The resting potential of a neuron refers to:
       a. a brief electrical charge that travels down the axon.
       b. the storage of neurotransmitter molecules within synaptic vesicles.
       c. the electrical imbalance between the inside and outside of the neural membrane.
       d. a capacity to reabsorb neurotransmitter molecules released into the synaptic gap.

Neurons, p. 49
Medium, Factual/Definitional, Objective 2, Ans: b
15.   The selective permeability of a neural membrane creates a(n):
       a. myelin sheath.
       b. resting potential.
       c. neural network.
       d. association area.
       e. lesion.

Neurons, p. 50
Easy, Factual/Definitional, Objective 2, Ans: d
16.   A neural impulse is generated only when excitatory minus inhibitory signals exceed a certain:
       a. action potential.
       b. synaptic gap.
       c. computed tomography.
       d. threshold.

Neurons, p. 50
Medium, Factual/Definitional, Objective 2, Ans: d
17.   An all-or-none response pattern is characteristic of the:
       a. activation of either the sympathetic or the parasympathetic system.
       b. release of endorphins into the central nervous system.
       c. release of hormones into the bloodstream.
       d. initiation of neural impulses.
       e. inheritance of behavioral predispositions.

How neurons communicate, p. 50
Easy, Factual/Definitional, Objective 3, Ans: c
18. The spatial junctions where impulses are chemically transmitted from one neuron to another
     are called:
     a. neurotransmitters.
     b. interneurons.
     d. dendrites.
     e. thresholds.

How neurons communicate, p. 50
Easy, Factual/Definitional, Objective 3, Ans: b
19. Neurotransmitters are chemical messengers that travel across the:
     a. cell body.
     b. synaptic gap.
     c. axon.
     d. myelin sheath.
     e. threshold.

How neurons communicate, p. 50
Medium, Factual/Definitional, Objective 3, Ans: a
20. Neurotransmitters influence the flow of _____ into receiving neurons.
     a. ions
     b. glial cells
     c. molecules
     d. hormones

How neurons communicate, p. 50
Medium, Factual/Definitional, Objective 3, Ans: a
21. Neurotransmitter receptor sites are located on the:
     a. dendrites.
     b. myelin sheath.
     c. cell body.
     d. axon.

How neurons communicate, p. 50
Difficult, Factual/Definitional, Objective 3, Ans: b
22. Research on neurotransmitters indicates that:
     a. a single synapse generally uses several dozen neurotransmitters.
     b. neurotransmitters can inhibit neural impulse transmission.
     c. less than a dozen neurotransmitters are involved in all neural transmission.
     d. the release of endorphins causes paralysis of the muscles.

How neurotransmitters influence us, p. 51
Difficult, Factual/Definitional, Objective 3, Ans: c
23. Prozac is an antidepressant drug that increases the level of the neurotransmitter:
     a. GABA.
     b. ACh.
     c. serotonin.
     d. dopamine.

How neurotransmitters influence us, p. 52
Easy, Factual/Definitional, Objective 3, Ans: d

24.   Acetylcholine is a(n):
      a. receptor.
      b. neurotransmitter.
      c. endorphin.
      d. hormone.

How neurotransmitters influence us, pp. 52, 81
Medium, Conceptual, Objective 3, Ans: d

25.   Epinephrine is to hormone as _____ is to neurotransmitter.
      a. curare
      b. botulin
      c. estrogen
      d. ACh

How neurotransmitters influence us, p. 52
Medium, Factual/Definitional, Objective 3, Ans: c

26.   When the release of ACh is blocked by botulin, the result is:
      a. depression.
      b. aggression.
      c. paralysis.
      d. schizophrenia.
      e. euphoria.

How neurotransmitters influence us, p. 52
Medium, Factual/Definitional, Objective 3, Ans: a

27.   The venom of the black widow spider causes violent muscle contractions by accelerating the release of:
      a. acetylcholine.
      b. serotonin.
      c. endorphins.
      d. epinephrine.

How neurotransmitters influence us, p. 52
Easy, Factual/Definitional, Objective 3, Ans: b

28.   Endorphins are most directly involved in the control of:
      a. body temperature.
      b. physical pain.
      c. muscle contraction.
      d. attention.

How neurotransmitters influence us, p. 52
Medium, Conceptual, Objective 3, Ans: b

29.   The pain of childbirth is most likely to be reduced by the accelerated release of:
      a. acetylcholine.
      b. endorphins.
      c. dopamine.
      d. estrogen.

How neurotransmitters influence us, p. 52
Medium, Conceptual, Objective 3, Ans: c

30. After 3 hours of playing a physically exhausting professional tennis match, Chitra began to experience a sense of physical exhilaration and pleasure. It is likely that her feelings were most directly linked to the release of:
    a. dopamine.
    b. acetylcholine.
    c. endorphins.
    d. insulin.

How neurotransmitters influence us, p. 52
Medium, Factual/Definitional, Objective 3, Ans: c

31. The body's own natural production of endorphins is likely to be suppressed by:
    a. physical pain.
    b. physical exercise.
    c. heroin usage.
    d. all the above.

How neurotransmitters influence us, p. 53
Easy, Factual/Definitional, Objective 3, Ans: d

32. Agonists mimic the activity of:
    a. motor neurons.
    b. glial cells.
    c. synapses.
    d. neurotransmitters.

How neurotransmitters influence us, p. 53
Difficult, Factual/Definitional, Objective 3, Ans: a

33. Morphine functions as an:
    a. endorphin agonist.
    b. endorphin antagonist.
    c. dopamine agonist.
    d. dopamine antagonist.

How neurotransmitters influence us, p. 54
Difficult, Factual/Definitional, Objective 3, Ans: b

34. L-dopa helps to control the:
    a. memory loss accompanying Alzheimer's disease.
    b. tremors accompanying Parkinson's disease.
    c. hallucinations accompanying schizophrenia.
    d. mood swings accompanying depression.

How neurotransmitters influence us, p. 54
Medium, Factual/Definitional, Objective 3, Ans: d

35. The tremors of Parkinson's disease result from the loss of nerve cells that produce the neurotransmitter:
    a. serotonin.
    b. ACh.
    c. GABA.
    d. dopamine.

The nervous system, p. 54
Easy, Factual/Definitional, Objective 4, Ans: d

36.   The body's speedy electrochemical information system is called the:
      a. circulatory system.
      b. reproductive system.
      c. cerebral cortex.
      d. nervous system.
      e. endocrine system.

The nervous system, p. 54
Medium, Factual/Definitional, Objective 4, Ans: d

37.   Nerves are neural cables containing many:
      a. hormones.
      b. endorphins.
      c. interneurons.
      d. axons.
      e. lesions.

The nervous system, p. 54
Easy, Factual/Definitional, Objective 4, Ans: b

38.   Information is carried from the tissues of the body to the central nervous
      system by:
      a. interneurons.
      b. sensory neurons.
      c. motor neurons.
      d. endocrine glands.

The nervous system, p. 54
Easy, Factual/Definitional, Objective 4, Ans: d

39.   Sensory neurons transmit signals to:
      a. glands.
      b. glial cells.
      c. motor neurons.
      d. interneurons.

The nervous system, p. 54
Medium, Conceptual, Objective 4, Ans: c

40.   When Jim was stung by a bee, the pain message was transmitted to his spinal cord by the
      _____ nervous system.
      a. sympathetic
      b. parasympathetic
      c. peripheral
      d. central

The nervous system, p. 54
Easy, Factual/Definitional, Objective 4, Ans: c

41.   The central nervous system largely consists of:
      a. sensory neurons.
      b. motor neurons.
      c. interneurons.
      d. glands.

The nervous system, p. 54
Medium, Conceptual, Objective 4, Ans: a
42. Information travels from the spinal cord to the brain via:
     a. interneurons.
     b. the circulatory system.
     c. sensory neurons.
     d. the sympathetic nervous system.
     e. the endocrine system.

The nervous system, p. 54
Medium, Conceptual, Objective 4, Ans: c
43. In order for you to be able to run, _____ must relay messages from your central nervous system to your leg muscles.
     a. interneurons
     b. the cerebellum
     c. motor neurons
     d. the reticular formation
     e. the autonomic nervous system

The nervous system, p. 54
Medium, Factual/Definitional, Objective 4, Ans: c
44. Motor neurons are an important part of the:
     a. limbic system.
     b. reticular formation.
     c. peripheral nervous system.
     d. sympathetic nervous system.

The nervous system, p. 54
Difficult, Conceptual, Objective 4, Ans: e
45. Motor neurons are to the _____ nervous system as interneurons are to the _____ nervous system.
     a. sympathetic; parasympathetic
     b. central; peripheral
     c. autonomic; somatic
     d. parasympathetic; sympathetic
     e. peripheral; central

The peripheral nervous system, p. 55
Medium, Conceptual, Objective 4, Ans: c
46. The part of the peripheral nervous system that controls the movement of your legs when you walk is the:
     a. reticular formation.
     b. sympathetic nervous system.
     c. somatic nervous system.
     d. parasympathetic nervous system.

The peripheral nervous system, p. 55
Medium, Factual/Definitional, Objective 4, Ans: a
47. The parasympathetic nervous system is a division of the _____ nervous system.
     a. autonomic
     b. somatic
     c. central
     d. sympathetic

The peripheral nervous system, p. 55
Medium, Conceptual, Objective 4, Ans: c

48.   Messages are transmitted from your spinal cord to your stomach muscles by the:
       a. limbic system.
       b. central nervous system.
       c. sympathetic nervous system.
       d. somatic nervous system.
       e. reticular formation.

The peripheral nervous system, p. 55
Difficult, Factual/Definitional, Objective 4, Ans: b

49.   The sympathetic nervous system _____ digestion and _____ heartbeat.
       a. accelerates; decelerates
       b. decelerates; accelerates
       c. accelerates; accelerates
       d. decelerates; decelerates

The peripheral nervous system, p. 55
Medium, Conceptual, Objective 4, Ans: b

50.   When Mr. Valdez thought his 1-year-old daughter had fallen down the stairs, his heartbeat
       accelerated, his blood pressure rose, and he began to perspire heavily. Mr. Valdez's state of
       arousal was activated by his _____ nervous system.
       a. parasympathetic
       b. sympathetic
       c. somatic
       d. sensorimotor
       e. central

The peripheral nervous system, p. 55
Difficult, Conceptual, Objective 4, Ans: e

51.   Accelerated digestion is to decelerated digestion as the _____ nervous system is to the
       _____ nervous system.
       a. somatic; autonomic
       b. autonomic; somatic
       c. central; peripheral
       d. sympathetic; parasympathetic
       e. parasympathetic; sympathetic

The peripheral nervous system, p. 55
Difficult, Conceptual, Objective 4, Ans: d

52.   The parasympathetic nervous system is to the sympathetic nervous system as _____ is to
       _____.
       a. pupil dilation; pupil contraction
       b. increasing blood pressure; decreasing blood pressure
       c. inhibition of digestion; stimulation of digestion
       d. lowering of blood sugar; raising of blood sugar

The central nervous system, p. 56
Easy, Factual/Definitional, Objective 5, Ans: c

53. The simplest neural pathways are those that govern our:
    a. thoughts.
    b. emotions.
    c. reflexes.
    d. sexual drives.

The central nervous system, p. 56
Medium, Factual/Definitional, Objective 5, Ans: a

54. The knee-jerk reflex requires the activity of the:
    a. central nervous system.
    b. autonomic nervous system.
    c. limbic system.
    d. cerebellum.

The central nervous system, p. 56
Difficult, Conceptual, Objective 5, Ans: a

55. Jerry was able to jerk his hand out of the scalding water before sensing any pain because this withdrawal reflex:
    a. was activated by interneurons in his spinal cord.
    b. did not involve any activity within the central nervous system.
    c. was activated by the rapidly responding reticular formation of the brain.
    d. was activated by the self-regulating autonomic nervous system.

The central nervous system, p. 57
Easy, Factual/Definitional, Objective 5, Ans: d

56. The neurons of the central nervous system cluster into functional systems known as:
    a. nerves.
    b. lesions.
    c. neurotransmitters.
    d. neural networks.

The central nervous system, p. 57
Easy, Factual/Definitional, Objective 5, Ans: b

57. The brain's information processing capacities are enhanced by:
    a. agonists.
    b. neural networks.
    c. endorphins.
    d. lesions.
    e. CT scans.

The tools of discovery, p. 58
Easy, Factual/Definitional, Objective 6, Ans: d

58. A brain lesion refers to _____ of brain tissue.
    a. electrical stimulation
    b. x-ray photography
    c. radioactive bombardment
    d. destruction

The tools of discovery, p. 59
Medium, Factual/Definitional, Objective 6, Ans: a
59. Recording electrodes are placed directly on the scalp to produce a(n):
    a. EEG.
    b. PET scan.
    c. MRI.
    d. CT scan.

The tools of discovery, p. 59
Medium, Factual/Definitional, Objective 6, Ans: c
60. X-ray photographs of the brain are necessary to produce a(n):
    a. EEG.
    b. PET scan.
    c. CT scan.
    d. lobotomy.

The tools of discovery, p. 59
Difficult, Factual/Definitional, Objective 6, Ans: d
61. The concentration of glucose in active regions of the brain underlies the special usefulness of a(n):
    a. MRI.
    b. CT scan.
    c. EEG.
    d. PET scan.

The tools of discovery, p. 59
Difficult, Conceptual, Objective 6, Ans: d
62. EEG is to PET scan as:
    a. x-ray photography is to amplified recording of brain waves.
    b. amplified recording of brain waves is to x-ray photography.
    c. measurement of radioactive emissions is to amplified recording of brain waves.
    d. amplified recording of brain waves is to measurement of radioactive emissions.

The tools of discovery, p. 59
Difficult, Factual/Definitional, Objective 6, Ans: a
63. Which technique involves the use of magnetic fields and radio waves to produce computer-generated images of the brain's soft tissues?
    a. MRI
    b. EEG
    c. CT scan
    d. PET scan

Lower-level brain structures, p. 61
Medium, Conceptual, Objective 7, Ans: d
64. Which part of the human brain is most similar to the brain of a frog?
    a. the occipital lobe
    b. the limbic system
    c. the parietal lobe
    d. the brainstem

The brainstem, p. 61
Medium, Factual/Definitional, Objective 7, Ans: e
65. Your life would be most immediately threatened if you suffered destruction of the:
    a. amygdala
    b. hippocampus.
    c. angular gyrus.
    d. corpus callosum.
    e. medulla.

The brainstem, p. 61
Medium, Factual/Definitional, Objective 7, Ans: d
66. In which brain structure are nerves from the left side of the brain routed to the right side of the body?
    a. thalamus
    b. cerebellum
    c. reticular formation
    d. brainstem

The brainstem, p. 61
Easy, Factual/Definitional, Objective 7, Ans: a
67. Which nerve network in the brainstem plays an important role in controlling arousal?
    a. reticular formation
    b. hypothalamus
    c. cerebellum
    d. medulla

The brainstem, p. 61
Medium, Factual/Definitional, Objective 7, Ans: a
68. Stimulation of the reticular formation will cause a:
    a. sleeping cat to awaken.
    b. hungry cat to stop eating.
    c. violent cat to become passive.
    d. thirsty cat to drink.

The thalamus, p. 62
Easy, Factual/Definitional, Objective 7, Ans: c
69. The thalamus serves as a:
    a. memory bank.
    b. pleasure center.
    c. sensory switchboard.
    d. master gland.

The thalamus, p. 62
Medium, Conceptual, Objective 7, Ans: e
70. Your ability to experience the physical pleasure of a hot shower is most likely to be disrupted by damage to your:
    a. corpus callosum.
    b. angular gyrus.
    c. hippocampus.
    d. cerebellum.
    e. thalamus.

The cerebellum, p. 62
Medium, Factual/Definitional, Objective 7, Ans: b
71.   A loss of physical coordination and balance is most likely to result from damage to the:
   a. hypothalamus.
   b. cerebellum.
   c. corpus callosum.
   d. amygdala.

Lower-level brain structures, pp. 62-63
Difficult, Conceptual, Objective 7, Ans: b
72.   The medulla is to the control of _____ as the cerebellum is to the control of _____.
   a. eating; sleeping
   b. breathing; walking
   c. emotion; motivation
   d. memory; attention
   e. hearing; seeing

The limbic system, pp. 62-63
Easy, Factual/Definitional, Objective 7, Ans: b
73.   The amygdala and hypothalamus are part of the:
   a. brainstem.
   b. limbic system.
   c. reticular formation.
   d. cerebral cortex.

The amygdala, pp. 62-63
Easy, Factual/Definitional, Objective 7, Ans: a
74.   Which neural center in the limbic system plays a central role in emotions such as rage and fear?
   a. amygdala
   b. thalamus
   c. cerebellum
   d. medulla

The amygdala, pp. 62-63
Difficult, Conceptual, Objective 7, Ans: d
75.   If Professor Conklin lesions the amygdala of a laboratory rat, it is most likely that the rat will become:
   a. hungry.
   b. aggressive.
   c. physically uncoordinated.
   d. less emotional.

The hypothalamus, p. 63
Medium, Factual/Definitional, Objective 7, Ans: a

76.   The activity of the hypothalamus most directly influences:
   a. hunger and thirst.
   b. muscular coordination.
   c. attention and memory.
   d. heartbeat and breathing.

The hypothalamus, p. 63
Medium, Factual/Definitional, Objective 7, Ans: b
77.   The secretions of the pituitary gland are most directly regulated by the:
      a. reticular formation.
      b. hypothalamus.
      c. amygdala.
      d. cerebellum.

The hypothalamus, p. 64
Difficult, Factual/Definitional, Objective 7, Ans: c
78.   Olds discovered that rats would willingly cross an electrified floor in order to electrically
      stimulate areas within their:
      a. reticular formation.
      b. cerebellum.
      c. hypothalamus.
      d. sensory cortex.

The hypothalamus, p. 64
Medium, Conceptual, Objective 7, Ans: d
79.   Alicia tends to binge on sweets. Her doctor thinks that her binging may be due to a genetically
      disposed deficiency in the brain systems for pleasure, referred to as:
      a. pleasure deduction syndrome.
      b. reward stimulation addiction.
      c. pleasure addiction.
      d. reward deficiency syndrome.

The cerebral cortex, p. 64
Easy, Factual/Definitional, Objective 8, Ans: b
80.   Which region of the human brain best distinguishes us from other animals?
      a. reticular formation
      b. cerebral cortex
      c. limbic system
      d. hypothalamus

The cerebral cortex, p. 65
Easy, Factual/Definitional, Objective 8, Ans: a
81.   Nerve cells in the brain receive life-supporting nutrients and insulating myelin from:
      a. glial cells.
      b. neurotransmitters.
      c. motor neurons.
      d. hormones.

The cerebral cortex, p. 65
Easy, Factual/Definitional, Objective 8, Ans: a
82.   Which regions of the cerebral cortex lie at the back of the head and receive visual information?
      a. occipital lobes
      b. parietal lobes
      c. temporal lobes
      d. association areas

The cerebral cortex, p. 65
Medium, Conceptual, Objective 8, Ans: a

83. Alicia suffered a brain disease that destroyed major portions of her temporal lobes. Alicia is most likely to suffer some loss of:
    a. auditory perception.
    b. hunger and thirst.
    c. pain sensations.
    d. muscular coordination.

The cerebral cortex, p. 65
Difficult, Conceptual, Objective 8, Ans: d

84. Seeing is to hearing as the _____ lobes are to the _____ lobes.
    a. frontal; temporal
    b. occipital; parietal
    c. frontal; parietal
    d. occipital; temporal

The cerebral cortex, p. 65
Difficult, Conceptual, Objective 8, Ans: b

85. The parietal lobes are to _____ as the occipital lobes are to _____.
    a. hearing; speaking
    b. sensing touch; seeing
    c. sensing pleasure; sensing pain
    d. tasting; smelling
    e. speaking; seeing

The cerebral cortex, p. 66
Medium, Conceptual, Objective 8, Ans: d

86. Direct stimulation of a part of the motor cortex would most likely result in:
    a. feelings of anger.
    b. acceleration of heartbeat.
    c. a sensation of being touched on the arm.
    d. movement of a hand.
    e. intense pain.

The cerebral cortex, p. 67
Medium, Factual/Definitional, Objective 8, Ans: a

87. In order to make a monkey smile, José Delgado stimulated the monkey's:
    a. motor cortex.
    b. hypothalamus.
    c. sensory cortex.
    d. reticular formation.
    e. limbic system.

The cerebral cortex, p. 67
Medium, Factual/Definitional, Objective 8, Ans: a

88. The sensory cortex is located in the _____ lobes.
    a. parietal
    b. temporal
    c. frontal
    d. occipital

The cerebral cortex, p. 67
Medium, Conceptual, Objective 8, Ans: c
89. Which part of your brain receives information as to whether or not you are moving your legs?
    a. limbic system
    b. motor cortex
    c. sensory cortex
    d. Broca's area

The cerebral cortex, p. 68
Medium, Factual/Definitional, Objective 9, Ans: d
90. The cortical regions that are not primarily concerned with sensory or motor functions are known as:
    a. interneurons.
    b. temporal lobes.
    c. frontal lobes.
    d. association areas.
    e. occipital lobes.

The cerebral cortex, p. 68
Medium, Factual/Definitional, Objective 9, Ans: a
91. Damage to the association areas in the frontal lobe is most likely to interfere with the ability to:
    a. formulate plans.
    b. recognize familiar faces.
    c. understand word meanings.
    d. experience emotion.

The cerebral cortex, p. 69
Medium, Factual/Definitional, Objective 9, Ans: d
92. Phineas Gage underwent a dramatic personality change after a tamping iron inflicted massive damage to his _____ lobe.
    a. parietal
    b. temporal
    c. occipital
    d. frontal

The cerebral cortex, p. 69
Medium, Conceptual, Objective 9, Ans: c
93. The process of comparing currently experienced visual input with past visual memories takes place within:
    a. Broca's area.
    b. the sensory cortex.
    c. the association area.
    d. the limbic system.

The cerebral cortex, p. 69
Difficult, Conceptual, Objective 9, Ans: e
94. The region of your right temporal lobe that enables you to recognize a person as your own mother is:
    a. Wernicke's area.
    b. the limbic system.
    c. the sensory cortex.
    d. Broca's area.
    e. an association area.

The cerebral cortex, p. 69
Medium, Factual/Definitional, Objective 9, Ans: a

95. Broca's area is located in the left _____ lobe.
    a. frontal
    b. occipital
    c. temporal
    d. parietal

The cerebral cortex, p. 69
Difficult, Conceptual, Objective 9, Ans: b

96. After she suffered a stroke, Mrs. Josephson had so much difficulty speaking that she had to communicate by writing. This suggests that her cortex was damaged in:
    a. the occipital lobe.
    b. Broca's area.
    c. the angular gyrus.
    d. Wernicke's area.

The cerebral cortex, p. 69
Easy, Factual/Definitional, Objective 9, Ans: d

97. In which of the following parts of the brain would a lesion most likely result in aphasia?
    a. corpus callosum
    b. sensory cortex
    c. hypothalamus
    d. Wernicke's area

The cerebral cortex, p. 69
Difficult, Conceptual, Objective 9, Ans: d

98. Temporal lobe is to _____ as frontal lobe is to _____.
    a. sensory cortex; motor cortex
    b. motor cortex; sensory cortex
    c. Broca's area; Wernicke's area
    d. Wernicke's area; Broca's area

The cerebral cortex, pp. 69-70
Difficult, Conceptual, Objective 9, Ans: d

99. After a sky-diving accident, Laurie was unable to make sense of other people's speech. It is likely that her cortex was damaged in:
    a. the sensory area.
    b. Broca's area.
    c. the angular gyrus.
    d. Wernicke's area.

The cerebral cortex, pp. 69-70
Difficult, Conceptual, Objective 9, Ans: d

100. After suffering a stroke that damaged his angular gyrus, Mr. Chang is likely to experience the greatest difficulty:
    a. recognizing familiar faces.
    b. speaking fluently.
    c. understanding other people when they speak.
    d. reading.

Brain reorganization, p. 71
Difficult, Factual/Definitional, Objective 10, Ans: c

101. Visual information processing within the temporal lobe of deaf people who communicate with sign language best illustrates:
    a. aphasia.
    b. tomography.
    c. plasticity.
    d. phrenology.
    e. hemispherectomy.

Brain reorganization, p. 71
Medium, Conceptual, Objective 10, Ans: d

102. After Terry lost a finger in an industrial accident, the area of his sensory cortex devoted to receiving input from that finger gradually became very responsive to sensory input from his adjacent fingers. This best describes the value of:
    a. phrenology.
    b. aphasia.
    c. hemispherectomy.
    d. tomography.

Brain reorganization, p. 71
Easy, Factual/Definitional, Objective 10, Ans: a

103. The aging brain can partially compensate for the gradual loss of neurons by:
    a. generating new brain cells.
    b. increasing the speed of the action potential.
    c. inhibiting the growth of glial cells.
    d. decreasing the production of acetylcholine.

Brain reorganization, p. 71
Medium, Conceptual, Objective 10, Ans: e

104. When Susan was a child, a brain disease required the surgical removal of her left cerebral hemisphere. Susan is now a successful college student who lives a normal life. Her success best illustrates the importance of:
    a. aphasia.
    b. hemispherectomy.
    c. phrenology.
    d. tomography.
    e. plasticity.

Our divided brains, p. 72
Easy, Factual/Definitional, Objective 11, Ans: d

105. The left cerebral hemisphere is typically superior to the right in:
    a. spatial reasoning.
    b. language comprehension.
    c. visual perception.
    d. musical abilities.

Splitting the brain, p. 72
Easy, Factual/Definitional, Objective 11, Ans: b
106. Information is most quickly transmitted from one cerebral hemisphere to the other by the:
a. medulla.
b. corpus callosum.
c. angular gyrus.
d. limbic system.
e. reticular formation.

Splitting the brain, p. 72
Easy, Factual/Definitional, Objective 11, Ans: c
107. Split-brain patients have had their _____ surgically cut.
a. cerebral lobes
b. limbic system
c. corpus callosum
d. sensory cortex
e. reticular formation

Splitting the brain, p. 73
Medium, Conceptual, Objective 11, Ans: d
108. If an individual's right cerebral hemisphere is completely destroyed by disease, that person is unable to see anything:
a. with his or her right eye.
b. with his or her left eye.
c. in his or her right field of vision.
d. in his or her left field of vision.

Splitting the brain, p. 73
Difficult, Conceptual, Objective 11, Ans: c
109. A picture of a cat is briefly flashed in the left visual field and a picture of a mouse is briefly flashed in the right visual field of a split-brain patient. The individual will be able to use her _____ hand to indicate she saw a _____.
a. right; cat
b. left; mouse
c. right; mouse
d. left or right; cat
e. left or right; mouse

Splitting the brain, p. 74
Medium, Factual/Definitional, Objective 11, Ans: b
110. The right hemisphere is superior to the left at:
a. solving arithmetic problems.
b. recognizing people's faces.
c. understanding simple verbal requests.
d. processing information in an orderly sequence.

Studying hemispheric differences in the intact brain, p. 74
Difficult, Conceptual, Objective 11, Ans: c
111. What will most likely happen as a neurosurgeon sedates the entire right cerebral hemisphere of a patient who is asked to count aloud with both arms extended upward?
    a. The patient's left arm will fall limp and he will become speechless.
    b. The patient's right arm will fall limp and he will become speechless.
    c. The patient's left arm will fall limp but he will continue counting aloud.
    d. The patient's right arm will fall limp but he will continue counting aloud.

Studying hemispheric differences in the intact brain, p. 74
Difficult, Factual/Definitional, Objective 11, Ans: c
112. When exposed to competing sounds presented to their right and left ears, _____ speakers more accurately recognized the "tsk" sound if it was presented in the _____ ear.
    a. Zulu; left
    b. English; left
    c. Zulu; right
    d. English; right

Brain organization and handedness, p. 75
Medium, Factual/Definitional, Objective 12, Ans: c
113. Research on left-handedness indicates that:
    a. twice as many women as men are left-handed.
    b. left-handers typically have a smaller corpus callosum than right-handers.
    c. left-handers are less likely than right-handers to process speech primarily in their left hemisphere.
    d. left-handers generally demonstrate less mathematical competence than right-handers.

Brain organization and handedness, p. 75
Medium, Factual/Definitional, Objective 12, Ans: a
114. In order to predict the hand preference of newborn infants, you would be best advised to observe how they:
    a. turn their heads.
    b. kick their feet.
    c. clench their fists.
    d. swallow their milk.

Brain organization and handedness, p. 76
Easy, Factual/Definitional, Objective 12, Ans: c
115. The percentage of left-handers is much lower among _____ than among _____.
    a. men; women
    b. black Americans; white Americans
    c. older people; younger people
    d. primates; humans

Thinking critically about left brain/right brain (Box), p. 78
Difficult, Conceptual, Objective 12, Ans: d
116. People should typically recognize familiar words more rapidly when they are spoken into the _____ ear; they should typically recognize familiar melodies more rapidly when they are played into the _____ ear.
    a. right; right
    b. left; left
    c. left; right
    d. right; left

Thinking critically about left brain/right brain (Box), p. 78
Medium, Conceptual, Objective 12, Ans: d

117. Performing scientific research involves brain activity in the _____ cerebral hemisphere(s); writing a story involves brain activity in the _____ cerebral hemisphere(s).
      a. left; right
      b. right; left
      c. left; right and left
      d. right and left; right and left

The endocrine system, p. 80
Easy, Factual/Definitional, Objective 13, Ans: c

118. The chemical messengers of the endocrine system are called:
      a. neurotransmitters.
      b. glial cells.
      c. hormones.
      d. agonists.
      e. genes.

The endocrine system, pp. 50, 80
Medium, Conceptual, Objective 13, Ans: b

119. Neurotransmitter is to hormone as _____ is to _____.
      a. pancreas; hypothalamus
      b. nervous system; endocrine system
      c. sympathetic; parasympathetic
      d. sensory neuron; motor neuron
      e. cerebral cortex; limbic system

The endocrine system, p. 81
Medium, Factual/Definitional, Objective 13, Ans: d

120. Epinephrine and norepinephrine are released by the _____ gland(s).
      a. thyroid
      b. pituitary
      c. parathyroid
      d. adrenal
      e. thymus

The endocrine system, p. 81
Medium, Factual/Definitional, Objective 13, Ans: d

121. The release of epinephrine into the bloodstream is most likely to:
      a. lower blood sugar.
      b. reduce blood pressure.
      c. stimulate digestion.
      d. accelerate heartbeat.

The endocrine system, pp. 52, 81
Medium, Conceptual, Objective 13, Ans: d

122. Neurotransmitter is to hormone as acetylcholine is to:
      a. glucose.
      b. endorphins.
      c. dopamine.
      d. epinephrine.
      e. agonist.

The endocrine system, pp. 63, 81
Difficult, Conceptual, Objective 13, Ans: d

123. Endocrine system is to nervous system as _____ is to _____.
    a. amygdala; limbic system
    b. neurotransmitter; hormone
    c. thalamus; cerebellum
    d. pituitary; hypothalamus

The endocrine system, p. 81
Medium, Factual/Definitional, Objective 13, Ans: d

124. Which gland regulates body growth and controls the functioning of other glands?
    a. parathyroid gland
    b. adrenal gland
    c. thyroid gland
    d. pituitary gland

CHAPTER 3

The Nature and Nurture of Behavior

Learning Objectives

Genes: Our Biological Blueprint (pp. 86-87)

1. Describe the composition and physical location of genes.

Evolutionary Psychology: Explaining Universal Behaviors (pp. 87-93)

2. Discuss the impact of evolutionary history on genetically predisposed behavioral tendencies.

3. Identify gender differences in sexual behavior and describe and evaluate evolutionary explanations for those differences.

Behavior Genetics: Explaining Individual Differences (pp. 93-101)

4. Describe how twin and adoption studies help us differentiate hereditary and environmental influences on human traits.

5. Discuss how differences in infant temperament illustrate the effect of heredity on development.

6. Describe how behavior geneticists estimate trait heritability, and discuss the interaction of genetic and environmental influences.

7. Discuss the potential promise and perils of molecular genetics.

Environmental Influence (pp. 102-110)

8. Explain why we should be cautious about attributing children's successes and failures to parental influence.

9. Explain how twins may experience different prenatal environments, and describe the effect of experience on brain development.

10. Describe how development is influenced by the individual's peer group and culture.

Gender (pp. 110-114)

11.   Explain how biological sex is determined, and describe the role of sex hormones in biological
       development and gender differences.

12.   Discuss the importance of gender roles and explain how social and cognitive factors contribute
       to gender identity and gender-typing.

Postscript: Reflections on Nature and Nurture (pp. 114-116)

13.   Discuss the danger of blaming nature and nurture for our own personal failings.

Genes: Our biological blueprint, p. 86
Easy, Factual/Definitional, Objective 1, Ans: c
1.   The threadlike structures that contain genes are called:
      a. memes.
      b. schemas.
      c. chromosomes.
      d. nucleotides.

Genes: Our biological blueprint, p. 86
Difficult, Conceptual, Objective 1, Ans: a
2.   Forty-six chromosomes are located within every human:
      a. blood cell.
      b. gene.
      c. nucleotide.
      d. sperm cell.
      e. synapse.

Genes: Our biological blueprint, p. 86
Difficult, Factual/Definitional, Objective 1, Ans: b
3.   Genes form templates for the production of:
      a. schemas.
      b. proteins.
      c. memes.
      d. egg cells.

Genes: Our biological blueprint, p. 86
Easy, Factual/Definitional, Objective 1, Ans: d
4.   Chromosomes are composed of:
      a. schemas.
      b. synapses.
      c. neurotransmitters.
      d. deoxyribonucleic acid.

Genes: Our biological blueprint, p. 86
Medium, Factual/Definitional, Objective 1, Ans: d
5.   Each of your body cells contains:
      a. DNA molecules.
      b. chromosomes.
      c. nucleotides.
      d. all of the above.

Genes: Our biological blueprint, p. 86
Difficult, Factual/Definitional, Objective 1, Ans: c

6. The human genome has about 3 billion pairs of:
    a. chromosomes.
    b. genes.
    c. nucleotides.
    d. synapses.
    e. memes.

Evolutionary psychology, p. 88
Medium, Factual/Definitional, Objective 2, Ans: a

7. Evolutionary psychologists emphasize that environmentally adaptive behaviors are those that have promoted:
    a. reproductive success.
    b. personal happiness.
    c. erotic plasticity.
    d. cultural diversity.
    e. genetic mutations.

Evolutionary psychology, p. 88
Medium, Factual/Definitional, Objective 2, Ans: b

8. The prevalence of genetically predisposed traits which have a reproductive advantage is best explained in terms of:
    a. gender-typing.
    b. natural selection.
    c. behavior genetics.
    d. gender schema theory.

Evolutionary psychology, p. 88
Medium, Conceptual, Objective 2, Ans: d

9. If a genetic predisposition to fear darkness contributes to reproductive success, that trait will likely be passed on to subsequent generations. This best illustrates:
    a. gender schema theory.
    b. behavior genetics.
    c. gender typing.
    d. natural selection.

Evolutionary psychology, p. 88
Medium, Factual/Definitional, Objective 2, Ans: c

10. Mutations are gene replication errors that lead to a change in the sequence of:
    a. memes.
    b. hormones.
    c. nucleotides.
    d. gender schemas.

Evolutionary psychology, p. 88
Medium, Conceptual, Objective 2, Ans: b

11. Evolutionary psychology would be most helpful for understanding the _____ human aggression.
    a. social causes of
    b. reproductive advantages of
    c. cross-cultural variations in
    d. remedial treatments of

Evolutionary psychology, p. 88
Easy, Factual/Definitional, Objective 2, Ans: c

12. Evolutionary psychologists are most directly concerned with the impact of _____ on behavior.
    a. gender schemas
    b. testosterone
    c. genetic predispositions
    d. erotic plasticity

Evolutionary psychology, p. 89
Medium, Conceptual, Objective 2, Ans: b

13. An evolutionary psychologist would be likely to suggest that human preferences for sweet-tasting foods:
    a. have hindered human reproduction.
    b. are genetically predisposed.
    c. vary widely across cultures.
    d. are influenced by gender schemas.

Evolutionary psychology, p. 89
Difficult, Conceptual, Objective 2, Ans: c

14. The principles of evolutionary psychology would suggest that parents experience the strongest grief over the deaths of their:
    a. infant sons.
    b. infant daughters.
    c. adolescent sons.
    d. adolescent daughters.

Evolution and sexuality, pp. 89-90
Medium, Factual/Definitional, Objective 3, Ans: a

15. Compared with men, women are _____ likely to read pornographic material and _____ likely to refuse direct requests for casual sex.
    a. less; more
    b. more; more
    c. less; less
    d. more; less

Evolution and sexuality, p. 90
Medium, Factual/Definitional, Objective 3, Ans: c

16. Compared with women, men are more likely to:
    a. report low levels of marital satisfaction.
    b. smile at members of the opposite sex.
    c. perceive simple friendliness as a sexual come-on.
    d. demonstrate erotic plasticity.

Evolution and sexuality, p. 90
Difficult, Conceptual, Objective 3, Ans: b

17. Men rape women much more frequently than women rape men. Evolutionary psychologists would most likely explain this in terms of sex differences in:
    a. erotic plasticity.
    b. reproductive capacity.
    c. gender-typing.
    d. body size.

Evolution and sexuality, p. 90
Medium, Conceptual, Objective 3, Ans: b
18. Professor Archibald suggests that men are more likely than women to initiate casual sex because this has proven to be a more successful reproductive strategy for men than for women. The professor's suggestion best illustrates a(n) _____ theory.
    a. social learning
    b. evolutionary
    c. gender schema
    d. psychodynamic

Evolution and sexuality, p. 91
Medium, Conceptual, Objective 3, Ans: d
19. It has been suggested that men in all cultures tend to marry women younger than themselves because they are naturally attracted to female features associated with youthful fertility. This suggestion best illustrates:
    a. erotic plasticity.
    b. gender schema theory.
    c. gender-typing.
    d. an evolutionary perspective.

Evolution and sexuality, p. 91
Easy, Factual/Definitional, Objective 3, Ans: d
20. Evolutionary psychologists suggest that when compared to women, men are _____ concerned with maintaining a youthful appearance and _____ concerned with achieving social power.
    a. more; more
    b. less; less
    c. more; less
    d. less; more

Evolution and sexuality, p. 91
Medium, Conceptual, Objective 3, Ans: b
21. Jack aspires to become a corporate executive because he wants to earn a huge salary. Evolutionary psychologists would most likely attribute Jack's motivation to:
    a. gender schemas.
    b. genetic predispositions.
    c. gender-typing.
    d. peer influence.

Critiquing the evolutionary explanation, p. 92
Medium, Factual/Definitional, Objective 3, Ans: a
22. Evolutionary psychologists are most likely to be criticized for:
    a. hindsight speculation.
    b. underestimating gender differences.
    c. overestimating cultural variations.
    d. all of the above.

Critiquing the evolutionary explanation, p. 92
Difficult, Conceptual, Objective 3, Ans: c
23.   Evolutionary psychology would probably have the most difficulty accounting for:
       a. differences in the sexual behavior patterns of males and females.
       b. similarities in the sexual behavior patterns of males and females.
       c. differences in the sexual behavior patterns of Americans and Russians.
       d. similarities in the sexual behavior patterns of Americans and Russians.

Behavior genetics, p. 93
Medium, Factual/Definitional, Objective 4, Ans: d
24.   Twin studies are of most direct concern to:
       a. evolutionary psychologists.
       b. molecular biologists.
       c. gender schema theorists.
       d. behavior geneticists.

Behavior genetics, p. 93
Medium, Conceptual, Objective 4, Ans: c
25.   A researcher who assesses the heritability of intelligence is most likely a(n):
       a. gender schema theorist.
       b. evolutionary psychologist.
       c. behavior geneticist.
       d. social learning theorist.

Twin studies, pp. 93-94
Easy, Conceptual, Objective 4, Ans: d
26.   Compared to identical twins, fraternal twins are _____ likely to be the same sex and
       _____ likely to be similar in extraversion.
       a. less; more
       b. more; less
       c. more; more
       d. less; less
       e. less; equally

Twin studies, p. 94
Easy, Conceptual, Objective 4, Ans: d
27.   Taro and Kiichi are fraternal twins being raised by the same parents; Helene and Victoire are
       identical twins being raised by the same parents. Helene and Victoire are more likely than Taro
       and Kiichi to be similar in:
       a. personality.
       b. abilities.
       c. interests.
       d. all the above.

Twin studies, p. 95
Medium, Factual/Definitional, Objective 4, Ans: e
28.   Studies of identical twins who had been reared apart most clearly highlight the importance of
       _____ in personality development.
       a. testosterone
       b. gender schema
       c. erotic plasticity
       d. parental influence
       e. genetic predispositions

Twin studies, p. 95
Medium, Conceptual, Objective 4, Ans: c
29. Identical twins separated at birth and raised in completely different cultures would be most likely to have similar:
   a. gender schemas.
   b. religious beliefs.
   c. temperaments.
   d. memes.

Adoption studies, p. 96
Difficult, Conceptual, Objective 4, Ans: d
30. We are likely to _____ the personality similarities among children in the same family and we are likely to _____ the personality similarities between parents and their children.
   a. overestimate; underestimate
   b. underestimate; overestimate
   c. underestimate; underestimate
   d. overestimate; overestimate

Adoption studies, p. 97
Difficult, Factual/Definitional, Objective 4, Ans: d
31. At the age of 3 months, Kevin is removed from the home of his abusive biological parents and placed with adoptive parents who provide a happy, stable environment. As Kevin matures, he will probably develop a:
   a. personality very similar to that of his biological father.
   b. personality very similar to that of his adoptive father.
   c. more introverted personality than that of his biological father.
   d. higher level of intelligence than that of his biological father.

Adoption studies, p. 97
Medium, Factual/Definitional, Objective 4, Ans: a
32. Adoptive parents are most likely to influence the _____ of their adopted children.
   a. generosity
   b. gender identity
   c. extraversion
   d. temperament

Temperament studies, p. 97
Medium, Factual/Definitional, Objective 5, Ans: b
33. A person's temperament is best illustrated by his or her characteristic level of:
   a. physical attractiveness.
   b. fearfulness.
   c. physical health.
   d. intelligence.

Temperament studies, p. 97
Medium, Conceptual, Objective 5, Ans: d
34. Lynnae is usually timid and fearful, whereas her sister Eileen is typically relaxed and fearless. The two sisters are most strikingly different in:
   a. brain maturation.
   b. gender schemas.
   c. physical health.
   d. temperament.
   e. erotic plasticity.

Temperament studies, p. 97
Medium, Factual/Definitional, Objective 5, Ans: a

35.   Exceptionally timid and cautious infants tend to become shy and unassertive adolescents. This
       best illustrates the long-term impact of:
       a. temperament.
       b. memes.
       c. gender schemas.
       d. the X chromosome.

Temperament studies, p. 98
Easy, Factual/Definitional, Objective 5, Ans: c

36.   Heredity most clearly contributes to individual difference in:
       a. memes.
       b. gender-typing.
       c. temperament.
       d. erotic plasticity.
       e. personal space.

Temperament studies, p. 98
Easy, Factual/Definitional, Objective 5, Ans: b

37.   Newborn Asian infants have been observed to be calmer and less reactive than newborn
       Caucasian infants. This best illustrates racial differences in:
       a. physical health.
       b. temperament.
       c. erotic plasticity.
       d. parenting style.
       e. gender schemas.

Heritability, p. 98
Difficult, Factual/Definitional, Objective 6, Ans: b

38.   The heritability of intelligence refers to:
       a. the percentage of a person's intelligence that is attributable to genetics.
       b. the percentage of differences in intelligence among a group of individuals that is
           attributable to genetics.
       c. the extent to which children can inherit the intellectual aptitude of their parents.
       d. the extent to which genetically distinctive ethnic groups differ in intellectual aptitude.

Heritability, p. 98
Difficult, Factual/Definitional, Objective 6, Ans: b

39.   The heritability of a specific trait will be lowest among genetically _____ individuals who
       have been raised in _____ environments.
       a. similar; similar
       b. similar; dissimilar
       c. dissimilar; similar
       d. dissimilar; dissimilar

Heritability, p. 98
Difficult, Factual/Definitional, Objective 6, Ans: d

40.   Racial differences in a highly heritable trait are not necessarily caused by:
       a. genetic differences between racial groups.
       b. cultural differences between racial groups.
       c. temperament differences between racial groups.
       d. any of the above.

Gene-environment interactions, pp. 99-100
Medium, Conceptual, Objective 6, Ans: b
41.   Our selective exposure to those life experiences that are best suited to our unique temperaments best illustrates the interaction of:
a. roles and norms.
b. nature and nurture.
c. plasticity and permanence.
d. natural selection and evolution.

Gene-environment interactions, p. 100
Medium, Conceptual, Objective 6, Ans: b
42.   Because Marla is the first girl in her fourth-grade class to sexually mature, she is sometimes teased and rejected by her classmates. Marla's sense of social isolation and embarrassment result from the interaction of:
a. gender identity and temperament.
b. nature and nurture.
c. schemas and roles.
d. norms and memes.

Molecular genetics, p. 100
Difficult, Conceptual, Objective 7, Ans: a
43.   Molecular geneticists would be most interested in studying:
a. nucleotide sequences.
b. sex hormones.
c. gender schemas.
d. erotic plasticity.

How much credit (or blame) do parents deserve?, pp. 102-103
Medium, Factual/Definitional, Objective 8, Ans: d
44.   Parents should not take too much blame for the failures and shortcomings of their children because:
a. their child-rearing mistakes simply reflect that they were not properly raised by their own parents.
b. children typically fail on purpose in order to establish a healthy independence from parents.
c. child-rearing practices have been shown to have little long-lasting effects on children's development.
d. parental behavior is only one of many factors that influence children's behavior.

How much credit (or blame) do parents deserve?, pp. 102-103
Difficult, Conceptual, Objective 8, Ans: b
45.   Those who inappropriately attribute children's troubling personality traits to inadequate parental nurture should be reminded of the importance of:
a. erotic plasticity.
b. temperament.
c. personal space.
d. the X chromosome.

Prenatal environment, p. 103
Easy, Factual/Definitional, Objective 9, Ans: a

46.   Identical twins who have separate placentas are somewhat less similar than identical twins who share a placenta. This best illustrates the influence of _____ on development.
      a. prenatal environments
      b. genetic predispositions
      c. gender schemas
      d. erotic plasticity

Prenatal environment, p. 103
Medium, Conceptual, Objective 9, Ans: b

47.   Carl and Shirley are both mentally retarded because their mothers drank heavily during their embryonic development. This best illustrates the potentially harmful influence of:
      a. natural selection.
      b. prenatal environments.
      c. infant temperaments.
      d. gender schemas.

Experience and brain development, p. 104
Easy, Factual/Definitional, Objective 9, Ans: d

48.   A stimulating environment is most likely to facilitate the development of a child's:
      a. nucleotides.
      b. genome.
      c. temperament.
      d. neural connections.

Experience and brain development, p. 104
Difficult, Factual/Definitional, Objective 9, Ans: a

49.   Research on brain development suggests that repeated learning experiences
      seem to:
      a. strengthen neural connections at the location that processes the experiences.
      b. dramatically increase the number of brain cells in the cerebral cortex.
      c. promote the formation of the brainstem but have no effect on the formation of the cortex.
      d. have no effect on the structure of neural tissue.

Experience and brain development, p. 104
Difficult, Conceptual, Objective 9, Ans: a

50.   Jason was born with cataracts in both eyes. Even though they were removed when he was 5, his lack of visual experiences during early childhood makes it likely that he has experienced:
      a. degeneration of neural connections in visual reception areas of the brain.
      b. an inability to develop heritable traits.
      c. difficulty incorporating new experiences into existing schemas.
      d. a massive loss of sensory neurons.

Peer influence, p. 105
Medium, Factual/Definitional, Objective 10, Ans: b

51.   Children's English accents are more likely to be influenced by their _____ than by their
      _____.
      a. genes; environment
      b. peers; parents
      c. temperament; gender
      d. X chromosome; Y chromosome

Peer influence, p. 105
Medium, Factual/Definitional, Objective 10, Ans: c
52. The remarkable academic and vocational successes of children of the refugee Asian boat people best illustrate the importance of:
   a. peer influence.
   b. temperament.
   c. family environment.
   d. personal space.

Culture, p. 106
Easy, Factual/Definitional, Objective 10, Ans: c
53. People are most likely to notice the impact of environmental influences on behavior when confronted by:
   a. identical twins.
   b. gender schemas.
   c. cultural diversity.
   d. human temperaments.

Culture, p. 106
Easy, Factual/Definitional, Objective 10, Ans: b
54. The ideas and traditions of a culture are typically perpetuated by means of:
   a. stereotypes.
   b. norms.
   c. schemas.
   d. temperaments.

Culture, pp. 106-107
Medium, Conceptual, Objective 10, Ans: e
55. The practice of covering your mouth when you cough best illustrates the impact of:
   a. genetic predispositions.
   b. roles.
   c. gender schemas.
   d. personal space.
   e. norms.

Culture, pp. 106-107
Easy, Factual/Definitional, Objective 10, Ans: d
56. Social norms have been found to:
   a. facilitate smooth social interaction.
   b. vary from one culture to another.
   c. free people from uncertainty about how they ought to behave.
   d. do all the above.

Culture, p. 107
Easy, Conceptual, Objective 10, Ans: c
57. Even though there are many unoccupied chairs in the library study area, Wang chooses to sit in a chair right next to Annest. Annest is most likely to feel uncomfortable because Wang has violated her:
   a. role.
   b. gender schema.
   c. personal space.
   d. temperament.
   e. gender identity.

Culture, p. 107
Difficult, Factual/Definitional, Objective 10, Ans: b
58.   In which of the following countries do people generally prefer to maintain the largest personal
      space?
      a. France
      b. England
      c. Mexico
      d. Saudi Arabia

Culture, p. 107
Medium, Factual/Definitional, Objective 10, Ans: c
59.   Compared with northern Europeans, people from Mediterranean cultures are _____ likely
      to be emotionally expressive and _____ likely to be punctual.
      a. more; more
      b. less; less
      c. more; less
      d. less; more

Culture, p. 108
Medium, Factual/Definitional, Objective 10, Ans: d
60.   In comparison to 40 years age, today American women are more likely to marry for the sake
      of:
      a. economic advantage.
      b. reproductive success.
      c. gender identity.
      d. love.

Culture, p. 108
Difficult, Conceptual, Objective 10, Ans: e
61.   Genes are to the perpetuation of individuals as _____ are to the perpetuation of cultures.
      a. synapses
      b. schemas
      c. nucleotides
      d. mutations
      e. memes

Culture and child-rearing, p. 108
Medium, Factual/Definitional, Objective 10, Ans: c
62.   Compared with many Asian and African parents, today's North American parents are more
      likely to teach their children to value:
      a. civil obedience.
      b. emotional closeness.
      c. personal independence.
      d. family traditions.

Culture and child-rearing, pp. 108-109
Medium, Factual/Definitional, Objective 10, Ans: c
63.   Compared to North American children, Chinese children are likely to exhibit _____ respect
      for authority and _____ shyness toward strangers.
      a. more; less
      b. less; more
      c. more; more
      d. less; less

Developmental similarities across groups, p. 109
Difficult, Factual/Definitional, Objective 10, Ans: b
64.   Cross-cultural research on human development indicates that:
    a. differences among cultural groups largely reflect genetic differences among racial groups.
    b. developmental processes are highly similar among individuals raised in different cultures.
    c. differences among cultural groups are greater than person-to-person differences within cultural groups.
    d. gender differences in behavior result from differences in biology rather than from differences in life experience.

The nature of gender, pp. 110-111
Medium, Factual/Definitional, Objective 11, Ans: d
65.   A baby girl receives a(n) _____ chromosome from her _____.
    a. Y; father
    b. Y; mother
    c. Y; father and mother
    d. X; father and mother

The nature of gender, p. 111
Easy, Factual/Definitional, Objective 11, Ans: c
66.   The prenatal development of the external male sex organs is stimulated by:
    a. gender schemas.
    b. the X chromosome.
    c. testosterone.
    d. endorphins.
    e. memes.

The nature of gender, p. 111
Medium, Factual/Definitional, Objective 11, Ans: d
67.   Prenatal testosterone secretions exert one of their earliest influences on:
    a. genes.
    b. memes.
    c. gender schemas.
    d. brain organization.

The nature of gender, p. 111
Medium, Factual/Definitional, Objective 11, Ans: d
68.   A genetically female child who receives excess testosterone during prenatal growth is subsequently likely to develop:
    a. greater erotic plasticity than most females.
    b. a female gender role, but a male gender identity.
    c. a male body with both X and Y chromosomes, unless there is corrective surgery.
    d. more aggressive behavior patterns than most girls.

Gender roles, p. 111
Easy, Factual/Definitional, Objective 12, Ans: b
69.   Sets of expected behaviors for males and for females are called:
    a. gender identities.
    b. gender roles.
    c. sexual norms.
    d. gender types.

Gender roles, pp. 111-112
Medium, Conceptual, Objective 12, Ans: b
70. Six-year-old Jennifer believes that men become doctors and women become nurses. Clearly, Jennifer is already acquiring a knowledge of traditional:
a. gender identities.
b. gender roles.
c. sexual orientations.
d. sexual norms.
e. gender types.

Gender roles, p. 112
Medium, Factual/Definitional, Objective 12, Ans: c
71. Women's leadership responsibilities have most clearly been limited by their:
a. erotic plasticity.
b. sex hormones.
c. gender roles.
d. reproductive strategies.

Gender and child-rearing, p. 113
Easy, Factual/Definitional, Objective 12, Ans: a
72. A person's sense of being male or female is his or her gender:
a. identity.
b. role.
c. type.
d. schema.

Gender and child-rearing, p. 113
Easy, Factual/Definitional, Objective 12, Ans: c
73. The acquisition of a masculine or a feminine gender role is referred to as:
a. sexual orientation.
b. erotic plasticity.
c. gender-typing.
d. gender identification.

Gender and child-rearing, p. 113
Medium, Conceptual, Objective 12, Ans: c
74. Six-year-old Tommy wants his hair cut and combed like his father's. He also wants a new cap, shirt, and sweater to match his father's. This best illustrates the process of:
a. stereotyping.
b. natural selection.
c. gender-typing.
d. sexual orientation.

Gender and child-rearing, p. 113
Easy, Factual/Definitional, Objective 12, Ans: d
75. The importance of rewards and punishments in gender-typing is emphasized by _____ theory.
a. evolutionary
b. gender schema
c. psychoanalytic
d. social learning

Gender and child-rearing, p. 113
Medium, Conceptual, Objective 12, Ans: b

76.   Edgar responds to his daughter's fistfight with, "Good girls don't fight!" but when his son has a
      fistfight he says, "Did you win?!" The role of Edgar's reactions in the gender-typing of his
      children would be of most direct concern to:
      a. behavior genetics theory.
      b. social learning theory.
      c. evolutionary theory.
      d. gender schema theory.

Gender and child-rearing, p. 113
Medium, Factual/Definitional, Objective 12, Ans: b

77.   According to gender schema theory, children become gender-typed because they:
      a. identify most strongly with their same-sex parent.
      b. perceive much of reality in terms of masculinity and femininity.
      c. are unable to assume the perspective of the opposite sex.
      d. grow up in a sexually oppressive family environment.

Gender and child-rearing, p. 114
Difficult, Conceptual, Objective 12, Ans: b

78.   Because he believes that "real men have no fears," 8-year-old George has difficulty accepting
      the fact that his father is fearful of losing his job. George's experience is most directly
      explained by:
      a. social learning theory.
      b. gender schema theory.
      c. evolutionary theory.
      d. behavior genetics theory.

Postscript: Reflections on nature and nurture, p. 115
Medium, Factual/Definitional, Objective 13, Ans: b

79.   By insisting that humans are "nothing but" products of nature and nurture, we run the greatest
      risk of undermining:
      a. personal space.
      b. individual responsibility.
      c. natural selection.
      d. gender identity.

CHAPTER **4**

The Developing Person

Learning Objectives

Prenatal Development and the Newborn (pp. 119-123)

1. Discuss the course of prenatal development and the destructive impact of teratogens.

2. Describe the capacities of the newborn and the use of habituation for assessing infant cognition.

Infancy and Childhood (pp. 123-140)

3. Describe the influence of maturation and experience on brain and motor development.

4. Describe Piaget's view of how the mind develops and discuss his stage theory of cognitive development, noting current thinking regarding cognitive stages.

5. Discuss the effect of body contact, familiarity, and responsive parenting on infant social attachments.

6. Describe the benefits of a secure attachment and the impact of parental neglect and separation, as well as day care on childhood development.

7. Describe the early development of a self-concept and discuss possible effects of different parenting styles on children.

Adolescence (pp. 140-152)

8. Define adolescence and identify the major physical changes that occur during this period of life.

9. Describe the adolescent's growing reasoning power and Kohlberg's theory of moral development, noting the relationship between thoughts and actions.

10. Discuss the search for identity and the development of intimate social relationships during the adolescent years.

Adulthood (pp. 152-167)

11.   Identify the major physical changes that occur in middle and older adulthood.

12.   Describe the impact of aging on adult memory and intelligence.

13.   Explain why the path of adult development need not be tightly linked to one's chronological age.

14.   Discuss the importance of family and work commitments in adult development.

15.   Describe people's life satisfaction across the life span and their reactions to death or the prospect of dying.

Reflections on Life-Span Development (pp. 167-169)

16.   Summarize current views regarding continuity versus stages and stability versus change in lifelong development.

The developing person, p. 119
Easy, Factual/Definitional, Objective 1, Ans: d
1.   The branch of psychology that systematically focuses on the physical, mental, and social changes that occur throughout the life cycle is called:
    a. clinical psychology.
    b. social psychology.
    c. personality psychology.
    d. developmental psychology.
    e. biological psychology.

Conception, p. 120
Medium, Factual/Definitional, Objective 1, Ans: d
2.   Boys first begin producing sperm during:
    a. embryonic development.
    b. fetal development.
    c. the first year after birth.
    d. puberty.

Prenatal development, p. 120
Medium, Factual/Definitional, Objective 1, Ans: b
3.   A fertilized egg is called a(n):
    a. embryo.
    b. zygote.
    c. teratogen.
    d. fetus.

Prenatal development, p. 120
Medium, Factual/Definitional, Objective 1, Ans: a

4.   From 10 days to 9 weeks after conception, the human organism is known as a(n):
    a. embryo.
    b. fetus.
    c. zygote.
    d. ovum.

Prenatal development, p. 121
Medium, Factual/Definitional, Objective 1, Ans: b

5. The developing human organism from 9 weeks after conception to birth is known as a(n):
    a. embryo.
    b. fetus.
    c. zygote.
    d. neonate.

Prenatal development, p. 121
Medium, Factual/Definitional, Objective 1, Ans: c

6. Newborn infants typically prefer their mother's voice over their father's voice because:
    a. their rooting reflex is naturally triggered by higher-pitched sounds.
    b. they rapidly habituate to lower-pitched male voices.
    c. they become familiar with their mother's voice before they are born.
    d. they form an emotional attachment to their mother during breast-feeding.
    e. they have difficulty hearing lower-pitched voices during the first few days after birth.

Prenatal development, p. 121
Easy, Conceptual, Objective 1, Ans: b

7. Phyllis, a 28-year-old heroin addict, is pregnant. Her baby will be born:
    a. with schizophrenia.
    b. a heroin addict.
    c. visually impaired.
    d. with Down syndrome.
    e. hyperactive.

Prenatal development, p. 121
Difficult, Factual/Definitional, Objective 1, Ans: e

8. Markedly increased violent crime rates among Danish men whose mothers smoked heavily during pregnancy best illustrate the lasting influence of:
    a. imprinting.
    b. crystallized intelligence.
    c. object permanence.
    d. egocentrism.
    e. teratogens.

Prenatal development, p. 121
Difficult, Conceptual, Objective 1, Ans: a

9. The symptoms of FAS demonstrate that alcohol is a:
    a. teratogen.
    b. form of DNA.
    c. hallucinogen.
    d. neurotransmitter.
    e. gene.

The competent newborn, p. 122
Easy, Conceptual, Objective 2, Ans: b

10. When Joan touched her infant's cheek, he turned his head toward the side that was touched and opened his mouth. Joan was eliciting the:
  a. startle reaction.
  b. rooting reflex.
  c. grasping reflex.
  d. attachment reflex.
  e. attention reflex.

The competent newborn, p. 122
Medium, Factual/Definitional, Objective 2, Ans: d

11. Research on the perceptual abilities of newborns indicates that they:
  a. see nothing for the first 12 hours.
  b. see only differences in brightness.
  c. recognize the outlines of objects but none of the details.
  d. look more at a human face than at a bull's-eye pattern.

The competent newborn, p. 122
Difficult, Factual/Definitional, Objective 2, Ans: a

12. Research indicates that 3-week-old human infants can distinguish:
  a. their mother's voice from that of a female stranger.
  b. differences in light intensity but not differences in shape.
  c. their mother's face from that of a female stranger.
  d. differences in sound intensity but not differences in sound quality.

Research strategies for understanding infants' thinking (Box), p. 123
Easy, Conceptual, Objective 2, Ans: d

13. Three-month-old Andrew was obviously startled by the first ring of the telephone, but with each subsequent ring he seemed to become less reactive. This best illustrates the process of:
  a. accommodation.
  b. conservation.
  c. imprinting.
  d. habituation.
  e. attachment.

Research strategies for understanding infants' thinking (Box), p. 123
Difficult, Factual/Definitional, Objective 2, Ans: e

14. The best evidence that day-old human infants possess visual memory capabilities comes from research on:
  a. imprinting.
  b. conservation.
  c. the rooting reflex.
  d. object permanence.
  e. habituation.

Brain development, p. 124
Easy, Factual/Definitional, Objective 3, Ans: d

15. Biological growth processes that are relatively uninfluenced by experience and that enable orderly changes in behavior are referred to as:
a. continuity.
b. imprinting.
c. generativity.
d. maturation.
e. fixation.

Brain development, p. 124
Medium, Factual/Definitional, Objective 3, Ans: d

16. The immaturity of an infant's nervous system is best demonstrated by its limited:
a. speed of neural transmission.
b. number of brain cells.
c. size of mental schemas.
d. complexity of neural networks.

Maturation and infant memory, p. 125
Medium, Factual/Definitional, Objective 3, Ans: b

17. Poor memory for early life experiences results from a baby's relative lack of:
a. brain cells.
b. neural connections.
c. perceptual abilities.
d. all the above.

Maturation and infant memory, p. 125
Difficult, Conceptual, Objective 3, Ans: a

18. Kristen is a normal, healthy newborn. Research indicates that:
a. she has most of the brain cells she is ever going to have.
b. the neural connections that will enable her to think and talk are already completely formed.
c. she is clearly capable of forming permanent lifelong memories.
d. all the above are true.

Motor development, p. 126
Medium, Factual/Definitional, Objective 3, Ans: b

19. Identical twins typically begin walking on nearly the same day. This best illustrates the importance of:
a. responsive parenting.
b. maturation.
c. accommodation.
d. secure attachment.
e. habituation.

Motor development, p. 126
Easy, Conceptual, Objective 3, Ans: d

20. It is difficult to successfully train many children to walk before they are 10 months old. This best illustrates the importance of:
a. assimilation.
b. habituation.
c. accommodation.
d. maturation.
e. secure attachments.

Motor development, p. 126
Medium, Conceptual, Objective 3, Ans: b
21.   The concept of maturation is most relevant to understanding the absence of:
       a. secure attachments among infants.
       b. bladder control among 2-year-olds.
       c. self-esteem among kindergarten students.
       d. moral behavior among adolescents.

Cognitive development, p. 127
Easy, Factual/Definitional, Objective 4, Ans: c
22.   Which psychologist was most influential in shaping our understanding of cognitive
       development?
       a. B. F. Skinner
       b. Konrad Lorenz
       c. Jean Piaget
       d. Sigmund Freud
       e. Erik Erikson

Cognitive development, p. 127
Easy, Factual/Definitional, Objective 4, Ans: d
23.   A concept or framework that organizes and interprets information is called a(n):
       a. assimilation.
       b. attachment.
       c. accommodation.
       d. schema.
       e. neural network.

Cognitive development, p. 127
Difficult, Conceptual, Objective 4, Ans: b
24.   Because her father was abusive, Edith has trouble perceiving that other men can be
       compassionate and nurturant. Piaget would have suggested that Edith is limited by:
       a. stranger anxiety.
       b. an inadequate schema.
       c. egocentrism.
       d. object permanence.

Cognitive development, p. 127
Medium, Factual/Definitional, Objective 4, Ans: c
25.   According to Piaget, assimilation involves:
       a. the absorption of nutrients into the body for growth and development.
       b. training children to behave in a socially acceptable manner.
       c. interpreting new experiences in terms of one's current understanding.
       d. altering existing schemas in order to incorporate new information.

Cognitive development, p. 127
Difficult, Conceptual, Objective 4, Ans: b

26.   Three-year-old Zara calls all four-legged animals "kitties." Her tendency to fit all four-legged
       animals into her existing conception of a kitten illustrates the process of:
       a. conservation.
       b. assimilation.
       c. accommodation.
       d. egocentrism.
       e. attachment.

Cognitive development, p. 127
Easy, Factual/Definitional, Objective 4, Ans: b

27.   Adjusting current schemas to make sense of new information is called:
a. habituation.
b. accommodation.
c. egocentrism.
d. assimilation.
e. maturation.

Cognitive development, p. 127
Difficult, Conceptual, Objective 4, Ans: e

28.   In recognizing the inaccuracies of one's own ethnic stereotypes and revising his or her beliefs, an individual most clearly illustrates the process of:
a. habituation.
b. attachment.
c. assimilation.
d. imprinting.
e. accommodation.

Piaget's theory and current thinking, p. 128
Easy, Factual/Definitional, Objective 4, Ans: b

29.   Cognition refers to:
a. an emotional tie linking one person with another.
b. the mental activities associated with thinking, knowing, and remembering.
c. any process that facilitates the physical development of the brain.
d. an awareness that we are constantly changing as we develop.

Piaget's theory and current thinking, p. 128
Medium, Factual/Definitional, Objective 4, Ans: b

30.   During which stage do children understand the world primarily by observing the effects of their own actions on other people, objects, and events?
a. concrete operational
b. sensorimotor
c. formal operational
d. preoperational

Piaget's theory and current thinking, pp. 128-129
Easy, Factual/Definitional, Objective 4, Ans: d

31.   The awareness that things continue to exist even when they are not perceived is known as:
a. attachment.
b. conservation.
c. assimilation.
d. object permanence.
e. habituation.

Piaget's theory and current thinking, pp. 128-129
Easy, Conceptual, Objective 4, Ans: b

32. Lisa attempts to retrieve her bottle after her father hides it under a blanket. This suggests that Lisa has developed a sense of:
    a. egocentrism.
    b. object permanence.
    c. conservation.
    d. accommodation.
    e. secure attachment.

Piaget's theory and current thinking, pp. 128-129
Easy, Conceptual, Objective 4, Ans: c

33. When Franklin's father hides a ball behind his back, Franklin quickly loses interest in the ball. This suggests that Franklin has not developed a sense of:
    a. basic trust.
    b. attachment.
    c. object permanence.
    d. curiosity.
    e. egocentrism.

Piaget's theory and current thinking, p. 129
Difficult, Factual/Definitional, Objective 4, Ans: c

34. The discovery that 5-month-old infants stare longer at numerically impossible outcomes suggests that Piaget:
    a. underestimated the importance of imprinting on infant attachment.
    b. overestimated the impact of culture on infant intelligence.
    c. underestimated the cognitive capacities of infants.
    d. overestimated the continuity of cognitive development.

Piaget's theory and current thinking, pp. 128, 130
Difficult, Factual/Definitional, Objective 4, Ans: a

35. According to Piaget, children in the preoperational stage are able to:
    a. represent objects with words and images.
    b. reason abstractly and test hypotheses.
    c. understand the world only by observing the consequences of their own actions.
    d. think logically about tangible things.

Piaget's theory and current thinking, p. 130
Medium, Factual/Definitional, Objective 4, Ans: c

36. The principle that properties such as mass, volume, and number remain the same despite changes in the forms of objects is called:
    a. perceptual constancy.
    b. object equivalence.
    c. conservation.
    d. object permanence.
    e. accommodation.

Piaget's theory and current thinking, p. 130
Medium, Conceptual, Objective 4, Ans: a

37. Five-year-old Tammy mistakenly believes that her short, wide glass contains less soda than her brother's tall, narrow glass. Actually, both glasses contain the same amount of soda. This illustrates that Tammy lacks the concept of:
    a. conservation.
    b. egocentrism.
    c. assimilation.
    d. object permanence.
    e. accommodation.

Piaget's theory and current thinking, p. 130
Difficult, Factual/Definitional, Objective 4, Ans: b

38. Current research on cognitive development indicates that:
    a. Piaget overestimated the cognitive competence of young children.
    b. mental skills develop earlier and more gradually than Piaget believed.
    c. Piaget's theory may apply only to middle-class male children.
    d. Piaget overlooked the importance of imprinting on cognitive development.

Piaget's theory and current thinking, p. 130
Medium, Factual/Definitional, Objective 4, Ans: d

39. According to Piaget, an egocentric child can best be described as:
    a. selfish.
    b. conceited.
    c. lacking in self-esteem.
    d. cognitively limited.

Piaget's theory and current thinking, pp. 130-131
Difficult, Conceptual, Objective 4, Ans: d

40. Although Mr. Tong was obviously busy reading an absorbing novel, his 5-year-old daughter kept interrupting him with comments and questions about the TV cartoons she was watching. Before Mr. Tong becomes irritated with his daughter for being inconsiderate, he should be alerted to Piaget's concept of:
    a. object permanence.
    b. habituation.
    c. conservation.
    d. egocentrism.
    e. accommodation.

Piaget's theory and current thinking, p. 131
Medium, Factual/Definitional, Objective 4, Ans: a

41. Children's ability to infer other people's intentions and feelings is indicative of their emerging:
    a. theory of mind.
    b. concept of conservation.
    c. practice of habituation.
    d. sense of object permanence.

Piaget's theory and current thinking, p. 131
Easy, Conceptual, Objective 4, Ans: c

42. The ability of preschool children to empathize with classmates who are feeling sad illustrates that preoperational children are not completely:
     a. habituated.
     b. assimilated.
     c. egocentric.
     d. imprinted.

Piaget's theory and current thinking, p. 131
Medium, Factual/Definitional, Objective 4, Ans: b

43. The ability of preschoolers to recognize that other children may hold false beliefs best illustrates that they are not completely:
     a. assimilated.
     b. egocentric.
     c. imprinted.
     d. habituated.
     e. accommodated.

Piaget's theory and current thinking, p. 131
Medium, Factual/Definitional, Objective 4, Ans: c

44. Autism is a disorder most strikingly characterized by an impaired:
     a. capacity for habituation.
     b. sense of object permanence.
     c. theory of mind.
     d. concept of conservation.

Piaget's theory and current thinking, p. 132
Difficult, Factual/Definitional, Objective 4, Ans: c

45. The Russian psychologist Vygotsky suggested that children's ability to solve problems is enhanced by:
     a. basic trust.
     b. egocentrism.
     c. inner speech.
     d. conservation.
     e. imprinting.

Piaget's theory and current thinking, p. 132
Medium, Factual/Definitional, Objective 4, Ans: c

46. Children acquire the mental operations needed to comprehend such things as mathematical transformations and conservation during the _____ stage.
     a. preoperational
     b. sensorimotor
     c. concrete operational
     d. formal operational

Piaget's theory and current thinking, p. 132
Difficult, Conceptual, Objective 4, Ans: a

47. Gilbert notices that his sausage is sliced into six pieces, whereas his brother's is sliced into nine pieces. He understands, however, that his brother's sausage is not actually any larger than his own. This indicates that Gilbert has by now reached the _____ stage of development.
    a. concrete operational
    b. sensorimotor
    c. formal operational
    d. preoperational

Piaget's theory and current thinking, pp. 130, 132
Difficult, Conceptual, Objective 4, Ans: c

48. According to Piaget, the preoperational stage is to the concrete operational stage as _____ is to _____.
    a. assimilation; accommodation
    b. object permanence; stranger anxiety
    c. egocentrism; conservation
    d. responsive parenting; temperament

Piaget's theory and current thinking, p. 132
Medium, Factual/Definitional, Objective 4, Ans: d

49. According to Piaget, during the concrete operational stage, a child is still unlikely to demonstrate:
    a. object permanence.
    b. comprehension of mathematical transformations.
    c. evidence of assimilation and accommodation.
    d. the ability to think hypothetically.
    e. any evidence of logic.

Piaget's theory and current thinking, pp. 128, 132
Easy, Factual/Definitional, Objective 4, Ans: c

50. According to Piaget, people are first able to reason abstractly and think hypothetically during the _____ stage.
    a. preoperational
    b. postconventional
    c. formal operational
    d. concrete operational

Piaget's theory and current thinking, pp. 132-133
Medium, Factual/Definitional, Objective 4, Ans: b

51. Contemporary research suggests that Piaget identified fairly accurately _____ of major cognitive developmental milestones.
    a. both the sequence and the age-related timing
    b. the sequence but not the age-related timing
    c. the age-related timing but not the sequence
    d. neither the sequence nor the age-related timing

Social Development, p. 134
Medium, Factual/Definitional, Objective 5, Ans: c

52. The acquisition of a sense of object permanence is most closely associated with the
     development of:
     a. conservation.
     b. concrete operational intelligence.
     c. stranger anxiety.
     d. self-awareness.
     e. egocentrism.

Social development, p. 134
Medium, Conceptual, Objective 5, Ans: b

53. Eighteen-month-old Justin follows his mother around the house, clinging tightly to her when he
     is frightened. This best illustrates:
     a. object permanence.
     b. attachment behavior.
     c. stranger anxiety.
     d. the rooting reflex.
     e. habituation.

Social development, p. 134
Medium, Factual/Definitional, Objective 5, Ans: d

54. Young children typically try to stay very close to their parents when they are in an unfamiliar
     setting. This best illustrates the adaptive value of:
     a. habituation.
     b. conservation.
     c. the rooting reflex.
     d. attachment.
     e. egocentrism.

Origins of attachment: body contact, pp. 134-135
Medium, Factual/Definitional, Objective 5, Ans: b

55. Harlow's studies of infant monkeys raised with artificial mothers suggests that body contact
     promotes:
     a. egocentrism.
     b. attachment.
     c. stranger anxiety.
     d. conservation.
     e. all the above.

Origins of attachment: body contact, p. 135
Medium, Factual/Definitional, Objective 5, Ans: b

56. Infant monkeys raised with a nourishing wire mother and a nonnourishing cloth mother:
     a. preferred the nourishing wire mother.
     b. preferred the nonnourishing cloth mother.
     c. showed no preference for one mother over the other.
     d. shifted their initial preference for the wire mother to the cloth mother as
         they matured.

Origins of attachment: body contact, pp. 135, 136
Medium, Conceptual, Objective 5, Ans: b

57.   Mr. Johnson spends time each day caressing and rocking his infant daughter. This time together should serve most directly to promote:
       a. habituation.
       b. secure attachment.
       c. stranger anxiety.
       d. egocentrism.
       e. conservation.

Origins of attachment: familiarity, p. 135
Medium, Factual/Definitional, Objective 5, Ans: b

58.   Which of the following factors is most important for the development of positive emotional bonds between human infants and their mothers?
       a. conservation
       b. familiarity
       c. egocentrism
       d. imprinting
       e. stranger anxiety

Origins of attachment: familiarity, p. 135
Medium, Conceptual, Objective 5, Ans: b

59.   Dr. Wong believes that children whose parents are not responsive to their needs during the first two months of life will never develop basic trust toward the world. Obviously, Dr. Wong believes that this developmental stage is a:
       a. preoperational stage.
       b. critical period.
       c. cognitive schema.
       d. maturational span.

Origins of attachment: familiarity, p. 135
Easy, Factual/Definitional, Objective 5, Ans: a

60.   The process by which certain birds form attachments during a critical period very early in life is called:
       a. imprinting.
       b. assimilation.
       c. habituation.
       d. bonding.
       e. the rooting reflex.

Origins of attachment: familiarity, p. 135
Difficult, Conceptual, Objective 5, Ans: b

61.   Lambs raised in the barn where the cattle are kept tend to stay near the cattle when subsequently placed in open pasture. This best illustrates a process known as:
       a. assimilation.
       b. imprinting.
       c. conservation.
       d. accommodation.
       e. the rooting reflex.

Origins of attachment: responsive parenting, p. 136
Medium, Conceptual, Objective 5, Ans: a

62. At 12 months of age Jeremy shows no more desire to be held by his own parents than by complete strangers. His behavior best illustrates:
    a. object permanence.
    b. insecure attachment.
    c. habituation.
    d. conservation.
    e. egocentrism.

Origins of attachment: responsive parenting, p. 136
Medium, Conceptual, Objective 5, Ans: a

63. Although Adam ventures away from his mother to explore the attractive toys located in the dentist's waiting room, he periodically returns to her side for brief moments. Adam most clearly displays signs of:
    a. secure attachment.
    b. habituation.
    c. egocentrism.
    d. conservation.
    e. stranger anxiety.

Origins of attachment: responsive parenting, p. 136
Medium, Conceptual, Objective 5, Ans: d

64. Even though Alicia was busy playing when her mother came to pick her up from her babysitter, she quickly ran to her mother, gesturing to be held. Alicia most clearly showed signs of:
    a. conservation.
    b. stranger anxiety.
    c. habituation.
    d. secure attachment.
    e. egocentrism.

Origins of attachment: responsive parenting, p. 136
Easy, Conceptual, Objective 5, Ans: b

65. Dr. Ensing studies the reactions of very young children who are briefly separated from their mothers while in an unfamiliar setting. It is most likely that Dr. Ensing is conducting research on:
    a. habituation.
    b. attachment.
    c. conservation.
    d. egocentrism.
    e. the rooting reflex.

Origins of attachment: responsive parenting, p. 136
Difficult, Factual/Definitional, Objective 5, Ans: d

66. In a pleasant but unfamiliar setting, infants with an insecure maternal attachment are most likely to:
    a. demonstrate unusually low levels of stranger anxiety.
    b. happily leave their mother's side and explore their new surroundings.
    c. feel immediately reassured and comforted when their mothers leave them.
    d. show indifference or hostility when their mothers approach them after a brief absence.

Origins of attachment: responsive parenting, pp. 119, 136
Medium, Conceptual, Objective 5, Ans: c

67. Questions about the extent to which secure attachments are influenced by infant temperament or by responsive parenting are most directly relevant to the issue of:
    a. continuity or stages.
    b. stability or change.
    c. nature or nurture.
    d. rationality or irrationality.
    e. assimilation or accommodation.

Origins of attachment: responsive parenting, p. 136
Easy, Factual/Definitional, Objective 5, Ans: d

68. Responsive parenting is most likely to contribute to:
    a. egocentrism.
    b. habituation.
    c. maturation.
    d. secure attachment.
    e. temperament.

Origins of attachment: responsive parenting, p. 136
Easy, Factual/Definitional, Objective 5, Ans: d

69. A mother who consistently responds supportively to her infant's cries for care and protection is most likely to encourage:
    a. egocentrism.
    b. habituation.
    c. stranger anxiety.
    d. secure attachment.
    e. conservation.

Origins of attachment: responsive parenting, p. 136
Medium, Conceptual, Objective 5, Ans: d

70. Babies who are unable to predict how their parents will react to their cries for care and attention are usually likely to show signs of:
    a. egocentrism.
    b. conservation.
    c. crystallized intelligence.
    d. insecure attachment.
    e. habituation.

Origins of attachment: responsive parenting, p. 136
Medium, Conceptual, Objective 5, Ans: a

71. When 1-year-old Andrea tries to talk, her mother talks back; when she smiles, her mother smiles in return. These maternal reactions are most relevant to Andrea's development of:
    a. secure attachment.
    b. conservation.
    c. accommodation.
    d. habituation.
    e. object permanence.

Origins of attachment: responsive parenting, p. 136
Medium, Conceptual, Objective 5, Ans: a
72. At 16 months of age, Edmund is uncertain whether his busy parents will take time to feed him when he is hungry. This is most indicative of:
   a. insecure attachment.
   b. imprinting.
   c. conservation.
   d. habituation.
   e. the rooting reflex.

Origins of attachment: responsive parenting, p. 137
Medium, Factual/Definitional, Objective 5, Ans: b
73. After the age of _____ months, anxiety over temporary separation from parents typically

   _____.
   a. 3; declines
   b. 13; declines
   c. 23; increases
   d. 33; increases

Effects of attachment, p. 137
Easy, Factual/Definitional, Objective 6, Ans: b
74. Compared to toddlers with an insecure parental attachment, those with a secure attachment are likely to be _____ sociable toward other children and _____ enthusiastic and persistent in tackling challenging tasks.
   a. less; more
   b. more; more
   c. more; less
   d. less; less

Effects of attachment, p. 137
Medium, Factual/Definitional, Objective 6, Ans: c
75. Erik Erikson suggested that children with a very secure attachment to their parents are especially likely to experience:
   a. stranger anxiety.
   b. egocentrism.
   c. basic trust.
   d. object permanence.
   e. habituation.

Effects of attachment, p. 137
Difficult, Factual/Definitional, Objective 6, Ans: c
76. Erik Erikson suggested that a sense of basic trust during infancy results from:
   a. habituation.
   b. object permanence.
   c. responsive parenting.
   d. inborn temperament.
   e. accommodation.

Effects of attachment, p. 137
Easy, Conceptual, Objective 6, Ans: e

77. Already at 15 months of age, Justin strongly senses that he can rely on his father to comfort and protect him. This most clearly contributes to:
   a. egocentrism.
   b. stranger anxiety.
   c. object permanence.
   d. habituation.
   e. basic trust.

Deprivation of attachment, p. 138
Difficult, Factual/Definitional, Objective 6, Ans: b

78. Monkeys raised in total isolation have been observed to:
   a. imprint to the first moving object they observe.
   b. become very fearful or aggressive when brought into close contact with other monkeys their age.
   c. form a close attachment to the first monkey with whom they experience bodily contact.
   d. show complete apathy and indifference to the first monkeys they encounter.

Deprivation of attachment, p. 138
Medium, Factual/Definitional, Objective 6, Ans: d

79. Research indicates that most abusive parents were:
   a. raised in a permissive and overindulgent environment.
   b. raised by their grandparents who provided inadequate role models.
   c. kept socially isolated as children and prevented from interacting with their peers.
   d. themselves battered or neglected as children.

Disruption of attachment, p. 138
Difficult, Factual/Definitional, Objective 6, Ans: d

80. When infants younger than 6 months of age are removed from their foster mothers and placed in stable adoptive homes, they typically show:
   a. initial distress in infancy and subsequent maladjustment at age 10.
   b. initial distress in infancy but no subsequent maladjustment at age 10.
   c. no initial distress in infancy but subsequent maladjustment at age 10.
   d. neither initial distress in infancy nor subsequent maladjustment at age 10.

Disruption of attachment, p. 139
Easy, Factual/Definitional, Objective 6, Ans: c

81. Foster care that moves a young child through a series of foster families is most likely to result in the disruption of:
   a. the rooting reflex.
   b. habituation.
   c. attachment.
   d. object permanence.
   e. assimilation.

Does day care affect attachment?, pp. 139-140
Easy, Factual/Definitional, Objective 6, Ans: c

82. Children's parental attachments are most likely to be disrupted if the children are provided with day care by:
     a. caregivers who demonstrate authoritative child-rearing practices.
     b. volunteer caregivers who become emotionally attached to children.
     c. poorly paid caregivers with high job turnover rates.
     d. grandparents who pay more attention to children than do parents.

Self-concept, p. 140
Medium, Conceptual, Objective 7, Ans: c

83. Dmitri is a typical 6-month-old. When he looks into a mirror he is likely to:
     a. recognize the image as himself.
     b. show no interest and ignore what he sees.
     c. reach toward the image as if it were another child.
     d. be somewhat frightened and turn away.

Self-concept, p. 140
Difficult, Conceptual, Objective 7, Ans: c

84. In order to recognize that a face seen in a mirror is one's own, a child must have a:
     a. theory of mind.
     b. secure attachment.
     c. self-schema.
     d. concept of conservation.

Self-concept, p. 140
Medium, Factual/Definitional, Objective 7, Ans: e

85. Researchers have sneakily dabbed rouge on young children's noses in order to study the developmental beginnings of:
     a. egocentrism.
     b. object permanence.
     c. habituation.
     d. conservation.
     e. self-awareness.

Child-rearing practices, p. 141
Easy, Factual/Definitional, Objective 7, Ans: d

86. Psychologists describe child-rearing in which rules are imposed without explanation as a(n) _____ style.
     a. authoritative
     b. egocentric
     c. disengaged.
     d. authoritarian

Child-rearing practices, p. 141
Medium, Conceptual, Objective 7, Ans: a

87. Authoritarian parents are especially likely to be:
     a. inflexible.
     b. educated.
     c. permissive.
     d. trusting.

Child-rearing practices, p. 141
Medium, Conceptual, Objective 7, Ans: a

88. Authoritative parents demonstrate _____ levels of parental control and _____ levels of parental responsiveness.
     a. high; high
     b. low; low
     c. high; low
     d. low; high

Child-rearing practices, p. 141
Medium, Conceptual, Objective 7, Ans: c

89. The Albertsons establish and enforce rules for their children to follow. They give reasons for the rules and invite their teenagers to join in the discussion when new rules are being made. Psychologists would characterize the Albertsons as _____ parents.
     a. authoritarian
     b. legalistic
     c. authoritative
     d. permissive

Child-rearing practices, p. 141
Medium, Factual/Definitional, Objective 7, Ans: b

90. Self-esteem in children is most positively correlated with _____ parenting.
     a. permissive
     b. authoritative
     c. paternal
     d. authoritarian

Child-rearing practices, p. 141
Easy, Factual/Definitional, Objective 7, Ans: a

91. Parents who discuss and negotiate family rules are especially likely to raise children who are:
     a. self-confident.
     b. insecurely attached.
     c. disobedient.
     d. egocentric.

Adolescence, p. 143
Easy, Factual/Definitional, Objective 8, Ans: b

92. Which of the following phases of development extends from the beginnings of sexual maturity to independent adulthood?
     a. puberty
     b. adolescence
     c. menopause
     d. menarche

Adolescence, p. 143
Medium, Conceptual, Objective 8, Ans: d

93. Compared to a century ago, menarche occurs _____ in life and marriage begins _____ in life.
     a. later; later
     b. earlier; earlier
     c. later; earlier
     d. earlier; later

Adolescent physical development, p. 144
Easy, Factual/Definitional, Objective 8, Ans: c
94. The term "puberty" refers to the period of:
   a. formal operations and the development of conventional morality.
   b. late adolescence when self-identity is formed.
   c. surging physical growth and the onset of reproductive capability.
   d. sexual attraction to the opposite-sex parent.

Adolescent physical development, p. 144
Medium, Conceptual, Objective 8, Ans: a
95. An example of a primary sex characteristic is a:
   a. woman's ovaries.
   b. man's larynx.
   c. woman's breasts.
   d. man's adrenal glands.

Adolescent physical development, p. 144
Easy, Factual/Definitional, Objective 8, Ans: b
96. Nonreproductive sexual characteristics such as the deepened male voice and facial hair on the male are called:
   a. masculine prototypes.
   b. secondary sex characteristics.
   c. primary sex characteristics.
   d. sex-linked traits.

Adolescent physical development, p. 145
Easy, Factual/Definitional, Objective 8, Ans: b
97. The term "menarche" refers to the:
   a. onset of male sexual potency.
   b. first menstrual period.
   c. development of the primary sex characteristics.
   d. cessation of menstruation.

Adolescent physical development, p. 145
Medium, Factual/Definitional, Objective 8, Ans: c
98. A man's first ejaculation:
   a. almost always produces feelings of guilt.
   b. typically results from masturbation.
   c. usually occurs as a nocturnal emission.
   d. signifies a physical readiness to father children.

Adolescent physical development, p. 145
Difficult, Conceptual, Objective 8, Ans: a
99. Who is likely to be the most popular student in the fifth-grade class?
   a. Helmut, who is the tallest boy in the class
   b. Jeff, who is the statistician for the basketball team
   c. Hara, who is below average in height and physical maturity
   d. Sally, who is the most sexually mature girl in the class

Developing reasoning power, p. 146
Easy, Conceptual, Objective 9, Ans: b

100. Vincent's ability to test hypotheses successfully in his geometry class indicates he is in the
_____ stage of development.
   a. concrete operational
   b. formal operational
   c. preconventional
   d. postconventional
   e. preoperational

Developing reasoning power, p. 146
Difficult, Conceptual, Objective 9, Ans: a

101. "If you're really concerned about the rights and dignity of women," Yigal asked his older
brother, "how can you justify buying pornographic magazines?" Yigal's question indicates
that he is in the _____ stage of development.
   a. formal operational
   b. conventional
   c. preconventional
   d. concrete operational
   e. early adulthood

Developing morality, p. 146
Easy, Factual/Definitional, Objective 9, Ans: a

102. Kohlberg emphasized that moral judgments are reflections of:
   a. cognitive development.
   b. social development.
   c. physical development.
   d. economic development.

Developing morality, p. 146
Medium, Conceptual, Objective 9, Ans: e

103. Cognitive development is to _____ as moral development is to _____.
   a. Gilligan; Kohlberg
   b. Kohlberg; Erikson
   c. Piaget; Erikson
   d. Erikson; Piaget
   e. Piaget; Kohlberg

Developing morality, p. 147
Difficult, Conceptual, Objective 9, Ans: c

104. Henry resists stealing jelly beans from his sister's Easter basket because he's afraid his mother
will spank him if he does. Henry's thinking best represents a(n) _____ morality.
   a. egocentric
   b. conventional
   c. preconventional
   d. concrete operational
   e. postconventional

Developing morality, p. 147
Medium, Factual/Definitional, Objective 9, Ans: c
105. According to Kohlberg, morality based on the need to gain social approval is characteristic of the _____ stage.
    a. preconventional
    b. preoperational
    c. conventional
    d. postconventional

Developing morality, p. 147
Medium, Conceptual, Objective 9, Ans: c
106. A student who does not cheat on tests because he fears what his friends will think of him if he gets caught is in Kohlberg's _____ stage.
    a. preconventional
    b. preoperational
    c. conventional
    d. postconventional

Developing morality, p. 147
Difficult, Factual/Definitional, Objective 9, Ans: d
107. Formal operational thought is most necessary for the development of _____ morality.
    a. preoperational
    b. conventional
    c. preconventional
    d. postconventional

Developing morality, p. 147
Difficult, Conceptual, Objective 9, Ans: d
108. Preconventional morality is to postconventional morality as _____ is to _____.
    a. social approval; ethical principles
    b. self-interest; social approval
    c. social approval; self-interest
    d. self-interest; ethical principles

Developing morality, p. 148
Difficult, Factual/Definitional, Objective 9, Ans: a
109. A postconventional level of morality is most likely to be found in cultures that value:
    a. individualism.
    b. utilitarianism.
    c. communism.
    d. social harmony.
    e. socialism.

Developing morality, p. 148
Difficult, Conceptual, Objective 9, Ans: d
110. Postconventional morality is likely to be most characteristic of the adult population of:
    a. China.
    b. Colombia.
    c. Mexico.
    d. Canada.

Developing morality, p. 148
Difficult, Factual/Definitional, Objective 9, Ans: c

111. The best basis for predicting whether a high school student will smoke marijuana would be the:
    a. attitude of the student's parents toward marijuana.
    b. student's attitudes toward his or her parents.
    c. number of the student's friends who smoke marijuana.
    d. extent to which the student has attained a postconventional level of morality.

Forming an identity, p. 148
Medium, Conceptual, Objective 10, Ans: d

112. Piaget is to cognitive development as Erikson is to _____ development.
    a. moral
    b. physical
    c. emotional
    d. psychosocial

Forming an identity, pp. 148-149
Easy, Conceptual, Objective 10, Ans: b

113. According to Erikson, infancy is to trust as adolescence is to:
    a. autonomy.
    b. identity.
    c. generativity.
    d. integrity.

Forming an identity, p. 149
Medium, Conceptual, Objective 10, Ans: e

114. According to Erikson, committing oneself to meaningful social roles would be most indicative of the achievement of:
    a. integrity.
    b. autonomy.
    c. competence.
    d. initiative.
    e. identity.

Forming an identity, p. 149
Medium, Factual/Definitional, Objective 10, Ans: b

115. According to Erikson, adolescents who are unable to develop a sense of identity experience:
    a. postconventional morality.
    b. role confusion.
    c. egocentrism.
    d. dementia.

Forming an identity, p. 149
Difficult, Conceptual, Objective 10, Ans: a

116. Fred has no meaningful occupational goals and has switched college majors several times. Erikson would have suggested that Fred lacks:
    a. identity.
    b. initiative.
    c. trust.
    d. autonomy.
    e. competence.

Forming an identity, p. 149
Difficult, Conceptual, Objective 10, Ans: b

117. Lolita vacillates between acting rebellious toward her parents and high school teachers and behaving with compliance and respect. Erikson would have suggested that Lolita's inconsistency illustrates:
    a. separation anxiety.
    b. role confusion.
    c. egocentricity.
    d. stagnation.
    e. inferiority.

Forming an identity, p. 149
Medium, Factual/Definitional, Objective 10, Ans: d

118. As individuals progress through their teen years into early adulthood, their self-concepts typically become:
    a. less personalized and unique.
    b. more fluid and changeable.
    c. less integrated.
    d. more positive.

Developing intimacy, pp. 149, 150
Medium, Conceptual, Objective 3, Ans: c

119. According to Erikson, later adulthood is to integrity as young adulthood is to:
    a. autonomy.
    b. initiative.
    c. intimacy.
    d. identity.

Developing intimacy, p. 150
Easy, Factual/Definitional, Objective 10, Ans: c

120. Compared to men, women are more likely to show obvious signs of:
    a. fluid intelligence.
    b. individualism.
    c. interdependence.
    d. postconventional morality.

Developing intimacy, p. 150
Medium, Conceptual, Objective 10, Ans: c

121. Male self-identity is to _____ as female self-identity is to _____.
    a. maturation; nurture
    b. integrity; generativity
    c. self-reliance; social connectedness
    d. crystallized intelligence; fluid intelligence

Developing intimacy, p. 150
Medium, Factual/Definitional, Objective 10, Ans: c

122. Men are typically _____ socially independent and _____ interested in religion than women.
    a. more; more
    b. less; less
    c. more; less
    d. less; more

Developing intimacy, p. 151
Medium, Factual/Definitional, Objective 10, Ans: a

123. Women report that their friendships with women are _____ enjoyable and intimate than their friendships with men. Men report that their friendships with men are _____ enjoyable and intimate than their friendships with women.
      a. more; less
      b. less; more
      c. more; more
      d. less; less

Developing intimacy, p. 151
Medium, Factual/Definitional, Objective 10, Ans: c

124. As people progress through adulthood, women become _____ assertive and men become _____ emphatic.
      a. less; less
      b. less; more
      c. more; more
      d. more; less

Separating from parents, p. 151
Easy, Factual/Definitional, Objective 10, Ans: d

125. Adolescents and their parents are most likely to have disagreements regarding:
      a. religious beliefs.
      b. career choices.
      c. college choices.
      d. homework.

Separating from parents, p. 152
Medium, Factual/Definitional, Objective 10, Ans: b

126. Research on social relationships indicates that most American adolescents:
      a. seldom experience feelings of loneliness.
      b. feel they get along well with their parents.
      c. want to avoid emotionally close relationships with peers.
      d. experience positive relationships with peers and negative relationships with parents.

Physical changes in middle adulthood, p. 154
Easy, Factual/Definitional, Objective 11, Ans: b

127. Which of the following is true of physical development in adult life?
      a. The outward signs of advancing years are psychologically stressful for adults in every culture.
      b. Sensory ability and reaction time reach their peak by the mid-twenties.
      c. Most adults are keenly aware of the first signs of physical decline.
      d. All the above are true.

Physical changes in middle adulthood, p. 154
Easy, Conceptual, Objective 11, Ans: c

128. Judy has recently had periods of mild physical discomfort and profuse sweating. Her doctor notes that her estrogen level is low. It is most likely that Judy is experiencing:
      a. postmenstrual stress syndrome.
      b. a generalized anxiety disorder.
      c. menopause.
      d. Alzheimer's disease.

Physical changes in middle adulthood, p. 154
Medium, Factual/Definitional, Objective 11, Ans: c

129. Menopause is associated with a reduction in:
      a. adrenaline.
      b. testosterone.
      c. estrogen.
      d. acetylcholine.
      e. dopamine.

Physical changes in middle adulthood, p. 155
Medium, Factual/Definitional, Objective 11, Ans: b

130. In surveying women who either had or had not yet experienced menopause, researchers have
      discovered that:
      a. premenopausal women generally look forward to the new level of maturity that menopause
          signifies.
      b. postmenopausal women frequently agree that after menopause women feel better than they
          have for years.
      c. postmenopausal women are generally unable to recall any unpleasant physical symptoms
          associated with menopause.
      d. all the above are true.

Physical changes in middle adulthood, p. 155
Easy, Factual/Definitional, Objective 11, Ans: c

131. In a study of 3000 midlife adults, most postmenopausal women recalled feelings of _____
      with the onset of menopause.
      a. regret
      b. panic
      c. relief
      d. pain

Physical changes in later life, pp. 155-156
Easy, Factual/Definitional, Objective 11, Ans: d

132. The infant female population is _____the infant male population, and female infants have a
      _____ life expectancy than do male infants.
      a. equal to; longer
      b. larger than; shorter
      c. equal to; shorter
      d. smaller than; longer

Physical changes in later life, p. 156
Medium, Factual/Definitional, Objective 11, Ans: b

133. Evolutionary biologists have suggested that the physiological degeneration and resulting death
      that accompany old age in humans are a:
      a. byproduct of crystallized intelligence.
      b. genetically predisposed outcome.
      c. hindrance to natural selection.
      d. threat to the survival of the human species.

Physical changes in later life, p. 156
Medium, Factual/Definitional, Objective 11, Ans: b

134. Research on people aged 65 and over has shown that:
    a. most elderly people become increasingly fearful of death as they age.
    b. most elderly people experience a noticeable loss of visual sensitivity.
    c. most victims of Alzheimer's disease can prevent their own mental deterioration by remaining physically and mentally active.
    d. only about 25 percent of those over 65 reside in heath care institutions such as nursing homes.

Physical changes in later life, p. 157
Difficult, Conceptual, Objective 11, Ans: b

135. Judson is a 70-year-old retired automobile mechanic. In contrast to when he was 20, he now probably:
    a. has a greater fear of death.
    b. is less susceptible to catching colds.
    c. experiences less life satisfaction.
    d. would not do as well on a vocabulary test.

Physical changes in later life, p. 157
Medium, Factual/Definitional, Objective 11, Ans: a

136. As people progress through late adulthood they typically experience a slight:
    a. decrease in brain weight.
    b. increase in colds and flu.
    c. increase in life satisfaction.
    d. increase in fluid intelligence.

Dementia and Alzheimer's disease, p. 158
Easy, Factual/Definitional, Objective 11, Ans: d

137. An irreversible brain disorder marked by a deterioration of reasoning and memory is called:
    a. aphasia.
    b. arteriosclerosis.
    c. psychogenic amnesia.
    d. Alzheimer's disease.

Dementia and Alzheimer's disease, p. 158
Easy, Factual/Definitional, Objective 11, Ans: c

138. The deterioration of memory, reasoning, and language that accompanies Alzheimer's disease is called:
    a. crystallized intelligence.
    b. role confusion.
    c. dementia.
    d. menarche.

Dementia and Alzheimer's disease, p. 158
Medium, Conceptual, Objective 11, Ans: d

139. An early sign of Alzheimer's disease would most likely be:
    a. an inability to recognize oneself in a mirror.
    b. the use of profane and abusive language.
    c. an increase in crystallized intelligence.
    d. difficulty in naming familiar objects or people.

Dementia and Alzheimer's disease, p. 158
Difficult, Factual/Definitional, Objective 11, Ans: d
140. In addition to relieving menopausal discomfort, estrogen supplements have been linked to reduced risk of:
    a. heart disease.
    b. osteoporosis.
    c. Alzheimer's disease.
    d. all the above.

Aging and memory, p. 159
Difficult, Conceptual, Objective 12, Ans: a
141. Twenty-year-olds would most likely outperform 60-year-olds on an art history exam in which they were asked to:
    a. list as many famous artists as possible.
    b. match paintings with famous painters.
    c. pick an artist's country of birth from a list of four possibilities.
    d. respond to true-false statements regarding important events in artists' lives.

Aging and memory, pp. 159, 160
Medium, Factual/Definitional, Objective 12, Ans: c
142. In recall and recognition tests of memory for recently learned material, older adults are more likely than young adults to have difficulty:
    a. recalling meaningful material.
    b. recognizing meaningful material.
    c. recalling meaningless material.
    d. recognizing meaningless material.

Aging and memory, p. 160
Difficult, Factual/Definitional, Objective 12, Ans: a
143. As adults grow older, they are most likely to show a decline in their ability to remember:
    a. nonsense syllables.
    b. musical lyrics.
    c. medical instructions.
    d. practical skills.

Aging and intelligence, p. 160
Medium, Conceptual, Objective 12, Ans: c
144. Tonya asks people of different ages to complete a measure of life satisfaction. She then looks for life satisfaction differences across different age levels. Tonya is conducting a _____ study.
    a. longitudinal
    b. factor-analytic
    c. cross-sectional
    d. psychohistorical
    e. chronological

Aging and intelligence, p. 160
Easy, Factual/Definitional, Objective 12, Ans: a
145. In which research method are the same people retested over a period of years?
    a. longitudinal
    b. experimental
    c. chronological
    d. cross-sectional

Aging and intelligence, pp. 160-161
Medium, Factual/Definitional, Objective 12, Ans: d
146. The idea that adult intelligence declines with age has been challenged most effectively by:
    a. cross-sectional research.
    b. research on fluid intelligence.
    c. tests that assess formal operational thinking.
    d. longitudinal research.

Aging and intelligence, p. 162
Medium, Factual/Definitional, Objective 12, Ans: a
147. Crystallized intelligence refers most directly to a person's:
    a. accumulated knowledge and verbal skills.
    b. ability to reason speedily and abstractly.
    c. ability to assume the perspective of others.
    d. willingness to revise beliefs in the light of new information.
    e. ability to master new information and to learn new skills.

Aging and intelligence, p. 162
Easy, Factual/Definitional, Objective 12, Ans: d
148. Which of the following terms refers to a person's ability to reason abstractly?
    a. crystallized intelligence
    b. concrete operational intelligence
    c. intelligence quotient
    d. fluid intelligence

Aging and intelligence, pp. 132, 162
Difficult, Conceptual, Objective 12, Ans: a
149. Formal operational thought is most similar to:
    a. fluid intelligence.
    b. generativity.
    c. conventional morality.
    d. autonomy.
    e. crystallized intelligence.

Aging and intelligence, p. 162
Medium, Factual/Definitional, Objective 12, Ans: a
150. Research suggests that during early and middle adulthood, crystallized intelligence _____ and fluid intelligence _____ .
    a. increases; decreases
    b. decreases; increases
    c. increases; increases
    d. decreases; decreases

Aging and intelligence, p. 162
Difficult, Conceptual, Objective 12, Ans: a
151. On which of the following tasks are 55-year-old adults most likely to perform just as effectively as they could 30 years earlier?
    a. writing a story
    b. solving an abstract geometry problem
    c. recalling previously presented nonsense syllables
    d. repeating numbers in the opposite order they were presented

Adulthood's ages and stages, p. 163
Difficult, Factual/Definitional, Objective 13, Ans: a

152. Adults are _____ likely to divorce in their early forties than in their early twenties. They are _____ likely to commit suicide in their early forties than in their early seventies.
    a. less; less
    b. more; more
    c. less; more
    d. more; less

Adulthood's ages and stages, p. 163
Medium, Factual/Definitional, Objective 13, Ans: e

153. Level of emotional instability is:
    a. highest among 35-year-olds.
    b. highest among 40-year-olds.
    c. highest among 50-year-olds.
    d. highest among 55-year-olds.
    e. similar among adults at all these ages.

Adulthood's ages and stages, p. 163
Medium, Factual/Definitional, Objective 13, Ans: a

154. The term *social clock* refers to:
    a. the culturally preferred timing for when one should leave home, marry, have children, and retire.
    b. the pace of life in a culture as assessed by its level of industrialization.
    c. the average age of people in different social groups and organizations.
    d. the different ways in which societies evaluate the physical and cognitive changes accompanying the aging process.

Adulthood's ages and stages, p. 163
Difficult, Factual/Definitional, Objective 13, Ans: b

155. Those who criticize stage theories of adulthood suggest that the pattern of adult development depends heavily on:
    a. genetic predispositions.
    b. unpredictable life events.
    c. fluid intelligence.
    d. secondary sex characteristics.

Adulthood's commitments, p. 163
Medium, Factual/Definitional, Objective 14, Ans: c

156. Erik Erikson maintained that the two basic aspects of life that dominate adulthood are:
    a. identity and independence.
    b. intimacy and identity.
    c. intimacy and generativity.
    d. independence and generativity.

Adulthood's commitments, p. 164
Medium, Factual/Definitional, Objective 14, Ans: c

157. Compared to 40 years ago, Americans are marrying at a(n) _____ age and are experiencing _____ marital satisfaction.
    a. older; more
    b. younger; less
    c. older; less
    d. younger; more

Adulthood's commitments, p. 164
Easy, Factual/Definitional, Objective 14, Ans: a

158. Rising divorce rates over the past 40 years are a consequence of _____ marital expectations and the _____ economic independence of women.
    a. increasing; increasing
    b. decreasing; decreasing
    c. increasing; decreasing
    d. decreasing; increasing

Adulthood's commitments, p. 164
Medium, Factual/Definitional, Objective 14, Ans: d

159. Adults are most likely to experience unhappiness and dissatisfaction with life if they are:
    a. married.
    b. single and have never married.
    c. divorced and remarried.
    d. separated or divorced.

Adulthood's commitments, p. 164
Medium, Factual/Definitional, Objective 14, Ans: e

160. Marriage bonds are especially likely to endure when members of a couple:
    a. avoid open disagreements and arguments.
    b. live together for a time before they marry.
    c. focus their time and energy on their growing children's needs.
    d. engage in less frequent sexual interactions.
    e. engage in more positive than negative interactions with each other.

Adulthood's commitments, p. 165
Difficult, Conceptual, Objective 14, Ans: c

161. Cecil and Astrud have a 4-year-old son and a 7-year-old daughter. If their experience is typical, their satisfaction with their marriage is:
    a. increasing greatly.
    b. increasing slightly.
    c. declining slightly.
    d. remaining constant.

Adulthood's commitments, p. 165
Medium, Conceptual, Objective 14, Ans: b

162. Kathryn and Rafael's third and last child is leaving home for college next year. Their empty nest is likely to be a(n) _____ place.
    a. depressed
    b. happy
    c. anxious
    d. boring

Adulthood's commitments, p. 165
Easy, Factual/Definitional, Objective 14, Ans: b

163. Research suggests that most beginning American college students:
    a. should develop clear occupational goals before starting college.
    b. will shift from their initially intended majors while in college.
    c. will complete a graduate school program after their college education.
    d. should pursue specific vocational training programs rather than a broad liberal arts education.

Well-being across the life span, p. 166
Easy, Factual/Definitional, Objective 15, Ans: e
164. There is very *little* relationship between the age of an adult and his or her:
   a. fluid intelligence.
   b. ability to recall meaningless information.
   c. susceptibility to colds and flu.
   d. susceptibility to accidental physical injury.
   e. level of life satisfaction.

Well-being across the life span, p. 166
Medium, Factual/Definitional, Objective 15, Ans: d
165. Research on people's feelings of satisfaction with their lives indicates that:
   a. adolescents report a greater sense of life satisfaction than do people over 65 years of age.
   b. people over 65 years of age report a greater sense of life satisfaction than do adolescents.
   c. middle-aged adults report a greater sense of life satisfaction than do both adolescents and people over 65 years of age.
   d. there is very little relationship between people's age and their level of life satisfaction.

Well-being across the life span, p. 166
Medium, Conceptual, Objective 15, Ans: e
166. At the age of 65, Mrs. Benvenisti is likely to experience _____ with less intensity than when she was a teenager.
   a. joy
   b. anger
   c. fear
   d. jealousy
   e. all the above

Well-being across the lifespan, p. 166
Medium, Factual/Definitional, Objective 15, Ans: a
167. As adults advance in age, their positive and negative moods become _____ extreme and _____ enduring.
   a. less; more
   b. more; less
   c. less; less
   d. more; more

Death and dying, p. 167
Medium, Factual/Definitional, Objective 15, Ans: a
168. In Erikson's theory, the sense of integrity achieved in late adulthood refers to the feeling that:
   a. one's life has been meaningful.
   b. one is healthy and not dependent upon others.
   c. one is acting ethically.
   d. one's life is full of close friendships.

Death and dying, p. 167
Medium, Factual/Definitional, Objective 15, Ans: b
169. According to Erikson, the elderly can most effectively cope with the prospect of their own death if they have achieved a sense of:
   a. identity.
   b. integrity.
   c. initiative.
   d. intimacy.
   e. autonomy.

Death and dying, p. 167
Difficult, Conceptual, Objective 15, Ans: a
170. Ralph, a 70-year-old retired accountant, feels that his life has been worthless and meaningless. According to Erikson, Ralph has failed to achieve a sense of:
   a. integrity.
   b. intimacy.
   c. initiative.
   d. autonomy.

Continuity and stages, p. 168
Medium, Conceptual, Objective 16, Ans: d
171. Ross believes that personality development is a matter of sudden qualitative changes at various turning points in the life span. His viewpoint is most directly relevant to the issue of:
   a. rationality or irrationality.
   b. nature or nurture.
   c. assimilation or accommodation.
   d. continuity or stages.

Continuity and stages, p. 168
Difficult, Factual/Definitional, Objective 16, Ans: a
172. Researchers who emphasize learning and experience tend to view development as a _____; those who emphasize maturation often view development as a _____.
   a. continuous process; sequence of stages
   b. sequence of stages; continuous process
   c. cognitive process; social process
   d. social process; cognitive process

Continuity and stages, p. 168
Easy, Factual/Definitional, Objective 16, Ans: d
173. A stage theory of development has been advanced by:
   a. Kohlberg.
   b. Erikson.
   c. Piaget.
   d. all the above.

Continuity and stages, p. 168
Medium, Factual/Definitional, Objective 16, Ans: c
174. Stage theories of adult development are most likely to be criticized for exaggerating the:
   a. importance of social influence.
   b. stability of personality.
   c. predictability of development.
   d. importance of fluid intelligence.
   e. interaction of nature and nurture.

Stability and change, p. 168
Medium, Conceptual, Objective 16, Ans: d
175. Questions about the extent to which maladaptive habits learned in childhood can be overcome in adulthood are most directly relevant to the issue of:
    a. continuity or stages.
    b. behavior or mental processes.
    c. rationality or irrationality.
    d. stability or change.
    e. nature or nurture.

Stability and change, p. 168
Medium, Conceptual, Objective 16, Ans: c
176. As boys with explosive tempers grow older, they are especially likely to have difficulty maintaining good jobs and happy marriages. This fact is most relevant to the issue of:
    a. conventional or postconventional morality.
    b. fluid or crystallized intelligence.
    c. stability or change.
    d. cross-sectional or longitudinal studies.
    e. concrete or formal operations.

Stability and change, p. 168
Difficult, Conceptual, Objective 16, Ans: b
177. The conflicting results of cross-sectional and longitudinal studies of aging and intelligence are of greatest relevance to the issue of:
    a. continuity or stages.
    b. stability or change.
    c. rationality or irrationality.
    d. concrete or formal operational thought.

Stability and change, p. 169
Medium, Factual/Definitional, Objective 16, Ans: d
178. Human personality shows the greatest stability during:
    a. preschool years.
    b. late childhood.
    c. teenage years.
    d. adulthood.

CHAPTER **5**

Sensation

Learning Objectives

Sensing the World: Some Basic Principles (pp. 172-177)

1. Contrast the processes of sensation and perception.

2. Distinguish between absolute and difference thresholds, and discuss research findings on subliminal stimulation.

3. Describe the phenomenon of sensory adaptation, and explain its functional value.

Vision (pp. 177-188)

4. Explain the visual process, including the stimulus input, the structure of the eye, and the transduction of light energy.

5. Discuss the different levels of visual information processing and the value of parallel processing.

6. Explain the Young-Helmholtz and opponent-process theories of color vision, and describe the nature of color constancy.

Hearing (pp. 189-196)

7. Explain the auditory process, including the stimulus input and the structure and function of the ear.

8. Explain the place and frequency theories of pitch perception, and describe how we locate sounds.

9. Discuss the nature and causes of hearing loss, and describe the effects of noise on hearing and behavior.

The Other Senses (pp. 196-206)

10. Describe the sense of touch, and explain the basis of pain.

11.   Describe the senses of taste and smell, and comment on the nature of sensory interaction.

12.   Distinguish between kinesthesis and the vestibular sense.

13.   Discuss the effects of sensory restriction.

Sensation and perception, p. 171
Medium, Factual/Definitional, Objective 1, Ans: b
1.   Sensation is the:
      a. transformation of sound and light into meaningful words and images.
      b. detection and encoding of stimulus energies by the nervous system.
      c. organization and interpretation of environmental events.
      d. recognition of specific features of a physical stimulus.

Sensation and perception, p. 171
Easy, Factual/Definitional, Objective 1, Ans: d
2.   The process by which we select, organize, and interpret sensory information in order to recognize meaningful objects and events is called:
      a. sensory adaptation.
      b. parallel processing.
      c. sensation.
      d. perception.
      e. accommodation.

Sensation and perception, p. 171
Medium, Conceptual, Objective 1, Ans: c
3.   Detection is to interpretation as _____ is to _____.
      a. absolute threshold; difference threshold
      b. transduction; accommodation
      c. sensation; perception
      d. wavelength; hue

Sensation and perception, p. 171
Difficult, Conceptual, Objective 1, Ans: c
4.   Experiencing an apple as being red is to _____ as recognizing an apple as being a fruit is to

      _____.
      a. absolute threshold; difference threshold
      b. accommodation; feature detection
      c. sensation; perception
      d. feature detection; difference threshold

Sensation and perception, p. 171
Medium, Factual/Definitional, Objective 1, Ans: d
5.   The effect of past experience and current expectations on perception best illustrates the importance of:
      a. accommodation.
      b. transduction.
      c. sensory thresholds.
      d. top-down processing.

Sensation and perception, p. 171
Difficult, Factual/Definitional, Objective 1, Ans: a

6. Damage to the temporal lobe region of the brain essential for facial recognition produces a loss of:
    a. perception.
    b. signal detection.
    c. transduction.
    d. accommodation.
    e. sensation.

Sensation and perception, p. 171
Difficult, Factual/Definitional, Objective 1, Ans: a

7. The patient "E.H." suffers from prosopagnosia and is unable to recognize her own face in a mirror. Her difficulty stems from a deficiency in:
    a. top-down processing.
    b. transduction.
    c. kinesthesis.
    d. sensation.
    e. accommodation.

Thresholds, p. 172
Medium, Factual/Definitional, Objective 2, Ans: d

8. Psychophysics is best defined as the study of relationships between:
    a. sensation and perception.
    b. stimulus energies and neural impulses.
    c. absolute thresholds and difference thresholds.
    d. physical stimuli and psychological experience.

Absolute thresholds, p. 173
Medium, Factual/Definitional, Objective 2, Ans: c

9. The absolute threshold is the minimum amount of stimulation that a person needs to detect a stimulus:
    a. at the beginning of a sensory experience.
    b. on a subliminal level.
    c. 50 percent of the time.
    d. reliably on any occasion.

Absolute thresholds, p. 173
Medium, Conceptual, Objective 2, Ans: c

10. Although Mandume was sitting right next to his parents, he smelled a skunk minutes before they did. Apparently, Mandume has a lower _____ for skunk odor than his parents have.
    a. accommodation level
    b. tolerance level
    c. absolute threshold
    d. olfactory saturation level
    e. feature detector

Absolute thresholds, p. 173
Difficult, Conceptual, Objective 2, Ans: a

11. ꞏ If an adult develops cataracts, his or her _____ threshold for light is likely to _____.
   a. absolute; increase
   b. difference; decrease
   c. absolute; remain unchanged
   d. difference; remain unchanged
   e. absolute; decrease

Signal detection, p. 173
Easy, Conceptual, Objective 2, Ans: c

12. An exhausted forest ranger may notice the faintest scent of a forest fire, whereas much stronger but less important odors fail to catch her attention. This fact would be of greatest relevance to:
   a. the Young-Helmholtz theory.
   b. opponent-process theory.
   c. signal detection theory.
   d. frequency theory.
   e. place theory.

Signal detection, p. 173
Medium, Conceptual, Objective 2, Ans: e

13. The fact that fear may increase your sensitivity to an almost imperceptible pain stimulus is of most relevance to:
   a. place theory.
   b. frequency theory.
   c. the Young-Helmhotz theory.
   d. opponent-process theory.
   e. signal detection theory.

Subliminal stimulation, p. 173
Easy, Factual/Definitional, Objective 2, Ans: c

14. Soothing musical audiotapes accompanied by faint and imperceptible verbal messages designed to increase a desire to lose weight best illustrate:
   a. kinesthesis.
   b. sensory interaction.
   c. subliminal stimulation.
   d. parallel processing.
   e. difference thresholds.

Subliminal stimulation, p. 173
Medium, Factual/Definitional, Objective 2, Ans: b

15. A subliminal message is one that is presented:
   a. while an individual is under hypnosis.
   b. below the absolute threshold for awareness.
   c. in a manner that is unconsciously persuasive.
   d. with very soft background music.
   e. repetitiously.

Subliminal stimulation, p. 173
Medium, Conceptual, Objective 2, Ans: d

16. Which of the following strategies best illustrates the use of subliminal stimulation?
     a. A department store places flashing red lights near its sale merchandise.
     b. A magazine ad pictures a pack of cigarettes with a beautiful mountain stream in the
         background.
     c. A church organist plays relaxing background music during a pastor's congregational prayer.
     d. A trim female figure is imperceptibly flashed on the TV screen during an ad for a weight-
         reduction clinic.

Subliminal stimulation, p. 174
Medium, Factual/Definitional, Objective 2, Ans: c

17. Those who believe in the value of subliminal audiotapes would be wrong to claim that:
     a. people are capable of parallel processing.
     b. signal detection is influenced by a person's motivational state.
     c. unconsciously processed information is unusually persuasive.
     d. sensory transduction can occur without conscious awareness.
     e. any of the above are true.

Subliminal stimulation, p. 174
Difficult, Factual/Definitional, Objective 2, Ans: c

18. Participants in one experiment felt more positively about people if their photographs had been
     associated with scenes of kittens rather than with scenes of werewolves. This study best
     illustrated:
     a. the difference between signal detection and feature detectors.
     b. a diminishing sensitivity to unchanging and familiar information.
     c. that information can be processed outside conscious awareness.
     d. the pervasive impact of sensory interaction.

Difference thresholds, p. 175
Easy, Conceptual, Objective 2, Ans: c

19. Some people are better than others at detecting slight variations in the taste of various blends of
     coffee. This best illustrates the importance of:
     a. sensory adaptation.
     b. subliminal stimulation.
     c. difference thresholds.
     d. parallel processing.
     e. the vestibular sense.

Difference thresholds, p. 175
Medium, Conceptual, Objective 2, Ans: a

20. Roger thinks 75-watt light bulbs give more light than 60-watt bulbs. His wife thinks both are
     equally bright. Roger apparently has a _____ threshold than his wife.
     a. lower difference
     b. lower absolute
     c. higher difference
     d. higher absolute

Difference thresholds, p. 175
Medium, Conceptual, Objective 2, Ans: d

21.   If the just noticeable difference for a 10-ounce weight is 1 ounce, the just noticeable difference for an 80-ounce weight would be _____ ounce(s).
      a. 1
      b. 2
      c. 4
      d. 8
      e. 10

Difference thresholds, p. 175
Difficult, Factual/Definitional, Objective 2, Ans: b

22.   Weber's law is relevant to an understanding of:
      a. absolute thresholds.
      b. difference thresholds.
      c. sensory adaptation.
      d. sensory interaction.
      e. all the above.

Sensory adaptation, p. 176
Easy, Factual/Definitional, Objective 3, Ans: c

23.   Diminished sensitivity to an unchanging stimulus is known as:
      a. accommodation.
      b. equilibrium.
      c. sensory adaptation.
      d. sensory transformation.
      e. sensory interaction.

Sensory adaptation, p. 176
Medium, Conceptual, Objective 3, Ans: c

24.   Which of the following is an example of sensory adaptation?
      a. enjoying a painting more the longer you study it
      b. responding vigorously every time a fire alarm is sounded
      c. not realizing how cold it is after you have been outdoors for a while in winter
      d. relying heavily on your hearing when you wear a blindfold

Sensory adaptation, p. 176
Medium, Factual/Definitional, Objective 3, Ans: a

25.   If we could stop our eyes from quivering as we stared at a stationary object, the object would probably:
      a. vanish from sight.
      b. stimulate feature detector cells located in the retina.
      c. appear more brilliantly colored.
      d. appear to change colors.

Sensory adaptation, p. 176
Medium, Factual/Definitional, Objective 3, Ans: c

26.   Sensory adaptation helps us to focus our attention on _____ stimuli.
      a. familiar
      b. subliminal
      c. novel
      d. intense

Vision, p. 177
Medium, Factual/Definitional, Objective 4, Ans: c
27. Transduction refers to the process:
  a. of organizing and interpreting sensory information.
  b. by which living organisms are exposed to stimulus energies.
  c. by which stimulus energies are converted into neural messages.
  d. whereby we can sense the position and movement of our muscles, tendons, and joints.

Vision, pp. 177, 180
Medium, Conceptual, Objective 4, Ans: c
28. The process by which rods and cones convert electromagnetic energy into neural signals is an example of:
  a. accommodation.
  b. sensory adaptation.
  c. transduction.
  d. sensory interaction.

The stimulus input: light energy (Figure 5.4), p. 178
Difficult, Conceptual, Objective 4, Ans: d
29. Green light is _____ in wavelength than _____ light.
  a. longer; yellow
  b. shorter; blue
  c. longer; orange
  d. shorter; red

The stimulus input: light energy, p. 178
Medium, Factual/Definitional, Objective 4, Ans: b
30. The amplitude of electromagnetic waves determines the _____ of light.
  a. absolute threshold
  b. brightness
  c. hue
  d. difference threshold
  e. wavelength

The stimulus input: light energy, p. 178
Medium, Conceptual, Objective 4, Ans: e
31. Brightness is to intensity as hue is to:
  a. amplitude.
  b. timbre.
  c. color.
  d. pitch.
  e. wavelength.

The stimulus input: light energy, pp. 178, 189
Difficult, Conceptual, Objective 4, Ans: a
32. Loudness is to pitch as brightness is to:
  a. hue.
  b. light.
  c. intensity.
  d. frequency.
  e. amplitude.

The eye, p. 179
Easy, Factual/Definitional, Objective 4, Ans: d

33.   The adjustable opening in the center of the eye is the:
      a. fovea.
      b. lens.
      c. cornea.
      d. pupil.
      e. blind spot.

The eye, p. 179
Easy, Factual/Definitional, Objective 4, Ans: d

34.   Dilation and constriction of the pupil are controlled by the:
      a. optic nerve.
      b. lens.
      c. retina.
      d. iris.
      e. cornea.

The eye, p. 179
Medium, Conceptual, Objective 4, Ans: d

35.   The iris constricts in response to visible _____ light waves.
      a. low frequency
      b. low amplitude
      c. high frequency
      d. high amplitude

The eye, p. 179
Medium, Factual/Definitional, Objective 4, Ans: b

36.   The process by which the lens changes shape so as to focus the image of an object on the retina
      is called:
      a. adaptation.
      b. accommodation.
      c. transduction.
      d. feature detection.

The eye, pp. 179-180
Easy, Factual/Definitional, Objective 4, Ans: d

37.   The light-sensitive inner surface of the eye, containing the rods and cones, is the:
      a. fovea.
      b. optic nerve.
      c. cornea.
      d. retina.
      e. iris.

The eye, p. 179
Medium, Conceptual, Objective 4, Ans: a

 38.   When Judy reads a book, the images of the printed words come into sharpest focus at a point
      behind her retina. This indicates that she:
      a. is farsighted.
      b. is nearsighted.
      c. usually has good visual activity.
      d. has a larger-than-normal blindspot.

The eye, p. 180
Medium, Factual/Definitional, Objective 4, Ans: c

39.   As people grow older, they are most likely to need glasses because:
    a. the iris loses its ability to contract the pupil.
    b. the blind spot increases in diameter.
    c. the lens loses its ability to change shape readily.
    d. the feature detectors progressively decrease in number.
    e. the cornea loses much of its transparency.

The retina, p. 180
Easy, Factual/Definitional, Objective 4, Ans: c

40.   The receptor cells that convert light energy into neural signals are called:
    a. bipolar cells.
    b. ganglion cells.
    c. rods and cones.
    d. feature detectors.

The retina, p. 180
Medium, Factual/Definitional, Objective 4, Ans: b

41.   Bipolar cells are located in the:
    a. optic nerve.
    b. retina.
    c. blind spot.
    d. lens.
    e. cochlea.

The retina, p. 180
Medium, Factual/Definitional, Objective 4, Ans: d

42.   Ganglion cells converge to form:
    a. the basilar membrane.
    b. bipolar cells.
    c. the auditory nerve.
    d. the optic nerve.
    e. the olfactory epithelium.

The retina, p. 181
Medium, Factual/Definitional, Objective 4, Ans: a

43.   The area of the retina where the optic nerve leaves the eye is called the:
    a. blind spot.
    b. pupil.
    c. visual cortex.
    d. cornea.
    e. lens.

The retina, p. 181
Medium, Conceptual, Objective 4, Ans: c

44.   Damage to the fovea would have the greatest effect on:
    a. night vision.
    b. peripheral vision.
    c. visual acuity.
    d. sensory adaptation.
    e. kinesthesis.

The retina, p. 181
Medium, Factual/Definitional, Objective 4, Ans: d

45. The most light-sensitive receptor cells are the:
    a. ganglion cells.
    b. cones.
    c. bipolar cells.
    d. rods.

The retina, p. 181
Medium, Factual/Definitional, Objective 4, Ans: d
46. Compared to rods, cones are _____ sensitive to dim light and _____ sensitive to fine detail.
    a. more; more
    b. less; less
    c. more; less
    d. less; more

The retina, p. 181
Difficult, Factual/Definitional, Objective 4, Ans: b
47. Under very dim levels of illumination:
    a. rods reach their maximum light sensitivity more rapidly than do cones.
    b. rods are more light sensitive than cones.
    c. it is particularly important to look straight at the objects we want to see.
    d. all the above are true.

Feature detection, p. 182
Medium, Factual/Definitional, Objective 5, Ans: d
48. Which of the following types of cells are located in the brain?
    a. rods and cones
    b. bipolar cells
    c. ganglion cells
    d. feature detectors

Feature detection, p. 182
Easy, Factual/Definitional, Objective 5, Ans: d
49. The nerve cells that respond to specific aspects of a visual stimulus, such as its shape or its movement, are:
    a. bipolar cells.
    b. rods and cones.
    c. ganglion cells.
    d. feature detectors.

Feature detection, pp. 182-183
Medium, Conceptual, Objective 5, Ans: a
50. When you look at a vertical line, you are probably activating different _____ than when you look at a horizontal line.
    a. feature detectors
    b. opponent processes
    c. sensory thresholds
    d. hair cells

Feature detection, p. 183
Difficult, Conceptual, Objective 5, Ans: d

51.   Our shifting perspective of a Necker cube best illustrates the importance of:
       a. sensory interaction.
       b. bottom-up processing.
       c. sensory adaptations.
       d. top-down processing.

Parallel processing, p. 184
Medium, Conceptual, Objective 5, Ans: c

52.   The ability to simultaneously recognize the color, shape, size, and speed of an oncoming
       automobile best illustrates:
       a. kinesthesis.
       b. sensory interaction.
       c. parallel processing.
       d. subliminal perception.
       e. accommodation.

Parallel processing, p. 185
Medium, Factual/Definitional, Objective 5, Ans: e

53.   People who demonstrate blindsight have most likely suffered damage to their:
       a. cornea.
       b. lens.
       c. fovea.
       d. optic nerve.
       e. visual cortex.

Parallel processing, p. 185
Difficult, Factual/Definitional, Objective 5, Ans: a

54.   The ability to process information automatically and without conscious awareness of doing so
       is best illustrated by:
       a. blindsight.
       b. sensory adaptation.
       c. serial processing.
       d. sensory interaction.

Parallel processing, p. 185
Difficult, Factual/Definitional, Objective 5, Ans: c

55.   The ability to almost instantly recognize a familiar face best illustrates the value of:
       a. bottom-up processing.
       b. sensory adaptation.
       c. parallel processing.
       d. sensory interaction.

Color vision, p. 186
Medium, Factual/Definitional, Objective 6, Ans: a

56.   According to the Young-Helmholtz theory:
       a. the retina contains three kinds of color receptors.
       b. color vision depends on pairs of opposing retinal processes.
       c. the size of the difference threshold is proportional to the intensity of the stimulus.
       d. certain nerve cells in the brain respond to specific features of a stimulus.

Color vision (Figure 5.15), p. 186
Difficult, Conceptual, Objective 6, Ans: d
57.   According to the Young-Helmholtz theory, when red-, green-, and blue-sensitive cones are all
       stimulated simultaneously, a person should see:
       a. yellow.
       b. red and blue, but not green.
       c. a full spectrum of colors.
       d. white.

Color vision, p. 186
Difficult, Factual/Definitional, Objective 6, Ans: b
58.   In additive color mixing, a combination of red and green forms _____; in subtractive color
       mixing, a combination of yellow and blue forms _____.
       a. green; yellow
       b. yellow; green
       c. white; black
       d. red; blue
       e. blue; red

Color vision, p. 186
Difficult, Factual/Definitional, Objective 6, Ans: a
59.   Dogs' limited color vision results from their lack of receptor cells for wavelengths of:
       a. red.
       b. blue.
       c. green.
       d. all the above hues.

Color vision, pp. 187, 198
Easy, Conceptual, Objective 6, Ans: e
60.   The gate-control theory is to our sense of pain as the opponent-process theory is to our sense
       of:
       a. equilibrium.
       b. taste.
       c. smell.
       d. pitch.
       e. color.

Color vision, p. 187
Medium, Conceptual, Objective 6, Ans: c
61.   When most people stare at a red square and then shift their eyes to a white surface, the
       afterimage of the square is:
       a. yellow.
       b. red.
       c. green.
       d. blue.
       e. white.

Color vision, p. 187
Medium, Factual/Definitional, Objective 6, Ans: a
62. Experiencing a green afterimage of a red object is most easily explained by:
    a. the opponent-process theory.
    b. the gate-control theory.
    c. place theory.
    d. the Young-Helmholtz theory.
    e. frequency theory.

Color vision, p. 187
Medium, Factual/Definitional, Objective 6, Ans: e
63. According to the opponent-process theory, cells that are stimulated by exposure to _____ light are inhibited by exposure to _____ light.
    a. red; yellow
    b. blue; green
    c. yellow; green
    d. red; blue
    e. yellow; blue

Color vision, p. 187
Difficult, Conceptual, Objective 6, Ans: d
64. The opponent-process theory would predict that you would have the greatest trouble experiencing a color as:
    a. greenish-blue.
    b. yellowish-red.
    c. greenish-yellow.
    d. yellowish-blue.

Color constancy, pp. 187-188
Medium, Conceptual, Objective 6, Ans: c
65. On a cloudy day, a yellow flower is likely to appear _____ it does on a bright sunny day.
    a. less colorful than
    b. less yellow than
    c. equally as yellow as
    d. more yellow than
    e. whiter than

Color constancy, p. 188
Medium, Factual/Definitional, Objective 6, Ans: a
66. The phenomenon of color constancy best demonstrates that:
    a. an object's perceived color is influenced by its surrounding context.
    b. the retina has three types of color receptors.
    c. the brain processes information about color and shape simultaneously.
    d. quivering eye movements help to maintain the perception of color.
    e. color vision depends on pairs of opposing retinal processes.

The stimulus input: sound waves, p. 189
Easy, Conceptual, Objective 7, Ans: c
67. The high notes on a piano always produce _____ sound waves than the low notes.
    a. higher-amplitude
    b. lower-amplitude
    c. higher-frequency
    d. lower-frequency

The stimulus input: sound waves, p. 189
Medium, Conceptual, Objective 7, Ans: a
68.   The low notes on a piano always produce _____ sound waves than the high notes.
      a. longer
      b. higher-amplitude
      c. shorter
      d. lower-amplitude

The stimulus input: sound waves, pp. 178, 189
Difficult, Conceptual, Objective 7, Ans: b
69.   A soprano's voice is to a bass's voice as _____ light is to _____ light.
      a. dim; bright
      b. blue; red
      c. bright; dim
      d. red; blue

The stimulus input: sound waves, p. 189
Easy, Conceptual, Objective 7, Ans: b
70.   Frequency is to pitch as amplitude is to:
      a. timbre.
      b. loudness.
      c. hue.
      d. wavelength.
      e. sound.

The stimulus input: sound waves, pp. 178, 189
Medium, Conceptual, Objective 7, Ans: d
71.   Hue is to light as _____ is to sound.
      a. wavelength
      b. loudness
      c. amplitude
      d. pitch
      e. frequency

The stimulus input: sound waves, p. 189
Difficult, Conceptual, Objective 7, Ans: e
72.   The 130-decibel sound of a rock band is about _____ times louder than the 100-decibel sound of a nearby subway train.
      a. 2
      b. 10
      c. 30
      d. 100
      e. 1000

The ear, p. 189
Easy, Factual/Definitional, Objective 7, Ans: d
73.   The coiled, fluid-filled tube in which sound waves trigger nerve impulses is called the:
      a. eustachian tube.
      b. auditory canal.
      c. semicircular canal.
      d. cochlea.
      e. vestibular apparatus.

The ear, pp. 179, 189
Medium, Conceptual, Objective 7, Ans: b
74.   The retina is to the eye as the _____ is to the ear.
a. auditory nerve
b. cochlea
c. auditory canal
d. eardrum
e. eustachian tube

The ear, p. 190
Easy, Factual/Definitional, Objective 7, Ans: c
75.   Hair cells protrude from the:
a. feature detectors.
b. eardrum.
c. basilar membrane.
d. auditory nerve.

The ear, p. 190
Medium, Factual/Definitional, Objective 7, Ans: d
76.   The basilar membrane is located in the:
a. middle ear.
b. auditory canal.
c. semicircular canal.
d. cochlea.

The ear, p. 190
Difficult, Factual/Definitional, Objective 7, Ans: a
77.   The mechanical vibrations triggered by sound waves are transduced into neural impulses by:
a. hair cells.
b. the eardrum.
c. the oval window.
d. the auditory cortex.
e. the vestibular apparatus.

Noise (Close-up), p. 191
Medium, Factual/Definitional, Objective 9, Ans: c
78.   Laboratory experiments have indicated that noise is particularly stressful and disruptive when it is:
a. high pitched.
b. repetitive.
c. uncontrollable.
d. between 40 and 60 decibels.

How do we perceive pitch?, p. 192
Easy, Factual/Definitional, Objective 8, Ans: e
79.   The discovery that high-frequency sounds trigger a wave of activity that peaks near the beginning of the basilar membrane supports the _____ theory.
a. gate-control
b. frequency
c. Young-Helmholtz
d. opponent-process
e. place

How do we perceive pitch?, pp. 192, 193
Difficult, Conceptual, Objective 8, Ans: d

80.   Many elderly people lose their hearing for high-pitched sounds due to the degeneration near the beginning of the basilar membrane. This is best explained by the _____ theory.
   a. Young-Helmholtz
   b. frequency
   c. opponent-process
   d. place

How do we perceive pitch? pp. 187, 192
Medium, Conceptual, Objective 8, Ans: b

81.   The opponent-process theory is to hue as place theory is to:
   a. brightness.
   b. pitch.
   c. amplitude.
   d. pain.
   e. kinesthesis.

How do we perceive pitch?, p. 192
Medium, Factual/Definitional, Objective 8, Ans: c

82.   According to the frequency theory:
   a. most sound waves are a complex mixture of many frequencies.
   b. high-frequency sounds trigger a wave of activity that peaks near the beginning of the basilar membrane.
   c. the rate at which impulses travel up the auditory nerve matches the frequency of the tone being heard.
   d. frequent or prolonged stimulation of a sensory receptor causes that receptor to become less sensitive.

How do we perceive pitch?, p. 192
Difficult, Factual/Definitional, Objective 8, Ans: d

83.   The volley principle is particularly relevant to the _____ theory.
   a. opponent-process
   b. place
   c. gate-control
   d. frequency

How do we locate sounds?, p. 192
Easy, Factual/Definitional, Objective 8, Ans: a

84.   Small differences in the loudness of a sound received by each ear enable us to identify the _____ of the sound.
   a. location
   b. amplitude
   c. pitch
   d. timbre

How do we locate sounds?, p. 193
Easy, Conceptual, Objective 8, Ans: a
85. You are in an unfamiliar setting and your eyes are closed. Which of the following sounds would be hardest for you to locate correctly?
     a. a bell ringing 6 feet directly in front of you
     b. a pen hitting the top of a table beside you
     c. a crying child standing 5 feet off to your right
     d. music from a loudspeaker 15 feet to your left

How do we locate sounds?, p. 193
Medium, Factual/Definitional, Objective 8, Ans: b
86. One neural pathway detects differences in the loudness of a sound received by each of our ears while another neural pathway simultaneously detects differences in the arrival time of a sound to each of our ears. This best illustrates:
     a. sensory interaction.
     b. parallel processing.
     c. kinesthesis.
     d. accommodation.

Hearing loss, p. 193
Medium, Factual/Definitional, Objective 9, Ans: c
87. Conduction hearing loss is most likely to result from damage to the:
     a. cochlea.
     b. auditory canal.
     c. eardrum.
     d. auditory nerve.

Hearing loss, p. 193
Difficult, Conceptual, Objective 9, Ans: c
88. Which of the following circumstances is most likely to contribute to conduction hearing loss?
     a. failure to use earplugs while working in a noisy factory
     b. exposure to very loud rock music
     c. misuse of Q-tips (cotton swabs) in cleaning your ears
     d. exposure to unpredictable or uncontrollable noise

Hearing loss, p. 193
Easy, Factual/Definitional, Objective 9, Ans: b
89. Nerve deafness is caused by damage to the:
     a. eardrum.
     b. cochlea.
     c. hammer, anvil, and stirrup.
     d. auditory canal.

Hearing loss (Figure 5.22), p. 193
Difficult, Conceptual, Objective 9, Ans: d
90. Jacob, a 60-year-old accountant, notices a loss of hearing only for higher-frequency sounds. It is most likely that this hearing loss involves problems in the:
     a. auditory canal.
     b. eardrum.
     c. tiny bones of the middle ear.
     d. cochlea.

Hearing loss, p. 194
Easy, Factual/Definitional, Objective 9, Ans: e
91.   A cochlear implant would be most helpful for those who suffer:
       a. loss of the sense of movement.
       b. loss of the sense of position.
       c. loss of the sense of balance.
       d. conduction hearing loss.
       e. sensorineural hearing loss.

Touch, p. 197
Medium, Factual/Definitional, Objective 10, Ans: a
92.   The sensation of wetness results from the simultaneous stimulation of adjacent _____
       sensitive spots on the skin.
       a. pressure and cold
       b. warmth and pressure
       c. cold and warmth
       d. pain and cold

Touch, p. 197
Medium, Factual/Definitional, Objective 10, Ans: a
93.   The simultaneous stimulation of adjacent cold and warmth spots on the skin produces the
       sensation of:
       a. hot.
       b. cold.
       c. pressure.
       d. wetness.

Touch, p. 197
Medium, Factual/Definitional, Objective 10, Ans: b
94.   The somatosensory cortex is activated by _____ stimulation.
       a. auditory
       b. tactile
       c. olfactory
       d. visual

Pain, p. 198
Medium, Factual/Definitional, Objective 10, Ans: c
95.   The importance of central nervous system activity for the experience of pain is best highlighted
       by:
       a. Weber's law.
       b. frequency theory.
       c. phantom limb sensations.
       d. the opponent-process theory.

Pain, p. 198
Difficult, Factual/Definitional, Objective 10, Ans: a
96.   There are no specialized neural receptor cells devoted solely to the sense of:
       a. pain.
       b. pressure.
       c. sight.
       d. hearing.

Pain, p. 198
Easy, Factual/Definitional, Objective 10, Ans: b
97.   The gate-control theory attempts to explain how:
   a. certain nerve cells in the brain respond to specific features of a visual stimulus.
   b. the nervous system blocks or allows pain signals to pass to the brain.
   c. the perception of pitch is related to the specific area of the basilar membrane that is activated.
   d. color vision depends on pairs of opposing neural processes.

Pain, p. 199
Medium, Conceptual, Objective 10, Ans: c
98.   On the day she is to be interviewed for an important new position, Rachel awakens with a severe toothache. During the interview she feels no pain; not until 30 minutes later does she become aware again of the troublesome toothache. Rachel's experience is best explained by:
   a. the opponent-process theory.
   b. Weber's law.
   c. the gate-control theory.
   d. the Young-Helmholtz theory.
   e. frequency theory.

Pain, p. 199
Medium, Factual/Definitional, Objective 10, Ans: c
99.   Our experience of pain may be intensified when we perceive that others are experiencing pain. This best illustrates the importance of:
   a. sensory adaptation.
   b. accommodation.
   c. top-down processing.
   d. kinesthesis.
   e. difference thresholds.

Pain, p. 199
Easy, Conceptual, Objective 10, Ans: d
100.   If Richard watches a nurse give him an injection, he experiences more pain than if he closes his eyes during the procedure and thinks about his favorite food. This illustrates the value of _____ for pain control.
   a. sensory adaptation
   b. perceptual adaptation
   c. subliminal stimulation
   d. distraction
   e. kinesthesis

Taste, p. 201
Easy, Factual/Definitional, Objective 11, Ans: e
101.   Heavy smoking is most likely to interfere with your sense of:
   a. equilibrium.
   b. vision.
   c. kinesthesis.
   d. hearing.
   e. taste.

Taste, p. 201
Easy, Conceptual, Objective 11, Ans: a

102. With her eyes closed and her nose plugged, Chandra was unable to taste the difference between an onion and a pear. Her experience best illustrates the importance of:
    a. sensory interaction.
    b. sensory transduction.
    c. sensory adaptation.
    d. kinesthesis.
    e. subliminal stimulation.

Taste, p. 201
Medium, Conceptual, Objective 11, Ans: d

103. The green-colored ham and eggs had such a strange appearance that they tasted terrible to Sam. This illustrates the importance of:
    a. difference thresholds.
    b. sensory adaptation.
    c. equilibrium.
    d. sensory interaction.
    e. accommodation.

Smell, p. 201
Easy, Factual/Definitional, Objective 11, Ans: b

104. Olfactory receptor cells are essential for our sense of:
    a. kinesthesis.
    b. smell.
    c. touch.
    d. hearing.
    e. equilibrium.

Smell, p. 203
Medium, Factual/Definitional, Objective 11, Ans: b

105. Areas of the brain involved in memory are located most closely to areas of the brain responsible for our sense of:
    a. touch.
    b. smell.
    c. vision.
    d. hearing.

Smell, p. 203
Difficult, Factual/Definitional, Objective 11, Ans: d

106. Damage to frontal areas of the temporal lobes is most likely to affect our:
    a. vision.
    b. hearing.
    c. sense of touch.
    d. sense of smell.
    e. vestibular sense.

Body position and movement, p. 203
Medium, Factual/Definitional, Objective 12, Ans: d

107. Kinesthesis refers to the:
    a. quivering eye movements that enable the retina to detect continuous stimulation.
    b. process by which stimulus energies are changed into neural signals.
    c. diminished sensitivity to an unchanging stimulus.
    d. system for sensing the position and movement of muscles, tendons, and joints.
    e. process of organizing and interpreting sensory information.

Body position and movement, p. 203
Medium, Conceptual, Objective 12, Ans: b

108. With her eyes closed, Sandra can accurately touch her mouth, nose, and chin with her index
    finger. Sandra's accuracy illustrates the importance of:
    a. accommodation.
    b. kinesthesis.
    c. sensory interaction.
    d. sensory adaptation.
    e. feature detectors.

Body position and movement, p. 203
Medium, Conceptual, Objective 12, Ans: c

109. The ability to detect whether your body is in a horizontal or vertical position depends most
    directly on:
    a. accommodation.
    b. sensory adaptation.
    c. the vestibular sense.
    d. olfactory receptors.
    e. subliminal stimulation.

Body position and movement, p. 204
Medium, Factual/Definitional, Objective 12, Ans: b

110. Receptor cells for the vestibular sense are located in the:
    a. fovea.
    b. inner ear.
    c. muscles and joints.
    d. olfactory epithelium.

Sensory restriction, p. 205
Easy, Factual/Definitional, Objective 13, Ans: b

111. In a form of therapy called REST, smokers heard antismoking messages while spending 24
    hours lying in bed. Which of the following factors appeared to play the biggest role in the
    effectiveness of this therapy?
    a. subliminal stimulation
    b. sensory restriction
    c. sensory adaptation
    d. sensory interaction

CHAPTER 6

Perception

Learning Objectives

Selective Attention and Perceptual Illusions (pp. 209-213)

1. Describe how the process of perception is directed and limited by selective attention.

2. Explain how illusions help us to understand perception.

Perceptual Organization (pp. 213-225)

3. Discuss Gestalt psychology's contribution to our understanding of perception.

4. Explain the figure-ground relationship, and identify principles of perceptual grouping in form perception.

5. Discuss research on depth perception involving the use of the visual cliff, and describe the binocular and monocular cues in depth perception.

6. Describe stroboscopic movement and the phi phenomenon.

7. Describe the perceptual constancies, and show how the perceived size-distance relationship operates in visual illusions.

Perceptual Interpretation (pp. 226-234)

8. Describe the debate over the role of nature and nurture in perception, and discuss what research findings on sensory deprivation and restored vision have contributed to this debate.

9. Explain what the use of distorting goggles indicates regarding the adaptability of perception.

10. Discuss the effects of experiences, assumptions, expectations, and context on our perceptions.

Is There Extrasensory Perception? pp. (234-238)

11. State the claims of ESP, and explain why most research psychologists remain skeptical.

Selective attention, p. 209
Medium, Factual/Definitional, Objective 1, Ans: e

1.   You typically fail to consciously perceive that your own nose is in your line of vision. This best illustrates:

     a. perceptual adaptation.
     b. visual capture.
     c. the phi phenomenon.
     d. convergence.
     e. selective attention.

Selective attention, p. 209
Medium, Conceptual, Objective 1, Ans: c

2.   Felix was so preoccupied with his girlfriend's good looks that he failed to perceive any of her less admirable characteristics. This best illustrates the dangers of:

     a. perceptual adaptation.
     b. figure-ground relationships.
     c. selective attention.
     d. the cocktail party effect.
     e. perceptual constancy.

Selective attention, p. 209
Easy, Factual/Definitional, Objective 1, Ans: e

3.   The ability to pay attention to only one voice at a time is called:

     a. perceptual set.
     b. convergence.
     c. perceptual adaptation.
     d. the phi phenomenon.
     e. the cocktail party effect.

Selective attention, p. 209
Difficult, Conceptual, Objective 1, Ans: e

4.   Because she was listening to the news on the radio, Mrs. Schultz didn't perceive a word of what her husband was saying. Her experience best illustrates:

     a. perceptual adaptation.
     b. perceptual constancy.
     c. relative clarity.
     d. the phi phenomenon.
     e. the cocktail party effect.

Selective attention, p. 210
Medium, Factual/Definitional, Objective 1, Ans: d

5.   Participants in an experiment were told to listen to and repeat a prose passage played in one ear, while a novel tune was played in their other ear. The results of this experiment indicated that the participants:

     a. suffered a sense of discomfort because the novel tune was subliminal.
     b. were able to identify exactly which tune had been played in their ear.
     c. produced an increasing level of alpha waves while exposed to the music.
     d. showed an increase in their liking for the novel tune.

Perceptual illusions, pp. 211, 222-223
Easy, Factual/Definitional, Objective 2, Ans: d

6.   The Müller-Lyer illusion involves the misperception of:
      a. figure-ground relationships.
      b. relative clarity.
      c. binocular distance cues.
      d. the length of lines.

Perceptual illusions, p. 213
Medium, Conceptual, Objective 2, Ans: d

7.   People are most likely to perceive the steady drip of a leaky water faucet as:
      a. speeding up over time.
      b. slowing down over time.
      c. becoming progressively louder.
      d. a repeating rhythm of two or more beats.

Perceptual illusions, p. 213
Medium, Factual/Definitional, Objective 2, Ans: c

8.   Visual capture refers to the tendency for:
      a. attention to be captured by novel or threatening stimuli in the visual field.
      b. visual deprivation early in life to limit later ability to perceive visual information.
      c. visual information to dominate other types of sensory information.
      d. people and other animals to have difficulty adjusting to lenses that displace their visual
          world.

Perceptual illusions, p. 213
Difficult, Conceptual, Objective 2, Ans: d

9.   As she gazed down from a bridge at the rapidly flowing river, Nancy felt as though she were
      moving. Her experience best illustrates the phenomenon of:
      a. retinal disparity.
      b. perceptual adaptation.
      c. location constancy.
      d. visual capture.
      e. the phi phenomenon.

Perceptual organization, p. 213
Easy, Factual/Definitional, Objective 3, Ans: c

10.   Which group of psychologists focused on principles of perceptual organization?
      a. structuralists
      b. psychoanalysts
      c. Gestalt psychologists
      d. parapsychologists

Perceptual organization, p. 213
Medium, Factual/Definitional, Objective 3, Ans: d

11.   Who emphasized that the whole exceeds the sum of its parts?
      a. evolutionary psychologists
      b. parapsychologists
      c. behaviorists
      d. Gestalt psychologists
      e. psychoanalysts

Perceptual organization, p. 213
Difficult, Factual/Definitional, Objective 3, Ans: d

12. Gestalt psychologists emphasized that:
    a. perception is independent of sensation.
    b. we learn to perceive the world through experience.
    c. the whole is equal to the sum of its parts.
    d. we organize sensations into meaningful patterns.

Perceptual organization, pp. 213, 215
Difficult, Conceptual, Objective 3, Ans: e

13. Which of the following concepts best illustrates the perspective of Gestalt psychologists?
    a. extrasensory perception
    b. retinal disparity
    c. visual capture
    d. convergence
    e. closure

Perceptual organization, p. 214
Difficult, Conceptual, Objective 3, Ans: d

14. The perception of illusory contours best demonstrates that:
    a. perception can occur apart from sensory input.
    b. we readily adjust to an artificially displaced visual field.
    c. binocular cues are more informative than monocular cues.
    d. the whole perception is more than the sum of its sensory elements.
    e. novel or threatening information is especially likely to capture our attention.

Perceptual organization, pp. 214-215
Difficult, Conceptual, Objective 3, Ans: e

15. The principles of continuity and closure best illustrate the importance of:
    a. binocular cues.
    b. perceptual adaptation.
    c. visual capture.
    d. perceptual constancy.
    e. top-down processing.

Figure and ground, p. 214
Easy, Conceptual, Objective 4, Ans: a

16. Although several students in the classroom are talking loudly, Jim's attention is focused only on what his girlfriend is saying. In this instance, the girlfriend's voice is a:
    a. figure.
    b. gestalt.
    c. perceptual set.
    d. perceptual adaptation.

Figure and ground, p. 214
Difficult, Conceptual, Objective 4, Ans: d

17. Moon is to sky as _____ is to _____.
    a. light and shadow; relative height
    b. closure; relative clarity
    c. lightness constancy; relative clarity
    d. figure; ground
    e. proximity; similarity

Figure and ground, p. 214
Medium, Conceptual, Objective 4, Ans: e
18. People are more likely to perceive a figure and ground illustration as reversible if they are told it is reversible. This best illustrates the importance of:
    a. visual capture.
    b. retinal disparity.
    c. perceptual adaptation.
    d. perceptual constancy.
    e. top-down processing.

Grouping, p. 215
Medium, Factual/Definitional, Objective 4, Ans: c
19. The Gestalt principles of proximity and similarity refer to ways in which we:
    a. adapt to perceptual changes.
    b. activate meaningful perceptual sets.
    c. organize stimuli into coherent groups.
    d. decompose whole objects into sensory stimuli.

Grouping, p. 215
Easy, Factual/Definitional, Objective 4, Ans: d
20. The perceptual tendency to group together stimuli that are near each other is called:
    a. closure.
    b. interposition.
    c. perceptual set.
    d. proximity.
    e. convergence.

Grouping, p. 215
Difficult, Conceptual, Objective 4, Ans: b
21. Because the football game was interrupted by a long half-time break, 5-year-old Mark mistakenly concluded that the second and third quarters of play were parts of two different games. His experience best illustrates the organizational principle of:
    a. continuity.
    b. proximity.
    c. similarity.
    d. convergence.
    e. closure.

Grouping, p. 215
Medium, Conceptual, Objective 4, Ans: c
22. Almost half the birds in the yard were brown and the rest were bright red cardinals, so Jimmy perceived them as two distinct groups of birds. This best illustrates the principle of:
    a. proximity.
    b. closure.
    c. similarity.
    d. connectedness.
    e. relative clarity.

Grouping, p. 215
Easy, Factual/Definitional, Objective 4, Ans: b
23. The principle of continuity refers to the perceptual tendency to:
   a. group things that are near each other.
   b. group stimuli into smooth, uninterrupted patterns.
   c. fill in gaps so as to perceive a complete, whole object.
   d. group elements that are similar to each other.

Grouping, p. 215
Difficult, Conceptual, Objective 4, Ans: d
24. The tendency to see all the spokes in a bicycle wheel as part of a single unit best illustrates the principle of:
   a. closure.
   b. continuity.
   c. convergence.
   d. connectedness.
   e. interposition.

Grouping, p. 215
Medium, Conceptual, Objective 4, Ans: a
25. The tendency to see complete letters on a neon sign, even though some of the bulbs are out, illustrates the principle of:
   a. closure.
   b. convergence.
   c. similarity.
   d. constancy.
   e. connectedness.

Grouping, p. 215
Difficult, Conceptual, Objective 4, Ans: b
26. During a radio ad listeners are repeatedly asked, "What would life be without Fletchers Ice Cream?" At the end of the ad the same question is cleverly interrupted immediately after the word "without." At that point many listeners mentally respond with the words "Fletchers Ice Cream." Their response best illustrates the principle of:
   a. convergence.
   b. closure.
   c. proximity.
   d. interposition.
   e. similarity.

Depth perception, p. 215
Easy, Factual/Definitional, Objective 5, Ans: b
27. The organization of two-dimensional retinal images into three-dimensional perceptions is called:
   a. retinal disparity.
   b. depth perception.
   c. perceptual constancy.
   d. visual capture.
   e. the phi phenomenon.

Depth perception, p. 215
Medium, Factual/Definitional, Objective 5, Ans: c
28. Experiments with the visual cliff suggest that:
    a. humans must learn to recognize depth.
    b. binocular cues are more important than monocular cues.
    c. the ability to perceive depth is at least partially innate.
    d. unlike other animals, humans do not perceive depth until about
       8 months of age.

Depth perception, pp. 216, 226
Difficult, Conceptual, Objective 5, Ans: b
29. During the first month of life, human infants will turn to avoid an
    object coming directly at them. This best serves to support the perspective
    advanced by:
    a. Freud.
    b. Kant.
    c. Locke.
    d. Aristotle.

Depth perception: binocular cues, p. 216
Easy, Factual/Definitional, Objective 5, Ans: b
30. Which of the following is a binocular cue for the perception of distance?
    a. relative size
    b. retinal disparity
    c. relative motion
    d. linear perspective

Depth perception: binocular cues, p. 216
Medium, Factual/Definitional, Objective 5, Ans: b
31. A 3-D movie enhances one's sense of depth perception by simulating the effects of:
    a. interposition.
    b. retinal disparity.
    c. linear perspective.
    d. convergence.
    e. perceptual constancy.

Depth perception: binocular cues, p. 217
Medium, Factual/Definitional, Objective 5, Ans: b
32. In the context of visual perception, convergence refers to the:
    a. tendency to perceive parallel lines as coming closer together in the distance.
    b. extent to which the eyes turn toward each other when looking at an object.
    c. current trend toward a combination of the theories supporting both the nature and the
       nurture positions.
    d. tendency to see stimuli that are very near to each other as parts of a unified object.

Depth perception: binocular cues, pp. 216, 217
Difficult, Conceptual, Objective 5, Ans: a
33. If Jill carefully watches Eduard as he runs directly toward her, she will experience a(n)
    _____ in retinal disparity and a(n) _____ in convergence.
    a. increase; increase
    b. decrease; decrease
    c. increase; decrease
    d. decrease; increase

Depth perception: monocular cues, p. 217
Easy, Factual/Definitional, Objective 5, Ans: b

34. Interposition is a cue for depth perception in which closer objects:
    a. create larger retinal images than do distant objects.
    b. obstruct our view of distant objects.
    c. reflect more light to our eyes than do distant objects.
    d. appear lower in the horizontal plane than do distant objects.

Depth perception: monocular cues, p. 217
Easy, Conceptual, Objective 5, Ans: a

35. Helen knew the red tulip was closer to her than the yellow tulip because the red one cast a larger retinal image than the yellow one. This illustrates the importance of the distance cue known as:
    a. relative size.
    b. interposition.
    c. proximity.
    d. relative height.
    e. linear perspective.

Depth perception: monocular cues, p. 217
Medium, Conceptual, Objective 5, Ans: b

36. In order to give greater depth to his painting, Shakir enveloped the background landscape in a misty haze. Shakir was making use of the distance cue known as:
    a. texture.
    b. relative clarity.
    c. interposition.
    d. closure.
    e. proximity.

Depth perception: monocular cues, p. 217
Difficult, Conceptual, Objective 5, Ans: d

37. In foggy weather, automobile drivers are especially likely to be misled by the distance cue known as:
    a. interposition.
    b. convergence.
    c. relative motion.
    d. relative clarity.
    e. relative size.

Depth perception: monocular cues, p. 218
Easy, Factual/Definitional, Objective 5, Ans: a

38. Texture gradient provides a cue for perceiving the _____ of objects.
    a. distance
    b. shape
    c. color
    d. overlap

Depth perception: monocular cues, p. 218
Difficult, Conceptual, Objective 5, Ans: e
39. The individual boulders and crevices of the huge and clearly visible mountain peak appeared so indistinct to the hikers that they knew it would take them another full day to reach it. This best illustrates the impact of _____ on distance perception.
     a. interposition
     b. continuity
     c. retinal disparity
     d. linear perspective
     e. texture gradient

Depth perception: monocular cues, p. 218
Medium, Factual/Definitional, Objective 5, Ans: c
40. Which of the following distance cues most likely contributes to the perception that the height of the St. Louis Gateway Arch is greater than its width?
     a. interposition
     b. convergence
     c. relative height
     d. linear perspective

Depth perception: monocular cues, p. 218
Medium, Conceptual, Objective 5, Ans: c
41. Cars are typically perceived as _____ if they have bright rather than dim headlights. Cars are typically perceived as _____ if they are higher rather than lower in our field of vision.
     a. closer; closer
     b. farther away; farther away
     c. closer; farther away
     d. farther away; closer

Depth perception: monocular cues, p. 218
Easy, Factual/Definitional, Objective 5, Ans: c
42. Relative motion provides a cue for perceiving the _____ of objects.
     a. weight
     b. speed
     c. distance
     d. shape

Depth perception: monocular cues, p. 218
Easy, Factual/Definitional, Objective 5, Ans: d
43. The convergence of parallel lines provides the distance cue known as:
     a. interposition.
     b. closure.
     c. relative height.
     d. linear perspective.
     e. continuity.

Depth perception: monocular cues, p. 218
Difficult, Conceptual, Objective 5, Ans: e

44.   The apparent narrowing of a river as it flows directly away from you into the distance best illustrates the depth cue known as:
      a. interposition.
      b. convergence.
      c. relative motion.
      d. continuity.
      e. linear perspective.

Depth perception: monocular cues, p. 218
Difficult, Conceptual, Objective 5, Ans: d

45.   If two identical objects are equally distant from a viewer, the more brightly illuminated object appears to be:
      a. larger.
      b. more finely textured.
      c. less colorful.
      d. closer.

Depth perception: monocular cues, p. 218
Easy, Factual/Definitional, Objective 5, Ans: c

46.   When viewing an object, we typically assume that the light originates from _____ the object.
      a. behind
      b. in front of
      c. above
      d. below

Motion perception, p. 220
Medium, Factual/Definitional, Objective 6, Ans: b

47.   If all the following oncoming vehicles were travelling at the same speed, which would most likely be perceived as moving the most slowly?
      a. a car
      b. a train
      c. a bus
      d. a motorcycle

Motion perception, p. 220
Medium, Conceptual, Objective 6, Ans: e

48.   The perception that Bugs Bunny is hopping across a movie screen best illustrates:
      a. visual capture.
      b. retinal disparity.
      c. perceptual adaptation.
      d. the Ponzo illusion.
      e. stroboscopic movement.

Motion perception, p. 220
Difficult, Conceptual, Objective 6, Ans: e
49. The illusion of movement in animated neon signs is known as:
   a. interposition.
   b. relative motion.
   c. retinal disparity.
   d. visual capture.
   e. the phi phenomenon.

Perceptual constancy, p. 221
Medium, Factual/Definitional, Objective 7, Ans: a
50. Shape constancy refers to our perception of an object as unchanging in shape regardless of changes in the:
   a. angle from which we view the object.
   b. distance from which we view the object.
   c. color of the object.
   d. extent to which our eyes converge inward when looking at the object.

Perceptual constancy, p. 221
Easy, Conceptual, Objective 7, Ans: c
51. As Sherod walked away from the camera, the image of his body filled a smaller area of the television screen. Nevertheless, viewers did not perceive Sherod as suddenly shrinking. This illustrates:
   a. perceptual adaptation.
   b. convergence.
   c. size constancy.
   d. relative clarity.
   e. visual capture.

Size-distance relationship, p. 221
Easy, Factual/Definitional, Objective 7, Ans: e
52. The visually perceived distance between ourselves and an object provides an important cue for our perception of the object's:
   a. brightness.
   b. shape.
   c. color.
   d. motion.
   e. size.

Size-distance relationship, p. 221
Difficult, Conceptual, Objective 7, Ans: c
53. If two different stars cast retinal images of the same size, the star that appears to be _____ is likely to be perceived as larger than the one that appears to be _____.
   a. brighter; dimmer
   b. moving; stationary
   c. farther away; closer
   d. high in the sky; near the horizon

Size-distance relationship, p. 222
Easy, Factual/Definitional, Objective 7, Ans: c
54.   The moon just above the horizon typically appears to be unusually _____, because we
       perceive it as unusually _____ ourselves.
       a. large; close to
       b. bright; close to
       c. large; far away from
       d. bright; far away from

Size-distance relationship, p. 222
Medium, Factual/Definitional, Objective 7, Ans: b
55.   The moon illusion can best be explained in terms of the relationship between _____ and
       _____.
       a. relative clarity; relative height
       b. perceived distance; perceived size
       c. proximity; closure
       d. atmospheric air pressure; diffusion of light waves
       e. selective attention; lightness constancy

Size-distance relationship, pp. 222-223
Easy, Factual/Definitional, Objective 7, Ans: c
56.   When observing buffalo, the African Pygmy Kenge most clearly failed to experience _____
       constancy.
       a. color
       b. shape
       c. size
       d. location
       e. brightness

Size-distance relationship, p. 223
Medium, Factual/Definitional, Objective 7, Ans: c
57.   The African Pygmy Kenge misperceived buffalo as rapidly increasing in size because of:
       a. a perceptual set provided by his belief in evil spirits.
       b. his intense hunger, which created in him a need to believe food would soon be plentiful.
       c. his limited experience in observing objects across large, wide-open distances.
       d. the absence of distance cues such as relative height and texture gradients.

Size-distance relationship, p. 224
Medium, Factual/Definitional, Objective 7, Ans: d
58.   The illusion of the shrinking and growing girls shown in the text can best be explained in terms
       of:
       a. shape constancy.
       b. retinal disparity.
       c. the principle of continuity.
       d. the misperception of distance.
       e. selective attention.

Lightness constancy, p. 224
Medium, Factual/Definitional, Objective 7, Ans: b

59. Lightness constancy refers to the fact that:
    a. the frequency of light waves has a fixed relationship to the brightness of the light.
    b. objects are perceived to have consistent lightness even if the amount of light they reflect changes.
    c. light waves reflected by an object remain constant despite changes in illumination levels.
    d. the perceived whiteness of an object has a constant relation to its lightness.

Lightness constancy, p. 224
Medium, Factual/Definitional, Objective 7, Ans: d

60. In order for us to experience lightness constancy, we should view things:
    a. for short periods of time.
    b. from very short distances.
    c. under high levels of illumination.
    d. in relation to surrounding objects.

Perceptual interpretation, p. 226
Difficult, Factual/Definitional, Objective 8, Ans: d

61. The philosopher Immanuel Kant emphasized that:
    a. perception is the same as sensation.
    b. we learn to perceive the world through experience.
    c. the whole is equal to the sum of its parts.
    d. perception depends on innate ways of organizing sensory experience.

Perceptual interpretation, p. 226
Medium, Factual/Definitional, Objective 8, Ans: c

62. Who emphasized that perceptions are learned through experience?
    a. Kant
    b. Gestalt psychologists
    c. Locke
    d. Plato

Perceptual interpretation, p. 226
Difficult, Conceptual, Objective 8, Ans: d

63. In the historical controversy over the dynamics of perception, _____ was to nature as _____ was to nurture.
    a. continuity; convergence
    b. Aristotle; Plato
    c. proximity; similarity
    d. Kant; Locke

Sensory deprivation and restored vision, p. 226
Difficult, Conceptual, Objective 8, Ans: c

64. Mr. Watkins had been blind from birth. While corrective eye surgery enabled him to see, he was unable to visually distinguish a spoon from a key. This fact would serve to support the position advanced by:
    a. Kant.
    b. Gestalt psychologists.
    c. Locke.
    d. parapsychologists.

Sensory deprivation and restored vision, p. 226
Medium, Factual/Definitional, Objective 8, Ans: c

65.   After corrective eye surgery, patients blind from birth have the greatest difficulty in visually
      distinguishing between stimuli that differ in:
      a. color.
      b. brightness.
      c. shape.
      d. size.

Sensory deprivation and restored vision, p. 226
Medium, Factual/Definitional, Objective 8, Ans: d

66.   When visually deprived infant monkeys were first allowed to see, they could not visually
      distinguish:
      a. between horizontal and vertical stripes.
      b. between different-colored objects.
      c. figures from backgrounds.
      d. circles from squares.

Sensory deprivation and restored vision, p. 227
Easy, Factual/Definitional, Objective 8, Ans: b

67.   Kittens raised in a visual environment consisting solely of vertical stripes subsequently had
      difficulty:
      a. seeing vertically oriented objects.
      b. seeing horizontally oriented objects.
      c. perceiving any figure-ground relationships.
      d. doing all the above.

Sensory deprivation and restored vision, p. 227
Difficult, Factual/Definitional, Objective 8, Ans: b

68.   The difficulties experienced by kittens raised without exposure to horizontal lines illustrated
      the functional significance of:
      a. visual capture.
      b. feature-detecting brain cells.
      c. retinal disparity.
      d. perceptual constancy.

Perceptual adaptation, p. 227
Easy, Factual/Definitional, Objective 9, Ans: d

69.   Perceptual adaptation refers to the:
      a. grouping of stimuli into smooth, uninterrupted patterns.
      b. perception of movement created by the successive blinking of adjacent lights.
      c. perception of an object as unchanging in shape regardless of our own viewing angle.
      d. perceptual adjustment to an artificially displaced visual field.
      e. tendency for novel or unfamiliar stimuli to capture our attention.

Perceptual adaptation, p. 227
Medium, Conceptual, Objective 9, Ans: d

70.   The impact of experience on perception is most clearly illustrated by:
      a. visual capture.
      b. retinal disparity.
      c. the phi phenomenon.
      d. perceptual adaptation.
      e. extrasensory perception.

Perceptual adaptation, p. 227
Medium, Factual/Definitional, Objective 9, Ans: d
71.   After chicks were fitted with special lenses that visually displaced objects to the left, they:
      a. quickly learned to compensate by pecking to the left of where the food appeared to be.
      b. only gradually learned to compensate by pecking to the right of where the food appeared to be.
      c. only gradually learned to compensate by pecking to the left of where the food appeared to be.
      d. never adapted to the visual distortion.

Perceptual adaptation, pp. 227-228
Medium, Conceptual, Objective 9, Ans: a
72.   After some practice, Carol was able to read books while holding them upside down. This best illustrates:
      a. perceptual adaptation.
      b. perceptual constancy.
      c. relative clarity.
      d. visual capture.

Perceptual set, p. 228
Medium, Factual/Definitional, Objective 10, Ans: d
73.   A perceptual set is a:
      a. tendency to fill in gaps so as to perceive a complete, whole object.
      b. readiness to perceive an object in an unfairly negative fashion.
      c. tendency to view similar elements as part of a single group.
      d. mental predisposition that influences what we perceive.

Perceptual set, pp. 226, 228
Medium, Conceptual, Objective 10, Ans: e
74.   John Locke would have suggested that a perceptual set results from:
      a. visual capture.
      b. relative clarity.
      c. natural selection.
      d. selective attention.
      e. prior experience.

Perceptual set, p. 229
Easy, Factual/Definitional, Objective 10, Ans: e
75.   In 1972, many people readily perceived photographs of a floating tree trunk as a partially submerged "Loch Ness Monster." The text mentions this in order to illustrate the powerful influence of:
      a. relative clarity.
      b. stroboscopic movement.
      c. bottom-up processing.
      d. visual capture.
      e. perceptual set.

Perceptual set, p. 229
Medium, Conceptual, Objective 10, Ans: a

76. After watching a scary television movie, Julie perceived the noise of the wind rattling her front windows as the sound of a burglar breaking into her house. Her mistaken interpretation best illustrates the influence of:
    a. perceptual set.
    b. visual capture.
    c. perceptual adaptation.
    d. bottom-up processing.
    e. stroboscopic movement.

Perceptual set, p. 229
Medium, Conceptual, Objective 10, Ans: b

77. After reading her horoscope in the morning newspaper, Nancy readily interpreted numerous experiences of that day as clear verifications of its accuracy. This best illustrates the dangers of:
    a. visual capture.
    b. perceptual set.
    c. the cocktail party effect.
    d. bottom-up processing.
    e. relative clarity.

Perceptual set, pp. 214, 229
Medium, Conceptual, Objective 10, Ans: d

78. The impact of a perceptual set on experience best illustrates the importance of:
    a. visual capture.
    b. linear perspective.
    c. relative clarity.
    d. top-down processing.
    e. the phi phenomenon.

Perceptual set, p. 229
Medium, Factual/Definitional, Objective 10, Ans: a

79. Schemas are best described as:
    a. concepts that organize sensory input.
    b. networks of interconnected brain cells.
    c. visual receptor cells located in the eye.
    d. genetic predispositions to perceive objects in a distorted fashion.
    e. monocular cues for depth perception.

Perceptual set, p. 229
Medium, Factual/Definitional, Objective 10, Ans: b

80. The perception of a humanlike face in the random configurations of the lunar landscape best illustrates the impact of _____ on visual perception.
    a. relative clarity
    b. perceptual schemas
    c. visual capture
    d. shape constancy
    e. stroboscopic movement

Context effects, p. 231
Medium, Conceptual, Objective 10, Ans: d
81. It wasn't until Clara heard some of her classmates laughing loudly during history class that she began to perceive the professor's ongoing lecture to be very funny. This provides an illustration of:
a. relative clarity.
b. the phi phenomenon.
c. perceptual adaptation.
d. context effects.
e. the cocktail party effect.

Context effects, p. 231
Medium, Conceptual, Objective 10, Ans: e
82. When Helen noticed that her classmates were all wearing expensive designer jeans, she suddenly perceived her own off-brand jeans to be very unattractive. This best illustrates the importance of:
a. convergence.
b. visual capture.
c. perceptual adaptation.
d. texture gradient.
e. context effects.

Context effects, p. 231
Medium, Conceptual, Objective 10, Ans: c
83. Numerous pedestrians calmly walked past an elderly gentleman lying on a city sidewalk without showing any concern. As a consequence, other passersby failed to perceive that the man was in obvious need of immediate medical assistance. This best illustrates the importance of:
a. perceptual adaptation.
b. relative clarity.
c. context effects.
d. visual capture.
e. perceptual constancy.

Context effects, pp. 224, 231
Difficult, Conceptual, Objective 10, Ans: e
84. The perceived lightness of an object depends on relative luminance. This provides an illustration of:
a. visual capture.
b. perceptual adaptation.
c. the phi phenomenon.
d. relative clarity.
e. context effects.

The human factor in operating machines (Close-up), p. 233
Medium, Factual/Definitional, Objective 10, Ans: c
85. Psychologists who help to design machines so that they make use of our natural perceptions are called:
a. parapsychologists.
b. Gestalt psychologists.
c. human factors psychologists.
d. psychophysicists.

Is there extrasensory perception?, p. 234
Easy, Factual/Definitional, Objective 11, Ans: a

86.   ESP refers to:
       a. perception that occurs apart from sensory input.
       b. the ability to move objects without touching them.
       c. a readiness to perceive an object in a distorted fashion.
       d. all the above.

Is there extrasensory perception?, p. 234
Medium, Factual/Definitional, Objective 11, Ans: a

87.   The study of phenomena such as clairvoyance and telepathy is called:
       a. parapsychology.
       b. Gestalt psychology.
       c. phenomenological psychology.
       d. psychokinesis.
       e. ESP.

Claims of ESP, p. 234
Easy, Factual/Definitional, Objective 11, Ans: c

88.   Telepathy, clairvoyance, and precognition are different forms of:
       a. parapsychology.
       b. psychokinesis.
       c. extrasensory perception.
       d. the Ponzo illusion.
       e. the phi phenomenon.

Claims of ESP, p. 234
Medium, Conceptual, Objective 11, Ans: a

89.   Sheryl claims that she knows at any given moment exactly what important political figures are
       thinking. Sheryl is claiming to possess the power of:
       a. telepathy.
       b. precognition.
       c. psychokinesis.
       d. clairvoyance.

Claims of ESP, p. 234
Medium, Factual/Definitional, Objective 11, Ans: b

90.   Clairvoyance refers to the:
       a. extrasensory transmission of thoughts from one mind to another.
       b. extrasensory perception of events that occur at places remote to the perceiver.
       c. perception of future events, such as a person's fate.
       d. ability to understand and share the emotions of another person.

Claims of ESP, pp. 234, 235
Medium, Conceptual, Objective 11, Ans: d

91.   Rudy claims that his special psychic powers enable him to correctly anticipate whether the
       outcome of a coin toss will be heads or tails. Rudy is claiming to possess the power of:
       a. psychokineses.
       b. clairvoyance.
       c. telepathy.
       d. precognition.

Claims of ESP, p. 234
Medium, Conceptual, Objective 11, Ans: c
92. Farouk insists that by intense mental concentration he can actually influence the mechanically generated outcomes of slot machines. Farouk is most specifically claiming to possess the power of:
    a. telepathy.
    b. clairvoyance.
    c. psychokinesis.
    d. precognition.

Claims of ESP, pp. 235-236
Easy, Factual/Definitional, Objective 11, Ans: e
93. Scientific analyses of the predictive powers of dreams offer support for the existence of:
    a. telepathy.
    b. clairvoyance.
    c. precognition.
    d. all of the above.
    e. none of the above.

Claims of ESP, p. 237
Medium, Factual/Definitional, Objective 11, Ans: c
94. Most research psychologists now believe that:
    a. many people have ESP.
    b. ESP exists only in a few specially gifted people.
    c. there is no reliable evidence that anyone possesses ESP.
    d. it is impossible to scientifically test claims of ESP.

Claims of ESP, p. 237
Medium, Factual/Definitional, Objective 11, Ans: e
95. The ganzfeld procedure has recently been used in studies of:
    a. perceptual adaptation.
    b. depth perception.
    c. the phi phenomenon.
    d. perceptual set.
    e. telepathy.

CHAPTER 7

States of Consciousness

Learning Objectives

Waking Consciousness (pp. 241-244)

1. Discuss the nature of consciousness and its significance in the history of psychology.

2. Contrast conscious and subconscious information processing.

3. Discuss the content and potential functions of daydreams and fantasies, and describe the fantasy-prone personality.

Sleep and Dreams (pp. 245-260)

4. Discuss the importance of seasonal, monthly, and daily biological rhythms.

5. Describe the cyclical nature and possible functions of sleep.

6. Identify the major sleep disorders.

7. Discuss the content and possible functions of dreams.

Hypnosis (pp. 261-270)

8. Discuss hypnosis, noting the behavior of hypnotized people and claims regarding its uses.

9. Discuss the controversy over whether hypnosis is an altered state of consciousness.

Drugs and Consciousness (pp. 270-282)

10. Discuss the nature of drug dependence, and identify some common misconceptions about addiction.

11. Describe the physiological and psychological effects of depressants, stimulants, and hallucinogens.

12. Discuss the factors that contribute to drug use.

Near-Death Experiences (pp. 283-284)

13. Describe the near-death experience and the controversy over whether it provides evidence for a mind-body dualism.

Waking consciousness, p. 241
Easy, Factual/Definitional, Objective 1, Ans: d

1.   By 1960 the study of consciousness had been revived by psychologists' renewed interest in:
      a. genetics.
      b. emotion.
      c. socialization.
      d. cognition.
      e. mental health.

Waking consciousness, p. 241
Difficult, Conceptual, Objective 1, Ans: e

2.   Behaviorism encouraged psychologists to ignore the study of:
      a. dreams.
      b. fantasies.
      c. hypnotic states.
      d. hallucinations.
      e. all the above.

Levels of information processing, p. 242
Medium, Factual/Definitional, Objective 2, Ans: d

3.   Subconscious information processing is more likely than conscious processing to:
      a. occur slowly.
      b. be limited in its capacity.
      c. contribute to effective problem solving.
      d. occur simultaneously on several parallel dimensions.

Levels of information processing, p. 242
Medium, Conceptual, Objective 2, Ans: c

4.   Parallel processing is to serial processing as _____ is to _____.
      a. daydream; sleep dream
      b. sleep dream; daydream
      c. subconsciousness; consciousness
      d. consciousness; subconsciousness

Levels of information processing, p. 242
Medium, Factual/Definitional, Objective 2, Ans: d

5.   Consciousness is most important for the correct performance of behaviors that:
      a. depend on information processing.
      b. require physical coordination skills.
      c. have been learned through repeated practice.
      d. are novel and challenging.

Daydreams and fantasies, p. 242
Medium, Factual/Definitional, Objective 3, Ans: b

6.   Research indicates that _____ spend more time daydreaming and admit to more sexual fantasies than do _____.
      a. males; females
      b. young adults; older adults
      c. drug addicts; nonaddicts
      d. the unmarried; the married

Daydreams and fantasies, p. 243
Easy, Factual/Definitional, Objective 3, Ans: c

7. Compared to others, those with a fantasy-prone personality are _____ likely to daydream and are _____ likely to report mystical or religious experiences.
    a. less; more
    b. more; less
    c. more; more
    d. less; less

Daydreams and fantasies, p. 244
Medium, Factual/Definitional, Objective 3, Ans: d

8. Studies of daydreaming indicate that:
    a. people prone to violent behavior tend to have more vivid fantasies.
    b. the frequency of daydreaming remains unchanged across the life span.
    c. daydreaming sometimes helps us escape reality but never helps us face it.
    d. daydreaming can positively influence a child's social and cognitive development.
    e. all the above are true.

Sleep and dreams, p. 245
Medium, Factual/Definitional, Objective 4, Ans: e

9. Research on sleep and dreams indicates that:
    a. occasional use of sleeping pills effectively reduces insomnia.
    b. the circadian rhythm has no influence on our patterns of sleep.
    c. sleepwalking involves the acting out of parts of our dreams.
    d. some people dream every night, whereas others seldom dream at all.
    e. none of the above are true.

Biological rhythms, p. 245
Medium, Conceptual, Objective 4, Ans: b

10. The impact of biological rhythms is best illustrated by:
    a. mood variations across the menstrual cycle.
    b. fluctuations in energy level and alertness across the span of a day.
    c. variations in study habits over the course of a school year.
    d. the different personalities of people born during different months of the calendar year.

PMS (Box), p. 246
Difficult, Factual/Definitional, Objective 4, Ans: d

11. The tendency to notice and remember instances that confirm our beliefs is most likely to contribute to overestimates of the prevalence of:
    a. narcolepsy.
    b. dissociation.
    c. REM sleep.
    d. PMS.

PMS (Box), p. 246
Medium, Factual/Definitional, Objective 4, Ans: c

12. Evidence of large cross-cultural differences in the prevalence of PMS most clearly serves to challenge the causal significance of _____ to this pattern of symptoms.
    a. REM sleep
    b. narcolepsy
    c. biological rhythms
    d. sleep apnea

Circadian rhythm, pp. 245, 247
Medium, Conceptual, Objective 4, Ans: d
13. Growth hormone secretions peak in women at predictable hours of each night. This best
     illustrates the dynamics of the:
     a. hypnogogic state.
     b. REM rebound.
     c. menstrual cycle.
     d. circadian rhythm.

Circadian rhythm, p. 245
Medium, Factual/Definitional, Objective 4, Ans: a
14. Human body temperatures typically rise with the approach of _____ and fall with the
     approach of _____.
     a. morning; night
     b. night; morning
     c. Stage 1 sleep; REM sleep
     d. REM sleep; Stage 1 sleep

Circadian rhythm, p. 245
Medium, Conceptual, Objective 4, Ans: c
15. Cindi prefers to take exams in the late afternoon rather than during the morning because her
     energy level and ability to concentrate are better at that time. Her experience most likely
     reflects the influence of the:
     a. REM rebound.
     b. menstrual cycle.
     c. circadian rhythm.
     d. hypnogogic state.

Circadian rhythm, p. 247
Easy, Conceptual, Objective 4, Ans: a
16. After four years of working nights, Raymond now works days. His present difficulty in getting
     to sleep at night is most likely due to a disruption of his normal:
     a. circadian rhythm.
     b. hypnogogic state.
     c. alpha wave pattern.
     d. general adaptation syndrome.

Circadian rhythm, p. 247
Difficult, Conceptual, Objective 4, Ans: d
17. The 25-hour cycle of our natural circadian rhythm helps explain why we are least likely to
     experience jet lag after we fly:
     a. north.
     b. south.
     c. east.
     d. west.

Sleep stages, p. 248
Difficult, Factual/Definitional, Objective 5, Ans: c
18. The act of yawning _____ your heart rate and _____ your alertness.
     a. increases; decreases
     b. decreases; increases
     c. increases; increases
     d. decreases; decreases

Sleep stages, p. 248
Medium, Factual/Definitional, Objective 5, Ans: e

19. Alpha waves are associated with:
    a. REM sleep.
    b. Stage 2 sleep.
    c. Stage 3 sleep.
    d. Stage 4 sleep.
    e. a relaxed but awake state.

Sleep stages, p. 249
Medium, Factual/Definitional, Objective 5, Ans: a

20. Fantastic images that are not part of our regular sleep dreams occur during _____ sleep.
    a. Stage 1
    b. Stage 2
    c. Stage 3
    d. Stage 4

Sleep stages, p. 249
Difficult, Factual/Definitional, Objective 5, Ans: e

21. Sleeptalking may occur during:
    a. Stage 1 sleep.
    b. Stage 2 sleep.
    c. REM sleep.
    d. Stage 4 sleep.
    e. any stage of sleep.

Sleep stages, p. 249
Medium, Factual/Definitional, Objective 5, Ans: d

22. The large, slow brain waves associated with deep sleep are called:
    a. alpha waves.
    b. beta waves.
    c. sleep spindles.
    d. delta waves.

Sleep stages, p. 249
Difficult, Factual/Definitional, Objective 5, Ans: a

23. Which of the following is most likely to be associated with slow-wave sleep?
    a. bedwetting
    b. sleep spindles
    c. hallucinations
    d. genital arousal

Sleep stages, p. 249
Difficult, Conceptual, Objective 5, Ans: b

24. Stage 2 sleep is to _____ as Stage 4 sleep is to _____.
    a. alpha waves; sleep spindles
    b. sleep spindles; delta waves
    c. delta waves; alpha waves
    d. alpha waves; rapid eye movements

Sleep stages, pp. 250-251
Easy, Conceptual, Objective 5, Ans: e
25.   After Carlos had been asleep for about an hour, his heart began to beat faster, his breathing became fast and irregular, and his closed eyes began to dart back and forth. Carlos was most likely experiencing:
a.   Stage 4 sleep.
b.   sleep apnea.
c.   narcolepsy.
d.   night terror.
e.   REM sleep.

Sleep stages, p. 251
Medium, Factual/Definitional, Objective 5, Ans: b
26.   Which of the following typically occur(s) during REM sleep?
a.   night terrors
b.   genital arousal
c.   bedwetting
d.   muscular tension

Sleep stages, p. 251
Medium, Factual/Definitional, Objective 5, Ans: d
27.   Which of the following is *not* characteristic of REM sleep?
a.   Heart and breathing rates increase.
b.   The eyes move rapidly under closed lids.
c.   Brain waves become more rapid.
d.   Voluntary muscles tense and become more active.

Sleep stages, pp. 249, 251
Difficult, Conceptual, Objective 4, Ans: e
28.   Paradoxical sleep is to slow-wave sleep as _____ sleep is to _____ sleep.
a.   REM; Stage 1
b.   Stage 1; REM
c.   REM; Stage 2
d.   Stage 2; REM
e.   REM; Stage 4

Sleep stages, p. 251
Easy, Factual/Definitional, Objective 5, Ans: b
29.   When people are experiencing vivid dreams:
a.   their bodies often move in accordance with what they dream.
b.   their eyes are likely to move under their closed eyelids.
c.   they are more likely to sleepwalk than during any other stage of sleep.
d.   their slow brain-wave patterns indicate that they are deeply asleep.
e.   all the above are true.

Sleep stages, p. 251
Easy, Conceptual, Objective 5, Ans: d
30.   Margie insists that she never dreams but her roommate feels she can prove otherwise. To prove that Margie does dream, the roommate should:
a.   feed Margie lots of rich food just before bedtime.
b.   make an all-night audiotape of the sounds Margie makes while sleeping.
c.   wake Margie after she has been asleep for about 5 minutes and ask her what she's dreaming.
d.   wake Margie after 5 minutes of REM sleep and ask her what she's dreaming.

Sleep stages, pp. 250, 251
Medium, Conceptual, Objective 5, Ans: c
31. Feli has been asleep for 3 hours. As he continues to sleep, we can expect that _____ sleep
     will diminish and that _____ sleep will increase in duration.
     a. Stage 4; Stage 3
     b. Stage 3; Stage 4
     c. Stage 4; REM
     d. REM; Stage 3

Why do we sleep?, p. 252
Easy, Factual/Definitional, Objective 5, Ans: b
32. When allowed to sleep 9 or 10 hours a night on a regular basis, people are most likely to:
     a. experience REM rebound.
     b. work more efficiently.
     c. show signs of sleep apnea.
     d. demonstrate apathy and loss of energy.

Why do we sleep?, p. 254
Medium, Conceptual, Objective 5, Ans: a
33. Terry has not slept for 72 hours. It is increasingly likely that he will be more susceptible to:
     a. viral infections.
     b. sleep apnea.
     c. insomnia.
     d. night terrors.
     e. dissociation.

Why do we sleep?, p. 254
Medium, Factual/Definitional, Objective 5, Ans: d
34. Chronic sleep deprivation is likely to _____ creativity and _____ hypertension.
     a. increase; increase
     b. decrease; decrease
     c. increase; decrease
     d. decrease; increase

Why do we sleep?, p. 254
Medium, Factual/Definitional, Objective 5, Ans: a
35. Humans sleep _____ than elephants and _____ than cats.
     a. more; less
     b. less; more
     c. more; more
     d. less; less

Why do we sleep?, p. 255
Difficult, Factual/Definitional, Objective 5, Ans: c
36. Caffeine boosts alertness by inhibiting the activity of:
     a. REM rebound.
     b. amphetamines.
     c. adenosine.
     d. epinephrine.

Why do we sleep?, p. 255
Easy, Factual/Definitional, Objective 5, Ans: e
37. Deep sleep appears to play an important role in:
    a. narcolepsy.
    b. sleep apnea.
    c. paradoxical sleep.
    d. posthypnotic amnesia.
    e. physical growth.

Why do we sleep?, p. 255
Medium, Factual/Definitional, Objective 5, Ans: c
38. The suggestion that sleep may play a role in physical growth is consistent with the observation that older adults spend relatively _____ amounts of their sleep time in _____ sleep.
    a. large; Stage 4
    b. large; REM
    c. small; Stage 4
    d. small; REM

Sleep disorders, p. 255
Easy, Factual/Definitional, Objective 6, Ans: b
39. Insomnia is a disorder involving:
    a. the excessive use of sleeping pills or other drugs that induce sleep.
    b. recurring difficulty in falling or staying asleep.
    c. the cessation of breathing during sleep.
    d. uncontrollable attacks of overwhelming sleepiness.

Sleep disorders, p. 255
Medium, Conceptual, Objective 6, Ans: a
40. To cure his insomnia, Mr. Ming-Hwei takes a sleeping pill just before bedtime. Research suggests that this practice:
    a. may actually make Mr. Ming-Hwei's insomnia worse when it is discontinued.
    b. may help Mr. Ming-Hwei permanently overcome his insomnia.
    c. has probably increased Mr. Ming-Hwei's REM sleep.
    d. may make Mr. Ming-Hwei more vulnerable to sleep apnea.

Sleep disorders, p. 255
Difficult, Conceptual, Objective 6, Ans: d
41. Eighty-year-old Mrs. West feels she has trouble falling asleep at night. She typically gets only 6 hours of sleep every 24 hours. What should she do about this?
    a. take a sleeping pill every night
    b. see a doctor who is a sleep specialist
    c. drink an alcoholic beverage before bedtime
    d. relax and remind herself that her sleep patterns are normal

Sleep disorders, p. 255
Easy, Factual/Definitional, Objective 6, Ans: a
42. The disorder involving uncontrollable attacks of overwhelming sleepiness is known as:
    a. narcolepsy.
    b. insomnia.
    c. sleep apnea.
    d. aphasia.

Sleep disorders, p. 255
Medium, Conceptual, Objective 6, Ans: d

43. Which of the following sleep disorders would be the most incapacitating for a commercial airline pilot?
     a. night terrors
     b. insomnia
     c. sleepwalking
     d. narcolepsy

Sleep disorders, p. 255
Medium, Factual/Definitional, Objective 6, Ans: a

44. Sleep apnea is a disorder involving:
     a. the cessation of breathing during sleep.
     b. periodic uncontrollable attacks of overwhelming sleepiness.
     c. hypnogogic sensations of falling or floating weightlessly.
     d. the excessive use of sleeping pills or other sleep-inducing drugs.

Sleep disorders, p. 256
Medium, Conceptual, Objective 6, Ans: a

45. Mr. Dayton occasionally stops breathing while sleeping. He wakes up to snort air for a few seconds before falling back to sleep. Mrs. Dayton complains that her husband snores. Clearly, Mr. Dayton suffers from:
     a. sleep apnea.
     b. narcolepsy.
     c. insomnia.
     d. night terrors.
     e. aphasia.

Sleep disorders, p. 256
Easy, Conceptual, Objective 6, Ans: a

46. About two hours after he falls asleep, Bobby often sits up in bed screaming incoherently. His mother tries to awaken him, but with no success. His pulse races and he gasps for breath. The next morning, he remembers nothing. It appears that Bobby suffers from:
     a. night terrors.
     b. narcolepsy.
     c. sleep spindles.
     d. sleep apnea.

Sleep disorders, p. 256
Difficult, Factual/Definitional, Objective 6, Ans: d

47. It has been found that night terrors:
     a. are usually recalled vividly for days following their occurrence.
     b. are typically accompanied by a state of temporary muscular immobility or paralysis.
     c. jolt the sleeper to a sudden state of full waking alertness.
     d. typically occur during Stage 4 sleep.

Sleep disorders, p. 256
Medium, Factual/Definitional, Objective 6, Ans: c

48. Which sleep disorder is more likely to be experienced by children than by adults?
     a. narcolepsy
     b. sleep apnea
     c. night terrors
     d. insomnia

What do we dream?, p. 257
Difficult, Factual/Definitional, Objective 7, Ans: a
49. Research on dreaming indicates that:
   a. some people are able to test their state of consciousness while dreaming.
   b. dreams cannot be confused with reality.
   c. about half the dreams reported by young men have sexual overtones.
   d. most dreams are unrelated to actual daily events.
   e. it is impossible to perceive color in dreams images.

What do we dream?, p. 257
Difficult, Factual/Definitional, Objective 7, Ans: b
50. Research studies of the content of dreams indicate that:
   a. men are less likely than women to report dreams with sexual overtones.
   b. females are more likely than males to dream about members of the opposite sex.
   c. the genital arousal that occurs during sleep is typically related to sexual dreams.
   d. most dreams are pleasant, exotic, and unrelated to ordinary daily life.

What do we dream?, p. 257
Easy, Factual/Definitional, Objective 7, Ans: a
51. Freud called the remembered story line of a dream its _____ content.
   a. manifest
   b. latent
   c. dissociated
   d. paradoxical
   e. delusional

What do we dream?, p. 257
Medium, Conceptual, Objective 7, Ans: e
52. Rodney, a straight-A student, remembers dreaming that he failed an important chemistry test. According to Freud, Rodney's account represents the _____ content of his dream.
   a. paradoxical
   b. dissociated
   c. delusional
   d. latent
   e. manifest

Why do we dream?, p. 258
Medium, Factual/Definitional, Objective 7, Ans: a
53. According to Freud, people dream in order to:
   a. give expression to personally threatening feelings and desires.
   b. prepare themselves for the challenges of the following day.
   c. strengthen their memories of the preceding day's events.
   d. do all the above.

Why do we dream?, p. 258
Easy, Factual/Definitional, Objective 7, Ans: c
54. According to Freud, the personally threatening and censored meaning of a dream is its:
   a. manifest content.
   b. dissociated content.
   c. latent content.
   d. hallucinatory content.

Why do we dream?, p. 258
Medium, Conceptual, Objective 7, Ans: b

55.   Josef, a high school student, tells his therapist that he has had a recurring dream in which he hunts and kills a ferocious tiger. The therapist explains that the dream reflects Josef's unresolved feelings of hostility toward his father. The therapist is revealing the possible _____ content of Josef's dream.
    a.   manifest
    b.   latent
    c.   regressive
    d.   dissociated

Why do we dream?, p. 258
Medium, Factual/Definitional, Objective 7, Ans: b

56.   Evidence indicates that REM sleep contributes to:
    a.   near-death experiences.
    b.   memory consolidation.
    c.   night terrors.
    d.   dissociation.
    e.   snoring.

Why do we dream?, p. 258
Difficult, Conceptual, Objective 7, Ans: a

57.   The stress and intense study periods of final exam week are likely to _____ among college students who manage to maintain their normal quota of sleep.
    a.   increase REM sleep
    b.   decrease REM sleep
    c.   increase night terrors
    d.   increase sleep spindles
    e.   decrease sleep spindles

Why do we dream?, p. 258
Medium, Factual/Definitional, Objective 7, Ans: a

58.   The theory that dreams result from bursts of neural activity that spread upward from the brainstem helps to explain why:
    a.   people often experience dramatic hallucinations during REM sleep.
    b.   birds and fish experience REM sleep.
    c.   most dreams are pleasant and unrelated to daily life events.
    d.   people spend progressively more of their sleep time in REM sleep as they grow older.
    e.   dreams frequently involve sexual images.

Why do we dream?, p. 258
Medium, Factual/Definitional, Objective 7, Ans: d

59.   Evidence that burst of rapid eye movements during REM sleep coincide with bursts of activity in the visual cortex is most directly supportive of:
    a.   social influence theory.
    b.   dissociation theory.
    c.   Freud's dream theory.
    d.   the activation-synthesis theory.

Why do we dream?, p. 259
Easy, Conceptual, Objective 7, Ans: a

60. As a sleep-research subject for the past three nights, Tim has been repeatedly disturbed during REM sleep. Tonight, when allowed to sleep undisturbed, Tim will likely experience:
   a. an increase in REM sleep.
   b. sleep apnea.
   c. insomnia.
   d. an increase in Stage 4 sleep.

Why do we dream?, p. 259
Medium, Factual/Definitional, Objective 7, Ans: d

61. The existence of REM rebound supports the notion that:
   a. as people grow older they need to spend progressively more time dreaming.
   b. dreams are triggered by random bursts of neural activity.
   c. dreams help to solidify our memories of daytime experiences.
   d. humans, like most other mammals, need REM sleep.

Hypnosis, p. 261
Easy, Factual/Definitional, Objective 8, Ans: d

62. The reported inability to recall what one experienced during hypnosis is called:
   a. dissociation.
   b. narcolepsy.
   c. age regression.
   d. posthypnotic amnesia.
   e. sleep apnea.

Hypnosis, p. 261
Medium, Factual/Definitional, Objective 8, Ans: e

63. Hypnosis has been associated with quackery thanks to the false claims made by:
   a. Sigmund Freud.
   b. Ernst Hilgard.
   c. Martin Orne.
   d. William Dement.
   e. Anton Mesmer.

Can anyone experience hypnosis?, p. 262
Easy, Factual/Definitional, Objective 8, Ans: c

64. Those who study hypnosis agree that it is a state of:
   a. amnesia.
   b. REM sleep.
   c. heightened suggestibility.
   d. physiological arousal.
   e. dissociation.

Can anyone experience hypnosis?, p. 262
Difficult, Conceptual, Objective 8, Ans: d

65. Twenty-two-year-old Milly scores high in hypnotic responsiveness as measured by the Stanford Hypnotic Susceptibility Scale. Research suggests that Milly also has:
   a. below-average intelligence.
   b. an above-average ability to hypnotize others.
   c. difficulty keeping her attention focused on any specific task.
   d. a rich fantasy life.

Can anyone experience hypnosis?, pp. 262-263
Medium, Factual/Definitional, Objective 8, Ans: a

66.   People are particularly responsive to hypnosis if they:
      a. strongly believe they can be hypnotized.
      b. are below average in intelligence and education.
      c. are easily distracted and have difficulty focusing attention.
      d. suffer a physical or psychological dependence on alcohol.

Can hypnosis enhance recall of forgotten events?, p. 263
Easy, Factual/Definitional, Objective 8, Ans: a

67.   Age regression refers to:
      a. the hypnotically induced reliving of earlier life experiences.
      b. the flashbacks to childhood that often occur during an LSD trip.
      c. our natural tendency to relive successful experiences in our daydreams.
      d. the life review that is reported in the near-death experience.

Can hypnosis enhance recall of forgotten events?, p. 263
Medium, Conceptual, Objective 8, Ans: a

68.   Under hypnosis, Mrs. Mohammed is encouraged by her therapist to vividly experience and
      describe the details of an argument she had with her father when she was a child. The therapist
      is employing a technique called:
      a. age regression.
      b. posthypnotic suggestion.
      c. temporal dissociation.
      d. dissociation.
      e. posthypnotic amnesia.

Can hypnosis enhance recall of forgotten events?, p. 263
Medium, Factual/Definitional, Objective 8, Ans: d

69.   Research indicates that memories retrieved during hypnosis are:
      a. forgotten again as soon as the person awakens from the hypnotic state.
      b. accurate recollections of information previously learned.
      c. experienced as being inaccurate even when they are true.
      d. often a combination of fact and fiction.

Can hypnosis force people to act against their will?, pp. 264, 266
Difficult, Factual/Definitional, Objective 8, Ans: d

70.   Research has indicated that when subjects are ordered to plunge their hands into what they
      think is acid or to throw acid in a bystander's face, they will:
      a. refuse to do either, even when hypnotized.
      b. plunge their hands into acid but will not throw it when hypnotized.
      c. do both, but only when hypnotized.
      d. do both, whether hypnotized or not.

Can hypnosis force people to act against their will?, p. 266
Medium, Conceptual, Objective 8, Ans: b

71.   While Bev was hypnotized, her therapist suggested that during the next several days she would
      have a strong desire to eat well-balanced meals. The therapist was apparently making use of:
      a. age regression.
      b. posthypnotic suggestion.
      c. a hidden observer.
      d. posthypnotic amnesia.
      e. paradoxical sleep.

Can hypnosis be therapeutic?, p. 266
Difficult, Conceptual, Objective 8, Ans: d

72.   In order to determine whether hypnosis can be therapeutic, researchers must compare the reactions of hypnotherapy recipients with the responses of:
       a.   a hidden observer.
       b.   drug addicts.
       c.   fantasy-prone personalities.
       d.   a control group.
       e.   insomniacs.

Can hypnosis alleviate pain?, p. 266
Easy, Factual/Definitional, Objective 8, Ans: d

73.   Research has indicated that hypnosis:
       a.   can force people to act against their will.
       b.   can block sensory input.
       c.   is helpful in overcoming nail biting but not smoking.
       d.   enables some people to undergo surgery without anesthesia.

Can hypnosis alleviate pain?, p. 266
Easy, Factual/Definitional, Objective 8, Ans: a

74.   Dissociation refers to:
       a.   a state of divided consciousness.
       b.   a state of paradoxical sleep.
       c.   conscious enactment of a hypnotic role.
       d.   nonconformity to social pressure.

Can hypnosis alleviate pain?, pp. 266-267
Difficult, Conceptual, Objective 8, Ans: a

75.   When subjected to a painful medical procedure without the benefit of an anesthetic, it is most likely that a hypnotized person would:
       a.   register physiological signs of arousal or tension.
       b.   exhibit a brain-wave pattern similar to that of Stage 4 sleep.
       c.   have no sensory experience of the pain-producing procedure.
       d.   be unable to remember anything that occurred during the procedure.

Hypnosis as a social phenomenon, pp. 267-268
Medium, Factual/Definitional, Objective 9, Ans: b

76.   Advocates of the social influence theory of hypnosis are likely to argue that:
       a.   hypnosis is a unique state of consciousness.
       b.   hypnotized people are simply enacting the role of good hypnotic subjects.
       c.   the process of dissociation best explains hypnotic phenomena.
       d.   most hypnotized people are consciously faking hypnosis.
       e.   hypnotic susceptibility is positively correlated with introversion.

Hypnosis as a social phenomenon, pp. 264, 266, 267-268
Medium, Conceptual, Objective 9, Ans: d

77.   Hypnotized people are no more likely to perform dangerous acts than those who are asked to simulate hypnosis. This fact is most consistent with:
       a.   the activation-synthesis theory.
       b.   dissociation theory.
       c.   Freud's dream theory.
       d.   social influence theory.

Hypnosis as a social phenomenon, pp. 267-268
Medium, Factual/Definitional, Objective 9, Ans: b
78.   People become unresponsive to hypnosis if told that those who are highly gullible are easily
       hypnotized. This fact is most consistent with the theory that hypnosis involves:
       a. dissociation.
       b. conscious role-playing.
       c. paradoxical sleep.
       d. psychological dependence.

Hypnosis as divided consciousness, p. 268
Easy, Factual/Definitional, Objective 9, Ans: b
79.   The divided-consciousness theory of hypnosis states that hypnosis involves:
       a. role-playing.
       b. dissociation.
       c. paradoxical sleep.
       d. motivational conflict.

Hypnosis as divided consciousness, p. 269
Difficult, Conceptual, Objective 9, Ans: c
80.   Evidence that people in posthypnotic state have no difficulty remembering everything they had
       learned while under hypnosis would most clearly serve to challenge:
       a. social influence theory.
       b. the activation-synthesis theory.
       c. dissociation theory.
       d. Freud's dream theory.

Hypnosis as divided consciousness, p. 269
Medium, Factual/Definitional, Objective 9, Ans: c
81.   In Hilgard's hidden observer studies, a person's hypnotized self usually indicated _____ to
       pain and a person's hidden observer indicated _____ to pain.
       a. insensitivity; insensitivity
       b. sensitivity; sensitivity
       c. insensitivity; sensitivity
       d. sensitivity; insensitivity

Hypnosis as divided consciousness, p. 269
Medium, Factual/Definitional, Objective 9, Ans: d
82.   Evidence that hypnotized subjects have a hidden observer has been used to support the theory
       that hypnosis involves a state of:
       a. paradoxical sleep.
       b. insomnia.
       c. conscious role-playing.
       d. dissociation.

Hypnosis as divided consciousness, p. 269
Medium, Conceptual, Objective 9, Ans: b
83.   Dr. Ganesh used hypnosis instead of an anesthetic when setting a patient's broken leg. The
       patient insisted that she felt no pain, but when asked to raise her hand if some part of her could
       feel pain, she raised her hand. This incident best illustrates the concept of:
       a. posthypnotic amnesia.
       b. the hidden observer.
       c. latent content.
       d. posthypnotic suggestion.
       e. paradoxical sleep.

Drugs and consciousness, p. 270
Easy, Factual/Definitional, Objective 10, Ans: c
84. Alcohol, marijuana, cocaine, and a wide variety of other chemical agents that alter perceptions and moods are called:
     a. stimulants.
     b. narcotic agents.
     c. psychoactive drugs.
     d. hallucinogens.

Dependence and addiction, p. 271
Easy, Factual/Definitional, Objective 10, Ans: d
85. Drug tolerance refers to the:
     a. absence of pain or anxiety following the use of a drug.
     b. loss of social inhibitions following drug use.
     c. discomfort and distress that follow the discontinued use of a drug.
     d. reduced effect of a drug resulting from its regular usage.

Dependence and addiction, p. 271
Easy, Conceptual, Objective 10, Ans: a
86. When Mark first tried to quit smoking, he experienced anxiety, irritability, and difficulty sleeping. Mark was experiencing:
     a. withdrawal.
     b. burnout.
     c. dissociation.
     d. post-traumatic stress disorder.

Dependence and addiction, p. 271
Easy, Conceptual, Objective 10, Ans: b
87. Although Mildred never experiences withdrawal symptoms when deprived of alcohol, every afternoon she needs at least one drink to relieve her stress. Mildred has developed:
     a. a physical dependence.
     b. a psychological dependence.
     c. both a psychological and a physical dependence.
     d. neither a psychological nor a physical dependence.

Misconceptions about addiction, p. 271
Easy, Conceptual, Objective 10, Ans: a
88. Which of the following provides the clearest indication of a drug addiction?
     a. physical dependence
     b. hallucinations
     c. narcolepsy
     d. daydreaming
     e. REM rebound

Misconceptions about addiction, p. 271
Difficult, Factual/Definitional, Objective 10, Ans: a
89. Research on the use of addictive drugs indicates that:
     a. many people use cocaine occasionally without becoming heavy users.
     b. individuals who are given morphine for pain relief usually develop the irresistible cravings of an addict.
     c. it is nearly impossible to discontinue heroin use without professional therapy.
     d. regular marijuana smokers typically experience an irresistible craving for THC.

Misconceptions about addiction, p. 271
Medium, Factual/Definitional, Objective 10, Ans: d

90.   Addictions to _____ are often overcome without professional help.
       a. nicotine
       b. heroin
       c. alcohol
       d. all the above

Depressants, p. 273
Medium, Factual/Definitional, Objective 11, Ans: d

91.   When moderately intoxicated by alcohol:
       a. an angry person tends to be more aggressive than usual.
       b. an altruistically inclined person tends to be more generous than usual.
       c. a sexually aroused person tends to be more sexually active than usual.
       d. all the above people tend to behave as stated.

Depressants, p. 273
Difficult, Conceptual, Objective 11, Ans: a

92.   Alcohol consumption is least likely to make people more:
       a. fearful.
       b. aggressive.
       c. self-conscious.
       d. sexually daring.
       e. self-disclosing.

Depressants, p. 273
Medium, Factual/Definitional, Objective 11, Ans: a

93.   Alcohol consumption _____ sympathetic nervous system activity and _____ self-
       awareness.
       a. decreases; decreases
       b. increases; increases
       c. decreases; increases
       d. increases; decreases

Depressants, p. 273
Difficult, Factual/Definitional, Objective 11, Ans: b

94.   Research indicates that alcohol:
       a. impairs short-term recall of what has just been said.
       b. disrupts the processing of recent experiences into long-term memories.
       c. impairs recall of existing long-term memories.
       d. does all the above.

Depressants, p. 273
Difficult, Conceptual, Objective 11, Ans: c

95.   After drinking three cans of beer, Akiva felt less guilty about the way he mistreated his wife
       and children. Akiva's reduced guilt most likely resulted from the fact that his alcohol
       consumption has:
       a. reduced his sexual desire.
       b. destroyed some of his brain cells.
       c. reduced his self-awareness.
       d. directed his attention to the future.
       e. increased his level of sympathetic nervous system arousal.

Depressants, p. 274
Easy, Factual/Definitional, Objective 11, Ans: a
96.   Which of the following drugs contributes to the greatest number of deaths?
      a. alcohol
      b. heroin
      c. cocaine
      d. marijuana
      e. LSD

Depressants, p. 275
Medium, Factual/Definitional, Objective 11, Ans: a
97.   Nembutal and Seconal, drugs prescribed to reduce insomnia, are:
      a. barbiturates.
      b. amphetamines.
      c. opiates.
      d. mild hallucinogens.

Depressants, p. 275
Difficult, Conceptual, Objective 11, Ans: a
98.   Sodium pentothal has sometimes been called a "truth serum" because it relaxes people and
      enables them to more freely disclose personally embarrassing experiences. It is most likely that
      sodium pentothal is a(n):
      a. barbiturate.
      b. amphetamine.
      c. endorphin.
      d. hallucinogen.

Depressants, p. 275
Easy, Factual/Definitional, Objective 11, Ans: d
99.   Taking an overdose of _____ is likely to result in death.
      a. barbiturates
      b. morphine
      c. heroin
      d. any of the above

Depressants, p. 275
Medium, Conceptual, Objective 11, Ans: b
100. Soon after taking a psychoactive drug, Larisa's breathing slowed, her pupils constricted, and
      her feelings of anxiety were replaced by blissful pleasure. Larisa most likely experienced the
      effects of:
      a. cocaine.
      b. heroin.
      c. LSD.
      d. nicotine.

Depressants, p. 275
Medium, Conceptual, Objective 11, Ans: a
101. Stimulants are to caffeine as depressants are to:
      a. heroin.
      b. cocaine.
      c. marijuana.
      d. LSD.

Depressants and stimulants, p. 275
Difficult, Conceptual, Objective 11, Ans: a

102. Pupil constriction is to pupil dilation as _____ is to _____.
    a. heroin; cocaine
    b. an amphetamine; a barbiturate
    c. nicotine; alcohol
    d. marijuana; morphine

Stimulants, p. 275
Medium, Factual/Definitional, Objective 11, Ans: d

103. Which of the following drugs is classified as a stimulant?
    a. marijuana
    b. morphine
    c. alcohol
    d. nicotine
    e. LSD

Stimulants, p. 275
Difficult, Conceptual, Objective 11, Ans: d

104. Who might be tempted to use a stimulant to help him achieve his personal goal?
    a. Victor, who wants relief from depression
    b. Karl, who wants to lose a lot of weight
    c. Milan, who wants to win his boxing match
    d. all the above

Stimulants, pp. 275-276
Medium, Factual/Definitional, Objective 11, Ans: b

105. A brief 15- to 30-minute rush of euphoria followed by a crash of agitated depression is most closely associated with the use of:
    a. marijuana.
    b. cocaine.
    c. LSD.
    d. barbiturates.

Stimulants, p. 276
Difficult, Factual/Definitional, Objective 11, Ans: a

106. Preventing the reuptake of dopamine leads mice to become:
    a. hyperactive.
    b. addicted.
    c. depressed.
    d. hungry.

Hallucinogens, p. 277
Easy, Factual/Definitional, Objective 11, Ans: b

107. LSD is most likely to produce:
    a. narcolepsy.
    b. hallucinations.
    c. dissociation.
    d. night terrors.
    e. age regression.

Hallucinogens, pp. 277, 283
Medium, Conceptual, Objective 11, Ans: e
108. An altered state of consciousness similar to that of a near-death experience is most likely to
      result from the use of:
      a. heroin.
      b. cocaine.
      c. barbiturates.
      d. marijuana.
      e. LSD.

Hallucinogens, p. 277
Medium, Factual/Definitional, Objective 11, Ans: c
109. In contrast to alcohol, marijuana:
      a. is rapidly eliminated from the body.
      b. does not impair motor coordination.
      c. amplifies sensitivity to sounds.
      d. does not impair memory.

Hallucinogens, p. 278
Difficult, Factual/Definitional, Objective 11, Ans: b
110. Studies of marijuana usage indicate that:
      a. daily use of the drug is currently higher than it has ever been among high school seniors.
      b. regular users may achieve a high with less of the drug than occasional users.
      c. regular usage has no serious negative effects on physical health.
      d. usage consistently reduces feelings of anxiety and depression.
      e. marijuana is the most commonly used psychoactive drug in North America.

Hallucinogens, p. 278
Medium, Factual/Definitional, Objective 11, Ans: a
111. Marijuana is _____ addictive than nicotine and _____ addictive than cocaine.
      a. less; less
      b. less; more
      c. more; more
      d. more; less

Influences on drug use, p. 280
Difficult, Factual/Definitional, Objective 12, Ans: c
112. Mice with _____ levels of _____ are especially likely to be attracted to alcohol.
      a. low; REM
      b. high; REM
      c. low; NPY
      d. high; NPY

Influences on drug use, p. 280
Medium, Factual/Definitional, Objective 12, Ans: b
113. Research suggests that an important factor in drug use among teenagers and young adults is:
      a. having a parent who suffers from narcolepsy.
      b. feeling that one's life is meaningless.
      c. being a fantasy-prone person.
      d. being socially unpopular.

Influences on drug use, p. 281
Easy, Factual/Definitional, Objective 12, Ans: a
114. The best predictor of an adolescent's pattern of drug usage is whether the adolescent:
     a. has close friends who use drugs.
     b. grows up in an intact two-parent family.
     c. is aware of the long-term costs of drug abuse.
     d. has religious beliefs that discourage drug use.
     e. owns his or her own car.

Near-death experiences, p. 283
Easy, Factual/Definitional, Objective 13, Ans: b
115. The altered state of consciousness that is most similar to a drug-induced hallucination is:
     a. REM sleep.
     b. the near-death experience.
     c. hypnosis.
     d. narcolepsy.

Near-death experiences, p. 284
Easy, Factual/Definitional, Objective 13, Ans: e
116. Plato's belief that death involves the separation of the mind from the body is known as:
     a. the circadian rhythm.
     b. age regression.
     c. reincarnation.
     d. dissociation.
     e. dualism.

Near-death experiences, p. 284
Medium, Conceptual, Objective 13, Ans: d
117. Monists are most likely to explain the near-death experience in terms of:
     a. spiritual forces that regulate life after death.
     b. the dissociation of brain and mind.
     c. the reunification of brain and mind.
     d. the activity of the brain under stress.

CHAPTER 8

Learning

Learning Objectives

Introduction to Learning (pp. 287-290)

1. Discuss the nature and importance of learning, and describe how behaviorism approached the study of learning.

Classical Conditioning (pp. 290-300)

2. Describe the general process of classical conditioning as demonstrated by Pavlov's experiments.

3. Explain the processes of acquisition, extinction, spontaneous recovery, generalization, and discrimination.

4. Discuss the importance of cognitive processes and biological predispositions in classical conditioning.

5. Explain the importance of Pavlov's work, and describe how it might apply to an understanding of human health and well-being.

Operant Conditioning (pp. 300-312)

6. Describe the process of operant conditioning, including the procedure of shaping, as demonstrated by Skinner's experiments.

7. Identify the different types of reinforcers, and describe the major schedules of partial reinforcement.

8. Discuss the effects of punishment on behavior.

9. Discuss the importance of cognitive processes and biological predispositions in operant conditioning.

10. Explain why Skinner's ideas were controversial, and describe some major applications of operant conditioning.

Learning by Observation (pp. 313-315)

11.   Describe the process of observational learning as demonstrated by Bandura's experiments, and discuss the impact of antisocial and prosocial models.

Introduction to learning, p. 287
Medium, Factual/Definitional, Objective 1, Ans: d

1.   The most crucial ingredient in all learning is:
      a. shaping.
      b. modeling.
      c. maturation.
      d. experience.
      e. continuous reinforcement.

Introduction to learning, pp. 288, 289
Difficult, Conceptual, Objective 1, Ans: d

2.   Classical and operant conditioning both illustrate:
      a. shaping.
      b. modeling.
      c. respondent behavior.
      d. associative learning.
      e. the overjustification effect.

Introduction to learning, p. 289
Difficult, Conceptual, Objective 1, Ans: b

3.   Classical conditioning is to _____ associations as operant conditioning is to _____ associations.
      a. stimulus-stimulus; response-response
      b. stimulus-stimulus; response-stimulus
      c. response-stimulus; stimulus-response
      d. response-response; stimulus-stimulus

Introduction to learning, p. 289
Easy, Factual/Definitional, Objective 1, Ans: d

4.   By directly experiencing a thunderstorm, we learn that a flash of lightning signals an impending crash of thunder. This best illustrates:
      a. operant conditioning.
      b. spontaneous recovery.
      c. observational learning.
      d. classical conditioning.
      e. generalization.

Introduction to learning, pp. 287, 289
Easy, Factual/Definitional, Objective 1, Ans: e

5.   Seals in an aquarium will repeat behaviors, such as slapping and barking, that prompt people to toss them a herring. This best illustrates:
      a. respondent behavior.
      b. spontaneous recovery.
      c. observational learning.
      d. latent learning.
      e. operant conditioning.

Introduction to learning, p. 290
Medium, Factual/Definitional, Objective 1, Ans: c

6.   Who was the first to emphasize that psychology should be restricted to the scientific study of observable behavior?
     a. Wundt
     b. Skinner
     c. Watson
     d. Bandura
     e. Garcia

Introduction to learning, p. 290
Difficult, Factual/Definitional, Objective 1, Ans: d

7.   John B. Watson emphasized that:
     a. learning depends on how predictably rather than how frequently events are associated.
     b. unlike lower animals, humans learn through a process of cognition.
     c. both humans and lower animals learn to expect that a CS will be followed by a UCS.
     d. learning should be explained without any reference to mental processes.

Classical conditioning, p. 290
Easy, Factual/Definitional, Objective 2, Ans: e

8.   The researcher most closely associated with the study of classical conditioning is:
     a. Thorndike.
     b. Wundt.
     c. Skinner.
     d. Bandura.
     e. Pavlov.

Pavlov's experiments, p. 291
Medium, Factual/Definitional, Objective 2, Ans: d

9.   If a ringing bell causes a dog to salivate because the bell has been regularly associated with food in the mouth, the UCR is the:
     a. ringing bell.
     b. salivation to the ringing bell.
     c. food in the mouth.
     d. salivation to the food in the mouth.

Pavlov's experiments, p. 291
Difficult, Conceptual, Objective 2, Ans: c

10. Which of the following is an unconditioned response?
     a. salivating at the sight of a lemon
     b. raising your hand to ask a question
     c. jerking your hand off a very hot stove
     d. walking into a restaurant to eat

Pavlov's experiments, p. 291
Easy, Factual/Definitional, Objective 2, Ans: a

11. In Pavlov's experiments, the taste of food triggered salivation in a dog. The food in the dog's mouth was the:
     a. UCS.
     b. UCR.
     c. CS.
     d. CR.

Pavlov's experiments, pp. 291, 292
Medium, Conceptual, Objective 2, Ans: b

12. Male Japanese quail became sexually aroused by a red light that had previously been associated with the presentation of a female quail. In this instance, the female quail is a:
   a. UCR.
   b. UCS.
   c. CR.
   d. CS.

Pavlov's experiments, p. 292
Medium, Conceptual, Objective 2, Ans: d

13. A dog's salivation at the sight of a food dish is a(n):
   a. conditioned stimulus.
   b. unconditioned stimulus.
   c. unconditioned response.
   d. conditioned response.

Pavlov's experiments, pp. 291, 292
Easy, Factual/Definitional, Objective 2, Ans: a

14. In Pavlov's experiments on the salivary conditioning of dogs, a CR was:
   a. salivation to the sound of a tone.
   b. salivation to the taste of food.
   c. the sound of a tone.
   d. the taste of food.

Pavlov's experiments, p. 292
Medium, Conceptual, Objective 2, Ans: a

15. If the sound of an electric can opener causes a cat to salivate because the can opener has been associated with the presentation of food, the cat's salivation to the sound of the can opener is a(n):
   a. conditioned response.
   b. unconditioned response.
   c. conditioned stimulus.
   d. unconditioned stimulus.

Pavlov's experiments, pp. 292, 298-299
Difficult, Conceptual, Objective 2, Ans: d

16. The infant Albert developed a fear of rats after a white rat was associated with a loud noise. In this example, fear of the white rat was the:
   a. UCS.
   b. UCR.
   c. CS.
   d. CR.

Pavlov's experiments, p. 292
Easy, Factual/Definitional, Objective 2, Ans: c

17. In Pavlov's experiments on the salivary conditioning of dogs, the CS was:
   a. the taste of food.
   b. salivation to the taste of food.
   c. the sound of a tone.
   d. salivation to the sound of a tone.

Pavlov's experiments, p. 292
Medium, Conceptual, Objective 2, Ans: a

18.   In Aldous Huxley's *Brave New World*, infants develop a fear of roses after roses are presented with electric shock. In this fictional example, the presentation of the roses is the:
  a. conditioned stimulus.
  b. unconditioned stimulus.
  c. unconditioned response.
  d. conditioned response.

Classical conditioning: acquisition, p. 292
Easy, Factual/Definitional, Objective 3, Ans: b

19.   The initial stage of classical conditioning during which a response to a neutral stimulus is established and gradually strengthened is called:
  a. association.
  b. acquisition.
  c. observational learning.
  d. shaping.

Classical conditioning: acquisition, p. 292
Medium, Factual/Definitional, Objective 3, Ans: c

20.   For the most rapid acquisition of a CR, the CS should be presented:
  a. shortly after the CR.
  b. shortly after the UCS.
  c. shortly before the UCS.
  d. at the same time as the UCS.

Classical conditioning: acquisition, p. 292
Difficult, Conceptual, Objective 3, Ans: b

21.   An experimenter plans to condition a dog to salivate to a light by pairing the light with food. The dog will learn to salivate to the light most quickly if the experimenter presents the light:
  a. 5 seconds before the food.
  b. 1/2 second before the food.
  c. at precisely the same time as the food.
  d. 1/2 second after the food.
  e. 5 seconds after the food.

Classical conditioning: extinction and spontaneous recovery, p. 293
Easy, Factual/Definitional, Objective 3, Ans: d

22.   When a CS is not followed by a UCS, the subsequent fading of a CR is called:
  a. discrimination.
  b. generalization.
  c. delayed reinforcement.
  d. extinction.

Classical conditioning: extinction and spontaneous recovery, p. 293
Medium, Factual/Definitional, Objective 3, Ans: d

23.   After Pavlov had conditioned a dog to salivate to a tone, he repeatedly sounded the tone without presenting the food. As a result, _____ occurred.
  a. generalization
  b. negative reinforcement
  c. latent learning
  d. extinction
  e. discrimination

Classical conditioning: extinction and spontaneous recovery, p. 293
Easy, Factual/Definitional, Objective 3, Ans: b

24.   The reappearance, after a time lapse, of an extinguished CR is called:
      a. generalization.
      b. spontaneous recovery.
      c. secondary reinforcement.
      d. latent learning.
      e. shaping.

Classical conditioning: extinction and spontaneous recovery, p. 293
Medium, Factual/Definitional, Objective 3, Ans: c

25.   Which of the following provides evidence that a CR is not completely eliminated during extinction?
      a. latent learning
      b. partial reinforcement
      c. spontaneous recovery
      d. generalization
      e. discrimination

Classical conditioning: extinction and spontaneous recovery, p. 293
Medium, Conceptual, Objective 3, Ans: c

26.   Long after being bitten by a stray dog, Allen found that his fear of dogs seemed to have disappeared. To his surprise, however, when he was recently confronted by a stray dog, he experienced a sudden twinge of anxiety. This sudden anxiety best illustrates:
      a. delayed reinforcement.
      b. latent learning.
      c. spontaneous recovery.
      d. shaping.

Classical conditioning: generalization, p. 294
Easy, Factual/Definitional, Objective 3, Ans: d

27.   The tendency for a CR to be evoked by stimuli similar to the CS is called:
      a. spontaneous recovery.
      b. conditioned reinforcement.
      c. latent learning.
      d. generalization.
      e. shaping.

Classical conditioning: generalization, p. 294
Medium, Conceptual, Objective 3, Ans: a

28.   Two-year-old Philip was recently clawed by the neighbor's cat. Philip's newly developed tendency to fear all small animals demonstrates the process of:
      a. generalization.
      b. latent learning.
      c. shaping.
      d. spontaneous recovery.
      e. secondary reinforcement.

Classical conditioning: generalization, p. 294
Medium, Conceptual, Objective 3, Ans: a
29. After receiving a painful shot from a female nurse in a white uniform, 3-year-old Vaclav experiences fear of any woman wearing a white dress. Vaclav's reaction best illustrates:
    a. generalization.
    b. extinction.
    c. shaping.
    d. latent learning.
    e. spontaneous recovery.

Classical conditioning: generalization, p. 294
Difficult, Conceptual, Objective 3, Ans: a
30. An allergy attack triggered by the sight of plastic flowers best illustrates the process of:
    a. generalization.
    b. latent learning.
    c. delayed reinforcement.
    d. the overjustification effect.
    e. spontaneous recovery.

Classical conditioning: discrimination, p. 294
Easy, Factual/Definitional, Objective 3, Ans: d
31. Some of Pavlov's dogs learned to salivate to the sound of one particular tone and not to other tones. This illustrates the process of:
    a. shaping.
    b. latent learning.
    c. secondary reinforcement.
    d. discrimination.
    e. extinction.

Classical conditioning: discrimination, p. 294
Medium, Conceptual, Objective 3, Ans: d
32. After recovering from a serious motorcycle accident, Gina was afraid to ride a motorcycle but not a bicycle. Gina's pattern of fear best illustrates:
    a. shaping.
    b. conditioned reinforcement.
    c. spontaneous recovery.
    d. discrimination.
    e. negative reinforcement.

Updating Pavlov's understanding: cognitive processes, p. 295
Difficult, Factual/Definitional, Objective 4, Ans: d
33. Research on the role of cognitive processes in learning indicates that the strength of a conditioned response depends primarily on the _____ of the CS-UCS association.
    a. frequency
    b. distinctiveness
    c. duration
    d. predictability

Updating Pavlov's understanding: cognitive processes, p. 295
Difficult, Factual/Definitional, Objective 4, Ans: d

34.   Classical conditioning occurs most rapidly when the learner perceives the _____ to cause the _____.
      a. UCS; UCR
      b. CS; CR
      c. UCR; CR
      d. CS; UCS

Updating Pavlov's understanding: cognitive processes, p. 295
Medium, Factual/Definitional, Objective 4, Ans: d

35.   After repeatedly taking alcohol spiked with a nausea-producing drug, alcoholics may fail to develop an aversive reaction to alcohol because they blame their nausea on the drug. This illustrates the importance of _____ in classical conditioning.
      a. biological predispositions
      b. the overjustification effect
      c. negative reinforcement
      d. cognitive processes
      e. spontaneous recovery

Updating Pavlov's understanding, biological predispositions, p. 296
Medium, Factual/Definitional, Objective 4, Ans: d

36.   Evidence that organisms are biologically predisposed to learn the particular associations that most readily facilitate their survival has been provided by:
      a. Watson and Rayner's study of fear conditioning in Little Albert.
      b. Bandura's study of observational learning and aggression in children.
      c. Pavlov's study of salivary conditioning in dogs.
      d. Garcia and Koelling's study of taste aversion in rats.

Updating Pavlov's understanding, biological predispositions, p. 296
Difficult, Factual/Definitional, Objective 4, Ans: b

37.   Garcia and Koelling's findings on taste aversion in rats challenged the previously accepted principle that:
      a. positive reinforcement is more effective than punishment in changing behavior.
      b. the UCS must immediately follow the CS for conditioning to occur.
      c. learning is influenced by the frequency of association between the CS and UCS.
      d. learning occurs only if a response is followed by reinforcement.

Updating Pavlov's understanding: biological predispositions, p. 296
Medium, Factual/Definitional, Objective 4, Ans: a

38.   It's easier to condition young children to fear snakes than to fear flowers. This best illustrates the importance of _____ in learning.
      a. biological predispositions
      b. primary reinforcement
      c. generalization
      d. spontaneous recovery
      e. punishment

Updating Pavlov's understanding: biological predispositions, p. 296
Easy, Factual/Definitional, Objective 4, Ans: b

39. Animals most readily learn the specific associations that promote:
     a. shaping.
     b. physical survival.
     c. social interaction.
     d. latent learning.
     e. the overjustification effect.

Pavlov's legacy, p. 297
Medium, Factual/Definitional, Objective 5, Ans: d

40. Pavlov's research on classical conditioning was important because:
     a. so many different species of animals, including humans, can be classically conditioned.
     b. so many different behaviors can be classically conditioned.
     c. it demonstrated that an internal psychological process could be studied with laboratory objectivity.
     d. of all the above reasons.

Applications of classical conditioning, p. 297
Medium, Conceptual, Objective 5, Ans: d

41. For drug addicts, the location in which a drug is frequently taken, for instance, a particular room, is likely to become a:
     a. primary reinforcer.
     b. cognitive map.
     c. UCS.
     d. CS.

Applications of classical conditioning, p. 298
Medium, Factual/Definitional, Objective 5, Ans: a

42. Little Albert developed a fear of rats after a white rat was presented with a loud noise. In this case, the loud noise was the:
     a. unconditioned stimulus.
     b. conditioned stimulus.
     c. conditioned reinforcer.
     d. delayed reinforcer.

Applications of classical conditioning, pp. 293, 298
Difficult, Conceptual, Objective 5, Ans: e

43. A patient who had long feared going into elevators was told by his therapist to force himself to go into 20 elevators a day. The therapist most likely wanted to encourage the _____ of the patient's fear.
     a. generalization
     b. negative reinforcement
     c. shaping
     d. secondary reinforcement
     e. extinction

Operant conditioning, p. 301
Easy, Factual/Definitional, Objective 6, Ans: d

44.   Learning associations between one's own personal actions and resulting events is most relevant to the process of:
a. classical conditioning.
b. latent learning.
c. observational learning.
d. operant conditioning.
e. habituation.

Operant conditioning, p. 301
Easy, Conceptual, Objective 6, Ans: d

45.   Ever since his mother began to give Julio gold stars for keeping his bed dry all night, Julio discontinued his habit of bedwetting. His change in behavior best illustrates the value of:
a. primary reinforcement.
b. classical conditioning.
c. spontaneous recovery.
d. operant conditioning.
e. latent learning.

Operant conditioning, p. 301
Medium, Conceptual, Objective 6, Ans: d

46.   Because Andrew was spanked on several occasions for biting electric cords, he no longer does so. Andrew's behavior change best illustrates the value of:
a. negative reinforcement.
b. classical conditioning.
c. conditioned reinforcers.
d. operant conditioning.
e. observational learning.

Classical and operant conditioning, pp. 290, 301
Medium, Conceptual, Objectives 2 & 6, Ans: d

47.   Pavlov is to _____ as Skinner is to _____.
a. operant conditioning; classical conditioning
b. latent learning; observational learning
c. observational learning; operant conditioning
d. respondent behavior; operant behavior

Classical and operant conditioning, pp. 290, 301
Difficult, Conceptual, Objectives 2 & 6, Ans: d

48.   The study of response-stimulus associations is to _____ as the study of stimulus-stimulus associations is to _____.
a. Pavlov; Bandura
b. Watson; Skinner
c. Watson; Bandura
d. Skinner; Pavlov

Skinner's experiments, p. 301
Easy, Factual/Definitional, Objective 6, Ans: a

49. The psychologist most closely associated with the study of operant conditioning was:
    a. Skinner.
    b. Pavlov.
    c. Watson.
    d. Bandura.
    e. Garcia.

Skinner's experiments, p. 301
Medium, Factual/Definitional, Objective 6, Ans: c

50. The law of effect refers to the tendency to:
    a. learn associations between consecutive stimuli.
    b. learn in the absence of reinforcement.
    c. repeat behaviors that are rewarded.
    d. lose intrinsic interest in an over-rewarded activity.

Skinner's experiments, p. 301
Easy, Conceptual, Objective 6, Ans: a

51. Dr. Raheja places a rat in a small, glass-enclosed chamber where it learns to press a bar to obtain a food pellet. Obviously, Dr. Raheja is using a _____ to study learning.
    a. Skinner box
    b. Bandura compartment
    c. Pavlovian maze
    d. Garcia operant chamber

Shaping, p. 302
Easy, Factual/Definitional, Objective 6, Ans: c

52. The process of reinforcing successively closer approximations to a desired behavior is called:
    a. generalization.
    b. intermittent reinforcement.
    c. shaping.
    d. secondary reinforcement.
    e. modeling.

Shaping, p. 302
Medium, Conceptual, Objective 6, Ans: e

53. In order to teach an animal to perform a complex sequence of behaviors, animal trainers are most likely to use a procedure known as:
    a. classical conditioning.
    b. delayed reinforcement.
    c. latent learning.
    d. generalization.
    e. shaping.

Shaping, p. 302
Medium, Conceptual, Objective 6, Ans: d

54.   On Monday, Johnny's mother gave him cookies and milk after he had played quietly for 10
       minutes. On Tuesday, she required 20 minutes of this quiet play before treat time, and on
       Wednesday, the cookies were given to him only after a full half hour of quiet play. Johnny was
       taught to play quietly for extended periods through:
       a. latent learning.
       b. secondary reinforcement.
       c. partial reinforcement.
       d. shaping.
       e. modeling.

Shaping, pp. 302-303
Medium, Factual/Definitional, Objective 6, Ans: d

55.   Teachers who effectively shape their students' study habits are most likely to:
       a. avoid the use of negative reinforcement to motivate effective study.
       b. reinforce effective study with primary rather than secondary reinforcers.
       c. reinforce effective study on a fixed-interval schedule.
       d. reinforce even minor improvements in students' study skills.

Principles of reinforcement, p. 303
Easy, Conceptual, Objective 7, Ans: c

56.   Because Carol would always pick up her newborn daughter when she began to cry, her
       daughter is now a real crybaby. In this case, picking up the infant served as a(n) _____ for
       crying.
       a. negative reinforcer
       b. conditioned stimulus
       c. positive reinforcer
       d. unconditioned stimulus

Principles of reinforcement, p. 303
Difficult, Conceptual, Objective 7, Ans: c

57.   The more often Matthew is scolded following a temper tantrum, the more frequently he loses
       his temper. In this case, the scolding serves as a _____ for Matthew's temper tantrums.
       a. negative reinforcer
       b. conditioned stimulus
       c. positive reinforcer
       d. punishment

Principles of reinforcement, p. 303
Medium, Factual/Definitional, Objective 7, Ans: b

58.   Escape from an aversive stimulus is a _____ reinforcer.
       a. positive
       b. negative
       c. secondary
       d. partial
       e. delayed

Principles of reinforcement, p. 303
Medium, Factual/Definitional, Objective 7, Ans: a

59. A negative reinforcer tends to _____ the behavior it follows.
    a. strengthen
    b. eliminate
    c. suppress but not eliminate
    d. have unpredictable effects on

Principles of reinforcement, p. 303
Difficult, Conceptual, Objective 7, Ans: c

60. Julie has a glass of wine after work because it relieves her anxiety. Her wine drinking is likely to continue because it is followed by a _____ reinforcer.
    a. secondary
    b. partial
    c. negative
    d. positive

Primary and conditioned reinforcers, p. 303
Easy, Factual/Definitional, Objective 7, Ans: b

61. Innately satisfying stimuli that satisfy biological needs are called _____ reinforcers.
    a. fixed
    b. primary
    c. positive
    d. continuous

Primary and conditioned reinforcers, p. 303
Easy, Conceptual, Objective 7, Ans: d

62. Which of the following is the best example of a primary reinforcer?
    a. applause for an excellent trumpet solo
    b. a grade of "A" for an excellent essay
    c. 5 dollars for washing the car
    d. a cold root beer for mowing the lawn on a hot day

Primary and conditioned reinforcers, p. 303
Difficult, Conceptual, Objective 7, Ans: d

63. Both the receipt of monetary rewards and the suspension of monetary fines most clearly serve as _____ reinforcers.
    a. partial
    b. primary
    c. negative
    d. conditioned
    e. continuous

Primary and conditioned reinforcers, p. 303
Medium, Conceptual, Objective 7, Ans: b

64. Money is to food as _____ is to _____.
    a. delayed reinforcer; immediate reinforcer
    b. secondary reinforcer; primary reinforcer
    c. discrimination; generalization
    d. partial reinforcement; continuous reinforcement
    e. operant conditioning; classical conditioning

Immediate and delayed reinforcers, pp. 303-304
Difficult, Conceptual, Objective 7, Ans: b

65.   As a hungry dog runs ever closer toward a bowl of food, the less likely it is to stop running until it reaches the food. This best illustrates that the dog's running behavior is most strongly affected by _____ reinforcers.
       a. conditioned
       b. immediate
       c. intermittent
       d. negative

Immediate and delayed reinforcers, p. 304
Medium, Conceptual, Objective 7, Ans: e

66.   Despite the painful hangovers that follow his use of alcohol, George continues to drink because he experiences a reduction of anxiety after just a couple of drinks. The continuation of his drinking habit most clearly illustrates the power of:
       a. generalization.
       b. spontaneous recovery.
       c. the overjustification effect.
       d. partial reinforcement.
       e. immediate reinforcement.

Immediate and delayed reinforcers, p. 304
Medium, Conceptual, Objective 7, Ans: c

67.   Janna's behavior is more strongly influenced by the momentary thrill of unprotected sex than by the prospect of an unwanted pregnancy or sexually transmitted disease. This best illustrates the impact of:
       a. classical conditioning.
       b. the overjustification theory.
       c. immediate reinforcement.
       d. a variable-interval schedule.
       e. spontaneous recovery.

Reinforcement schedules, p. 304
Medium, Factual/Definitional, Objective 7, Ans: d

68.   Intermittent reinforcement is associated with _____ acquisition and _____ extinction than continuous reinforcement.
       a. slower; faster
       b. faster; slower
       c. faster; faster
       d. slower; slower

Reinforcement schedules, p. 304
Medium, Conceptual, Objective 7, Ans: c

69.   A trainer wants to train a chicken to peck a key to obtain food. If she wants the chicken to learn this trick quickly and also to be resistant to extinction, she should use _____ reinforcement until the response is mastered and then follow with a period of _____ reinforcement.
       a. positive; negative
       b. negative; positive
       c. continuous; partial
       d. partial; continuous
       e. primary; secondary

Reinforcement schedules, p. 304
Difficult, Conceptual, Objective 7, Ans: c

70. When the Zantays eat dinner, the family dog begs for food. Sometimes, but not often, the children give in to the dog's begging and pass their pet a tasty morsel. You would be most justified in predicting that:
    a. the dog is eventually going to stop begging for food.
    b. as soon as the children stop reinforcing the dog's begging, it will stop begging.
    c. the dog is going to be quite persistent in its begging in the future.
    d. the dog will always beg for food even if the Zantays never reinforce the begging.

Reinforcement schedules, p. 305
Medium, Factual/Definitional, Objective 7, Ans: c

71. People paid on a piecework basis are reinforced on a _____ schedule.
    a. fixed-interval
    b. variable-interval
    c. fixed-ratio
    d. variable-ratio

Reinforcement schedules, p. 305
Medium, Conceptual, Objective 7, Ans: b

72. Jennifer edits manuscripts for a publisher and is paid $5 for every three pages she edits. Jennifer is reinforced on a _____ schedule.
    a. fixed-interval
    b. fixed-ratio
    c. variable-interval
    d. variable-ratio

Reinforcement schedules, p. 305
Easy, Factual/Definitional, Objective 7, Ans: d

73. A variable-ratio schedule of reinforcement is one in which a response is reinforced only after a(n):
    a. specified time period has elapsed.
    b. unpredictable time period has elapsed.
    c. specified number of responses have been made.
    d. unpredictable number of responses have been made.

Reinforcement schedules, p. 305
Medium, Factual/Definitional, Objective 7, Ans: b

74. Which of the following behaviors is typically reinforced on a variable-ratio schedule?
    a. studying for unexpected quizzes
    b. inserting coins into a slot machine
    c. paying a cashier for a candy bar
    d. checking the mailbox to see if the mail has arrived

Reinforcement schedules, p. 305
Medium, Conceptual, Objective 7, Ans: d

75. Basketball players are typically reinforced with game points for their shots on a _____ schedule.
    a. fixed-interval
    b. fixed-ratio
    c. variable-interval
    d. variable-ratio

Reinforcement schedules, (Figure 8.8), p. 305
Difficult, Factual/Definitional, Objective 7, Ans: b
76.   A choppy stop-start pattern of operant responding is associated with the _____ schedule of reinforcement.
      a. fixed-ratio
      b. fixed-interval
      c. variable-ratio
      d. variable-interval

Reinforcement schedules, p. 305
Difficult, Conceptual, Objective 7, Ans: a
77.   Glancing at the television in the next room in hopes of observing the beginning of the evening news is likely to be reinforced on a _____ schedule.
      a. fixed-interval
      b. fixed-ratio
      c. variable-interval
      d. variable-ratio

Reinforcement schedules, p. 305
Easy, Factual/Definitional, Objective 7, Ans: d
78.   A variable-interval schedule of reinforcement is one in which a response is reinforced only after a(n):
      a. specified time period has elapsed.
      b. unpredictable number of responses has been made.
      c. specified number of responses has been made.
      d. unpredictable time period has elapsed.

Reinforcement schedules, p. 305
Difficult, Conceptual, Objective 7, Ans: b
79.   A small-town radio disc jockey frequently announces how much money is currently in a jackpot. Every day several residents, randomly selected, are called and asked to identify the amount, and thereby win it. Those who keep track of the jackpot amount are most likely to be reinforced on a _____ schedule.
      a. fixed-ratio
      b. variable-interval
      c. variable-ratio
      d. fixed-interval

Reinforcement schedules (Figure 8.8), p. 305
Difficult, Factual/Definitional, Objective 7, Ans: d
80.   The lowest rates of operant responding are associated with the _____ schedule of reinforcement.
      a. fixed-ratio
      b. fixed-interval
      c. variable-ratio
      d. variable-interval

Reinforcement schedules, p. 305
Difficult, Factual/Definitional, Objective 7, Ans: c
81. Rates of operant responding are _____ for variable-ratio than for fixed-ratio schedules; they
     are _____ for variable-interval than for fixed-interval schedules.
     a. lower; higher
     b. higher; lower
     c. lower; lower
     d. higher; higher

Punishment, p. 306
Easy, Factual/Definitional, Objective 8, Ans: c
82. Which of the following decreases the recurrence of the behavior it follows?
     a. positive reinforcer
     b. negative reinforcer
     c. punishment
     d. both b. and c.

Punishment, p. 306
Medium, Conceptual, Objective 8, Ans: d
83. The introduction of an unpleasant stimulus is to _____ as the withdrawal of an unpleasant
     stimulus is to _____.
     a. acquisition; extinction
     b. negative reinforcer; positive reinforcer
     c. primary reinforcer; secondary reinforcer
     d. punishment; reinforcement
     e. partial reinforcement; continuous reinforcement

Punishment, p. 306
Easy, Conceptual, Objective 8, Ans: b
84. Masako was hit with a baseball last week during practice and now refuses to play. This
     behavior best illustrates the effects of:
     a. latent learning.
     b. punishment.
     c. primary reinforcers.
     d. delayed reinforcers.
     e. negative reinforcers.

Punishment, p. 306
Medium, Factual/Definitional, Objective 8, Ans: c
85. Punishment is a potentially hazardous way for parents to control their young children's
     behaviors because:
     a. the more severely children are punished for undesirable behaviors, the more likely they will
         exhibit those behaviors.
     b. children will forget how to perform punished behaviors in circumstances where they are
         justified and necessary.
     c. the use of punishment could condition children to fear and avoid their parents.
     d. punishment cannot even temporarily restrain undesirable behaviors.

Punishment, p. 307
Medium, Factual/Definitional, Objective 8, Ans: d
86.   Most psychologists think that the use of punishment is:
    a. ineffective in even temporarily restraining unwanted behavior.
    b. more effective than negative reinforcers in shaping behavior.
    c. the opposite of positive reinforcers and thus is its psychological equivalent in terms of
        changing behavior.
    d. less effective than positive reinforcers in promoting desirable behavior.

Updating Skinner's understanding: cognition, p. 307
Medium, Conceptual, Objective 9, Ans: b
87.   Jason has learned to expect that whenever he studies diligently for tests, he will receive good
       grades. This suggests that associative learning involves:
    a. respondent behavior.
    b. cognitive processes.
    c. primary reinforcers.
    d. intermittent reinforcement.
    e. shaping.

Updating Skinner's understanding: cognition, p. 307
Easy, Factual/Definitional, Objective 9, Ans: e
88.   Some psychologists believe that rats develop mental representations of mazes they have
       explored. These representations have been called:
    a. perceptual sets.
    b. successive approximations.
    c. discriminative surveys.
    d. geographic heuristics.
    e. cognitive maps.

Updating Skinner's understanding: cognition, pp. 307-308
Medium, Factual/Definitional, Objective 9, Ans: d
89.   The fact that rats can learn the layout of a maze while passively riding through it in a wire
       basket highlights the importance of:
    a. shaping.
    b. secondary reinforcers.
    c. spontaneous recovery.
    d. cognitive processes.
    e. primary reinforcers.

Updating Skinner's understanding: cognition, p. 308
Medium, Factual/Definitional, Objective 9, Ans: c
90.   The best evidence that animals develop cognitive maps consists of:
    a. shaping.
    b. generalization.
    c. latent learning.
    d. secondary reinforcement.
    e. spontaneous recovery.

Updating Skinner's understanding: cognition, p. 308
Medium, Factual/Definitional, Objective 9, Ans: a

91. Latent learning can occur in the absence of:
    a. reinforcement.
    b. cognition.
    c. experience.
    d. any of the above.

Updating Skinner's understanding: overjustification, p. 308
Easy, Factual/Definitional, Objective 9, Ans: b

92. Promising people rewards for doing what they already enjoy doing is likely to produce:
    a. overlearning.
    b. the overjustification effect.
    c. latent learning.
    d. generalization.
    e. spontaneous recovery.

Updating Skinner's understanding: overjustification, p. 308
Medium, Conceptual, Objective 9, Ans: c

93. What is the greatest danger associated with using small bribes to entice children to read good books?
    a. latent learning
    b. delayed reinforcement
    c. the overjustification effect
    d. respondent behavior
    e. discrimination

Updating Skinner's understanding: overjustification, p. 308
Difficult, Factual/Definitional, Objective 9, Ans: e

94. The overjustification effect best illustrates the importance of _____ in operant conditioning.
    a. spontaneous recovery
    b. generalization
    c. biological predispositions
    d. primary reinforcers
    e. cognitive processes

Updating Skinner's understanding: biological predispositions, p. 309
Medium, Conceptual, Objective 9, Ans: c

95. It is easier to train a dog to bark for food than to train it to stand on its hind legs for food. This best illustrates the importance of _____ in learning.
    a. primary reinforcement
    b. generalization
    c. biological predispositions
    d. negative reinforcement
    e. spontaneous recovery

Updating Skinner's understanding: biological predispositions, p. 309
Medium, Factual/Definitional, Objective 9, Ans: b
96. Pigeons learn to flap their wings to avoid shock _____ easily than they learn to peck a disk
     to avoid shock. They learn to flap their wings to obtain food _____ easily than they learn to
     peck a disk to obtain food.
     a. more; more
     b. more; less
     c. less; less
     d. more; less
     e. less; more

Skinner's legacy, p. 309
Easy, Factual/Definitional, Objective 10, Ans: c
97. B. F. Skinner discounted the role of _____ in learning.
     a. negative reinforcement
     b. punishment
     c. cognitive processes
     d. conditioned reinforcers
     e. effective parenting

Skinner's legacy, p. 309
Difficult, Conceptual, Objective 10, Ans: e
98. In explaining prosocial behavior, B. F. Skinner would most likely have emphasized:
     a. genetic influences.
     b. empathy and compassion.
     c. an unconscious need for social approval.
     d. the internalization of moral norms.
     e. the beneficial consequences of prosocial behavior.

Skinner's legacy, p. 309
Medium, Factual/Definitional, Objective 10, Ans: d
99. B. F. Skinner recommended that we control behavior with _____ rather than with
     _____.
     a. primary reinforcers; secondary reinforcers
     b. delayed reinforcement; immediate reinforcement
     c. modeling; conditioning
     d. reinforcement; punishment

Applications of operant conditioning, p. 310
Medium, Factual/Definitional, Objective 10, Ans: d
100. The use of online testing is most likely to involve an application of _____ principles.
     a. delayed reinforcement
     b. classical conditioning
     c. latent learning
     d. operant conditioning

Applications of operant conditioning, p. 310
Easy, Factual/Definitional, Objective 10, Ans: b
101. Golf instruction that reinforces short putts before attempting to reinforce fairway drives best illustrates the process of:
      a. generalization.
      b. shaping.
      c. modeling.
      d. discrimination.
      e. delayed reinforcement.

Applications of operant conditioning, p. 310
Medium, Conceptual, Objective 10, Ans: d
102. Mr. Schlenker has improved worker productivity at his furniture manufacturing plant by occasionally sending notes of appreciation to his hard-working employees. Mr. Schlenker has improved productivity by means of:
      a. latent learning.
      b. classical conditioning.
      c. modeling.
      d. operant conditioning.

Applications of operant conditioning, p. 311
Medium, Conceptual, Objective 10, Ans: a
103. Although 5-year-old Susy is not really thirsty, she frequently begins whining for a glass of water about 10 minutes after being put to bed. Her parents would be best advised to:
      a. simply ignore her complaining.
      b. provide her with a very small drink of water.
      c. close her bedroom door to indicate that they disapprove of her whining.
      d. read her a short story so she forgets about wanting a drink.

Applications of operant conditioning, p. 311
Medium, Factual/Definitional, Objective 10, Ans: a
104. In order to modify your own behavior using operant conditioning principles, you should:
      a. monitor and record the actual frequency of the operant behavior you wish to promote.
      b. formulate goals for behavior change that are a bit more ambitious than what you can actually accomplish.
      c. carefully observe and imitate the specific behaviors practiced by others who have successfully achieved your goals.
      d. systematically reinforce the operant behavior you wish to promote with delayed rather than immediate reinforcers.

Learning by observation, p. 313
Medium, Conceptual, Objective 11, Ans: a
105. Without any explicit training from adults, many 8-year-old children know how to turn the ignition key in order to start their parents' cars. This best illustrates the importance of:
      a. observational learning.
      b. classical conditioning.
      c. operant conditioning.
      d. spontaneous recovery.
      e. the overjustification effect.

Learning by observation, p. 313
Easy, Factual/Definitional, Objective 11, Ans: b

106. The tendency for children to imitate behaviors seen on television best illustrates the importance of:
    a. shaping.
    b. modeling.
    c. respondent behavior.
    d. immediate reinforcement.
    e. spontaneous recovery.

Learning by observation, p. 313
Medium, Conceptual, Objective 11, Ans: d

107. Reinforcement is to operant conditioning as _____ is to observational learning.
    a. prosocial behavior
    b. punishment
    c. respondent behavior
    d. modeling

Learning by observation, p. 313
Difficult, Factual/Definitional, Objective 11, Ans: e

108. Rapid changes in memes best illustrate the impact of:
    a. respondent behavior.
    b. immediate reinforcement.
    c. spontaneous recovery.
    d. primary reinforcers.
    e. observational learning.

Bandura's experiments, p. 313
Medium, Conceptual, Objective 11, Ans: c

109. Pavlov is to classical conditioning as _____ is to _____.
    a. Thorndike; modeling
    b. Skinner; latent learning
    c. Bandura; observational learning
    d. Garcia; computer-assisted instruction

Bandura's experiments, p. 314
Easy, Factual/Definitional, Objective 11, Ans: c

110. Bandura's experiments indicate that _____ is important in the process of learning.
    a. shaping
    b. generalization
    c. modeling
    d. respondent behavior
    e. secondary reinforcement

Applications of observational learning, p. 314
Medium, Conceptual, Objective 11, Ans: b

111. Mr. Zandee has stopped smoking because he wants to model healthy behavior patterns for his children. Mr. Zandee is apparently aware of the importance of _____ in his children's development.
    a. shaping
    b. observational learning
    c. generalization
    d. delayed reinforcement
    e. spontaneous recovery

Applications of observational learning, p. 314
Medium, Factual/Definitional, Objective 11, Ans: b

112. European Christians who risked their lives to rescue Jews from the Nazis and civil rights activists of the 1960s had parents who:
    a. consistently used reinforcement in combination with punishment to shape their children's moral behavior.
    b. modeled a strong moral or humanitarian concern.
    c. consistently used psychological punishment rather than physical punishment in shaping their children's behavior.
    d. consistently used permissive rather than authoritarian child-rearing practices.
    e. consistently explained to their children the harsh consequences of immoral behavior.

Applications of observational learning, p. 314
Medium, Factual/Definitional, Objective 11, Ans: d

113. Children exposed to a model who preached one thing and did another:
    a. ignored both what the model said and did.
    b. ignored what the model did and both talked and acted in ways consistent with what the model said.
    c. ignored what the model said and both talked and acted in ways consistent with what the model did.
    d. said what the model said and did what the model did.

CHAPTER 9

Memory

Learning Objectives

The Phenomenon of Memory (pp. 318-320)

1. Describe memory in terms of information processing, and distinguish among sensory memory, short-term memory, and long-term memory.

Encoding: Getting Information In (pp. 321-327)

2. Distinguish between automatic and effortful processing, and discuss the importance of rehearsal.

3. Explain the importance of meaning, imagery, and organization in the encoding process.

Storage: Retaining Information (pp. 328-334)

4. Describe the limited nature of sensory memory and short-term memory.

5. Describe the capacity and duration of long-term memory, and discuss the biological changes that may underlie memory formation and storage.

6. Distinguish between implicit and explicit memory, and identify the different brain structures associated with each.

Retrieval: Getting Information Out (pp. 335-338)

7. Contrast recall, recognition, and relearning measures of memory.

8. Describe the importance of retrieval cues and the impact of environmental contexts and internal emotional states on retrieval.

Forgetting (pp. 338-344)

9. Explain why the capacity to forget can be beneficial, and discuss the role of encoding failure and storage decay in the process of forgetting.

10. Explain what is meant by retrieval failure, and discuss the effects of interference and motivated forgetting on retrieval.

Memory Construction (pp. 345-353)

11.   Describe the evidence for the constructive nature of memory and the impact of imagination and
       leading questions on eyewitness recall.

12.   Describe the difficulties in discerning true memories from false ones and the reliability of
       children's eyewitness recall.

13.   Discuss the controversy over reports of repressed and recovered memories of childhood sexual
       abuse.

Improving Memory (pp. 354-355)

14.   Explain how an understanding of memory can contribute to effective study techniques.

Information processing, p. 319
Easy, Factual/Definitional, Objective 1, Ans: c
1.   The process of getting information into memory is called:
      a. priming.
      b. chunking.
      c. encoding.
      d. registering.
      e. storage.

Information processing, pp. 319-320
Medium, Conceptual, Objective 1, Ans: d
2.   According to the information-processing model of memory, acquisition is to retention as
      _____ is to _____.
      a. recall; recognition
      b. rehearsal; relearning
      c. interference; repression
      d. encoding; storage

Information processing, p. 319
Easy, Factual/Definitional, Objective 1, Ans: c
3.   The process of retrieval refers to:
      a. the persistence of learning over time.
      b. the organization of information into manageable units.
      c. getting information out of memory storage.
      d. conscious repetition of information to be remembered.
      e. the identification of information previously learned.

Information processing, p. 320
Easy, Factual/Definitional, Objective 1, Ans: c
4.   The relatively permanent and limitless storehouse of the memory system is called _____
      memory.
      a. sensory
      b. state-dependent
      c. long-term
      d. flashbulb
      e. implicit

Information processing, pp. 320, 328-329
Medium, Factual/Definitional, Objective 1, Ans: a

5. Short-term memory is _____ permanent and _____ limited than long-term memory.
   a. less; more
   b. more; less
   c. less; less
   d. more; more

Information processing, p. 320
Medium, Conceptual, Objective 1, Ans: b

6. After looking up his friend's phone number, Alex was able to remember it only long enough to dial it correctly. In this case, the telephone number was clearly stored in his _____ memory.
   a. echoic
   b. short-term
   c. flashbulb
   d. long-term
   e. implicit

Information processing, p. 320
Medium, Factual/Definitional, Objective 1, Ans: d

7. The three-stage processing model suggests that information from long-term memory can be _____ into _____ memory.
   a. encoded; sensory
   b. retrieved; sensory
   c. encoded; short-term
   d. retrieved; short-term

Information processing, p. 320
Difficult, Factual/Definitional, Objective 1, Ans: b

8. Short-term memory could best be characterized _____ memory.
   a. iconic
   b. working
   c. flashbulb
   d. implicit
   e. long-term

Automatic processing, p. 321
Easy, Factual/Definitional, Objective 2, Ans: c

9. Automatic processing involves:
   a. unconsciously deleting information from the memory system.
   b. a tendency to recall emotionally significant events.
   c. the effortless encoding of certain types of information.
   d. all the above.

Automatic processing, p. 321
Medium, Factual/Definitional, Objective 2, Ans: c

10. Encoding that occurs with no effort or a minimal level of conscious attention is known as:
    a. implicit memory.
    b. long-term potentiation.
    c. automatic processing.
    d. state-dependent memory.
    e. chunking.

Automatic processing, p. 321
Difficult, Conceptual, Objective 2, Ans: b

11.   While reading a novel at a rate of nearly 500 words per minute, Megan effortlessly understands the meaning of almost every word. This ability highlights the importance of:
      a.   flashbulb memory.
      b.   automatic processing.
      c.   the spacing effect.
      d.   iconic memory.

Automatic processing, p. 321
Difficult, Factual/Definitional, Objective 2, Ans: d

12.   Hasher and Zacks observed that people recall the frequency of specific words in a list just as accurately whether or not they are forewarned of the recall task prior to seeing the list. This finding provides evidence for:
      a.   implicit memory.
      b.   the serial position effect.
      c.   the spacing effect.
      d.   automatic processing.
      e.   state-dependent memory.

Effortful processing, p. 321
Easy, Factual/Definitional, Objective 2, Ans: b

13.   Effortful processing can only occur with:
      a.   implicit memory.
      b.   conscious attention.
      c.   visual imagery.
      d.   chunking.

Effortful processing, p. 321
Easy, Conceptual, Objective 2, Ans: e

14.   When first introduced to someone, Marcel effectively remembers the person's name by repeating it to himself several times. Marcel makes use of a strategy called:
      a.   chunking.
      b.   automatic processing.
      c.   the method of loci.
      d.   the next-in-line effect.
      e.   rehearsal.

Effortful processing, pp. 321, 336
Medium, Conceptual, Objective 2, Ans: c

15.   Priming is to retrieval as _____ is to encoding.
      a.   repression
      b.   amnesia
      c.   rehearsal
      d.   recall

Effortful processing, p. 321
Medium, Factual/Definitional, Objective 2, Ans: e
16.   Which pioneering researcher made extensive use of nonsense syllables in the study of human memory?
a. Pavlov
b. James
c. Loftus
d. Freud
e. Ebbinghaus

Effortful processing, p. 322
Difficult, Factual/Definitional, Objective 2, Ans: d
17.   Ebbinghaus's retention curve best illustrates the value of:
a. chunking.
b. imagery.
c. priming.
d. rehearsal.
e. implicit memory.

Effortful processing, pp. 322, 339
Difficult, Conceptual, Objective 2, Ans: a
18.   The next-in-line effect best illustrates:
a. encoding failure.
b. long-term potentiation.
c. automatic processing.
d. retroactive interference.
e. source amnesia.

Effortful processing, p. 322
Medium, Factual/Definitional, Objective 2, Ans: d
19.   Taped information played during sleep is registered by the ears but is not remembered. This illustrates that the retention of information often requires:
a. proactive interference.
b. state-dependent memory.
c. chunking.
d. effortful processing.
e. priming.

Effortful processing, p. 322
Easy, Factual/Definitional, Objective 2, Ans: c
20.   The tendency for distributed study to yield better long-term retention than massed study is known as:
a. the serial position effect.
b. state-dependent memory.
c. the spacing effect.
d. the method of loci.
e. priming.

Effortful processing, p. 322
Medium, Conceptual, Objective 2, Ans: e

21. Students often remember more information from a course that spans an entire semester than from a course that is completed in an intensive three-week learning period. This best illustrates the importance of:
    a. chunking.
    b. the serial position effect.
    c. automatic processing.
    d. implicit memory.
    e. the spacing effect.

Effortful processing, pp. 322-323
Medium, Conceptual, Objective 2, Ans: c

22. On the telephone, Melvin rattles off a list of 10 grocery items for Pilar to bring home from the store. Immediately after hearing the list, Pilar attempts to write down the items. She is most likely to forget the items:
    a. at the beginning of the list.
    b. at the end of the list.
    c. in the middle of the list.
    d. at the beginning and in the middle of the list.

Effortful processing, pp. 322-323
Difficult, Factual/Definitional, Objective 2, Ans: a

23. The serial position effect best illustrates the importance of:
    a. rehearsal.
    b. chunking.
    c. visual imagery.
    d. automatic processing.
    e. flashbulb memory.

Effortful processing, pp. 322-323, 342
Difficult, Conceptual, Objective 2, Ans: c

24. Proactive and retroactive interference contribute most strongly to the:
    a. next-in-line effect.
    b. self-reference effect.
    c. serial position effect.
    d. spacing effect.

Encoding meaning, pp. 319, 323
Medium, Factual/Definitional, Objective 3, Ans: d

25. Most people misrecall the sentence, "The angry rioter threw the rock at the window" as "The angry rioter threw the rock through the window." This best illustrates the importance of:
    a. iconic memory.
    b. retroactive interference.
    c. source amnesia.
    d. semantic encoding.
    e. mood-congruent memory.

Encoding meaning, p. 323
Easy, Factual/Definitional, Objective 3, Ans: e

26. The process by which information is encoded by its meaning is called:
    a. long-term potentiation.
    b. automatic processing.
    c. priming.
    d. mnemonic encoding.
    e. semantic encoding.

Encoding meaning, pp. 323-324
Difficult, Conceptual, Objective 3, Ans: c

27. Wei Dong was asked to memorize a long list of words that included "ship, effort, professor, and inquire." He later recalled these words as "boat, work, teacher, and question." This suggests that the four original words had been encoded:
    a. acoustically.
    b. visually.
    c. semantically.
    d. automatically.

Encoding meaning, p. 323
Medium, Conceptual, Objective 3, Ans: d

28. Your ability to immediately recognize the voice over the phone as your mother's illustrates the value of:
    a. flashbulb memory.
    b. the next-in-line effect.
    c. state-dependent memory.
    d. acoustic encoding.
    e. chunking.

Encoding meaning, p. 323
Difficult, Conceptual, Objective 3, Ans: a

29. After Jackie was presented with the letters "g, c, k, p, and d," she recalled them as "g, c, j, t, and d." Her recall errors best illustrate the importance of:
    a. acoustic encoding.
    b. implicit memory.
    c. automatic processing.
    d. iconic memory.

Encoding meaning, p. 323
Medium, Conceptual, Objective 3, Ans: e

30. Semantic encoding is to visual encoding as _____ is to _____.
    a. implicit memory; explicit memory
    b. effortful processing; automatic processing
    c. the serial position effect; the spacing effect
    d. iconic memory; flashbulb memory
    e. meaning; imagery

Encoding meaning, p. 324
Medium, Conceptual, Objective 3, Ans: c

31. Which of the following questions about the word *pen* would best prepare you to correctly remember tomorrow that you had seen that word in today's test?
     a. Does the word consist of three letters?
     b. Is the word written in capital letters?
     c. Would the word fit in this sentence: "The boy put the _____ on his desk"?
     d. Does the word rhyme with *den*?

Encoding meaning, p. 324
Medium, Conceptual, Objective 3, Ans: a

32. Rephrasing text material in your own words is an effective way to facilitate:
     a. semantic encoding.
     b. automatic processing.
     c. mood-congruent memory.
     d. proactive interference.
     e. implicit memory.

Encoding meaning, pp. 323-324, 334
Difficult, Conceptual, Objective 3, Ans: e

33. One reason adults typically recall little of their first 2 or 3 years of life is that during infancy they were unable to verbally label most of their experiences. This best illustrates that the formation of long-term memories often requires:
     a. automatic processing.
     b. implicit memory.
     c. acoustic encoding.
     d. source amnesia.
     e. semantic encoding.

Encoding meaning, p. 324
Medium, Conceptual, Objective 3, Ans: a

34. The self-reference effect best illustrates the value of:
     a. semantic encoding.
     b. source amnesia.
     c. the method of loci.
     d. flashbulb memory.
     e. repression.

Encoding imagery, p. 325
Medium, Factual/Definitional, Objective 3, Ans: b

35. We remember words that lend themselves to mental images better than we remember abstract low-imagery words. This best illustrates the value of:
     a. iconic memory.
     b. visual encoding.
     c. flashbulb memory.
     d. long-term potentiation.

Encoding imagery, p. 325
Easy, Factual/Definitional, Objective 3, Ans: d

36. Memory aids that involve the use of vivid imagery or clever ways of organizing material are called:
      a. semantic techniques.
      b. iconic traces.
      c. organizational cues.
      d. mnemonic devices.

Encoding imagery, p. 325
Medium, Conceptual, Objective 3, Ans: a

37. Tim, a third-grader, learns the sentence "George Eats Old Gray Rats And Paints Houses Yellow" to help him remember the spelling of "geography." Tim is using:
      a. a mnemonic device.
      b. the "peg-word" system.
      c. the spacing effect.
      d. the method of loci.
      e. the next-in-line effect.

Encoding imagery, p. 325
Medium, Factual/Definitional, Objective 3, Ans: b

38. Developed by the ancient Greeks, the method of loci is an illustration of:
      a. the spacing effect.
      b. a mnemonic device.
      c. flashbulb memory.
      d. automatic processing.
      e. the serial position effect.

Encoding imagery, p. 325
Difficult, Conceptual, Objective 3, Ans: d

39. In order to remember a list of the school supplies she needs, Marcy mentally visualizes each item at a certain location in her house. Marcy's tactic best illustrates the use of:
      a. iconic memory.
      b. state-dependent memory.
      c. the serial position effect.
      d. the method of loci.
      e. the spacing effect.

Encoding imagery, p. 325
Difficult, Factual/Definitional, Objective 3, Ans: b

40. Mnemonic devices such as the "peg-word" system make effective use of:
      a. flashbulb memory.
      b. visual imagery.
      c. state-dependent memory.
      d. the serial position effect.
      e. implicit memory.

Organizing information for encoding, p. 326
Easy, Factual/Definitional, Objective 3, Ans: c

41.   The organization of information into meaningful units is called:
       a. automatic processing.
       b. the spacing effect.
       c. chunking.
       d. the method of loci.
       e. the "peg-word" system.

Organizing information for encoding, p. 326
Difficult, Factual/Definitional, Objective 3, Ans: b

42.   The use of acronyms to improve one's memory of unfamiliar material best illustrates the value of:
       a. imagery.
       b. chunking.
       c. the spacing effect.
       d. the serial position effect.
       e. the method of loci.

Organizing information for encoding, p. 326
Medium, Conceptual, Objective 3, Ans: a

43.   The letters Y, M, O, M, R, E are presented. Jill remembers them by rearranging them to spell the word "MEMORY." This provides an illustration of:
       a. chunking.
       b. the "peg-word" system.
       c. automatic processing.
       d. the spacing effect.
       e. the method of loci.

Organizing information for encoding, p. 326
Difficult, Factual/Definitional, Objective 3, Ans: e

44.   Dario Donatelli could recall more than 70 sequentially presented digits by using the technique of:
       a. acoustic encoding.
       b. automatic processing.
       c. priming.
       d. visual imagery.
       e. chunking.

Organizing information for encoding, p. 327
Medium, Conceptual, Objective 3, Ans: d

45.   By creating an outline in which specific facts and theories are located within the larger framework of major topics and subtopics, Jasmine can remember much more of what she reads in her college textbooks. This best illustrates the benefits of:
       a. automatic processing.
       b. the method of loci.
       c. the serial position effect.
       d. hierarchical organization.
       e. the spacing effect.

Sensory memory storage, p. 328
Medium, Factual/Definitional, Objective 4, Ans: d
46. By presenting research participants with three rows of three letters each for only a fraction of a second, Sperling demonstrated that people have _____ memory.
    a. echoic
    b. flashbulb
    c. state-dependent
    d. iconic
    e. implicit

Sensory memory storage, p. 328
Medium, Factual/Definitional, Objective 4, Ans: b
47. Iconic memory refers to:
    a. the encoded meanings of words and events in short-term memory.
    b. photographic, or picture-image, memory that lasts for only about a second.
    c. the effortlessly processed incidental information about the timing and frequency of events.
    d. the visually encoded images in long-term memory.

Sensory memory storage, p. 328
Medium, Conceptual, Objective 4, Ans: a
48. For a fraction of a second after the lightning flash disappeared, Ileana retained a vivid mental image of its ragged edges. Her experience most clearly illustrates the nature of _____ memory.
    a. iconic
    b. flashbulb
    c. echoic
    d. explicit
    e. implicit

Sensory memory storage, p. 328
Easy, Factual/Definitional, Objective 4, Ans: b
49. Sounds and words that are not immediately attended to can still be recalled a brief moment later because of our _____ memory.
    a. flashbulb
    b. echoic
    c. implicit
    d. state-dependent
    e. iconic

Sensory memory storage, p. 328
Medium, Conceptual, Objective 4, Ans: c
50. Iconic memory is to echoic memory as _____ is to _____.
    a. short-term memory; long-term memory
    b. explicit memory; implicit memory
    c. visual stimulation; auditory stimulation
    d. automatic processing; effortful processing
    e. flashbulb memory; implicit memory

Short-term memory storage, pp. 328-329
Medium, Factual/Definitional, Objective 4, Ans: d

51. Peterson and Peterson asked people to count aloud backward after they were presented with three consonants. This study was designed to study the durability of _____ memory.
     a. echoic
     b. long-term
     c. mood-congruent
     d. short-term
     e. flashbulb

Short-term memory storage, p. 329
Easy, Factual/Definitional, Objective 4, Ans: b

52. Our immediate short-term memory for new material is limited to roughly _____ units of information.
     a. 3
     b. 7
     c. 12
     d. 24
     e. 50

Short-term memory storage, p. 329
Difficult, Factual/Definitional, Objective 4, Ans: a

53. Short-term memory is slightly better:
     a. for auditory information than for visual information.
     b. for random letters than for random digits.
     c. in children than in adults.
     d. in females than in males.

Long-term memory storage, p. 329
Medium, Factual/Definitional, Objective 5, Ans: a

54. The human capacity for storing long-term memories is:
     a. essentially unlimited.
     b. roughly equal to 7 units of information.
     c. typically much greater in young children than in adults.
     d. greatly reduced after people reach the age of 65.

Storing memories in the brain, p. 330
Difficult, Factual/Definitional, Objective 5, Ans: d

55. Which of the following provided evidence that past experiences were permanently and accurately stored in memory?
     a. the detailed reports of childhood experiences given by adults under hypnosis
     b. the recovery of painful unconscious childhood memories by Freud's adult clients
     c. Penfield's discovery that electrical stimulation of the brain activates vivid recollections of the distant past
     d. none of the above

Storing memories in the brain: synaptic changes, pp. 330-331
Medium, Factual/Definitional, Objective 5, Ans: a

56. Research on sea snails suggests that memory formation is facilitated by:
     a. RNA molecules.
     b. serotonin.
     c. alcohol.
     d. chunking.
     e. priming.

Storing memories in the brain: synaptic changes, p. 331
Easy, Factual/Definitional, Objective 5, Ans: d

57. The increased efficiency of neural circuitry that contributes to memory storage is known as:
     a. chunking.
     b. the next-in-line effect.
     c. automatic processing.
     d. long-term potentiation.
     e. proactive interference.

Storing memories in the brain: synaptic changes, p. 331
Medium, Factual/Definitional, Objective 5, Ans: c

58. Long-term potentiation refers to:
     a. the impact of overlearning on retention.
     b. an automatic tendency to recall emotionally significant events.
     c. an increased neural readiness for impulse transmission.
     d. the process of learning something without any conscious memory of having learned it.
     e. the relatively permanent and limitless storehouse of the memory system.

Storing memories in the brain: synaptic changes, p. 331
Easy, Conceptual, Objective 5, Ans: d

59. A baseball strikes Carol in the head and she is momentarily knocked unconscious. The physical injury, though not serious, is most likely to interfere with Carol's _____ memory.
     a. flashbulb
     b. implicit
     c. mood-congruent
     d. short-term

Storing memories in the brain: synaptic changes and stress hormones, p. 331
Difficult, Factual/Definitional, Objective 5, Ans: d

60. The temporary release of serotonin has been found to _____ memory formation, and the temporary release of stress hormones has been found to _____ memory formation.
     a. disrupt; facilitate
     b. facilitate; disrupt
     c. disrupt; disrupt
     d. facilitate; facilitate

Stress hormones and memory, p. 331
Medium, Factual/Definitional, Objective 5, Ans: e
61. The accuracy of the flashbulb memories of those who directly experienced the 1989 San Francisco Bay earthquake best illustrates that memory formation is facilitated by:
   a. chunking.
   b. hierarchical organization.
   c. the serial position effect.
   d. the method of loci.
   e. the body's release of stress hormones.

Storing implicit and explicit memories, p. 332
Easy, Factual/Definitional, Objective 6, Ans: c
62. Conscious memory of factual information is called _____ memory.
   a. state-dependent
   b. flashbulb
   c. explicit
   d. implicit
   e. iconic

Storing implicit and explicit memories, pp. 332-333
Medium, Conceptual, Objective 6, Ans: a
63. Many people retain their classically conditioned fears without any conscious recollection of how or when those fears were learned. This best illustrates _____ memory.
   a. implicit
   b. short-term
   c. sensory
   d. flashbulb
   e. state-dependent

Storing implicit and explicit memories, p. 332
Medium, Factual/Definitional, Objective 6, Ans: d
64. Implicit memory is to explicit memory as _____ is to _____.
   a. hippocampus; brainstem
   b. short-term memory; long-term memory
   c. effortful processing; automatic processing
   d. skill memory; fact memory

Storing implicit and explicit memories, p. 333
Medium, Factual/Definitional, Objective 6, Ans: a
65. Unlike implicit memories, explicit memories are processed by the:
   a. hippocampus.
   b. cerebellum.
   c. hypothalamus.
   d. motor cortex.

Storing implicit and explicit memories, p. 333
Difficult, Conceptual, Objective 6, Ans: d
66. Damage to the hippocampus would most likely interfere with a person's ability to learn:
   a. to ride a bike.
   b. to read mirror-image writing.
   c. the procedures for solving a jigsaw puzzle.
   d. the names of the fifty United States.

Storing implicit and explicit memories, p. 333
Medium, Conceptual, Objective 6, Ans: d
67. Although Mr. Yanagita has recently learned to play poker quite well, he cannot consciously remember ever having played poker. It is likely that he has suffered damage to his:
    a. brainstem.
    b. cerebellum.
    c. hypothalamus.
    d. hippocampus.
    e. motor cortex.

Storing implicit and explicit memories, p. 334
Easy, Factual/Definitional, Objective 6, Ans: b
68. The cerebellum plays a critical role in _____ memory.
    a. echoic
    b. implicit
    c. iconic
    d. explicit

Storing implicit and explicit memories, pp. 333, 334
Difficult, Conceptual, Objective 6, Ans: e
69. Explicit memory is to _____ as implicit memory is to _____.
    a. epinephrine; serotonin
    b. skill memory; fact memory
    c. automatic processing; effortful processing
    d. long-term memory; short-term memory
    e. hippocampus; cerebellum

Storing implicit and explicit memories, p. 334
Medium, Factual/Definitional, Objective 6, Ans: d
70. Infantile amnesia is largely associated with a lack of _____ memory.
    a. iconic
    b. echoic
    c. implicit
    d. explicit

Retrieval: getting information out, p. 335
Medium, Conceptual, Objective 7, Ans: c
71. An eyewitness to a grocery store robbery is asked to identify the suspects in a police lineup. Which test of memory is being utilized?
    a. recall
    b. relearning
    c. recognition
    d. rehearsal
    e. reconstruction

Retrieval: getting information out, p. 335
Medium, Conceptual, Objective 7, Ans: b
72. Fill-in-the-blank test questions measure _____; matching concepts with their definitions measures _____.
    a. recognition; relearning
    b. recall; recognition
    c. recall; relearning
    d. relearning; recall

Retrieval: getting information out, pp. 332, 335
Difficult, Factual/Definitional, Objective 7, Ans: c

73. Which measure of memory did Ebbinghaus use in order to assess the impact of rehearsal on retention?
    a. recall
    b. recognition
    c. relearning
    d. reconstruction

Retrieval cues, p. 335
Easy, Conceptual, Objective 8, Ans: c

74. The smell of freshly baked bread awakened in Mr. Hutz vivid memories of his early childhood. The aroma apparently acted as a powerful:
    a. sensory memory.
    b. reconstructive signal.
    c. retrieval cue.
    d. implicit memory.
    e. schema.

Retrieval cues, p. 336
Medium, Factual/Definitional, Objective 8, Ans: d

75. The often unconscious activation of particular associations in memory is called:
    a. chunking.
    b. automatic processing.
    c. repression.
    d. priming.
    e. state-dependent memory.

Retrieval cues, p. 336
Medium, Factual/Definitional, Objective 8, Ans: e

76. Retrieval cues are most likely to facilitate a process known as:
    a. automatic processing.
    b. repression.
    c. chunking.
    d. relearning.
    e. priming.

Retrieval cues, pp. 321, 336
Difficult, Conceptual, Objective 8, Ans: c

77. Rehearsal is to encoding as retrieval cues are to:
    a. chunking.
    b. relearning.
    c. priming.
    d. repression.
    e. the spacing effect.

Retrieval cues, p. 336
Medium, Factual/Definitional, Objective 8, Ans: a

78.   Shortly after you see a missing child poster you are more likely to interpret an ambiguous adult-child interaction as a possible kidnapping. This best illustrates the impact of:
    a. priming.
    b. state-dependent memory.
    c. source amnesia.
    d. retroactive interference.
    e. the self-reference effect.

Retrieval cues, p. 336
Difficult, Conceptual, Objective 8, Ans: a

79.   Reading a romantic novel caused Consuela to recall some old experiences with a high school boyfriend. The effect of the novel on Consuela's memory retrieval is an illustration of:
    a. priming.
    b. chunking.
    c. source amnesia.
    d. automatic processing.
    e. the spacing effect.

Context effects, p. 336
Medium, Factual/Definitional, Objective 8, Ans: d

80.   The discovery that words heard underwater are later better recalled underwater than on land best illustrates the value of:
    a. the method of loci.
    b. state-dependent memory.
    c. the spacing effect.
    d. retrieval cues.
    e. implicit memory.

Context effects, p. 337
Easy, Factual/Definitional, Objective 8, Ans: e

81.   The eerie sense of having previously experienced a situation is known as:
    a. the next-in-line effect.
    b. the serial position effect.
    c. mood-congruent memory.
    d. source amnesia.
    e. déjà vu.

Moods and memories, p. 337
Medium, Factual/Definitional, Objective 8, Ans: e

82.   Information learned while a person is _____ is best recalled when that person is _____.
    a. sad; happy
    b. drunk; sober
    c. angry; calm
    d. fearful; happy
    e. drunk; drunk

Moods and memories, p. 337
Medium, Conceptual, Objective 8, Ans: a

83. Zuhair was feeling depressed at the time he read a chapter of his history textbook. Zuhair is likely to recall best the contents of that chapter when he is:
   a. depressed.
   b. happy.
   c. relaxed.
   d. unemotional.

Moods and memories, p. 337
Easy, Factual/Definitional, Objective 8, Ans: e

84. The association of sadness with negative life events contributes to:
   a. the self-reference effect.
   b. retroactive interference.
   c. repression.
   d. source amnesia.
   e. mood-congruent memory.

Moods and memories, p. 337
Medium, Factual/Definitional, Objective 8, Ans: e

85. Compared to formerly depressed people, those who are currently depressed are more likely to recall their parents as rejecting and punitive. This best illustrates:
   a. retroactive interference.
   b. source amnesia.
   c. repression.
   d. the self-reference effect.
   e. mood-congruent memory.

Forgetting, p. 339
Easy, Factual/Definitional, Objective 9, Ans: a

86. In describing what he calls the seven sins of memory, Daniel Schacter suggests that encoding failure results from the sin of:
   a. absent-mindedness.
   b. transience.
   c. blocking.
   d. repression.

Forgetting, p. 339
Medium, Conceptual, Objective 9, Ans: c

87. In considering the seven sins of memory, transience is to the sin of _____ as suggestibility is to the sin of _____.
   a. distortion; intrusion
   b. proactive interference; retroactive interference
   c. forgetting; distortion
   d. retroactive interference; proactive interference

Encoding failure, p. 339
Easy, Factual/Definitional, Objective 9, Ans: c

88. An inability to recall the location of the number 0 on your calculator is most likely due to:
   a. source amnesia.
   b. proactive interference.
   c. encoding failure.
   d. memory decay.

Encoding failure, p. 339
Medium, Conceptual, Objective 9, Ans: c

89. George can't remember Jack Smith's name because he wasn't paying attention when Jack was formally introduced. George's poor memory is best explained in terms of:
    a. repression.
    b. proactive interference.
    c. encoding failure.
    d. retroactive interference.
    e. source amnesia.

Encoding failure, p. 339
Difficult, Conceptual, Objective 9, Ans: a

90. Although Arturo has looked at his watch thousands of times, he is unable to recall whether the watch features Arabic or Roman numerals. This is most likely due to a failure in:
    a. encoding.
    b. storage.
    c. retrieval.
    d. iconic memory.
    e. implicit memory.

Storage decay, p. 340
Medium, Factual/Definitional, Objective 9, Ans: d

91. Using nonsense syllables to study memory, Ebbinghaus found that:
    a. our sensory memory capacity is essentially unlimited.
    b. iconic memory fades more rapidly than echoic memory.
    c. what is learned in one mood is most easily retrieved while in that same mood.
    d. the most rapid memory loss for novel information occurs shortly after it is learned.

Storage decay, pp. 340-341
Medium, Factual/Definitional, Objective 9, Ans: d

92. Harry Bahrick observed that 3 years after people completed a Spanish course, they had forgotten much of the vocabulary they had learned. This finding indicates that information is lost while it is:
    a. encoded.
    b. rehearsed.
    c. retrieved.
    d. stored.

Retrieval failure, p. 341
Medium, Conceptual, Objective 10, Ans: d

93. When Jake applied for a driver's license, he was embarrassed by a momentary inability to remember his address. Jake's memory difficulty most likely resulted from a(n) _____ failure.
    a. rehearsal
    b. storage
    c. encoding
    d. retrieval
    e. automatic processing

Retrieval failure, p. 341
Medium, Conceptual, Objective 10, Ans: e
94. Although Yusef was having difficulty recalling the capital of The Netherlands, he quickly and correctly identified it after being given a list of cities in The Netherlands. Yusef's initial inability to recall the answer was due to a failure in:
   a. implicit memory.
   b. storage.
   c. encoding.
   d. state-dependent memory.
   e. retrieval.

Interference, p. 342
Medium, Conceptual, Objective 10, Ans: c
95. Professor Maslova has so many vivid memories of former students that she has difficulty remembering the names of new students. The professor's difficulty best illustrates:
   a. retroactive interference.
   b. mood-congruent memory.
   c. proactive interference.
   d. the spacing effect.
   e. source amnesia.

Interference, p. 342
Difficult, Conceptual, Objective 10, Ans: c
96. Which of the following best explains why Ebbinghaus found the task of learning new lists of nonsense syllables increasingly difficult as his research career progressed?
   a. the spacing effect
   b. source amnesia
   c. proactive interference
   d. retroactive interference
   e. motivated forgetting

Interference, p. 342
Easy, Factual/Definitional, Objective 10, Ans: c
97. Retroactive interference refers to the:
   a. decay of physical memory traces.
   b. disruptive effect of previously learned material on the recall of new information.
   c. disruptive effect of new learning on the recall of previously learned material.
   d. blocking of painful memories from conscious awareness.

Interference, p. 342
Medium, Conceptual, Objective 10, Ans: b
98. After studying biology all afternoon, Abba is having difficulty remembering details of the chemistry lecture he heard that morning. Abba's difficulty best illustrates:
   a. encoding failure.
   b. retroactive interference.
   c. the spacing effect.
   d. proactive interference.
   e. source amnesia.

Interference, p. 343

Easy, Factual/Definitional, Objective 10, Ans: d

99.   In order to reduce interference, between the time you study for a test and the time you take the test you should:

a. eat.

b. engage in physical exercise.

c. relax and watch television.

d. sleep.

Motivated forgetting, p. 343

Medium, Conceptual, Objective 10, Ans: d

100.   Motivated forgetting provides an example of forgetting caused by a failure in:

a. automatic processing.

b. encoding.

c. storage.

d. retrieval.

Motivated forgetting, p. 343

Difficult, Factual/Definitional, Objective 10, Ans: c

101.   Research participants who were exposed to very convincing arguments about the desirability of frequent toothbrushing misrecalled how frequently they had brushed their teeth in the preceding two weeks. This best illustrates:

a. the self-reference effect.

b. proactive interference.

c. motivated forgetting.

d. the spacing effect.

Motivated forgetting, p. 344

Medium, Conceptual, Objective 10, Ans: b

102.   Repression involves a failure in:

a. encoding.

b. retrieval.

c. storage.

d. all the above.

Motivated forgetting, p. 344

Easy, Factual/Definitional, Objective 10, Ans: e

103.   Who emphasized that we repress painful memories in order to minimize our own anxiety?

a. Ebbinghaus

b. Loftus

c. Peterson

d. Sperling

e. Freud

Motivated forgetting, p. 344
Easy, Conceptual, Objective 10, Ans: a

104. Philippe has just completed medical school. In reflecting on his years of formal education, he is able to recall the names of all his instructors except the fifth-grade teacher who flunked him. According to Freud, his forgetting illustrates:
   a. repression.
   b. proactive interference.
   c. retroactive interference.
   d. the serial position effect.
   e. the spacing effect.

Memory construction, p. 345
Medium, Factual/Definitional, Objective 11, Ans: d

105. We often alter our memories as we withdraw them from storage. This best illustrates:
   a. the self-reference effect.
   b. automatic processing.
   c. long-term potentiation.
   d. memory construction.
   e. priming.

Memory construction, p. 345
Difficult, Conceptual, Objective 11, Ans: a

106. When recalling a pleasant experience, we may picture ourselves in the scene. At the time of the experience we were not looking at ourselves, so our recollection illustrates:
   a. memory construction.
   b. mood-congruent memory.
   c. automatic processing.
   d. iconic memory.
   e. the spacing effect.

Misinformation and imagination effects, p. 345
Medium, Factual/Definitional, Objective 11, Ans: d

107. When Loftus and Palmer asked observers of a filmed car accident how fast the vehicles were going when they "smashed" into each other, the observers developed memories of the accident that:
   a. omitted some of the most painful aspects of the event.
   b. were more accurate than the memories of subjects who had not been immediately questioned about what they saw.
   c. were influenced by whether or not Loftus and Palmer identified themselves as police officers.
   d. portrayed the event as more serious than it had actually been.

Misinformation and imagination effects, p. 345
Medium, Conceptual, Objective 11, Ans: b

108. An attorney's use of misleading questions may distort a court witness's recall of a previously observed crime. This best illustrates:
   a. state-dependent memory.
   b. the misinformation effect.
   c. proactive interference.
   d. the next-in-line effect.
   e. the serial position effect.

Misinformation and imagination effects, p. 345
Medium, Conceptual, Objective 11, Ans: b

109. When Sharon told her roommate about the chemistry exam she had just completed, she knowingly exaggerated its difficulty. Subsequently, her memory of the exam was that it *was* as difficult as she had reported it to be. This best illustrates:

a. flashbulb memory.
b. the misinformation effect.
c. mood-congruent memory.
d. the self-reference effect.
e. proactive interference.

Misinformation and imagination effects, p. 346
Medium, Factual/Definitional, Objective 11, Ans: d

110. Researchers asked university students to recall childhood events, including a false event such as having spilled a punch bowl at a wedding. They discovered that:

a. events from the distant past are less vulnerable to memory distortion than more recent events.
b. people can easily distinguish between their own true and false memories.
c. hypnotic suggestion is an effective technique for accurate memory retrieval.
d. it is surprisingly easy to lead people to construct false memories.

Source amnesia, p. 347
Medium, Factual/Definitional, Objective 11, Ans: e

111. After hearing stories of things they both had and had not actually experienced with "Mr. Science," preschool children spontaneously recalled him doing things that were only mentioned in the story. This best illustrates:

a. the self-reference effect.
b. mood-congruent memory.
c. proactive interference.
d. implicit memory.
e. source amnesia.

Source amnesia, p. 347
Medium, Conceptual, Objective 11, Ans: a

112. After repeatedly hearing false, detailed accusations that he had sexually abused his daughter, Mr. Busker began to mistakenly recollect that such events had actually occurred. This best illustrates the dangers of:

a. source amnesia.
b. proactive interference.
c. implicit memory.
d. mood-congruent memory.
e. the self-reference effect.

Discerning true and false memories, p. 348
Difficult, Factual/Definitional, Objective 11, Ans: c

113. Compared to false memories, true memories are more likely to:

a. persist over time.
b. have emotional overtones.
c. contain detailed information.
d. be reported with confidence.

Discerning true and false memories, p. 348
Difficult, Factual/Definitional, Objective 11, Ans: d

114. One indication that an individual is falsely remembering a word is the lack of increased brain activity in the:
    a. hippocampus.
    b. cerebellum.
    c. hypothalamus.
    d. left temporal lobe.

Discerning true and false memories, p. 348
Medium, Conceptual, Objective 11, Ans: b

115. Those who are eager to use hypnosis in order to facilitate eyewitness recollections of the details of a crime should first be warned of the dangers of:
    a. the self-reference effect.
    b. the misinformation effect.
    c. proactive interference.
    d. state-dependent memory.
    e. the spacing effect.

Discerning true and false memories, p. 348
Medium, Factual/Definitional, Objective 12, Ans: e

116. When we fall in love, we tend to overestimate how much we liked our partner when we first began dating. This best illustrates the dynamics of:
    a. automatic processing.
    b. the spacing effect.
    c. proactive interference.
    d. the serial position effect.
    e. memory construction.

Discerning true and false memories, p. 348
Medium, Factual/Definitional, Objective 12, Ans: d

117. Donald Thompson, an Australian psychologist, was an initial suspect in a rape case. The rape victim confused her memories of Thompson and the actual rapist because she had seen Thompson's image on TV shortly before she was attacked. The victim's false recollection best illustrates:
    a. implicit memory.
    b. mood-congruent memory.
    c. the self-reference effect.
    d. source amnesia.
    e. the serial position effect.

Children's eyewitness recall, p. 349
Easy, Factual/Definitional, Objective 12, Ans: c

118. Compared to adults, children are more susceptible to:
    a. long-term potentiation.
    b. automatic processing.
    c. the misinformation effect.
    d. proactive interference.
    e. the self-reference effect.

Children's eyewitness recall, p. 349
Difficult, Conceptual, Objective 12, Ans: c

119. When children are officially interviewed about their recollections of possible sexual abuse, their reports are especially *unreliable* if:
    a. involved adults have not discussed the issue with them prior to the interview.
    b. they are asked general questions about the issue rather than more specific questions about details.
    c. after responding to an interviewer, they are repeatedly asked the same question they just answered.
    d. they disclose details of the abuse in the very first interview.

Children's eyewitness recall, p. 349
Medium, Factual/Definitional, Objective 12, Ans: a

120. In one study, children were periodically asked whether they remembered going to the hospital with a mousetrap on their finger. This experiment best illustrated the dynamics of:
    a. memory construction.
    b. long-term potentiation.
    c. flashbulb memory.
    d. sensory memory.
    e. mood-congruent memory.

Repressed or constructed memories of abuse?, pp. 350-351
Easy, Factual/Definitional, Objective 13, Ans: e

121. Adult incest survivors who have trouble remembering incidences of childhood sexual abuse have often been led to believe that their memory difficulties are due to:
    a. memory storage failure.
    b. the misinformation effect.
    c. memory encoding failure.
    d. proactive interference.
    e. repression.

Repressed or constructed memories of abuse?, p. 351
Medium, Factual/Definitional, Objective 13, Ans: c

122. Those who experience a so-called "false memory syndrome" are most likely to have:
    a. a sense of anxiety regarding the reliability of their own memories.
    b. feelings of personal power and self-importance.
    c. an excessive preoccupation with their false memory.
    d. a history of real sexual and physical abuse.

Repressed or constructed memories of abuse?, p. 351
Medium, Factual/Definitional, Objective 13, Ans: c

123. Memory experts who express skepticism regarding reports of repressed and recovered memories emphasize that:
    a. there is very little people can do to relieve the distress resulting from traumatic memories.
    b. most extremely traumatic life experiences are never encoded into long-term memory.
    c. therapeutic techniques such as guided imagery and dream analysis can easily encourage the construction of false memories.
    d. people rarely recall memories of long-forgotten unpleasant events.

Repressed or constructed memories of abuse?, pp. 351-352
Difficult, Factual/Definitional, Objective 13, Ans: c

124. Psychologists on both sides of the controversy regarding reports of repressed and recovered memories of childhood sexual abuse agree that:
    a. the accumulated experiences of our lives are all preserved somewhere in our minds.
    b. repression is the most common mechanism underlying the failure to recall early childhood sexual abuse.
    c. we commonly recover memories of long-forgotten unpleasant events.
    d. the more stressful an experience is, the more quickly it will be consciously forgotten.
    e. professional therapists can reliably distinguish between their clients' true and false childhood memories.

Repressed or constructed memories of abuse?, p. 352
Easy, Conceptual, Objective 13, Ans: d

125. Mrs. Ramos claims to remember being sexually abused by her father when she was less than a year old. Memory experts are most likely to doubt the reliability of her memory due to their awareness of:
    a. implicit memory.
    b. the self-reference effect.
    c. long-term potentiation.
    d. infantile amnesia.
    e. the spacing effect.

Repressed or constructed memories of abuse?, p. 352
Medium, Conceptual, Objective 13, Ans: c

126. Participants in one experiment were given entirely fabricated accounts of an occasion in which they had been lost in a shopping mall during their childhood. Many of these participants later falsely recollected vivid details of the experience as having actually occurred. This experiment best illustrated:
    a. the self-reference effect.
    b. mood-congruent memory.
    c. the misinformation effect.
    d. proactive interference.
    e. the spacing effect.

Repressed or constructed memories of abuse?, p. 353
Easy, Factual/Definitional, Objective 13, Ans: b

127. Memories of stressful and unpleasant life experiences are not likely to be:
    a. encoded.
    b. repressed.
    c. stored.
    d. retrieved.

Improving memory, p. 354
Easy, Factual/Definitional, Objective 14, Ans: d

128. Answering practice test questions about textbook material you have studied is a useful strategy for:
    a. automatically processing complex information.
    b. facilitating the development of implicit memory.
    c. activating your state-dependent memory.
    d. becoming aware of what you still need to learn.

CHAPTER **10**

Thinking and Language

Learning Objectives

Thinking (pp. 358-372)

1. Describe the nature of concepts and the role of prototypes in concept formation.

2. Discuss how we use trial and error, algorithms, heuristics, and insight to solve problems.

3. Describe how the confirmation bias and fixation can interfere with effective problem solving.

4. Explain how the representativeness and availability heuristics influence our judgments.

5. Describe the effects that overconfidence and framing can have on our judgments and decisions.

6. Discuss how our beliefs distort logical reasoning, and describe the belief perseverance phenomenon.

7. Describe artificial intelligence, and contrast the human mind and the computer as information processors.

Language (pp. 373-380)

8. Describe the structure of language in terms of sounds, meanings, and grammar.

9. Trace the course of language acquisition from the babbling stage through the two-word stage.

10. Explain how the nature-nurture debate is illustrated in theories of language development.

Thinking and Language (pp. 380-384)

11. Discuss Whorf's linguistic relativity hypothesis and the relationship between thought and language.

Animal Thinking and Language (pp. 384-389)

12. Describe the research on animal cognition and communication, and discuss the controversy over whether animals can use language.

Thinking, p. 358
Easy, Factual/Definitional, Objective 1, Ans: e

1. Cognitive psychologists are most directly concerned with the study of:
    a. emotion.
    b. genetics.
    c. the unconscious.
    d. brain chemistry.
    e. thinking.

Thinking, p. 358
Medium, Conceptual, Objective 1, Ans: b

2. Professor Thompson's research activities involve the use of computers to simulate human decision-making strategies. Which specialty area does this research best represent?
    a. personality psychology
    b. cognitive psychology
    c. biological psychology
    d. clinical psychology
    e. developmental psychology

Concepts, p. 358
Easy, Factual/Definitional, Objective 1, Ans: d

3. A mental grouping of similar objects, events, or people is a(n):
    a. algorithm.
    b. prototype.
    c. heuristic.
    d. concept.

Concepts, p. 358
Medium, Conceptual, Objective 1, Ans: a

4. When we use the term *Hispanic* to refer to a category of people, we are using this word as a(n):
    a. concept.
    b. heuristic.
    c. algorithm.
    d. prototype.
    e. stereotype.

Concepts, p. 358
Medium, Factual/Definitional, Objective 1, Ans: d

5. To promote cognitive efficiency, concepts are typically organized into:
    a. mental sets.
    b. algorithms.
    c. neural networks.
    d. hierarchies.

Concepts, p. 358
Medium, Factual/Definitional, Objective 1, Ans: c

6. A best example of a category of objects, events, or people is called a(n):
    a. algorithm.
    b. concept.
    c. prototype.
    d. model.
    e. heuristic.

Concepts, p. 358
Medium, Factual/Definitional, Objective 1, Ans: e
7. Prototypes are especially important in the process of:
    a. belief perseverance.
    b. trial and error.
    c. constructing algorithms.
    d. choosing heuristics.
    e. classifying objects.

Concepts, p. 358
Difficult, Conceptual, Objective 1, Ans: d
8. Christmas is to holiday as _____ is to _____.
    a. category; prototype
    b. availability heuristic; representativeness heuristic
    c. algorithm; heuristic
    d. prototype; category

Concepts, p. 358
Medium, Conceptual, Objective 1, Ans: d
9. When someone mentions *Ivy League colleges*, Trisha immediately thinks of Harvard University. In this instance, Harvard University is a:
    a. fixation.
    b. belief bias.
    c. heuristic.
    d. prototype.
    e. mental set.

Concepts, pp. 358-359
Medium, Conceptual, Objective 1, Ans: a
10. Most people take less time to identify a cow as a mammal than a mouse as a mammal because a cow more closely resembles their _____ of a mammal.
    a. prototype
    b. mental set
    c. heuristic
    d. algorithm

Concepts, pp. 358-359
Medium, Factual/Definitional, Objective 1, Ans: d
11. People more easily detect male prejudice against women than female prejudice against men because the former more closely resembles their _____ of prejudice.
    a. syntax
    b. heuristic
    c. algorithm
    d. prototype
    e. mental set

Solving problems, p. 359
Easy, Factual/Definitional, Objective 2, Ans: b
12. In testing thousands of different materials for use as lightbulb filaments, Thomas Edison best illustrated a problem-solving approach known as:
    a. the representativeness heuristic.
    b. trial and error.
    c. functional fixedness.
    d. the confirmation bias.
    e. belief perseverance.

Solving problems, p. 359
Easy, Factual/Definitional, Objective 2, Ans: d

13. Logical, methodical step-by-step procedures for solving problems are called:
    a. heuristics.
    b. semantics.
    c. prototypes.
    d. algorithms.
    e. fixations.

Solving problems, p. 359
Medium, Conceptual, Objective 2, Ans: b

14. Darla systematically tried each successive key on her dad's key ring until she found the one that unlocked his office door. This best illustrates problem solving by means of:
    a. belief perseverance.
    b. an algorithm.
    c. the representativeness heuristic.
    d. the availability heuristic.
    e. functional fixedness.

Solving problems, p. 359
Medium, Factual/Definitional, Objective 2, Ans: d

15. Heuristics are:
    a. methodical step-by-step procedures for solving problems.
    b. mental groupings of similar objects, events, or people.
    c. problem-solving strategies involving the use of trial and error.
    d. rule-of-thumb strategies for solving problems quickly and efficiently.

Solving problems, p. 359
Medium, Conceptual, Objective 2, Ans: b

16. In trying to solve a potentially complicated problem quickly, we are most likely to rely on:
    a. prototypes.
    b. heuristics.
    c. phonemes.
    d. algorithms.
    e. fixations.

Solving problems, p. 359
Difficult, Conceptual, Objective 2, Ans: d

17. Ruth resisted changing her answer to a test question after reminding herself that "it's always best to stick with your first answer." Ruth's decision best illustrates the use of:
    a. insight.
    b. an algorithm.
    c. trial and error.
    d. a heuristic.
    e. a prototype.

Solving problems, p. 359
Easy, Factual/Definitional, Objective 2, Ans: b

18. A sudden realization of the solution to a problem is called:
    a. framing.
    b. insight.
    c. a heuristic.
    d. belief perseverance.
    e. an algorithm.

Solving problems, p. 359
Medium, Factual/Definitional, Objective 2, Ans: e

19.   The sudden comprehension of the double meaning of a humorous pun best illustrates:
   a. the representativeness heuristic.
   b. belief perseverance.
   c. the availability heuristic.
   d. the framing effect.
   e. insight.

Confirmation bias, p. 360
Easy, Factual/Definitional, Objective 3, Ans: c

20.   The tendency to search for information consistent with our preconceptions is called:
   a. functional fixedness.
   b. the availability heuristic.
   c. confirmation bias.
   d. the representativeness heuristic.
   e. overconfidence.

Confirmation bias, p. 360
Medium, Conceptual, Objective 3, Ans: c

21.   Fred cites his cousin Millie's many car accidents as evidence that women are worse drivers than men. He overlooks the fact that his wife and three daughters have had far fewer car accidents than he and his two sons. Fred's prejudicial conclusion about women's driving skills best illustrates the effects of:
   a. functional fixedness.
   b. algorithms.
   c. confirmation bias.
   d. the framing effect.
   e. the representativeness heuristic.

Confirmation bias, p. 360
Medium, Factual/Definitional, Objective 3, Ans: d

22.   Business managers are more likely to track the career achievements of those they once hired than the accomplishments of those they once rejected. This best illustrates:
   a. the representativeness heuristic.
   b. functional fixedness.
   c. the framing effect.
   d. confirmation bias.
   e. neural networks.

Confirmation bias, p. 360
Difficult, Conceptual, Objective 3, Ans: a

23.   Myra has such a low level of self-esteem that she is typically on the lookout for critical comments about her appearance and behavior. Myra best illustrates the dangers of:
   a. confirmation bias.
   b. the framing effect.
   c. functional fixedness.
   d. algorithms.
   e. the representativeness heuristic.

Fixation, p. 361
Medium, Conceptual, Objective 3, Ans: e
24.   Brainstorming sessions that encourage people to spontaneously suggest new and unusual
      solutions to a problem are designed to avoid:
      a. heuristics. ·
      b. algorithms.
      c. prototypes.
      d. semantics.
      e. fixations.

Fixation, p. 361
Difficult, Conceptual, Objective 3, Ans: e
25.   Professor Santos talks very loudly in her unsuccessful efforts to get her students to listen
      carefully. Her failure to recognize that speaking softly would be a more effective way to gain
      her student's attention best illustrates the negative consequences of:
      a. the availability heuristic.
      b. framing.
      c. overconfidence.
      d. the representativeness heuristic.
      e. fixations.

Fixation, p. 361
Medium, Factual/Definitional, Objective 3, Ans: c
26.   A mental set is a:
      a. methodical step-by-step procedure for solving problems.
      b. mental grouping of similar objects, events, or people.
      c. tendency to approach a problem in a way that has been successful in the past.
      d. group of conclusions derived from certain assumptions or general principles.

Fixation, p. 361
Easy, Factual/Definitional, Objective 3, Ans: d
27.   Stress and anxiety are most likely to contribute to:
      a. linguistic relativity.
      b. artificial intelligence.
      c. overconfidence.
      d. fixation.

Fixation, p. 361
Medium, Factual/Definitional, Objective 3, Ans: d
28.   The Korean War paratrooper who fell to his death with a left-handed parachute apparently
      suffered the consequences of:
      a. overconfidence.
      b. functional fixedness.
      c. the representativeness heuristic.
      d. a mental set.
      e. the framing effect.

Fixation, pp. 361, 362
Medium, Factual/Definitional, Objective 3, Ans: b

29.   When given a candle, tacks, and a box of matches and asked to mount the candle on a wall, people often fail to think of using the matchbox as a candleholder. This best illustrates:
    a. overconfidence.
    b. functional fixedness.
    c. confirmation bias.
    d. the availability heuristic.
    e. the framing effect.

Fixation, p. 361
Difficult, Conceptual, Objective 3, Ans: d

30.   Raul and Sophia were having a picnic when it started to rain. They did not think of using their big plastic tablecloth as a temporary rain shelter and so were drenched within minutes. Their oversight best illustrates:
    a. the availability heuristic.
    b. confirmation bias.
    c. belief perseverance.
    d. functional fixedness.
    e. overconfidence.

The representativeness heuristic, p. 362
Medium, Factual/Definitional, Objective 4, Ans: e

31.   Judging the likelihood that things fall into a certain category on the basis of how well they seem to match a particular prototype refers to the use of the:
    a. framing effect.
    b. availability heuristic.
    c. confirmation bias.
    d. belief perseverance phenomenon.
    e. representativeness heuristic.

The representativeness heuristic, p. 362
Medium, Factual/Definitional, Objective 4, Ans: e

32.   The tendency to conclude that a person who likes to read poetry is more likely to be a college professor of classics than a construction worker illustrates the use of:
    a. the availability heuristic.
    b. confirmation bias.
    c. the framing effect.
    d. belief perseverance.
    e. the representativeness heuristic.

The representativeness heuristic, p. 362
Difficult, Conceptual, Objective 4, Ans: d

33.   Jerome believes that his 4-year-old grandson is a hyperactive child because the boy's constant movement resembles Jerome's prototype of hyperactivity. Jerome's thinking best illustrates:
    a. belief perseverance.
    b. the availability heuristic.
    c. confirmation bias.
    d. the representativeness heuristic.
    e. the framing effect.

The representativeness heuristic, p. 362
Difficult, Conceptual, Objective 4, Ans: c
34.   Because Ken is 6′6″, people often mistakenly assume that he must be a member of his college's basketball team. This mistaken judgment best illustrates the impact of:
   a. confirmation bias.
   b. the belief perseverance phenomenon.
   c. the representativeness heuristic.
   d. the availability heuristic.
   e. framing.

The availability heuristic, p. 363
Easy, Factual/Definitional, Objective 4, Ans: b
35.   The availability heuristic refers to our tendency to:
   a. judge the likelihood of category membership by how closely an object or event resembles a particular prototype.
   b. judge the likelihood of an event in terms of how readily instances of its occurrence are remembered.
   c. search for information that is consistent with our preconceptions.
   d. cling to our initial conceptions, even though they have been discredited.

The availability heuristic, p. 363
Easy, Conceptual, Objective 4, Ans: c
36.   Many people overestimate how long they actually remain awake during restless nights because their moments of wakefulness are easier to recall than their moments of sleep. This best illustrates the impact of:
   a. the representativeness heuristic.
   b. confirmation bias.
   c. the availability heuristic.
   d. functional fixedness.
   e. overconfidence.

The availability heuristic, p. 363
Medium, Factual/Definitional, Objective 4, Ans: b
37.   The tendency to estimate that the letter "k" appears more often as the first letter of words than as the third letter best illustrates our use of:
   a. the representativeness heuristic.
   b. the availability heuristic.
   c. prototypes.
   d. algorithms.
   e. semantics.

The availability heuristic, p. 363
Medium, Conceptual, Objective 4, Ans: d
38.   State lottery officials send residents a facsimile of a contest-winning check for over $5 million so as to encourage them to imagine themselves as possible winners. The lottery promoters are most clearly exploiting the influence of:
   a. functional fixedness.
   b. belief perseverance.
   c. mental set.
   d. the availability heuristic.
   e. the representativeness heuristic.

The availability heuristic, p. 363
Difficult, Conceptual, Objective 4, Ans: b

39.   After learning that her two best friends had recently lost their jobs, Julia began to grossly
       overestimate the national rate of unemployment. Julia's reaction best illustrates the
       consequences of:
       a. confirmation bias.
       b. the availability heuristic.
       c. the representativeness heuristic.
       d. the belief perseverance phenomenon.
       e. the framing effect.

Thinking Critically About Risks (Box), p. 364
Medium, Factual/Definitional, Objective 4, Ans: e

40.   Which of the following contributes most directly to people's exaggerated perceptions of the
       likelihood of air travel disasters, nuclear power accidents, and terrorist violence?
       a. the belief perseverance phenomenon
       b. the representativeness heuristic
       c. overconfidence
       d. the framing effect
       e. the availability heuristic

Overconfidence, p. 365
Easy, Conceptual, Objective 5, Ans: a

41.   The human tendency toward intellectual arrogance is best demonstrated by:
       a. overconfidence.
       b. brief perseverance.
       c. the framing effect.
       d. functional fixedness.
       e. the availability heuristic.

Overconfidence, p. 365
Easy, Conceptual, Objective 5, Ans: e

42.   Although Steve was certain that he answered between 70 and 80 items correctly on his biology
       test, he actually was right on only 55 items. Steve's misjudgment of his test performance
       illustrates:
       a. the representativeness heuristic.
       b. confirmation bias.
       c. the belief perseverance phenomenon.
       d. the framing effect.
       e. overconfidence.

Overconfidence, p. 365
Easy, Conceptual, Objective 5, Ans: d

43.   After taking two years of college economics courses, Lionel thinks he knows enough about
       business to become a millionaire. Lionel should become more aware of:
       a. the representativeness heuristic.
       b. functional fixedness.
       c. the belief perseverance phenomenon.
       d. overconfidence.
       e. the framing effect.

Overconfidence, p. 366
Difficult, Factual/Definitional, Objective 5, Ans: b

44. In studies where people have judged whether another is lying or telling the truth, participants have demonstrated high levels of:
     a. insight.
     b. overconfidence.
     c. functional fixedness.
     d. artificial intelligence.

Overconfidence, p. 366
Easy, Factual/Definitional, Objective 5, Ans: e

45. College students routinely underestimate how much time it will take them to complete assigned course projects. This best illustrates the impact of:
     a. framing.
     b. functional fixedness.
     c. the availability heuristic.
     d. the representativeness heuristic.
     e. overconfidence.

Framing decisions, p. 366
Medium, Factual/Definitional, Objective 5, Ans: a

46. Framing refers to:
     a. the way in which a problem or issue is phrased or worded.
     b. a methodical step-by-step procedure for solving problems.
     c. the grouping of similar objects, events, or people into a category.
     d. a rule-of-thumb strategy for solving problems efficiently.

Framing decisions, p. 366
Medium, Conceptual, Objective 5, Ans: d

47. Ojinska sold many more raffle tickets when she told potential buyers they had a 10 percent chance of winning a prize than when she told them they had a 90 percent chance of not winning. This best illustrates:
     a. the representativeness heuristic.
     b. the belief perseverance phenomenon.
     c. confirmation bias.
     d. the framing effect.
     e. the availability heuristic.

Framing decisions, p. 366
Medium, Conceptual, Objective 5, Ans: b

48. A woman is more likely to abort a pregnancy when informed there is a 50 percent chance of producing an abnormal child than when told there is a 50 percent chance of producing a normal offspring. This best illustrates the significance of:
     a. functional fixedness.
     b. framing.
     c. overconfidence.
     d. belief perseverance.
     e. the confirmation bias.

Framing decisions, p. 366
Difficult, Conceptual, Objective 5, Ans: e

49. Professional pollsters and survey takers are especially likely to be aware of:
    a. the representativeness heuristic.
    b. the belief perseverance phenomenon.
    c. the confirmation bias.
    d. functional fixedness.
    e. the framing effect.

Belief bias, p. 367
Medium, Factual/Definitional, Objective 6, Ans: c

50. We often consider illogical conclusions that happen to agree with our personal opinions to be logically valid. This is known as:
    a. the availability heuristic.
    b. linguistic relativity.
    c. belief bias.
    d. framing.
    e. functional fixedness.

Belief bias, p. 367
Difficult, Conceptual, Objective 6, Ans: e

51. Mr. Potter thinks that all socialists are political liberals and that the governor of his state is a political liberal. Mr. Potter's fear of socialism is so strong that he readily accepts the clearly illogical conclusion that his state governor must be a socialist. His difficulty best illustrates:
    a. confirmation bias.
    b. functional fixedness.
    c. the availability heuristic.
    d. the framing effect.
    e. belief bias.

The belief perseverance phenomenon, p. 368
Medium, Factual/Definitional, Objective 6, Ans: d

52. Experimental participants reviewed two research studies, one supporting and the other refuting the crime-deterring effectiveness of capital punishment. Afterwards, the opinions of those who initially favored the use of capital punishment became _____ favorable toward its use. The opinions of those who initially opposed the use of capital punishment became _____ favorable toward its use.
    a. more; more
    b. less; more
    c. less; less
    d. more; less

The belief perseverance phenomenon, p. 368
Difficult, Factual/Definitional, Objective 6, Ans: a

53. Anderson, Lepper, and Ross gave experimental participants evidence that either risk-prone or cautious people make better fire fighters. Participants were later informed that the evidence was fictitious. This experiment was designed to illustrate:
    a. the belief perseverance phenomenon.
    b. confirmation bias.
    c. the framing effect.
    d. the representativeness heuristic.
    e. the availability heuristic.

The belief perseverance phenomenon, p. 368
Medium, Conceptual, Objective 6, Ans: c
54.   Despite overwhelming and highly publicized evidence that Senator McEwan was guilty of
      serious political corruption and misconduct, many who had supported her in past elections
      remained convinced of her political integrity. Their reaction best illustrates:
      a. functional fixedness.
      b. the representativeness heuristic.
      c. the belief perseverance phenomenon.
      d. the availability heuristic.
      e. the framing effect.

The belief perseverance phenomenon, p. 368
Medium, Factual/Definitional, Objective 6, Ans: d
55.   Encouraging people to explain why their own personal views on an issue are correct is most
      likely to promote:
      a. functional fixedness.
      b. use of the representativeness heuristic.
      c. linguistic relativity.
      d. the belief perseverance phenomenon.
      e. the framing effect.

The belief perseverance phenomenon, p. 369
Difficult, Conceptual, Objective 6, Ans: b
56.   The difficulty involved in efforts to modify an unrealistically negative self-image best
      illustrates:
      a. functional fixedness.
      b. the belief perseverance phenomenon.
      c. the framing effect.
      d. the representativeness heuristic.
      e. overconfidence.

Simulating thinking: artificial intelligence, p. 370
Easy, Conceptual, Objective 7, Ans: e
57.   A computer program that employs heuristics to correctly solve a crossword puzzle illustrates an
      application of:
      a. the framing effect.
      b. functional fixedness.
      c. parallel processing.
      d. linguistic relativity.
      e. artificial intelligence.

Simulating thinking: artificial intelligence, pp. 370-371
Medium, Factual/Definitional, Objective 7, Ans: a
58.   Unlike conventional computers, people are capable of:
      a. processing numerous informational units simultaneously.
      b. using heuristics to arrive at solutions to problems.
      c. retrieving detailed facts from memory.
      d. following precise rules of logic.

Simulating thinking: artificial intelligence, p. 371
Difficult, Factual/Definitional, Objective 7, Ans: b
59.   The most exciting feature of computer neural networks is their capacity to mimic the human
      ability to:
      a. make rule-based decisions.
      b. learn from experience.
      c. retrieve information from memory.
      d. use algorithms to solve problems.

Language structure, p. 373
Easy, Factual/Definitional, Objective 8, Ans: b

60.   Phonemes are:
      a. the best examples of particular categories of objects.
      b. the smallest distinctive sound units of a language.
      c. rules for combining words into grammatically correct sentences.
      d. the smallest speech units that carry meaning.

Language structure, p. 373
Medium, Conceptual, Objective 8, Ans: e
61.   When Fred pronounced the words "this" and "that," he noticed that they share a common:
      a. prototype.
      b. phenotype.
      c. morpheme.
      d. algorithm.
      e. phoneme.

Language structure, p. 373
Difficult, Conceptual, Objective 8, Ans: b
62.   The English language has _____ letters than phonemes, and the consonant phonemes
      generally carry _____ information than the vowel phonemes.
      a. more; more
      b. fewer; more
      c. more; less
      d. fewer; less

Language structure, p. 373
Easy, Factual/Definitional, Objective 8, Ans: b
63.   The smallest speech units that carry meaning are called:
      a. phonemes.
      b. morphemes.
      c. prototypes.
      d. concepts.
      e. phenotypes.

Language structure, p. 373
Medium, Conceptual, Objective 8, Ans: d
64.   In the words "lightly," "neatly," and "shortly," the "ly" ending is a(n):
      a. algorithm.
      b. phenotype.
      c. phoneme.
      d. morpheme.
      e. prototype.

Language structure, p. 374
Medium, Conceptual, Objective 8, Ans: a

65.   When her teacher mentioned the arms race, Krista understood that the word "arms" referred to weapons and not to body parts. Krista's correct interpretation best illustrates the importance of:
       a. semantics.
       b. the representativeness heuristic.
       c. syntax.
       d. morphemes.
       e. prototypes.

Language structure, p. 374
Medium, Factual/Definitional, Objective 8, Ans: a

66.   Syntax refers to the:
       a. orderly arrangement of words into grammatically sensible sentences.
       b. derivation of meaning from morphemes, words, and sentences.
       c. smallest speech unit that carries meaning.
       d. most logical and methodical procedure for solving a problem.

Language structure, p. 374
Difficult, Conceptual, Objective 8, Ans: b

67.   A European visitor to the United States asked a taxi driver, "Can you please a ride to the airport me give?" This visitor has apparently not yet mastered the _____ of the English language.
       a. phonemes
       b. syntax
       c. semantics
       d. phenotypes
       e. nomenclature

Language structure, p. 374
Difficult, Conceptual, Objective 8, Ans: d

68.   Word meaning is to word order as _____ is to _____.
       a. concept; prototype
       b. phoneme; grammar
       c. morpheme; phoneme
       d. semantics; syntax
       e. nomenclature; semantics

Acquiring language, p. 374
Easy, Factual/Definitional, Objective 9, Ans: b

69.   The spontaneous utterance of a variety of sounds by infants is called:
       a. universal grammar.
       b. babbling.
       c. telegraphic speech.
       d. semantics.

Acquiring language, p. 374
Medium, Factual/Definitional, Objective 9, Ans: d

70.   During the earliest stage of speech development, infants:
       a. speak in single words that may be barely recognizable.
       b. begin to imitate adult syntax.
       c. make speech sounds only if their hearing is unimpaired.
       d. make some speech sounds that do not occur in their parents' native language.
       e. do all the above.

Acquiring language, p. 375
Medium, Conceptual, Objective 9, Ans: c
71.   At 17 months of age, Julie says "wada" whenever she wants a drink of water. Julie is most
       likely in the _____ stage of language development.
       a. semantic
       b. babbling
       c. one-word
       d. telegraphic speech
       e. phonetic

Acquiring language, p. 376
Easy, Conceptual, Objective 9, Ans: c
72.   Two-year-old Stephen's sentences—"Dad come," "Mom laugh," and "Truck gone"—are
       examples of:
       a. babbling.
       b. artificial grammar.
       c. telegraphic speech.
       d. universal grammar.

Acquiring language, p. 376
Difficult, Factual/Definitional, Objective 9, Ans: c
73.   Children begin to demonstrate appropriate use of syntax during the _____ stage.
       a. babbling
       b. syntactic
       c. two-word
       d. three-word
       e. phonetic

Explaining language development, p. 376
Difficult, Factual/Definitional, Objective 10, Ans: d
74.   Behaviorists such as B. F. Skinner have emphasized that the acquisition of language can be
       explained in terms of:
       a. the association of word sounds with various objects, events, actions, and qualities.
       b. children's imitation of the words and grammar modeled by parents and others.
       c. the positive reinforcement that adults give children for speaking correctly.
       d. all the above.

Explaining language development, pp. 376-377
Difficult, Factual/Definitional, Objective 10, Ans: c
75.   Which linguistic theorist was most impressed by the underlying similarities of all human
       language systems?
       a. Skinner
       b. Whorf
       c. Chomsky
       d. Bandura

Explaining language development, p. 377
Medium, Factual/Definitional, Objective 10, Ans: a
76.   According to Chomsky, the fact that young children overgeneralize certain rules of
       grammatical structure suggests that:
       a. language skills are not developed simply through the processes of imitation and
           reinforcement.
       b. language acquisition does not proceed in an orderly sequence.
       c. language acquisition develops normally even in the absence of social interaction.
       d. parents overemphasize correct grammatical usage.

Explaining language development, p. 377
Medium, Conceptual, Objective 10, Ans: d

77. Four-year-old Sarah told her mom, "The doggy runned away." Which theory would most likely emphasize the significance of Sarah's misapplication of a grammatical rule?
     a. Frisch's biological theory
     b. Skinner's language acquisition theory
     c. Whorf's linguistic relativity theory
     d. Chomsky's language acquisition theory

Explaining language development, p. 377
Medium, Factual/Definitional, Objective 10, Ans: c

78. After two minutes of exposure to an unbroken, monotone string of nonsense syllables, infants could recognize three-syllable sequences that appeared repeatedly. This best illustrates the importance of _____ in language development.
     a. reinforcement
     b. inborn universal grammar
     c. statistical learning
     d. imitation

Explaining language development, p. 377
Difficult, Factual/Definitional, Objective 10, Ans: d

79. The statistical learning explanation of language development _____ claims for an inborn universal grammar and _____ claims for a built-in readiness to learn grammatical rules.
     a. supports; supports
     b. challenges; challenges
     c. supports; challenges
     d. challenges; supports

Explaining language development, pp. 378-379
Easy, Factual/Definitional, Objective 10, Ans: a

80. Research suggests that humans can most easily master the grammar of a second language during:
     a. childhood.
     b. adolescence.
     c. early adulthood.
     d. late adulthood.

Explaining language development, p. 380
Medium, Factual/Definitional, Objective 10, Ans: b

81. The principles of learning emphasized by behaviorists would be most helpful in explaining why children:
     a. master the complicated rules of grammar with ease.
     b. add new words to their vocabulary.
     c. make systematic speech errors because they overgeneralize grammatical rules.
     d. babble even when they have deaf parents.

Language influences thinking, p. 381
Easy, Factual/Definitional, Objective 11, Ans: d

82. The suggestion that language determines the way we think is known as the _____ hypothesis.
     a. language acquisition
     b. social-cognitive
     c. belief perseverance
     d. linguistic relativity
     e. telegraphic speech

Language influences thinking, p. 381
Medium, Conceptual, Objective 11, Ans: d

83.   The linguistic relativity hypothesis is most consistent with the suggestion that "words are the
       _____ of ideas."
       a. brothers
       b. daughters
       c. husbands
       d. mothers

Language influences thinking, p. 381
Difficult, Factual/Definitional, Objective 11, Ans: c

84.   Which of the following would most likely be cited as evidence in support of the linguistic
       relativity hypothesis?
       a. The generic pronoun "he" is just as likely to trigger images of women as of men.
       b. People with no words for colors can still perceive color differences.
       c. Hopi Indians cannot readily think about the past because their language has no past tense for
           verbs.
       d. Chimpanzees can use signs and gestures to communicate with other members of their own
           species.

Language influences thinking, p. 381
Difficult, Conceptual, Objective 11, Ans: d

85.   Leland's language does not distinguish between "family love" and "romantic love," so he has
       difficulty realizing that he deeply loves his sister. Which of the following is most relevant to
       Leland's difficulty?
       a. the representativeness heuristic
       b. the belief perseverance phenomenon
       c. functional fixedness
       d. the linguistic relativity hypothesis

Language influences thinking, p. 382
Easy, Factual/Definitional, Objective 11, Ans: b

86.   When English-speaking Canadian children were taught by a French-speaking teacher during
       their early school years, researchers found that they experienced a(n):
       a. confused sense of cultural identity.
       b. improvement in intellectual aptitude.
       c. slight loss of verbal fluency in English.
       d. smaller-than-average improvement in mathematical ability.

Thinking without language, p. 383
Medium, Factual/Definitional, Objective 11, Ans: e

87.   Many successful athletes prepare for contests by imagining themselves performing their events.
       This mental rehearsal best illustrates the effectiveness of:
       a. the representativeness heuristic.
       b. the belief perseverance phenomenon.
       c. algorithms.
       d. the framing effect.
       e. thinking without language.

Do animals think?, p. 385
Medium, Factual/Definitional, Objective 12, Ans: a
88. The chimpanzee Sultan used a short stick to retrieve a long stick, then used the long stick to retrieve a piece of fruit. Sultan's successful acquisition of the fruit was said to be the result of:
   a. insight.
   b. a fixation.
   c. artificial intelligence.
   d. trial and error.
   e. the availability heuristic.

Do animals think?, p. 385
Medium, Factual/Definitional, Objective 12, Ans: a
89. Psychologists are most likely to question whether chimps have the capacity to:
   a. infer another chimp's mental states.
   b. discern numerical order.
   c. invent and transmit customs.
   d. form concepts.

Do animals exhibit language?, p. 386
Easy, Factual/Definitional, Objective 12, Ans: b
90. Karl von Frisch discovered that _____ communicate by means of an intricate dance.
   a. ants
   b. honeybees
   c. spiders
   d. flamingos
   e. butterflies

Do animals exhibit language?, p. 387
Medium, Factual/Definitional, Objective 12, Ans: d
91. Chimpanzees are capable of learning to:
   a. understand spoken words.
   b. string signs together into a meaningful sequence.
   c. use computer keyboards to communicate with other chimps.
   d. do all the above.

Do animals exhibit language?, p. 387
Medium, Factual/Definitional, Objective 12, Ans: d
92. Research on the language capabilities of apes indicates that they cannot:
   a. translate spoken words into signs.
   b. acquire a vocabulary of more than two dozen signs.
   c. use signs to communicate with other members of their own species.
   d. grammatically order language symbols as well as most 3-year-old children.

CHAPTER 11

Intelligence

Learning Objectives

The Origins of Intelligence Testing (pp. 391-394)

1. Trace the origins of intelligence testing, and describe Stern's formula for the intelligence quotient.

What Is Intelligence? (pp. 394-400)

2. Describe the nature of intelligence, and discuss whether it should be considered a general mental ability or many specific abilities.

3. Describe efforts to correlate intelligence with brain anatomy, brain functioning, and cognitive processing speed.

Assessing Intelligence (pp. 401-405)

4. Distinguish between aptitude and achievement tests, and describe modern tests of mental abilities such as the WAIS.

5. Describe test standardization, and explain the importance of appropriate standardization samples for effectively interpreting intelligence test scores.

6. Distinguish between the reliability and validity of intelligence tests, and explain how reliability and validity are assessed.

The Dynamics of Intelligence (pp. 405-410)

7. Discuss the stability of intelligence scores, and describe the two extremes of the normal distribution of intelligence.

8. Identify the factors associated with creativity, and describe the relationship between creativity and intelligence.

Genetic and Environmental Influences on Intelligence (pp. 410-421)

9. Discuss evidence for both genetic and environmental influences on intelligence.

10.   Describe group differences in intelligence test scores, and show how they can be explained in terms of environmental factors.

11.   Discuss whether intelligence tests are culturally biased.

The origins of intelligence testing, p. 392
Easy, Factual/Definitional, Objective 1, Ans: d

1.   The French government commissioned Binet to develop an intelligence test that would:
     a.   demonstrate the innate intellectual superiority of western European races.
     b.   effectively distinguish between practical and creative intelligence.
     c.   provide an objective measure of teaching effectiveness in the public school system.
     d.   reduce the need to rely on teachers' subjectively biased judgments of students' learning potential.

The origins of intelligence testing, p. 392
Easy, Conceptual, Objective 1, Ans: a

2.   Intelligence tests were initially designed by Binet and Simon to assess:
     a.   academic aptitude.
     b.   intellectual creativity.
     c.   academic achievement.
     d.   heritability.
     e.   savant syndrome.

The origins of intelligence testing, p. 392
Medium, Factual/Definitional, Objective 1, Ans: c

3.   In developing a test of intellectual ability for Parisian school children, Binet and Simon assumed that:
     a.   the test would measure capacities that were determined by heredity and thus unalterable.
     b.   the test would yield an intelligence quotient consisting of chronological age divided by mental age multiplied by 100.
     c.   a bright child would perform like a normal child of an older age.
     d.   measures of physical and sensory skills would be good predictors of school achievement.

The origins of intelligence testing, p. 392
Medium, Factual/Definitional, Objective 1, Ans: d

4.   Binet used the term mental age to refer to:
     a.   the average chronological age of children who completed a particular grade in school.
     b.   the years of formal education successfully completed by a child.
     c.   the total number of items correctly answered on an intelligence test divided by the respondent's chronological age.
     d.   the chronological age that most typically corresponds to a given level of intelligence-test performance.

The origins of intelligence testing, pp. 392-393
Difficult, Conceptual, Objective 1, Ans: c

5.   Binet's "mental orthopedics" is to _____ as Terman's "eugenics" is to _____.
     a.   mental age; chronological age
     b.   aptitude; achievement
     c.   nurture; nature
     d.   reliability; validity
     e.   academic intelligence; emotional intelligence

The origins of intelligence testing, p. 393
Easy, Factual/Definitional, Objective 1, Ans: c

6. Lewis Terman's widely used American revision of Binet's original intelligence test was the:
   a. WISC.
   b. WAIS.
   c. Stanford-Binet.
   d. Scholastic Aptitude Test.
   e. American College Testing Exam.

The origins of intelligence testing, p. 393
Medium, Conceptual, Objective 1, Ans: e

7. A 6-year-old who responded to the original Stanford-Binet with the proficiency typical of an average 8-year-old was said to have an IQ of:
   a. 75.
   b. 85.
   c. 115.
   d. 125.
   e. 133.

The origins of intelligence testing, p. 393
Difficult, Conceptual, Objective 1, Ans: b

8. Ko has a mental age of 10 and an IQ of 125 as measured by the Stanford-Binet. Ko's chronological age is:
   a. 6.
   b. 8.
   c. 9.
   d. 10.
   e. 12.5.

The origins of intelligence testing, p. 393
Medium, Conceptual, Objective 1, Ans: d

9. The eugenics movement most clearly demonstrated an interest in:
   a. emotional intelligence.
   b. savant syndrome.
   c. factor analysis.
   d. inherited traits.
   e. reification.

The origins of intelligence testing, p. 393
Medium, Conceptual, Objective 1, Ans: d

10. The original IQ formula would be least appropriate for representing the intelligence test performance of:
    a. kindergartners.
    b. grade school students.
    c. high school students.
    d. college students.

The origins of intelligence testing, pp. 391-393
Medium, Factual/Definitional, Objective 1, Ans: a

11. A survey of the history of intelligence testing reinforces the important lesson that:
    a. although science strives for objectivity, scientists can be influenced by their personal biases.
    b. the experiment is the most powerful tool available for examining cause-effect relationships.
    c. different theoretical perspectives on behavior may be complementary rather than competing.
    d. scientists are more concerned with the development of theory than with its practical application.

What is intelligence?, p. 394
Medium, Factual/Definitional, Objective 2, Ans: d

12. To regard an abstract concept as if it were a real, concrete thing is called:
    a. the naturalistic fallacy.
    b. heritability.
    c. factor analysis.
    d. reification.
    e. standardization.

What is intelligence?, p. 394
Easy, Conceptual, Objective 2, Ans: c

13. Intelligence tests have traditionally been designed to measure:
    a. social aptitude.
    b. moral achievement.
    c. cognitive aptitude.
    d. economic achievement.

Is intelligence one general or several specific abilities?, p. 395
Medium, Factual/Definitional, Objective 2, Ans: e

14. A statistical procedure that identifies clusters of test items that seem to tap a common ability is called:
    a. correlational measurement.
    b. standardization.
    c. reliability assessment.
    d. criterion-based validation.
    e. factor analysis.

Is intelligence one general or several specific abilities?, p. 395
Medium, Factual/Definitional, Objective 2, Ans: b

15. Psychologists have made extensive use of factor analysis to assess whether:
    a. intelligence is determined primarily by heredity or by experience.
    b. intelligence is a single trait or a collection of distinct abilities.
    c. intelligence scores remain stable over the life span.
    d. differences in intellectual ability exist between groups of individuals.

Is intelligence one general or several specific abilities?, p. 395
Easy, Factual/Definitional, Objective 2, Ans: c

16. Spearman referred to the general capacity that may underlie all the specific mental abilities as:
    a. IQ.
    b. heritability.
    c. the *g* factor.
    d. factor analysis.
    e. emotional intelligence.

Is intelligence one general or several specific abilities?, p. 395
Medium, Conceptual, Objective 2, Ans: d

17. Those who score above average on tests of mathematical aptitude are also likely to score above average on tests of verbal aptitude. According to Spearman, this best illustrates the importance of:
    a. predictive validity.
    b. factor analysis
    c. heritability.
    d. the *g* factor.
    e. reliability.

Is intelligence one general or several specific abilities?, p. 395
Difficult, Conceptual, Objective 2, Ans: d

18. Those who emphasize the importance of the *g* factor are most likely to be enthusiastic about:
    a. the discontinuation of "gifted child" programs for intellectually advantaged children.
    b. the derivation of adult intelligence test scores from the ratio of mental age to chronological age.
    c. the utilization of a small standardization sample in the process of intelligence-test construction.
    d. the quantification of intelligence with a single numerical score.

Is intelligence one general or several specific abilities?, p. 395
Easy, Factual/Definitional, Objective 2, Ans: b

19. A person with savant syndrome is one who:
    a. is capable of becoming socially and vocationally successful.
    b. possesses an amazing specific skill.
    c. suffers no obvious physical or emotional defects.
    d. is unable to profit from special educational training.
    e. is born with an extra chromosome.

Is intelligence one general or several specific abilities?, pp. 395-396
Medium, Conceptual, Objective 2, Ans: c

20. Psychological tests show that 18-year-old Tim has an intelligence score of 65. Nevertheless, Tim can, with a few seconds of mental calculation, accurately tell the day of the week on which Christmas falls for any year in the next two centuries. It would be fair to conclude that:
    a. the intelligence test Tim was given has no validity.
    b. intelligence tests are generally good measures of verbal but not of mathematical intelligence.
    c. Tim is a person with savant syndrome.
    d. Tim is suffering from Down syndrome.

Is intelligence one general or several specific abilities?, p. 396
Difficult, Factual/Definitional, Objective 2, Ans: c

21. The characteristics of savant syndrome have been used to support:
    a. Spearman's belief in a general intelligence, or *g*, factor.
    b. Cantor and Kihlstrom's distinction between academic and social intelligence.
    c. Gardner's argument for multiple intelligences.
    d. Eysenck's idea that intelligence is linked to information-processing speed.

Is intelligence one general or several specific abilities?, p. 397
Difficult, Conceptual, Objective 2, Ans: d

22.   Of the following, who best illustrates Sternberg and Wagner's concept of analytical
       intelligence?
       a. Trudy, a high school student who receives lower grades in physical education than in any
          other course
       b. Freda, a business executive who effectively motivates her sales staff
       c. Wilma, a schoolteacher who refuses to pay taxes because they are used to develop new
          weapons
       d. Selma, a fifth-grader who solves complicated mathematical problems in record time
       e. Nicole, a teenager who completes the road test for her driver's license without a single error

Is intelligence one general or several specific abilities?, pp. 397-398
Easy, Conceptual, Objective 2, Ans: e

23.   In very stressful or embarrassing situations, Julie is able to maintain her poise and help others
       to feel comfortable. Julie's ability best illustrates the value of:
       a. the *g* factor.
       b. heritability.
       c. mental age.
       d. savant syndrome.
       e. emotional intelligence.

Is intelligence one general or several specific abilities?, p. 398
Medium, Conceptual, Objective 2, Ans: c

24.   The ability to control one's impulses and deal effectively with social conflict is not likely to be
       reflected in one's performance on the WAIS. This best illustrates that intelligence is:
       a. impossible to measure with any reliability.
       b. unrelated to the speed of cognitive processing.
       c. a collection of distinctly different abilities.
       d. a joint function of nature and nurture.

Is intelligence neurologically measurable?, p. 398
Medium, Factual/Definitional, Objective 3, Ans: b

25.   The phrenologist Franz Gall suspected that intelligence differences among humans might result
       from individual differences in:
       a. language systems.
       b. brain structures.
       c. educational experiences.
       d. neural processing speeds.

Is intelligence neurologically measurable?, p. 399
Medium, Factual/Definitional, Objective 3, Ans: d

26.   Studies suggest that intelligence test scores are negatively correlated with:
       a. height.
       b. nearsightedness.
       c. head size.
       d. the brain's rate of glucose consumption.

Is intelligence neurologically measurable?, p. 399
Medium, Factual/Definitional, Objective 3, Ans: d

27.   In order to test whether intelligence is related to information-processing capacities, researchers have tested subjects to determine how long it takes them to:
a. copy the letters of the alphabet.
b. detect and identity familiar odors.
c. type written paragraphs presented on a computer monitor.
d. perceive briefly presented visual images.

Modern tests of mental abilities, p. 401
Easy, Factual/Definitional, Objective 4, Ans: a

28.   Aptitude tests are specifically designed to:
a. predict ability to learn a new skill.
b. compare an individual's abilities with those of highly successful people.
c. assess learned knowledge or skills.
d. assess the ability to produce novel and valuable ideas.

Modern tests of mental abilities, p. 401
Easy, Conceptual, Objective 4, Ans: d

29.   Molly has just taken a test of her capacity to learn to be a computer programmer. This is an example of an _____ test.
a. applied intelligence
b. achievement
c. interest
d. aptitude

Modern tests of mental abilities, p. 401
Easy, Factual/Definitional, Objective 4, Ans: d

30.   Tests designed to assess what a person has learned are called _____ tests.
a. ability
b. aptitude
c. standardized
d. achievement
e. intelligence

Modern tests of mental abilities, p. 401
Medium, Conceptual, Objective 4, Ans: b

31.   The final exam in a calculus course would be an example of a(n) _____ test.
a. aptitude
b. achievement
c. standardized
d. general intelligence

Modern tests of mental abilities, p. 401
Medium, Conceptual, Objective 4, Ans: d

32.   Assessing current competence is to _____ tests as predicting future performance is to _____ tests.
a. intelligence; standardized
b. aptitude; achievement
c. standardized; intelligence
d. achievement; aptitude

Modern tests of mental abilities, p. 401
Medium, Conceptual, Objective 4, Ans: e

33.   WAIS is to WISC as _____ is to _____.
      a. intelligence; creativity
      b. aptitude; achievement
      c. Binet-Simon; Stanford-Binet
      d. verbal; mathematical
      e. adult; child

Modern tests of mental abilities, p. 401
Medium, Factual/Definitional, Objective 4, Ans: a

34.   The test that provides separate "verbal" and "performance" intelligence scores, as well as an
      overall intelligence score, is the:
      a. WAIS.
      b. Stanford-Binet.
      c. SAT.
      d. GRE.

Modern tests of mental abilities, p. 401
Medium, Conceptual, Objective 4, Ans: a

35.   Twenty-two-year-old Bernie takes a test that includes measures of his ability in terms of digit
      span, vocabulary, and object assembly. Bernie has completed the:
      a. WAIS.
      b. SAT.
      c. Stanford-Binet.
      d. GRE.

Standardization, p. 402
Easy, Factual/Definitional, Objective 5, Ans: b

36.   When a person's test performance can be compared with that of a representative, pretested
      group, the test is:
      a. reliable.
      b. standardized.
      c. valid.
      d. normalized.
      e. internally consistent.

Standardization, p. 402
Medium, Conceptual, Objective 5, Ans: c

37.   Dr. Zimmer has designed a test to measure knowledge of American history. In order to
      interpret scores on it, he is presently administering the test to a representative sample of all
      Americans. Dr. Zimmer is clearly in the process of:
      a. establishing the test's validity.
      b. conducting a factor analysis of the test.
      c. standardizing the test.
      d. establishing the test's reliability.

Standardization, p. 402

Easy, Factual/Definitional, Objective 5, Ans: b

38. The bell-shaped curve that characterizes a large sample of intelligence test scores is a graphic representation of a:
  a. factor analysis.
  b. normal distribution.
  c. heritability estimate.
  d. savant syndrome.
  e. *g* factor.

Standardization, pp. 402-403

Difficult, Conceptual, Objective 5, Ans: e

39. Dr. Benthem reports that the scores of 100 males and females on his new test of mechanical reasoning form a normal curve. From his statement we may conclude:
  a. that the average male score was better than the average female score.
  b. that the scores were about the same as those obtained by a representative sample of adult Americans.
  c. that the average score on the test was 50 percent correct.
  d. that there were equal numbers of very high, very low, and average scores on the test.
  e. none of the above.

Standardization (Figure 11.4), p. 403

Difficult, Factual/Definitional, Objective 5, Ans: d

40. About _____ percent of WAIS scores fall between 70 and 130.
  a. 30
  b. 60
  c. 70
  d. 95

Standardization, p. 403

Medium, Factual/Definitional, Objective 5, Ans: e

41. The widespread increase in intelligence test performance during this century is called:
  a. the bell curve.
  b. reification.
  c. the *g* factor.
  d. standardization.
  e. the Flynn effect.

Standardization, p. 403

Difficult, Factual/Definitional, Objective 5, Ans: b

42. The Flynn effect best illustrates that the process of intelligence testing requires up-to-date:
  a. factor analyses.
  b. standardization samples.
  c. reliability indices.
  d. heritability estimates.

Standardization, p. 403
Difficult, Conceptual, Objective 5, Ans: a

43.   Effie, a high school senior, received an average score on the verbal and performance portions
of the WAIS. It would be most reasonable to predict that her college entrance aptitude test
scores will be:
a. below average.
b. average.
c. above average.
d. below average on math subtests and above average on verbal subtests.

Standardization, p. 403
Easy, Factual/Definitional, Objective 5, Ans: a

44.   The improvement in intelligence test performance among North Americans during the last 60
years most likely results from:
a. the increased level of education received by North Americans.
b. standardization of intelligence tests on international rather than national population samples.
c. the increase in the racial diversity of the North American population.
d. the introduction of easier test questions in contemporary intelligence tests.

Reliability, p. 404
Medium, Factual/Definitional, Objective 6, Ans: b

45.   A test is reliable if it:
a. measures what it claims to measure or predicts what it is supposed to predict.
b. yields consistent results every time it is used.
c. has been standardized on a representative sample of all those who are likely to take the test.
d. samples the behavior that is being assessed.
e. produces a normal distribution of scores.

Reliability, p. 404
Medium, Factual/Definitional, Objective 6, Ans: e

46.   Psychologists assess the correlation between scores obtained on alternate forms of the same test
in order to measure the _____ of the test.
a. content validity
b. predictive validity
c. normal distribution
d. standardization
e. reliability

Reliability, p. 404
Difficult, Conceptual, Objective 6, Ans: b

47.   Dr. Bronfman has administered her new 100-item test of abstract reasoning to a large sample of
college students. She is presently comparing their scores on the odd-numbered questions with
those on the even-numbered questions in an effort to:
a. determine the test's validity.
b. determine the test's reliability.
c. standardize the test.
d. factor-analyze the test.

Reliability, p. 404
Easy, Factual/Definitional, Objective 6, Ans: d
48.   Which test has been demonstrated to be a highly reliable measure?
a. Stanford-Binet
b. WAIS
c. WISC
d. all the above

Reliability and validity, p. 404
Medium, Conceptual, Objective 6, Ans: c
49.   Consistency is to accuracy as _____ is to _____.
a. aptitude; achievement
b. standardization; reliability
c. reliability; validity
d. factor analysis; standardization
e. content validity; predictive validity

Validity, p. 404
Medium, Factual/Definitional, Objective 6, Ans: a
50.   A test has a high degree of validity if it:
a. measures or predicts what it is supposed to measure or predict.
b. yields consistent results every time it is used.
c. produces a normal distribution of scores.
d. has been standardized on a representative sample of all those who are likely to take the test.

Validity, p. 404
Easy, Conceptual, Objective 6, Ans: c
51.   After learning about his low score on the Wechsler Adult Intelligence Scale, Gunter complained, "I don't believe that test is a measure of intelligence at all." Gunter's statement is equivalent to saying that the WAIS lacks:
a. standardization.
b. reliability.
c. validity.
d. a normal distribution.

Validity, p. 404
Medium, Conceptual, Objective 6, Ans: b
52.   College grades are the major criterion for the:
a. WISC.
b. SAT.
c. GRE.
d. MMPI.

Validity, p. 404
Medium, Conceptual, Objective 6, Ans: b
53.   A college administrator is trying to assess whether an admissions test accurately predicts how well applicants will perform at his school. The administrator is most obviously concerned that the test is:
a. standardized.
b. valid.
c. factor-analyzed.
d. normally distributed.
e. reliable.

Validity, p. 404
Medium, Factual/Definitional, Objective 6, Ans: d

54. The correlation is likely to be lowest between the:
    a. Stanford-Binet IQ scores and grades of elementary school children.
    b. Wechsler intelligence scores and grades of junior high school students.
    c. SAT scores and grades of college freshmen.
    d. GRE scores and grades of graduate students.

Validity, p. 404
Medium, Factual/Definitional, Objective 6, Ans: b

55. The relatively restricted range of aptitudes among the college seniors who take the Graduate
    Record Exam serves to _____ the _____ of the Graduate Record Exam.
    a. increase; reliability
    b. decrease; predictive validity
    c. increase; the normal distribution
    d. decrease; the standardization sample

Validity, pp. 404-405
Difficult, Conceptual, Objective 6, Ans: d

56. The correlation between intelligence test scores and annual income will probably be highest if
    computed for a group having test scores ranging from:
    a. 130 to 160.
    b. 70 to 100.
    c. 100 to 130.
    d. 80 to 120.

The dynamics of intelligence: stability or change?, p. 406
Easy, Conceptual, Objective 7, Ans: c

57. The Wilsons note that their 6-month-old daughter Beth seems to be developing more slowly
    and is not as playful as other infants her age. Research suggests that:
    a. Beth's intelligence score will be below average in childhood but not necessarily in
       adulthood.
    b. Beth's intelligence score will be below average in both childhood and adulthood.
    c. casual observation of Beth's behavior cannot be used to predict her later intelligence score.
    d. Beth's performance intelligence score but not necessarily her verbal intelligence score will
       be below average in both childhood and adulthood.

The dynamics of intelligence: stability or change?, p. 406
Medium, Factual/Definitional, Objective 7, Ans: d

58. Research has indicated that seventh- and eighth-graders who outscored most high school
    seniors on the SAT had begun _____ at an unusually early age.
    a. crawling
    b. walking
    c. talking
    d. reading

The dynamics of intelligence: stability or change?, p. 406
Medium, Factual/Definitional, Objective 7, Ans: a
59.   The stability of children's intelligence test scores over time is most positively correlated with their:
   a.   chronological age.
   b.   mental age.
   c.   head size.
   d.   brain size.

Extremes of intelligence (Table 11.1), p. 407
Difficult, Conceptual, Objective 7, Ans: c
60.   Hanan, a 22-year-old, is mentally retarded. Although not fully self-supporting, she earns some money by working in a sheltered workshop. She has been able to master basic skills equivalent to those of a second-grader. Hanan's intelligence test score is most likely between:
   a.   5 and 20.
   b.   20 and 34.
   c.   35 and 49.
   d.   50 and 70.

Extremes of intelligence, p. 407
Easy, Factual/Definitional, Objective 7, Ans: c

61.   A condition involving mental retardation caused by an extra chromosome in one's genetic makeup is known as:
   a.   the Flynn effect.
   b.   emotional intelligence.
   c.   Down syndrome.
   d.   savant syndrome.

Extremes of intelligence, p. 407
Medium, Factual/Definitional, Objective 7, Ans: d
62.   Research on mental retardation indicates that:
   a.   most mentally retarded individuals are unable to profit from vocational training.
   b.   most mentally retarded individuals are unable to function within mainstream society.
   c.   most mentally retarded individuals suffer from savant syndrome.
   d.   none of the above is true.

Extremes of intelligence, p. 407
Medium, Factual/Definitional, Objective 7, Ans: b
63.   Terman observed that children with IQ scores over 135 are likely to be:
   a.   athletically uncoordinated.
   b.   academically successful.
   c.   socially isolated and unpopular.
   d.   all the above.

Extremes of intelligence, p. 408
Easy, Factual/Definitional, Objective 7, Ans: c
64.   Educational programs for gifted children are most likely to be criticized for:
   a.   assuming that intelligence test scores can predict children's academic success.
   b.   underestimating the extent to which a *g* factor underlies success in a wide variety of tasks.
   c.   encouraging the segregation and academic tracking of intellectually advantaged students.
   d.   overemphasizing the genetic determinants of giftedness.

Creativity and intelligence, p. 409
Easy, Factual/Definitional, Objective 8, Ans: b
65. People who make outstanding creative contributions to the arts or sciences are most likely to:
     a. be unusually sensitive to criticism of their ideas.
     b. receive above-average scores on standard tests of intelligence.
     c. receive only average scores on standard tests of intelligence.
     d. be strongly motivated to attain fame and fortune.

Creativity and intelligence, p. 409
Medium, Factual/Definitional, Objective 8, Ans: b
66. The components of creativity include:
     a. impulsivity and empathy.
     b. expertise and a venturesome personality.
     c. competitiveness and dogmatism.
     d. imagination and extrinsic motivation.
     e. competitiveness and empathy.

Creativity and intelligence, p. 409
Difficult, Factual/Definitional, Objective 8, Ans: a
67. In one experiment, college students were either aware or unaware that experts would evaluate their creativity in constructing paper collages. This experiment most directly illustrated that creativity is facilitated by:
     a. intrinsic motivation.
     b. emotional intelligence.
     c. the Flynn effect.
     d. a venturesome personality.
     e. imaginative thinking skills.

Creativity and intelligence, p. 409
Medium, Conceptual, Objective 8, Ans: c
68. Cynthia, a high school English teacher, is particularly eager to promote creativity in her writing-class students. Which of the following reminders is likely to do most to accomplish her goal?
     a. "Your final essay will be evaluated by a well-known author."
     b. "Many of the best jobs demand good writing skills."
     c. "You are able to achieve new insights through your writing."
     d. "Admission to the most prestigious colleges demands some creative ability."

Creativity and intelligence, p. 409
Medium, Conceptual, Objective 8, Ans: e
69. Whenever Jacob reminded himself that his musical skills could earn him fame and fortune, the creativity of his musical performance suffered. This best illustrates that creativity may be inhibited by:
     a. the Flynn effect.
     b. a venturesome personality.
     c. the *g* factor.
     d. emotional intelligence.
     e. extrinsic motivation.

Genetic and environmental influences on intelligence, p. 411
Easy, Factual/Definitional, Objective 9, Ans: b
70. Research on the determinants of intelligence indicates that:
    a. concern over the nature-nurture issue has declined significantly during the past 10 years.
    b. both genes and environment have some influence on intelligence scores.
    c. there are no scientific methods for answering the nature-nurture question for a particular range of individuals or situations.
    d. there is no relationship between people's position on the nature-nurture issue and their social or political attitudes.

Genetic and environmental influences on intelligence, p. 411
Medium, Factual/Definitional, Objective 9, Ans: d
71. The similarity between intelligence scores of fraternal twins reared together is:
    a. equal to that between identical twins reared apart.
    b. less than that between children and their biological parents.
    c. equal to that between ordinary siblings reared together.
    d. less than that between identical twins reared apart.

Genetic and environmental influences on intelligence, p. 411
Difficult, Factual/Definitional, Objective 9, Ans: a
72. Which of the following observations provides the best evidence that intelligence test scores are influenced by environment?
    a. Fraternal twins are more similar in their intelligence scores than are ordinary siblings.
    b. The intelligence scores of children are positively correlated with those of their parents.
    c. Identical twins are more similar in their intelligence scores than are fraternal twins.
    d. The intelligence scores of siblings reared together are positively correlated.
    e. Different national groups have different average intelligence scores.

Genetic and environmental influences on intelligence, p. 412
Difficult, Factual/Definitional, Objective 9, Ans: a
73. The intelligence scores of adopted children are least likely to correlate positively with the intelligence scores of their:
    a. adoptive parents.
    b. biological parents.
    c. biologically related siblings.
    d. biologically unrelated siblings.

Genetic and environmental influences on intelligence, p. 412
Difficult, Factual/Definitional, Objective 9, Ans: c
74. With increasing age, identical twins' intelligence test scores become _____ positively correlated and adoptive siblings' scores become _____ positively correlated.
    a. more; more
    b. less; less
    c. more; less
    d. less; more

Genetic and environmental influences on intelligence, p. 412
Easy, Factual/Definitional, Objective 9, Ans: b

75. The extent to which differences in intelligence among a group of people is attributable to genetic factors is known as:
  a. the normal distribution.
  b. heritability.
  c. predictive validity.
  d. the Flynn effect.
  e. factor analysis.

Genetic and environmental influences on intelligence, pp. 412-413
Difficult, Factual/Definitional, Objective 9, Ans: c

76. The heritability of intelligence is greatest among genetically _____ individuals who have been raised in _____ environments.
  a. similar; similar
  b. similar; dissimilar
  c. dissimilar; similar
  d. dissimilar; dissimilar

Genetic and environmental influences on intelligence, p. 414
Difficult, Factual/Definitional, Objective 9, Ans: c

77. Research indicates that Head Start programs:
  a. fail to produce any short-term improvements in participants' mental skills.
  b. contribute to dramatic long-term gains in participants' intelligence test scores.
  c. are most beneficial to participants from disadvantaged home environments.
  d. are most beneficial to participants from intellectually stimulating home environments.

Genetic and environmental influences on intelligence, p. 414
Easy, Factual/Definitional, Objective 9, Ans: e

78. Children's intelligence test scores tend to _____ during the school year and _____ during the summer months.
  a. rise; rise
  b. remain unchanged; remain unchanged
  c. rise; remain unchanged
  d. remain unchanged; fall
  e. rise; fall

Ethnic similarities and differences, p. 415
Medium, Conceptual, Objective 10, Ans: e

79. The normal curve represents the distribution of U.S. intelligence test scores among:
  a. Asians.
  b. Whites.
  c. Hispanics.
  d. Blacks.
  e. all the above.

Ethnic similarities and differences, p. 415
Medium, Factual/Definitional, Objective 10, Ans: c
80.   Research on racial differences in intelligence indicates that:
   a.   American Blacks typically receive higher scores than Whites on nonverbal intelligence test questions.
   b.   there is currently no difference in the average SAT scores received by Blacks and Whites.
   c.   American Blacks average 10 points lower than Whites on intelligence tests.
   d.   among American Blacks those with African ancestry receive the highest intelligence scores.
   e.   all the above are true.

Ethnic similarities and differences, p. 416
Difficult, Factual/Definitional, Objective 10, Ans: d
81.   If the heritability of intelligence within both group A and group B is 100 percent, differences in average intelligence between these groups might result from:
   a.   environmental differences if the two groups are genetically similar.
   b.   genetic differences if the two groups have similar environments.
   c.   both genetic and environmental differences between the two groups.
   d.   any of the above.

Ethnic similarities and differences, p. 416
Medium, Factual/Definitional, Objective 10, Ans: a
82.   The Flynn effect is *least* likely to be explained in terms of:
   a.   changes in human genetic characteristics.
   b.   increasing educational opportunities.
   c.   reductions in family size.
   d.   improvements in infant nutrition.
   e.   changing communication technologies.

Ethnic similarities and differences, p. 417
Medium, Factual/Definitional, Objective 10, Ans: d
83.   The average intellectual aptitude gap between graduating white and black college graduates has been observed to _____ during their years in high school and to _____ their years in college.
   a.   decrease; decrease
   b.   increase; increase
   c.   decrease; increase
   d.   increase; decrease

Gender similarities and differences, p. 417
Easy, Conceptual, Objective 10, Ans: b
84.   On which of the following tasks are females most likely to perform as well or better than males?
   a.   playing checkers
   b.   interpreting poetry
   c.   playing video games
   d.   copying geometric designs

Gender similarities and differences, p. 417
Medium, Factual/Definitional, Objective 10, Ans: c

85. Among children with a very low level of verbal ability, there are _____ boys than girls; among children with a very high level of math problem-solving ability, there are _____ boys than girls.
     a. more; fewer
     b. fewer; more
     c. more; more
     d. fewer; fewer

Gender similarities and differences, p. 417
Difficult, Factual/Definitional, Objective 10, Ans: d

86. In terms of math computation, women perform _____ than men; in terms of solving math problems, women perform _____ than men.
     a. worse; worse
     b. better; better
     c. worse; better
     d. better; worse

Gender similarities and differences, p. 418
Medium, Factual/Definitional, Objective 10, Ans: d

87. On which of the following tasks are males most likely to outperform females?
     a. speed reading
     b. interpreting literature
     c. learning a foreign language
     d. mentally rotating three-dimensional objects

The question of bias, p. 419
Difficult, Conceptual, Objective 11, Ans: a

88. Intelligence tests are most likely to be considered culturally biased in terms of their:
     a. content validity.
     b. predictive validity.
     c. normal distribution.
     d. reliability.

The question of bias, p. 419
Medium, Factual/Definitional, Objective 11, Ans: b

89. Experts who defend intelligence tests against accusations of racial bias are most likely to note that racial differences in intelligence test scores:
     a. have increased in the past decade despite the introduction of less culturally biased test items.
     b. occur on nonverbal as well as verbal intelligence test subscales.
     c. are a clear indication that the heritability of intelligence approaches 100 percent.
     d. are just as significant as intelligence differences among members of a single race.

The question of bias, p. 419
Medium, Factual/Definitional, Objective 11, Ans: b
90.   Psychologists generally agree that intelligence test scores are _____ in terms of being sensitive to differences caused by cultural experiences and are _____ in terms of their predictive validity for different groups.
    a. biased; biased
    b. biased; not biased
    c. not biased; biased
    d. not biased; not biased

The question of bias, p. 419
Medium, Factual/Definitional, Objective 11, Ans: b
91.   Psychologists would be likely to agree that:
    a. intelligence tests have greater predictive validity for males than for females.
    b. intelligence tests have comparable predictive validity for Whites and Blacks.
    c. intelligence tests have less predictive validity for high school students than for college students.
    d. all the above are true.

CHAPTER 12

Motivation

Learning Objectives

Motivational Concepts (pp. 424-427)

1. Define motivation, and identify several theories of motivated behavior.

2. Describe Maslow's hierarchy of motives.

Hunger (pp. 427-434)

3. Describe the physiological determinants of hunger.

4. Discuss the impact of external incentives and culture on hunger, and describe the symptoms of anorexia nervosa and bulimia nervosa.

Sexual Motivation (pp. 435-447)

5. Describe how researchers have attempted to assess common sexual practices.

6. Describe the human sexual response cycle, and discuss the impact of both hormones and psychological factors on sexual motivation.

7. Identify factors contributing to increased rates of pregnancy and sexually transmitted disease among today's adolescents.

8. Describe research findings on the nature and dynamics of sexual orientation, and discuss the place of values in sex research.

The Need to Belong (pp. 448-449)

9. Describe the adaptive value of social attachments, and identify both healthy and unhealthy consequences of our need to belong.

Achievement Motivation (pp. 450-456)

10. Describe the nature and sources of achievement motivation.

11.   Distinguish between extrinsic and intrinsic achievement motivation, and identify factors that
      encourage each.

12.   Discuss how managers can create a motivated, productive, and satisfied work force, and
      identify various styles of management.

Motivation, p. 423
Medium, Conceptual, Objective 1, Ans: d

1.   Dr. Ligorano has devoted his professional life to researching the wants and needs that energize
     and direct behavior. His area of research has obviously been:
     a. adaptation.
     b. emotion.
     c. cognition.
     d. motivation.
     e. behavior genetics.

Instincts and evolutionary psychology, p. 424
Easy, Factual/Definitional, Objective 1, Ans: d

2.   An instinctive behavior is one that is:
     a. common to an entire species.
     b. developed without practice.
     c. rigidly patterned.
     d. characterized by all the above.

Instincts and evolutionary psychology, p. 424
Medium, Conceptual, Objective 1, Ans: e

3.   It is characteristic of robins to build nests. This provides an example of:
     a. intrinsic motivation.
     b. homeostasis.
     c. a drive.
     d. a need.
     e. an instinct.

Instincts and evolutionary psychology, p. 424
Medium, Factual/Definitional, Objective 1, Ans: a

4.   Contemporary psychologists are most likely to consider _____ to be a human instinct.
     a. infant sucking
     b. curiosity
     c. the need to belong
     d. religious ritual
     e. intrinsic motivation

Instincts and evolutionary psychology, p. 424
Easy, Factual/Definitional, Objective 1, Ans: e

5.   Instinct theory most clearly assumes that behavior is influenced by:
     a. homeostasis.
     b. extrinsic motivation.
     c. incentives.
     d. intrinsic motivation.
     e. genetic predispositions.

Drives and incentives, p. 425
Easy, Factual/Definitional, Objective 1, Ans: a
6.   Which of the following refers to a physiological state that usually triggers a state of
     motivational arousal?
     a. need
     b. homeostasis
     c. instinct
     d. drive
     e. incentive

Drives and incentives, p. 425
Medium, Conceptual, Objective 1, Ans: d
7.   Lack of body fluids is an example of a(n):
     a. drive.
     b. incentive.
     c. instinct.
     d. need.
     e. extrinsic motive.

Drives and incentives p. 425
Medium, Factual/Definitional, Objective 1, Ans: d
8.   A drive refers to:
     a. a rigidly patterned behavior characteristic of a species and developed without practice.
     b. a physiological need that usually triggers a state of motivational arousal.
     c. anything that is perceived as having positive or negative value in motivating behavior.
     d. an aroused or activated state that is often triggered by a physiological need.
     e. a desire to perform a behavior for its own sake.

Drives and incentives, p. 425
Difficult, Conceptual, Objective 1, Ans: b
9.   Lack of body fluids is to thirst as _____ is to _____.
     a. motivation; emotion
     b. need; drive
     c. homeostasis; hunger
     d. incentive; instinct
     e. pornography; lust

Drives and incentives, p. 425
Easy, Factual/Definitional, Objective 1, Ans: d
10. The body's tendency to maintain a constant internal state is known as:
     a. refractory period.
     b. instinct.
     c. intrinsic motivation.
     d. homeostasis.
     e. metabolism.

Drives and incentives, p. 425
Medium, Factual/Definitional, Objective 1, Ans: c

11. The term *homeostasis* literally means:
     a. "common to all."
     b. "unique to humans."
     c. "staying the same."
     d. "motivational dynamics."
     e. "constant stimulation."

Drives and incentives, p. 425
Medium, Conceptual, Objective 1, Ans: c

12. Perspiring and blood vessel constriction serve to:
     a. preserve body warmth.
     b. arouse drives.
     c. maintain homeostasis.
     d. lower the set point.

Drives and incentives, p. 425
Difficult, Factual/Definitional, Objective 1, Ans: b

13. Which theory most clearly emphasizes the importance of homeostasis in motivation?
     a. instinct theory
     b. drive-reduction theory
     c. arousal theory
     d. incentive theory

Drives and incentives, p. 425
Easy, Factual/Definitional, Objective 1, Ans: c

14. An incentive is a(n):
     a. rigidly patterned behavioral urge characteristic of an entire species.
     b. state of deprivation that triggers arousal.
     c. environmental stimulus that motivates behavior.
     d. state of arousal triggered by deprivation.
     e. desire to perform a behavior for its own sake.

Drives and incentives, p. 425
Difficult, Conceptual, Objective 1, Ans: c

15. Which of the following is most clearly *not* an example of an incentive?
     a. a crossword puzzle
     b. a pornographic movie
     c. low blood glucose level
     d. the smell of rotten eggs

Drives and incentives, p. 425
Medium, Factual/Definitional, Objective 1, Ans: c

16. The influence of personal and cultural experience on our wants and desires can most clearly be seen in the influence of _____ on motivation.
     a. instincts
     b. homeostasis
     c. incentives
     d. drives
     e. needs

Drives and incentives, p. 425
Difficult, Conceptual, Objective 1, Ans: b
17. A thick, juicy hamburger is to hunger as _____ is to _____.
    a. need; drive
    b. incentive; drive
    c. extrinsic motivation; intrinsic motivation
    d. homeostasis; thirst
    e. incentive; instinct

Drives and incentives, p. 425
Medium, Conceptual, Objective 1, Ans: e
18. Internal push is to external pull as _____ is to _____.
    a. incentive; extrinsic motivation
    b. task leadership; social leadership
    c. instinct; need
    d. need; drive
    e. need; incentive

Optimum arousal, p. 425
Easy, Factual/Definitional, Objective 1, Ans: d
19. The arousal theory of motivation would be most useful for explaining very young children's urge to:
    a. cry.
    b. sleep.
    c. eat.
    d. explore.

Optimum arousal, p. 425
Medium, Conceptual, Objective 1, Ans: a
20. The arousal theory of motivation would be most helpful for explaining why:
    a. recreational skydivers jump out of airplanes.
    b. hungry fishermen venture across dangerous ocean waters.
    c. starving prisoners are preoccupied with thoughts of food.
    d. sexually active teens learn to practice effective birth control.

Optimum arousal, p. 425
Difficult, Conceptual, Objective 1, Ans: d
21. The desire to avoid stress is to _____ theory as the desire to avoid boredom is to _____ theory.
    a. arousal; incentive
    b. instinct; drive-reduction
    c. incentive; instinct
    d. drive-reduction; arousal

A hierarchy of motives, p. 426
Easy, Conceptual, Objective 2, Ans: b

22.   Professor Sanford explains that the need for physical safety must be met before city dwellers will be motivated to form close friendships with fellow citizens. Professor Sanford is providing an example of:
a. task leadership.
b. a hierarchy of motives.
c. homeostasis.
d. extrinsic motivation.
e. instincts.

A hierarchy of motives, p. 426
Medium, Factual/Definitional, Objective 2, Ans: a

23.   According to Maslow, our need for _____ must be met before we are prompted to satisfy our need for _____.
a. food; love
b. self-esteem; adequate clothing
c. self-actualization; economic security
d. political freedom; economic security
e. religious fulfillment; adequate housing

A hierarchy of motives, p. 426
Difficult, Conceptual, Objective 2, Ans: b

24.   Maslow's hierarchy of needs suggests that people are unlikely to be motivated to obtain _____ if they are deprived of _____.
a. sexual gratification; self-esteem
b. good grades in school; love and safety
c. food and shelter; political freedom
d. friendship and love; religious fulfillment

Hunger, p. 428
Easy, Conceptual, Objective 3, Ans: c

25.   Prisoners of war placed on a semistarvation diet in which their food intake is cut in half are likely to:
a. lose half their original body weight.
b. show an increased interest in sex and politics.
c. spend a great deal of time daydreaming about food.
d. do all the above.

The physiology of hunger, p. 428
Medium, Factual/Definitional, Objective 3, Ans: c

26.   In looking at the relationship between hunger and conditions of the stomach, researchers have discovered that:
a. hunger cannot be experienced if one's stomach is full.
b. stomach contractions are necessary for experiencing hunger.
c. rats whose stomachs are removed continue to eat regularly.
d. humans and animals without stomachs lose the capacity to feel hungry.

The physiology of hunger: body chemistry, p. 429
Easy, Factual/Definitional, Objective 3, Ans: b
27. What two substances in the blood are critical in regulating hunger levels?
   a. adrenaline and insulin
   b. insulin and glucose
   c. sucrose and adrenaline
   d. glucose and estrogen

The physiology of hunger: body chemistry, p. 429
Medium, Factual/Definitional, Objective 3, Ans: d
28. An increase in insulin triggers a(n) _____ in blood glucose levels and a(n) _____ in feelings of hunger.
   a. decrease; decrease
   b. increase; increase
   c. increase; decrease
   d. decrease; increase

The physiology of hunger: the brain, p. 429
Easy, Factual/Definitional, Objective 3, Ans: a
29. Hunger controls are located within the:
   a. hypothalamus.
   b. medulla.
   c. temporal lobe.
   d. amygdala.
   e. hippocampus.

The physiology of hunger: the brain, p. 429
Medium, Factual/Definitional, Objective 3, Ans: c
30. Electrical stimulation of the _____ causes an animal to _____.
   a. lateral hypothalamus; stop eating
   b. ventromedial hypothalamus; start eating
   c. lateral hypothalamus; start eating
   d. ventromedial hypothalamus; overeat

The physiology of hunger: the brain, p. 429
Difficult, Factual/Definitional, Objective 3, Ans: c
31. Rats become very hungry when they experience _____ levels of _____.
   a. elevated; leptin
   b. reduced; insulin
   c. elevated; orexin
   d. reduced; estrogen

The physiology of hunger: the brain, p. 429
Difficult, Conceptual, Objective 3, Ans: a
32. Inhibition of hunger is to overeating as _____ is to _____.
   a. destruction of the lateral hypothalamus; destruction of the ventromedial hypothalamus
   b. destruction of the ventromedial hypothalamus; destruction of the lateral hypothalamus
   c. a low blood glucose level; a high blood insulin level
   d. a high blood glucose level; a low blood insulin level

The physiology of hunger: the brain, p. 429
Difficult, Factual/Definitional, Objective 3, Ans: a
33. Which of the following events would most likely cause an animal to eat voraciously and become obese?
     a. destruction of its ventromedial hypothalamus
     b. lowering its set point
     c. stimulation of its ventromedial hypothalamus
     d. destruction of its lateral hypothalamus

The physiology of hunger: the brain, pp. 429, 430
Difficult, Factual/Definitional, Objective 3, Ans: b
34. Increases in _____ increase hunger, whereas increases in _____ decrease hunger.
     a. insulin; orexin
     b. orexin; leptin
     c. leptin; glucose
     d. glucose; insulin

The physiology of hunger: the brain and set point, p. 430
Easy, Factual/Definitional, Objective 3, Ans: a
35. The specific body weight maintained automatically by most adults over long periods of time is known as the:
     a. set point.
     b. homeostatic constant.
     c. hypothalamic plateau.
     d. basal metabolic rate.

The physiology of hunger: the brain, p. 430
Medium, Conceptual, Objective 3, Ans: c
36. The concept of a set point best illustrates an explanation of motivation in terms of:
     a. instincts.
     b. incentives.
     c. homeostasis.
     d. refractory periods.

The physiology of hunger: the brain, pp. 429, 430
Difficult, Conceptual, Objective 3, Ans: b
37. As part of a research project, Dr. Smirnov destroys part of the ventromedial hypothalamus of a laboratory rat. This operation is most likely to:
     a. cause the animal to eat excessively until it becomes obese.
     b. lower the animal's set point for body weight.
     c. raise the animal's blood insulin levels.
     d. raise the animal's set point for body weight.

The physiology of hunger: the brain, p. 430
Medium, Factual/Definitional, Objective 3, Ans: c
38. When an organism's weight falls below its set point, the organism is likely to experience a(n) _____ in hunger and a(n) _____ in its basal metabolic rate.
     a. increase; increase
     b. decrease; decrease
     c. increase; decrease
     d. decrease; increase

External incentives and hunger, p. 431
Medium, Factual/Definitional, Objective 4, Ans: d

39. In the context of hunger motivation, an "external" person is an individual:
   a. who is particularly sensitive to the social norm of slimness.
   b. whose basal metabolic rate is more sensitive to exercise than to internal factors.
   c. whose dieting can be maintained only by external, social support.
   d. whose eating is triggered more by the presence of food stimuli than by internal factors.

External incentives and hunger, p. 431
Medium, Factual/Definitional, Objective 4, Ans: a

40. Judith Rodin observed that the sight and smell of a sizzling steak were especially likely to
   _____ the blood insulin levels of individuals identified as _____.
   a. increase; externals
   b. decrease; internals
   c. increase; internals
   d. decrease; externals

Taste preference: biology or culture?, p. 431
Medium, Factual/Definitional, Objective 4, Ans: c

41. As a meal progresses, people are increasingly likely to:
   a. experience a drop in their basal metabolic rate.
   b. enjoy the taste of each bite of food.
   c. chew longer on each bite of food.
   d. experience a rising blood insulin level.

Taste preference: biology or culture?, p. 431
Medium, Factual/Definitional, Objective 4, Ans: c

42. The consumption of carbohydrates is most likely to:
   a. lower the body's set point.
   b. decrease blood glucose levels.
   c. reduce tension and anxiety.
   d. prevent bulimia nervosa.

Eating disorders, p. 432
Medium, Conceptual, Objective 4, Ans: d

43. Chiara, a 14-year-old, is of average height but weighs only 80 pounds. She has lost 30 pounds over the last 6 months by eating very little and running 5 miles a day. She is determined not to become overweight and ignores her parents' suggestion that she should eat well-balanced meals. Chiara suffers from:
   a. bulimia nervosa.
   b. obesity.
   c. an abnormally low set point.
   d. anorexia nervosa.
   e. hypermetabolism.

Eating disorders, p. 432
Difficult, Factual/Definitional, Objective 4, Ans: b
44. Bulimia nervosa is characterized by:
     a. losses of 25 percent or more of normal weight.
     b. episodes of overeating followed by vomiting.
     c. the loss of regular menstrual periods.
     d. all the above.

Eating disorders, p. 432
Medium, Conceptual, Objective 4, Ans: b
45. Sixteen-year-old Jill loves ice cream and other rich foods, but she has become increasingly anxious about gaining too much weight. Jill frequently overeats and then intentionally vomits in an attempt to control her weight. Jill most clearly suffers from:
     a. hypermetabolism.
     b. bulimia nervosa.
     c. an abnormally high set point.
     d. anorexia nervosa.
     e. obesity.

Eating disorders, p. 432
Medium, Factual/Definitional, Objective 4, Ans: a
46. Bulimia nervosa is _____ common and _____ difficult to detect than anorexia nervosa.
     a. more; more
     b. less; less
     c. more; less
     d. less; more

Eating disorders, p. 432
Difficult, Factual/Definitional, Objective 4, Ans: c
47. Compared to the families of anorexia patients, the families of bulimia patients are _____ likely to be obese and _____ likely to be alcoholics.
     a. more; less
     b. less; more
     c. more; more
     d. less; less

Eating disorders, p. 433
Medium, Conceptual, Objective 4, Ans: c
48. If Marla is a typical female college student, it is most probable that she:
     a. would like to weigh more than what she thinks men prefer her to weigh.
     b. thinks she weighs less than what she would like to weigh.
     c. would like to weigh less than what men actually prefer her to weigh.
     d. thinks men prefer her to weigh more than they really do.

Describing sexual behavior, p. 435
Difficult, Factual/Definitional, Objective 5, Ans: c
49. Alfred Kinsey's study of American sexual practices in the 1940s indicated that:
     a. women who reported masturbating before marriage typically had difficulties experiencing orgasm after marriage.
     b. a majority of married women reported that they had never had an orgasm.
     c. a majority of both women and men reported that they masturbated.
     d. all the above were true.

Describing sexual behavior, p. 436
Medium, Factual/Definitional, Objective 5, Ans: d

50.   Recent surveys regarding marital infidelity in America suggest that:
       a. nearly half of all women and a small minority of men disapprove of extramarital sex.
       b. the majority of women and a minority of men disapprove of extramarital sex.
       c. the vast majority of women and about half of all men disapprove of extramarital sex.
       d. the vast majority of both men and women disapprove of extramarital sex.

The sexual response cycle, p. 436
Difficult, Factual/Definitional, Objective 6, Ans: c

51.   In a complete sexual response cycle, _____ immediately precedes _____.
       a. the excitement phase; orgasm
       b. orgasm; the excitement phase
       c. the plateau phase; orgasm
       d. the excitement phase; the resolution phase
       e. the plateau phase; the excitement phase

The sexual response cycle, p. 436
Medium, Factual/Definitional, Objective 6, Ans: c

52.   Research on the human sexual response cycle indicates that:
       a. blood pressure rates decrease during the plateau phase and increase during orgasm.
       b. conception is not possible without the occurrence of male orgasm.
       c. female orgasm increases the actual likelihood of conception.
       d. the resolution phase of the female sexual response cycle is especially lengthy following
          multiple orgasms.

The sexual response cycle, p. 437
Easy, Factual/Definitional, Objective 6, Ans: e

53.   The time span after orgasm during which a male cannot be aroused to another orgasm is called:
       a. the plateau phase.
       b. coitus interruptus.
       c. the set point.
       d. homeostasis.
       e. the refractory period.

The sexual response cycle, p. 437
Difficult, Factual/Definitional, Objective 6, Ans: c

54.   The male refractory period lasts anywhere from a few:
       a. seconds to a few minutes.
       b. minutes to a couple of hours.
       c. minutes to a day or more.
       d. hours to a week or more.

Hormones and sexual behavior, p. 437
Difficult, Factual/Definitional, Objective 6, Ans: a

55.   Research on sex hormones and animal sexual behavior indicates that:
       a. most female mammals are sexually receptive only at the time of ovulation.
       b. the level of testosterone is the most important factor determining the sexual receptivity of
          female mammals.
       c. castrated male rats show virtually no reduction in sexual motivation.
       d. sex hormones have very little influence on the sexual behavior of most female mammals.

Hormones and sexual behavior, p. 437
Easy, Conceptual, Objective 6, Ans: d

56.   Testosterone is to _____ as estrogen is to _____.
       a. hunger; sex
       b. premature ejaculation; impotence
       c. refractory period; orgasm
       d. males; females

Hormones and sexual behavior, p. 437
Medium, Factual/Definitional, Objective 6, Ans: c

57.   Research on sex hormones and human sexual behavior indicates that:
       a. the sexual desire of human females is much higher at the time of ovulation than at other
           times in the menstrual cycle.
       b. male sex offenders typically have lower-than-normal testosterone levels.
       c. adult males who suffer castration experience a decline in their sex drive.
       d. sexual interests are aroused by decreased testosterone levels in women and increased
           testosterone levels in men.

The psychology of sex: external stimuli, p. 438
Medium, Conceptual, Objective 6, Ans: b

58.   Mr. and Mrs. Kohl plan to spend their evening watching X-rated sex movies. Watching these
       films is most likely to increase:
       a. their appreciation of each other as highly desirable sexual partners.
       b. their levels of sexual arousal.
       c. their feelings that sexual promiscuity is morally wrong.
       d. Mr. Kohl's sexual arousal, while decreasing Mrs. Kohl's.
       e. Mrs. Kohl's estrogen levels and decrease Mr. Kohl's testosterone levels.

The psychology of sex: external stimuli, p. 438
Difficult, Conceptual, Objective 6, Ans: d

59.   Research suggests that after 18-year-old Ralph has looked at magazine pictures of sexually
       attractive women, he will be _____ likely to perceive _____ as attractive.
       a. more; himself
       b. more; his girlfriend
       c. less; himself
       d. less; his girlfriend

The psychology of sex: imagined stimuli, p. 439
Easy, Factual/Definitional, Objective 6, Ans: c

60.   Women are more likely than men to experience:
       a. genital arousal during their dreams.
       b. sexually vivid dreams that lead to orgasm.
       c. fantasies of being sexually taken by a passionate lover.
       d. fantasies of coercing someone else into having sex.

The psychology of sex: imagined stimuli, p. 439
Easy, Factual/Definitional, Objective 6, Ans: c

61.   Compared to women, men fantasize about sex _____ frequently and _____
       romantically.
       a. more; more
       b. less; less
       c. more; less
       d. less; more

Sexual disorders and therapy (Close-up), p. 439
Easy, Factual/Definitional, Objective 6, Ans: d
62.   The sexual disorders of _____ seem to involve a personality disorder.
   a. both men and women
   b. men but not women
   c. women but not men
   d. neither men nor women

Sexual disorders and therapy (Close-up), p. 439
Medium, Conceptual, Objective 6, Ans: b
63.   Amy, a 23-year-old married high school teacher, experiences orgasmic disorder. Recent
       research suggests that she is most likely to be helped by:
   a. drug therapy, which increases her estrogen level.
   b. therapy that trains her to enjoy her body and give herself orgasms.
   c. psychoanalysis, which uncovers the unconscious conflict causing her problem.
   d. nondirective therapy that raises her self-esteem.
   e. behavior therapy that encourages her to be sexually active only during ovulation.

Adolescent sexuality, p. 440
Medium, Factual/Definitional, Objective 7, Ans: d
64.   Sexual chastity is most common among teens in:
   a. Canada.
   b. Britain.
   c. the United States.
   d. China.

Adolescent sexuality, p. 441
Easy, Factual/Definitional, Objective 7, Ans: c
65.   A high sense of premarital sex guilt _____ sexual abstinence and _____ planned
       contraceptive use.
   a. encourages; encourages
   b. discourages; discourages
   c. encourages; discourages
   d. discourages; encourages

Adolescent sexuality, p. 441
Easy, Factual/Definitional, Objective 7, Ans: d
66.   Premarital sexual activity is higher among American teens who:
   a. have college-educated rather than high school-educated parents.
   b. frequently rather than seldom attend religious services.
   c. earn high rather than low grades in school.
   d. consume rather than abstain from alcohol.

Adolescent sexuality, p. 441
Medium, Factual/Definitional, Objective 7, Ans: d
67.   Research on American adolescent sexuality and pregnancy indicates that:
   a. high sex guilt can inhibit planning for birth control.
   b. sexually active teens are usually alcohol-using teens.
   c. fewer than half of adolescents can identify the safe and risky times of the menstrual cycle.
   d. all the above are true.

Adolescent sexuality, p. 441
Easy, Factual/Definitional, Objective 7, Ans: d

68. Teen sexual promiscuity contributes to:
    a. premature infertility.
    b. cervical cancer.
    c. HIV transmission.
    d. all the above

Sexual orientation, p. 442
Easy, Factual/Definitional, Objective 8, Ans: e

69. Our sexual attraction toward members of either the same sex or the opposite sex is called our:
    a. intrinsic motivation.
    b. gender identity.
    c. extrinsic motivation.
    d. sexual identity.
    e. sexual orientation.

Sexual orientation, p. 442
Medium, Factual/Definitional, Objective 8, Ans: d

70. Most homosexual people first begin thinking of themselves as gay or lesbian during:
    a. early childhood.
    b. middle childhood.
    c. late adolescence.
    d. early adulthood.

Sexual orientation, p. 442
Medium, Factual/Definitional, Objective 8, Ans: a

71. The proportion of adult Americans that occasionally or frequently engage in homosexual
    activity is roughly _____ percent.
    a. 3 or 4
    b. 10 or 11
    c. 25 or 26
    d. 33 or 34

Understanding sexual orientation, p. 443
Medium, Conceptual, Objective 8, Ans: e

72. Emma and Nanette are sisters and both are lesbians. According to the research on the origins of
    sexual orientation, it is highly likely that:
    a. they grew up without any brothers.
    b. they have higher testosterone levels than most adult women.
    c. they were sexually abused in childhood by a close female relative.
    d. their father was not present during their childhood.
    e. none of the above is true.

Understanding sexual orientation, p. 444
Medium, Factual/Definitional, Objective 8, Ans: d

73. The incidence of male homosexuality has been found to be slightly higher than usual among:
    a. physicians.
    b. professional athletes.
    c. residents of small villages.
    d. men who have older brothers.

The brain and sexual orientation, p. 444
Medium, Factual/Definitional, Objective 8, Ans: c

74. A neural cell cluster located in the _____ was discovered by _____ to be larger in heterosexual than in homosexual men.
    a. cerebellum; Kinsey
    b. amygdala; Masters
    c. hypothalamus; Le Vay
    d. medulla; Johnson
    e. thalamus; Dorner

Genes and sexual orientation, p. 445
Medium, Factual/Definitional, Objective 8, Ans: e

75. Research on the causes of homosexuality suggests that:
    a. homosexuality develops most readily in families with domineering mothers and weak, ineffectual fathers.
    b. homosexuality arises from a fear of members of the opposite sex.
    c. male homosexuality results from abnormally high levels of testosterone in the blood.
    d. childhood sexual victimization contributes strongly to homosexual development.
    e. sexual orientation may be genetically influenced.

Genes and sexual orientation, p. 445
Medium, Factual/Definitional, Objective 8, Ans: a

76. The fraternal twin brothers of homosexual men experience an _____ rate of homosexuality. The fraternal twin sisters of homosexual women experience an _____ rate of homosexuality.
    a. above average; above average
    b. average; average
    c. above average; average
    d. average; above average

Prenatal hormones and sexual orientation, p. 445
Difficult, Factual/Definitional, Objective 8, Ans: e

77. Evidence that homosexual men have spatial abilities like those typical of heterosexual women is most consistent with the hypothesized linkage between sexual orientation and:
    a. blood glucose levels.
    b. artistic skills.
    c. hypothalamic activity.
    d. the refractory period.
    e. prenatal hormones.

Sex and human values, p. 446
Medium, Factual/Definitional, Objective 8, Ans: d

78. A review of sex research and education indicates that:
    a. sexual activity is largely a medical issue, not a moral issue.
    b. public standards of morality are irrelevant to something as private and personal as human sexual behavior.
    c. scientific methods prevent sex research from being influenced by psychologists' personal values.
    d. the labels researchers use to describe sexual behavior are often value-laden.

The need to belong, p. 448
Medium, Conceptual, Objective 9, Ans: b
79. Those who trace the origins of social bonding to its survival value are most likely to agree that the need to belong is:
a. an incentive.
b. genetically influenced.
c. an instinct.
d. an extrinsic motive.
e. Maslow's highest-level need.

The need to belong, p. 448
Medium, Factual/Definitional, Objective 9, Ans: e
80. Our _____ serves as a gauge of how socially accepted we feel.
a. set point
b. basal metabolic rate
c. sexual response cycle
d. intrinsic motivation
e. self-esteem

The need to belong, p. 449
Easy, Conceptual, Objective 9, Ans: c
81. Sheila is more fearful of loneliness than of remaining in a physically abusive relationship with her boyfriend. This best illustrates the potentially harmful impact of _____ needs.
a. self-actualization
b. achievement
c. belongingness
d. sexual
e. safety

Identifying achievement motivation, p. 450
Easy, Conceptual, Objective 10, Ans: c
82. At the age of 13, Jeff plays tennis for nearly 3 hours every day because he wants to become the best player he can possibly be. His goal and behavior most clearly suggest that he has a high level of:
a. extrinsic motivation.
b. task leadership.
c. achievement motivation.
d. social leadership.
e. self-esteem.

Identifying achievement motivation, p. 450
Difficult, Factual/Definitional, Objective 10, Ans: a
83. In order to measure the strength of the need for achievement, McClelland and Atkinson asked subjects to:
a. invent stories about ambiguous pictures.
b. indicate their eagerness to engage in easy, moderately challenging, or difficult tasks.
c. draw pictures of men and women engaging in different behaviors.
d. indicate their current annual income and the annual income they expected to earn in the future.

Identifying achievement motivation, p. 450
Medium, Factual/Definitional, Objective 10, Ans: b

84. In a ring-toss game, people with a high need for achievement prefer to stand _____ the stake on which the ring is to be tossed.
    a. close to
    b. at an intermediate distance from
    c. far away from
    d. either close to or far from

Identifying achievement motivation, p. 450
Medium, Conceptual, Objective 10, Ans: c

85. Creative writers with a high need for achievement would be especially motivated to attempt a literary project that involved _____ risk of failure.
    a. no
    b. a very low
    c. a moderate
    d. a very high

Sources of achievement motivation, p. 451
Medium, Conceptual, Objective 10, Ans: c

86. Which mother is most likely to have a child who is high in achievement motivation?
    a. Gloria, who is very permissive with her 8-year-old son and pays little attention to his performance in school
    b. Milly, who sets high goals for her 4-year-old daughter and punishes her when she fails
    c. Lalita, who encourages her 6-year-old daughter to be independent and praises her when she masters a new task at school
    d. Nicole, who does not expect her 7-year-old son to assume new responsibilities until he says he is ready and then quickly helps him if he experiences any frustration

Sources of achievement motivation, p. 451
Medium, Conceptual, Objective 10, Ans: b

87. Attributing good grades in school to one's own academic efforts and abilities serves as an important _____ source of academic achievement motivation.
    a. instinctive
    b. cognitive
    c. extrinsic
    d. homeostatic
    e. emotional

Intrinsic motivation and achievement, p. 451
Medium, Factual/Definitional, Objective 11, Ans: e

88. Intrinsic motivation refers to:
    a. the body's tendency to maintain a constant internal state.
    b. a physiological need that triggers arousal.
    c. a state of arousal triggered by physiological need.
    d. a rigidly patterned behavioral urge characteristic of an entire species.
    e. a desire to perform a behavior for its own sake.

Intrinsic motivation and achievement, p. 451
Easy, Conceptual, Objective 11, Ans: d

89.   Because Yuri was curious about human behavior, he enrolled in an introductory psychology course. George registered because he heard it was an easy course that would boost his grade point average. In this instance, Yuri's behavior was a reflection of _____, whereas George's behavior was a reflection of _____.
       a. theory X; theory Y
       b. Maslow's lower-level motives; Maslow's higher-level motives
       c. task leadership; social leadership
       d. intrinsic motivation; extrinsic motivation

Intrinsic motivation and achievement, pp. 451-452
Medium, Conceptual, Objective 11, Ans: e

90.   The skyrocketing salaries of major league baseball players are most likely to reduce the athletes':
       a. achievement motivation.
       b. social leadership.
       c. extrinsic motivation.
       d. task leadership.
       e. intrinsic motivation.

Intrinsic motivation and achievement, p. 452
Easy, Conceptual, Objective 11, Ans: b

91.   Which of the following individuals best illustrates an extrinsic religious motivation?
       a. Dorothy, who donates money to charity in order to affirm her spiritual values
       b. Rhonda, who attends religious services in order to promote her business contacts
       c. Judy, who reads devotional materials in order to understand the meaning of life
       d. Carol, who prays in order to increase her awareness of God

Motivating people: cultivate intrinsic motivation, p. 453
Medium, Conceptual, Objective 12, Ans: d

92.   At the Pamuk Manufacturing Company, employees are under constant surveillance by supervisors in order to ensure that every worker contributes his or her fair share to company productivity. This is most likely to _____ the employees' _____.
       a. increase; achievement motivation
       b. decrease; productivity
       c. increase; self-esteem
       d. decrease; intrinsic motivation

Motivating people: cultivate intrinsic motivation, p. 453
Medium, Factual/Definitional, Objective 12, Ans: b

93.   Extrinsic rewards are not likely to reduce intrinsic motivation if they are:
       a. large.
       b. informative.
       c. frequently given.
       d. perceived as manipulative.

Motivating people: cultivate intrinsic motivation, p. 453
Difficult, Conceptual, Objective 12, Ans: d
94.   Informative reward is to controlling reward as _____ is to _____.
a. need; incentive
b. incentive; drive
c. social leadership; task leadership
d. intrinsic motivation; extrinsic motivation

Motivating people: choose an appropriate leadership style, p. 454
Easy, Conceptual, Objective 12, Ans: d
95.   Managers with a social leadership style would be most likely to:
a. ensure that individual employees contribute their fair share to group projects.
b. discourage employees from critically discussing controversial company policies.
c. inform employees of the exact deadlines for the completion of work projects.
d. mediate a personal dispute between two argumentative employees.
e. provide employees with relatively easy work assignments.

Motivating people: choose an appropriate leadership style, p. 454
Medium, Factual/Definitional, Objective 12, Ans: a
96.   In a group discussion, women are _____ likely than men to express support for others' opinions. As group leaders, women are _____ likely than men to promote a democratic leadership style.
a. more; more
b. less; more
c. less; less
d. more; less

Motivating people: choose an appropriate leadership style, p. 454
Medium, Factual/Definitional, Objective 12, Ans: b
97.   In everyday behavior, men are *less* likely than women to:
a. stare at others.
b. smile at others.
c. interrupt others.
d. initiate touching others.

Motivating people: choose an appropriate leadership style, p. 454
Easy, Conceptual, Objective 12, Ans: a
98.   During the course of a conversation between Lola, Martha, and Gus, which of the following events is most likely to occur?
a. Gus interrupts Lola.
b. Lola interrupts Martha.
c. Martha interrupts Gus.
d. All the above are equally likely to occur.

Motivating people: choose an appropriate leadership style, p. 454
Medium, Factual/Definitional, Objective 12, Ans: b
99.   Female managers more often excel at _____ than do their male counterparts; male
      managers more often excel at _____ than do their female counterparts.
      a.   extrinsic motivation; intrinsic motivation
      b.   social leadership; task leadership
      c.   directive management; participative management
      d.   mastery orientation; work orientation

Motivating people: choose an appropriate leadership style, p. 455
Medium, Factual/Definitional, Objective 12, Ans: d
100. Theory X managers are more likely than theory Y managers to assume that employees are
      motivated by:
      a.   challenging work assignments.
      b.   satisfying social relations.
      c.   a need for self-esteem.
      d.   a desire for higher wages.

Motivating people: choose an appropriate leadership style, p. 455
Difficult, Conceptual, Objective 12, Ans: b
101. Theory X is to _____ as theory Y is to _____.
      a.   intrinsic motivation; extrinsic motivation
      b.   directive management; participative management
      c.   social leadership; task leadership
      d.   informative rewards; controlling rewards

Motivating people: choose an appropriate leadership style, p. 455
Medium, Conceptual, Objective 12, Ans: a
102. Intrinsic motivation is to _____ as extrinsic motivation is to _____.
      a.   theory Y; theory X
      b.   directive management; participative management
      c.   task leadership; social leadership
      d.   controlling reward; informative reward

Motivating people: choose an appropriate leadership style, p. 455
Difficult, Conceptual, Objective 12, Ans: b
103. Theory X is to _____ as theory Y is to _____.
      a.   social leadership; task leadership
      b.   Maslow's lower-level needs; Maslow's higher-level needs
      c.   participative management; directive management
      d.   informative reward; controlling reward
      e.   intrinsic motivation; extrinsic motivation

Motivating people: choose an appropriate leadership style, p. 455
Easy, Factual/Definitional, Objective 12, Ans: c
104. Employee achievement motivation is most likely to be facilitated by:
      a.   task leadership.
      b.   directive management.
      c.   participative management.
      d.   theory X managers.

Motivating people: choose an appropriate leadership style, p. 455
Difficult, Conceptual, Objective 12, Ans: d

105. Directive management is to _____ as participative management is to _____.
      a. informative reward; controlling reward
      b. social leadership; task leadership
      c. theory Y; theory X
      d. extrinsic motivation; intrinsic motivation

Motivating people: choose an appropriate leadership style, p. 455
Difficult, Conceptual, Objective 12, Ans: b

106. Maslow's higher-level needs are to _____ as Maslow's lower-level needs are to _____.
      a. theory X; theory Y
      b. participative management; directive management
      c. task leadership; social leadership
      d. controlling reward; informative reward
      e. extrinsic motivation; intrinsic motivation

Motivating people: choose an appropriate leadership style, p. 455
Medium, Factual/Definitional, Objective 12, Ans: a

107. Theory Y managers are most likely to _____ employees' _____.
      a. increase; intrinsic motivation
      b. decrease; achievement motivation
      c. increase; fear of failure
      d. decrease; productivity

Motivating people: choose an appropriate leadership style, p. 455
Medium, Factual/Definitional, Objective 12, Ans: c

108. Theory Y managers are more likely than theory X managers to:
      a. closely observe individual employees in order to monitor their productivity.
      b. discourage employees from critically discussing controversial company policies.
      c. give employees a high degree of responsibility for developing their own work procedures.
      d. remind employees of the exact deadlines for the completion of work projects.

Motivating people: choose an appropriate leadership style, p. 455
Medium, Conceptual, Objective 12, Ans: a

109. In terms of Maslow's motivational hierarchy, the higher-level needs of employees are most likely to be satisfied by:
      a. theory Y managers.
      b. monetary incentives.
      c. task leadership.
      d. directive management.

CHAPTER **13**

Emotion

Learning Objectives

Theories of Emotion (pp. 459-465)

1. Identify the three components of emotions and contrast the James-Lange and Cannon-Bard theories of emotion.

2. Describe Schachter's two-factor theory of emotion, and discuss evidence suggesting that some emotional reactions involve no conscious thought.

3. Describe how emotions can be differentiated along the dimensions of valence and arousal level.

The Physiology of Emotion (pp. 465-470)

4. Describe the physiological changes that occur during emotional arousal, and discuss the relationship between arousal and performance.

5. Describe the relationship between physiological states and specific emotions, and discuss the effectiveness of the polygraph in detecting lies.

Expressing Emotion (pp. 470-476)

6. Describe some nonverbal indicators of emotion, and discuss the extent to which people from different cultures display and interpret facial expressions of emotion in a similar manner.

7. Describe the effects of facial expressions on emotional experience.

Experiencing Emotion (pp. 477-487)

8. Discuss the significance of environmental and biological factors in the acquisition of fear.

9. Discuss the catharsis hypothesis, and identify some of the advantages and disadvantages of openly expressing anger.

10. Identify some potential causes and consequences of happiness, and describe how happiness is influenced by our prior experiences and by others' attainments.

Theories of emotion, p. 460
Easy, Factual/Definitional, Objective 1, Ans: b
1. Which of the following is *not* one of the basic components of emotion identified in the text?
   a. physiological arousal
   b. pupil contraction
   c. conscious experience
   d. expressive behavior

The James-Lange theory, p. 460
Easy, Factual/Definitional, Objective 1, Ans: c
2. Which theory suggests that the experience of emotion results from an awareness of one's own physiological responses to an emotion-arousing event?
   a. the Cannon-Bard theory
   b. the opponent-process theory
   c. the James-Lange theory
   d. the adaptation-level theory

The James-Lange theory, p. 460
Medium, Conceptual, Objective 1, Ans: b
3. Ten-year-old Kevin tells his friend, "You know you are scared when your knees knock, your hands sweat, and your stomach is in knots." This statement best illustrates the:
   a. Cannon-Bard theory.
   b. James-Lange theory.
   c. catharsis hypothesis.
   d. opponent-process theory.
   e. adaptation-level principle.

The James-Lange theory, p. 460
Difficult, Factual/Definitional, Objective 1, Ans: d
4. Which theory would be most threatened by evidence that highly similar patterns of physiological activity are associated with uniquely different emotional states?
   a. the two-factor theory
   b. the Cannon-Bard theory
   c. the opponent-process theory
   d. the James-Lange theory

The James-Lange theory, p. 460
Medium, Conceptual, Objective 1, Ans: d
5. The suggestion that "a happy face creates a merry soul" is most consistent with the:
   a. Cannon-Bard theory.
   b. catharsis hypothesis.
   c. adaptation-level principle.
   d. James-Lange theory.
   e. opponent-process theory.

The James-Lange theory, p. 460
Medium, Conceptual, Objective 1, Ans: d
6. The James-Lange theory is most consistent with the suggestion that:
   a. big fish are happiest in small ponds.
   b. behind dark clouds the sun still shines.
   c. expressing angry feelings reduces rage.
   d. a gloomy face saddens the soul.
   e. going through the motions eliminates emotions.

The James-Lange theory, pp. 460-461
Difficult, Factual/Definitional, Objective 1, Ans: d
7.   Which of the following research findings is consistent with the James-Lange theory of emotion?
a. Facial expressions intensify felt emotion.
b. Distinct patterns of physiological activity are associated with distinctly different emotions.
c. People with neck-level spinal cord injuries experience a considerable decrease in emotion.
d. All the above are consistent with the James-Lange theory.

The Cannon-Bard theory, p. 460
Easy, Factual/Definitional, Objective 1, Ans: c
8.   According to the Cannon-Bard theory, the experience of an emotion:
a. depends on the intensity of body arousal.
b. can occur only after body arousal.
c. occurs simultaneously with body arousal.
d. precedes body arousal.

The Cannon-Bard theory, p. 460
Medium, Conceptual, Objective 1, Ans: b
9.   According to the Cannon-Bard theory, bodily arousal is to the subjective awareness of emotion as the _____ is to the _____.
a. parasympathetic nervous system; thalamus
b. sympathetic nervous system; cortex
c. thalamus; hypothalamus
d. cerebellum; cortex
e. parasympathetic nervous system; sympathetic nervous system

The Cannon-Bard theory, p. 460
Medium, Factual/Definitional, Objective 1, Ans: d
10. According to the Cannon-Bard theory:
a. you experience fear because your heart begins pounding.
b. your heart begins pounding because you experience fear.
c. both of the above are true.
d. neither a. nor b. is true.

The Cannon-Bard theory, pp. 460-461
Difficult, Factual/Definitional, Objective 1, Ans: d
11. Evidence that neck-level spinal cord injuries reduce the intensity with which people experience certain emotions most directly refutes the:
a. James-Lange theory.
b. catharsis hypothesis.
c. two-factor theory.
d. Cannon-Bard theory.

The James-Lange and Cannon-Bard theories, pp. 460-461
Difficult, Factual/Definitional, Objective 1, Ans: a
12. Hohmann discovered that the _____ an individual's spinal cord injury, the more feelings of anger tended to _____ in intensity following the injury.
a. higher; decrease
b. higher; increase
c. lower; decrease
d. lower; increase

Schachter's two-factor theory of emotion, p. 462
Easy, Factual/Definitional, Objective 2, Ans: d

13. Which theory states that emotion results from a conscious interpretation of our bodily arousal?
   a. adaptation-level
   b. opponent-process
   c. Cannon-Bard
   d. two-factor

Schachter's two-factor theory of emotion, pp. 460, 462
Medium, Factual/Definitional, Objective 2, Ans: a

14. Both the James-Lange and the two-factor theories of emotion maintain that:
   a. the experience of emotion grows from an awareness of our bodily arousal.
   b. distinct physiological differences exist among the emotions.
   c. some emotions can be experienced apart from cognition.
   d. all the above are true.

Schachter's two-factor theory of emotion, p. 462
Medium, Conceptual, Objective 2, Ans: e

15. When students perceive the arousal that accompanies test-taking as energizing rather than debilitating, they experience much less anxiety. This is best understood in terms of the:
   a. relative deprivation principle.
   b. James-Lange theory.
   c. adaptation-level principle.
   d. opponent-process theory.
   e. two-factor theory.

Schachter's two-factor theory of emotion, p. 462
Medium, Conceptual, Objective 2, Ans: b

16. John experienced excessive fear while flying because he interpreted his rapid heart rate, shallow breathing, and heavy perspiration as a reaction to the imminent danger of an air accident. When his psychotherapist convinced him that this physical arousal was simply a harmless reaction to acceleration, cabin pressure, and confined space, his fear of flying was greatly reduced. The reduction in John's fear is best understood in terms of the:
   a. James-Lange theory.
   b. two-factor theory.
   c. adaptation-level principle.
   d. relative deprivation principle.
   e. catharsis hypothesis.

Schachter's two-factor theory of emotion, p. 462
Medium, Factual/Definitional, Objective 2, Ans: b

17. Which theory can best explain the results of the experiment in which subjects were injected with epinephrine prior to spending time with either a euphoric or an irritated person?
   a. the Cannon-Bard theory
   b. the two-factor theory
   c. the James-Lange theory
   d. the opponent-process theory

Schachter's two-factor theory of emotion, p. 462
Medium, Factual/Definitional, Objective 2, Ans: c

18. College men given injections of epinephrine felt happiest if they were told the injection would produce _____ and if they were in the company of a(n) _____ person.
    a. arousal; euphoric
    b. arousal; irritated
    c. no effects; euphoric
    d. no effects; irritated

Schachter's two-factor theory of emotion, p. 462
Medium, Conceptual, Objective 2, Ans: d

19. Marsha was emotionally aroused by a TV horror movie. She became extremely angry when her younger brother momentarily blocked her view of the screen. When her movie viewing was interrupted by a phone call from her boyfriend, however, she experienced unusually intense romantic feelings. Marsha's emotional reactivity to her brother and her boyfriend is best explained by the:
    a. catharsis hypothesis.
    b. James-Lange theory.
    c. adaptation-level principle.
    d. two-factor theory.
    e. Cannon-Bard theory.

Schachter's two-factor theory of emotion, p. 462
Difficult, Factual/Definitional, Objective 2, Ans: c

20. In anger-provoking situations, sexually aroused people experience more intense hostility than those who are not sexually aroused. This is best explained by the:
    a. Cannon-Bard theory.
    b. James-Lange theory.
    c. two-factor theory.
    d. catharsis hypothesis.
    e. relative deprivation principle.

Must cognition precede emotion?, pp. 463-464
Medium, Factual/Definitional, Objective 2, Ans: a

21. In their dispute over the nature of emotion, Zajonc and Lazarus disagree on whether:
    a. cognition must precede emotion.
    b. the physiological states underlying specific emotions are distinguishable.
    c. genetic or environmental factors are more important in shaping our emotions.
    d. intensity and valence are the basic dimensions of our emotional experience.

Must cognition precede emotion?, p. 463
Difficult, Factual/Definitional, Objective 2, Ans: d

22. Evidence that visual input is routed from the thalamus directly to an emotional control center in the brain has been used to support the claim that:
    a. emotion always involves a visual stimulus.
    b. emotion tends to bias our perceptions of the world.
    c. a visual stimulus always triggers a stronger emotional response than does an auditory stimulus.
    d. some emotional reactions may occur without conscious thinking.
    e. blind people's expressions of emotion must be learned.

Must cognition precede emotion?, p. 464
Difficult, Factual/Definitional, Objective 2, Ans: c

23. Which of the following emotional reactions is most likely to precede any conscious thinking?
     a. guilt
     b. love
     c. fear
     d. happiness

Two dimensions of emotion, p. 464
Easy, Factual/Definitional, Objective 3, Ans: c

24. The emotion of sadness is characterized by negative valence and _____ arousal.
     a. high
     b. positive
     c. low
     d. negative

Two dimensions of emotion, p. 464
Medium, Conceptual, Objective 3, Ans: b

25. As a seasoned professor, Dr. Jones experiences his prelecture arousal as a sign that he is ready for an effective performance. As a new professor, Dr. Lovelace experiences her prelecture arousal as a sign that she is inadequately prepared for her performance. The emotional experiences of the two professors are likely to differ the most with respect to:
     a. intensity.
     b. valence.
     c. duration.
     d. adaptation level.

Two dimensions of emotion, p. 464
Easy, Conceptual, Objective 3, Ans: e

26. Fear is to terror as anger is to:
     a. shame.
     b. grief.
     c. guilt.
     d. pain.
     e. rage.

The physiology of emotion: arousal, pp. 465-466
Difficult, Conceptual, Objective 4, Ans: c

27. An inexperienced pilot prepares for an emergency landing after her single-engine plane loses power. Her increasing level of emotional arousal is likely to be accompanied by:
     a. a decreased respiration rate.
     b. constriction of her pupils.
     c. increases in her blood sugar level.
     d. increased salivation.
     e. all the above.

The physiology of emotion: arousal, p. 466
Easy, Factual/Definitional, Objective 4, Ans: c

28. During a state of emotional arousal, the adrenal glands release _____ into the bloodstream.
    a. insulin
    b. acetylcholine
    c. epinephrine
    d. glucose
    e. testosterone

The physiology of emotion: arousal, p. 466
Easy, Factual/Definitional, Objective 4, Ans: a

29. Which division of the nervous system arouses the body and mobilizes its energy in emotionally stressful situations?
    a. sympathetic
    b. central
    c. somatic
    d. parasympathetic

The physiology of emotion: arousal, p. 466
Easy, Conceptual, Objective 4, Ans: b

30. Walking home from work late one night, Tilly suddenly hears footsteps behind her. Her heart pounds, her muscles tense, and her mouth goes dry. These bodily responses are activated by which nervous system?
    a. central
    b. sympathetic
    c. parasympathetic
    d. somatic

The physiology of emotion: arousal, p. 466
Medium, Conceptual, Objective 4, Ans: d

31. Turning in at her street, Heidi saw six fire trucks in front of her apartment building. Her heart beat wildly until someone yelled, "Just a false alarm." Her pulse then began to return to normal, due to the action of her _____ nervous system.
    a. central
    b. somatic
    c. sympathetic
    d. parasympathetic

The physiology of emotion: arousal, p. 466
Difficult, Factual/Definitional, Objective 4, Ans: b

32. Activation of the parasympathetic nervous system _____ heart rate and _____ digestion.
    a. accelerates; slows
    b. slows; accelerates
    c. slows; slows
    d. accelerates; accelerates

The physiology of emotion: arousal, pp. 465-466
Difficult, Conceptual, Objective 4, Ans: a

33. The sympathetic nervous system is to the parasympathetic nervous system as _____ is to
    _____.
    a. inhibition of digestion; acceleration of digestion
    b. decreasing heart rate; increasing heart rate
    c. decreasing blood sugar; increasing blood sugar
    d. contraction of pupils; dilation of pupils

The physiology of emotion: arousal, p. 466
Medium, Conceptual, Objective 4, Ans: a

34. Sondra will be taking an entrance exam for law school this afternoon. Her performance is likely
    to be _____ if during the exam her physiological arousal is _____.
    a. best; moderate
    b. worst; moderate
    c. mediocre; moderate
    d. best; very low
    e. best; very high

The physiology of emotion: arousal, p. 466
Difficult, Factual/Definitional, Objective 4, Ans: c

35. The level of arousal typically associated with optimal performance tends to be _____ on
    tasks that are _____.
    a. lower; relatively easy
    b. higher; relatively difficult
    c. higher; well learned
    d. lower; well learned

The physiology of emotion: arousal, p. 466
Difficult, Conceptual, Objective 4, Ans: b

36. Relatively high levels of physiological arousal would be most likely to improve performance
    in a:
    a. violin recital.
    b. bicycle race.
    c. chess tournament.
    d. basketball game.
    e. debate.

The physiology of emotion: arousal, p. 466
Difficult, Conceptual, Objective 4, Ans: c

37. Nikolaus, a high school junior, is on both the track and golf teams. A high level of
    physiological arousal is likely to _____ his running the 100-meter dash and _____ his
    accuracy in making long putts.
    a. have no effect on; interfere with
    b. enhance; enhance
    c. enhance; interfere with
    d. interfere with; enhance
    e. enhance; have no effect on

Physiological states accompanying specific emotions, p. 467
Easy, Factual/Definitional, Objective 5, Ans: b
38.   The emotions of anger and fear involve similar:
a. subjective thoughts and experiences.
b. patterns of autonomic arousal.
c. hormone secretions.
d. patterns of brain activity.

Physiological states accompanying specific emotions, p. 467
Medium, Conceptual, Objective 5, Ans: a
39.   Dr. Jacobs is electrically stimulating parts of a cat's brain. A cat that becomes enraged—pupils dilated, claws out, hissing—has most likely been stimulated in the:
a. limbic system.
b. cerebellum.
c. thalamus.
d. medulla.

Physiological states accompanying specific emotions, p. 467
Medium, Factual/Definitional, Objective 5, Ans: c
40.   Research on the physiological states accompanying specific emotions indicates that:
a. each emotion has a unique pattern of sympathetic nervous system activity.
b. emotions such as happiness and surprise are accompanied by different blood pressure levels.
c. different emotions arise through different brain circuits.
d. every emotion has precisely the same pattern of limbic system activity.

Physiological states accompanying specific emotions, p. 467
Difficult, Factual/Definitional, Objective 5, Ans: b
41.   When people experience positive emotions, the _____ hemisphere of the brain becomes _____ electrically active.
a. right; more
b. left; more
c. right; less
d. left; less

Physiological states accompanying specific emotions, p. 467
Medium, Conceptual, Objective 5, Ans: b
42.   Emotional disgust is to emotional delight as _____ is to _____.
a. blood sugar decrease; blood sugar increase
b. right hemisphere activation; left hemisphere activation
c. sympathetic nervous system; parasympathetic nervous system
d. the relative deprivation principle; the adaptation-level principle

Thinking critically about lie detection (Box), p. 468
Easy, Conceptual, Objective 5, Ans: c
43.   Mr. Robinson, an employee of the U.S. Defense Department, is strongly suspected of selling classified information to China. He has denied the allegation. To determine whether he is lying, the Defense Department is most likely to invite Mr. Robinson to take a(n) _____ test.
a. electrocardiograph
b. electroencephalograph
c. polygraph
d. myograph
e. tomograph

Thinking critically about lie detection (Box), p. 468
Medium, Factual/Definitional, Objective 5, Ans: d

44.   The polygraph measures the changes in _____ that accompany emotion.
a. blood sugar level
b. hormone secretions
c. pupil dilation
d. blood pressure
e. facial expression

Thinking critically about lie detection (Box), p. 468
Easy, Factual/Definitional, Objective 5, Ans: a

45.   The assumption underlying the use of the polygraph in criminal investigations is that denial of involvement in a crime is most likely to _____ arousal in suspects who are actually

_____.
a. increase; guilty
b. decrease; guilty
c. increase; innocent
d. decrease; innocent

Thinking critically about lie detection (Box), p. 469
Difficult, Factual/Definitional, Objective 5, Ans: c

46.   Research on the accuracy of lie detector tests indicates that they:
a. are rarely wrong.
b. err about 10 percent of the time.
c. err about one-third of the time.
d. are no more accurate than a 50-50 coin toss.

Thinking critically about lie detection (Box), p. 469
Easy, Conceptual, Objective 5, Ans: d

47.   Although newspapers reported that a murder victim had been stabbed with a knife, two police investigators knew that the actual murder weapon was a letter opener. While carefully monitoring the blood pressure and pulse rate of a prime suspect, the investigators asked him if he typically used a letter opener on his mail. The investigators were making use of:
a. the two-factor theory.
b. the adaptation-level phenomenon.
c. the relative deprivation principle.
d. the guilty knowledge test.
e. catharsis.

Thinking critically about lie detection (Box), p. 469
Difficult, Factual/Definitional, Objective 5, Ans: d

48.   When guilty knowledge tests are used in criminal investigations, _____ suspects are _____ judged guilty by polygraph examiners.
a. innocent; typically
b. guilty; always
c. guilty; seldom
d. innocent; seldom

Nonverbal communication, p. 470

Easy, Factual/Definitional, Objective 6, Ans: d
49. Couples who are passionately in love are most likely to communicate intimacy nonverbally by means of:
   a. averted glances.
   b. contraction of the pupils.
   c. winking.
   d. prolonged eye-gazing.
   e. raising just the inner parts of the eyebrows.

Nonverbal communication, p. 471
Difficult, Factual/Definitional, Objective 6, Ans: d
50. Comparing introverts and extraverts, we can say that the nonverbal expressions of emotion conveyed by _____ are easier to read, and _____ are better at reading other people's nonverbal expressions of emotion.
   a. introverts; introverts
   b. extraverts; extraverts
   c. introverts; extraverts
   d. extraverts; introverts

Nonverbal communication, p. 471
Medium, Conceptual, Objective 6, Ans: a
51. Compared to men, women would probably be better at:
   a. detecting the emotions of two people having a discussion over lunch.
   b. controlling their physiological responses on a guilty knowledge test.
   c. interpreting the polygraph test of a suspected criminal.
   d. overcoming the negative effects described by the adaptation-level principle.
   e. all the above.

Nonverbal communication, p. 471
Easy, Factual/Definitional, Objective 6, Ans: b
52. Women show _____ facial expression of emotion than men while viewing frightening films, and they show _____ facial expression of emotion than men while viewing happy films.
   a. more; less
   b. more; more
   c. less; more
   d. less; less

Nonverbal communication, p. 472
Medium, Factual/Definitional, Objective 6, Ans: d
53. The most unambiguous nonverbal clue to our specific emotional state is provided by our:
   a. respiration rate.
   b. hand gestures.
   c. body posture.
   d. facial muscles.
   e. pupil contraction and dilation.

Nonverbal communication, p. 473
Difficult, Factual/Definitional, Objective 6, Ans: e

54. University students who watched either an enjoyable or an emotionally upsetting film were instructed to talk and act as if they were enjoying the film. By simply observing the students' nonverbal behavior, who was able to detect whether they were lying about their true emotions?
     a. psychiatrists
     b. court judges
     c. federal polygraphers
     d. other university students
     e. none of the above

Culture and emotional expression, p. 474
Easy, Factual/Definitional, Objective 6, Ans: c

55. The facial expressions associated with particular emotions are:
     a. learned in early childhood.
     b. different in Eastern and Western cultures.
     c. the same throughout the world.
     d. more similar in adults than they are in children or adolescents.
     e. more similar in women than in men.

Culture and emotional expression, p. 474
Easy, Conceptual, Objective 6, Ans: b

56. As a member of the diplomatic corps, Jonas was given special training in the customs, language, and religions of the Third World country to which he was going. However, Jonas probably needed little training to correctly interpret his hosts' expressions of emotion as revealed by their:
     a. body postures.
     b. facial expressions.
     c. hand gestures.
     d. tones of voice.
     e. dancing.

Culture and emotional expression, pp. 474, 475
Medium, Conceptual, Objective 6, Ans: d

57. It has been suggested that raising the eyebrows is universally associated with the expression of surprise because this facial expression effectively widens the eyes to enhance the perception of unexpected circumstances. This suggestion best illustrates the:
     a. catharsis hypothesis.
     b. adaptation-level principle.
     c. two-factor theory.
     d. evolutionary perspective.
     e. relative deprivation principle.

Culture and emotional expression, p. 474
Medium, Factual/Definitional, Objective 6, Ans: e

58. Who suggested that baring the teeth is universally associated with the expression of anger because this ability to convey threats has helped humans to survive?
     a. Stanley Schachter
     b. William James
     c. Walter Cannon
     d. Richard Solomon
     e. Charles Darwin

Culture and emotional expression, p. 475
Easy, Factual/Definitional, Objective 6, Ans: a
59.   Americans are more likely than Asians to:
      a. openly display their feelings by their facial expressions.
      b. recognize facial expressions of happiness.
      c. repress their negative emotions.
      d. react with sympathetic nervous system arousal to a dangerous situation.
      e. work most effectively when highly aroused.

Culture and emotional expression, p. 475
Medium, Conceptual, Objective 6, Ans: c
60.   North Americans are more likely than Japanese citizens to display their feelings of anger and
      distress. This cultural difference best reflects the American culture's greater emphasis on:
      a. communication.
      b. role-playing.
      c. individuality.
      d. materialism.
      e. success and failure.

Culture and emotional expression, p. 475
Medium, Conceptual, Objective 6, Ans: c
61.   Compared with Asians, Americans are especially likely to display their feelings of:
      a. shame.
      b. respect.
      c. pride.
      d. sympathy.

The effects of facial expressions, p. 475
Medium, Factual/Definitional, Objective 7, Ans: b
62.   In order to effectively manage their emotions, people would be best advised to control their:
      a. tone of voice.
      b. facial expressions.
      c. body posture.
      d. blood pressure.

The effects of facial expressions, p. 475
Easy, Factual/Definitional, Objective 7, Ans: e
63.   Research on the effects of nonverbal emotional expressions most clearly supports the idea that:
      a. emotional suppression facilitates depression.
      b. expressing anger reduces rage.
      c. going through the motions simply dampens the emotions.
      d. behind dark clouds the sun still shines.
      e. a merry face makes a happy soul.

The effects of facial expressions, p. 475
Medium, Conceptual, Objective 7, Ans: a
64.   If you display a fearful facial expression while taking a difficult exam, this facial expression is
      likely to cause you to experience:
      a. increasingly intense feelings of fear.
      b. less difficulty recalling the correct answers to the exam questions.
      c. a decrease in your blood sugar levels.
      d. all the above.

The effects of facial expressions, pp. 475-476
Medium, Factual/Definitional, Objective 7, Ans: c

65. Researchers have found that people experience cartoons as more amusing while holding a pen with their teeth than while holding it with their lips. This best illustrates the:
   a. catharsis hypothesis.
   b. relative deprivation principle.
   c. facial feedback effect.
   d. adaptation level phenomenon.
   e. feel good, do good phenomenon.

Fear, p. 478
Medium, Factual/Definitional, Objective 8, Ans: b

66. People are fearful of so many different objects and events because:
   a. the nervous system is naturally aroused by novel and unfamiliar stimuli.
   b. they learn to fear things associated with naturally painful or traumatic experiences.
   c. they are biologically predisposed to be most fearful of things that most threaten their physical survival.
   d. they are biologically predisposed to fear almost anything.

Fear, p. 478
Medium, Factual/Definitional, Objective 8, Ans: a

67. In experiments with adult monkeys who were fearful of snakes and their offspring who were not, Susan Mineka discovered that the younger monkeys developed a fear of snakes through the process of:
   a. observational learning.
   b. classical conditioning.
   c. relative deprivation.
   d. catharsis.
   e. shaping.

Fear, p. 478
Medium, Factual/Definitional, Objective 8, Ans: b

68. People are most biologically predisposed to learn to fear:
   a. guns.
   b. spiders.
   c. electricity.
   d. other people.

Fear, p. 478
Medium, Factual/Definitional, Objective 8, Ans: b

69. Which brain structure has been found to be especially important in learning to fear specific objects?
   a. hypothalamus
   b. amygdala
   c. corpus callosum
   d. hippocampus
   e. thalamus

Fear, p. 478
Difficult, Factual/Definitional, Objective 8, Ans: d

70.   After learning to associate a blue slide with a blaring horn, people who have suffered damage
      to the amygdala _____ show a fear reaction to the blue slide, and they _____ be able to
      remember the previous pairing of the blue slide with the blaring horn.
      a. will; will
      b. will not; will not
      c. will; will not
      d. will not; will

Fear, p. 479
Medium, Factual/Definitional, Objective 8, Ans: c

71.   Individual differences in temperament suggest that the experience of fear is influenced by:
      a. relative deprivation.
      b. opponent processes.
      c. genetic predispositions.
      d. classical conditioning.
      e. catharsis.

Anger, p. 479
Medium, Factual/Definitional, Objective 9, Ans: c

72.   People report that they are especially likely to experience anger when they suffer from a
      misdeed that is perceived as:
      a. unusual.
      b. unintended.
      c. unjustified.
      d. unavoidable.

Anger, p. 480
Medium, Factual/Definitional, Objective 9, Ans: c

73.   The catharsis hypothesis refers to the idea that:
      a. every emotion is preceded by cognition.
      b. humans tend to adapt to a given level of stimulation.
      c. anger is reduced by aggressive action or fantasy.
      d. successful performance is influenced by level of physiological arousal.

Anger, p. 480
Difficult, Conceptual, Objective 9, Ans: b

74.   In which country would parents be least likely to advocate catharsis as a way of helping their
      children reduce their anger?
      a. the United States
      b. Japan
      c. Australia
      d. France

Anger, p. 480

Medium, Conceptual, Objective 9, Ans: d

75. A television producer believes that violent TV programs provide viewers an opportunity to reduce their own anger through fantasy. The producer appears to accept the:
     a. opponent-process theory.
     b. adaptation-level principle.
     c. relative deprivation principle.
     d. catharsis hypothesis.
     e. two-factor theory.

Anger, p. 480

Medium, Factual/Definitional, Objective 9, Ans: d

76. Verbal and nonverbal expressions of anger can:
     a. calm emotions and reduce anger.
     b. become habitual if they successfully reduce anger.
     c. increase immediate feelings of anger.
     d. do any of the above.

Anger, p. 480

Easy, Factual/Definitional, Objective 9, Ans: c

77. Experts suggest that an intensely angry person should:
     a. avoid the offending person so as to alleviate the problem.
     b. release the anger through some aggressive action or fantasy.
     c. take time to let the anger and emotional arousal subside.
     d. mentally rehearse the exact reasons for the anger.

Anger, pp. 480-481

Medium, Conceptual, Objective 9, Ans: a

78. Milan is upset with his wife because she was over an hour late in picking him up at the airport. He is likely to deal most effectively with his feelings of irritation toward her by telling her:
     a. "I'm really angry that I had to wait so long for you to get here."
     b. "From now on, I'll ask someone at the office to pick me up."
     c. "Darn it, why can't you be more responsible?"
     d. "I'm dying of hunger! It's 7:45 and I haven't had dinner yet."
     e. "I was starting to worry that you had a car accident on your way over here."

Happiness, p. 481

Easy, Conceptual, Objective 10, Ans: d

79. Mrs. Chen asks her teenage son, Keith, to rake leaves in the yard. Keith is most likely to want to help his mother after:
     a. washing the family's dishes.
     b. bringing home a less-than-satisfactory report card from school.
     c. hearing that a friend was involved in a minor automobile accident.
     d. receiving news that he has just won $1000 in a state lottery.

Happiness, p. 481

Medium, Conceptual, Objective 10, Ans: c

80. After receiving an unexpected "A" on his psychology test, Ted was easily persuaded to baby-sit his little sister while his parents went out for dinner. This best illustrates the:
    a. catharsis hypothesis.
    b. adaptation-level phenomenon.
    c. feel-good, do-good phenomenon.
    d. relative deprivation principle.
    e. two-factor theory.

Happiness, pp. 481, 483

Easy, Conceptual, Objective 10, Ans: c

81. Objective well-being is to economic status as subjective well-being is to:
    a. educational status.
    b. physical health.
    c. life satisfaction.
    d. ethnic identity.

Happiness, p. 481

Medium, Factual/Definitional, Objective 10, Ans: d

82. People's long-term feelings of life satisfaction are typically _____ by a tragic event and _____ by a dramatically positive event.
    a. decreased; largely unchanged
    b. decreased; increased
    c. largely unchanged; increased
    d. largely unchanged; largely unchanged

Happiness (Figure 13.15), p. 482

Difficult, Factual/Definitional, Objective 10, Ans: a

83. Over the last 30 years, American college freshmen have expressed a(n) _____ desire to be wealthy and a(n) _____ desire to develop a meaningful life philosophy.
    a. increasing; decreasing
    b. increasing; increasing
    c. decreasing; decreasing
    d. decreasing; increasing

Happiness, p. 483

Medium, Factual/Definitional, Objective 10, Ans: d

84. Research on the well-being of Americans indicates that the:
    a. vast majority of Americans currently declare themselves to be very happy.
    b. personal happiness of Americans has been increasing over the last 40 years.
    c. spendable income of Americans (adjusted for inflation) has been decreasing over the last 40 years.
    d. increase in the personal income of Americans over the past 40 years has provided no apparent boost to Americans' personal happiness.

Happiness and the adaptation-level principle, p. 484
Medium, Factual/Definitional, Objective 10, Ans: b

85. The adaptation-level phenomenon refers to the tendency for judgments of objects and events to be heavily influenced by:
    a. genetics.
    b. previous experiences.
    c. current level of happiness.
    d. current level of physiological arousal.
    e. an understanding of how others judge those same objects and events.

Happiness and the adaptation-level principle, p. 484
Medium, Conceptual, Objective 10, Ans: a

86. When Mrs. Van Dyke first acquired a new luxury car, she was ecstatic. After several months, however, she took the car for granted and it gave her little sense of emotional excitement. This change in her feelings can best be explained in terms of the:
    a. adaptation-level principle.
    b. relative deprivation principle.
    c. opponent-process theory.
    d. James-Lange theory.
    e. two-factor theory.

Happiness and the adaptation-level principle, p. 484
Difficult, Conceptual, Objective 10, Ans: e

87. Juan and Milly were millionaires until they lost everything in a stock market crash. Which of the following best explains why after 3 years Juan and Milly seem to have suffered no permanent loss of contentment?
    a. relative deprivation principle
    b. two-factor theory
    c. James-Lange theory
    d. opponent-process theory
    e. adaptation-level phenomenon

Happiness and the adaptation-level principle, p. 484
Difficult, Conceptual, Objective 10, Ans: b

88. A disturbing implication of the adaptation-level phenomenon is that:
    a. rich people who must give up their wealth will never experience normal levels of happiness and life satisfaction.
    b. seeking happiness through financial security requires an ever-increasing abundance of wealth.
    c. both rich and poor people are destined to be perpetually dissatisfied with their lives.
    d. comparing ourselves with those who are less fortunate simply increases our insecurity.

Happiness and the relative deprivation principle, p. 485
Easy, Factual/Definitional, Objective 10, Ans: c

89. The concept of relative deprivation refers to the perception that:
    a. yesterday's luxuries are today's necessities.
    b. things are never quite as bad as they could be.
    c. one is worse off than those with whom one compares oneself.
    d. happiness is simply a state of mind.
    e. happiness can't last forever.

Happiness and the relative deprivation principle, p. 485
Medium, Conceptual, Objective 10, Ans: c

90.   You were happy with your grade of "B" on the psychology test until you learned that everyone else in class received an "A." This illustrates that happiness is influenced by:
a. opponent-process effects.
b. the adaptation-level phenomenon.
c. relative deprivation.
d. the "feel-good, do-good" phenomenon.
e. catharsis.

Happiness and the relative deprivation principle, p. 485
Medium, Conceptual, Objective 10, Ans: e

91.   When the mayor ordered a salary increase for the city's police officers, there was a sudden loss of morale among the city's fire fighters. The fire fighters' sudden dissatisfaction best illustrates the:
a. James-Lange theory.
b. adaptation-level phenomenon.
c. opponent-process theory.
d. two-factor theory.
e. relative deprivation principle.

Happiness and the relative deprivation principle, p. 485
Medium, Factual/Definitional, Objective 10, Ans: d

92.   In order to increase your happiness and satisfaction with life, you would be best advised to:
a. recall past moments when your life was much more pleasant than it is now.
b. imagine what your life might be like if you were rich and famous.
c. observe children who are happily playing with each other.
d. compare yourself with people who are much less fortunate than you.

Opponent-process theory of emotion (Close-up), p. 486
Medium, Factual/Definitional, Objective 10, Ans: d

93.   The opponent-process theory of emotion suggests that every initial emotional reaction triggers an opposing emotion that:
a. is experienced with the same intensity as the initial emotional reaction.
b. is experienced for the same duration of time as the initial emotional reaction.
c. strengthens the intensity of the initial emotional reaction.
d. diminishes the intensity of the initial emotional reaction.

Opponent-process theory of emotion (Close-up), p. 486
Medium, Factual/Definitional, Objective 10, Ans: b

94.   Which theory predicts that the pleasurable highs produced by addictive drugs will tend to diminish in intensity with repeated drug usage?
a. two-factor theory
b. opponent-process theory
c. James-Lange theory
d. Cannon-Bard theory
e. relative deprivation principle

Opponent-process theory of emotion (Close-up), p. 486
Medium, Conceptual, Objective 10, Ans: b

95.   Qian has donated blood several times at the campus health center. He finds that he is becoming less fearful prior to each donation and increasingly relaxed and warm-hearted afterwards. Qian's experience is most directly explained in terms of:
       a. the accommodation principle.
       b. the opponent-process theory.
       c. catharsis.
       d. relative deprivation.
       e. the assimilation principle.

Opponent-process theory of emotion (Close-up), p. 486
Medium, Factual/Definitional, Objective 10, Ans: c

96.   The opponent-process theory would predict that with repeated jumps the fear aroused by parachuting would _____ and the exhilaration after landing would _____.
       a. increase; increase
       b. increase; decrease
       c. decrease; increase
       d. decrease; decrease

Opponent-process theory of emotion (Close-up), p. 486
Difficult, Conceptual, Objective 10, Ans: b

97.   The fear Bart experiences just before a street fight is replaced by a sense of joyful relief immediately afterwards. The opponent-process theory would predict that with repeated involvement in street fights, the intensity of joyful relief Bart experiences immediately after each fight will _____ and the intensity of fear he experiences immediately before will

       _____.
       a. increase; increase
       b. increase; decrease
       c. decrease; increase
       d. decrease; decrease

Predictors of happiness, p. 486
Easy, Factual/Definitional, Objective 10, Ans: d

98.   Research suggests that people experience the most happiness when they are:
       a. eating.
       b. daydreaming.
       c. highly self-aware.
       d. engaged in challenging activities.

Predictors of happiness, p. 487
Easy, Factual/Definitional, Objective 10, Ans: c

99.   Researchers have found that certain factors are related to happiness. One of these is that happy people tend to:
       a. be well educated.
       b. have many children.
       c. have a satisfying marriage or close friendship.
       d. be over 50 years old.
       e. be physically attractive.

CHAPTER 14

Personality

Learning Objectives

The Psychoanalytic Perspective (pp. 490-501)

1. Describe what is meant by personality, and explain how Freud's treatment of psychological disorders led to his study of the unconscious.

2. Describe personality structure in terms of the interactions of the id, ego, and superego.

3. Identify Freud's psychosexual stages of development, and describe the effects of fixation on behavior.

4. Explain how defense mechanisms protect the individual from anxiety.

5. Explain how projective tests are used to assess personality.

6. Discuss the contributions of the neo-Freudians, and describe the strengths and weaknesses of Freud's ideas.

The Trait Perspective (pp. 502-511)

7. Discuss psychologists' descriptions of personality in terms of types and traits.

8. Explain how personality inventories are used to assess traits, and discuss research regarding the consistency of behavior over time and across situations.

The Humanistic Perspective (pp. 512-521)

9. Describe the humanistic perspective on personality in terms of Maslow's focus on self-actualization and Rogers' emphasis on people's potential for growth.

10. Describe humanistic psychologists' approach to personality assessment, and discuss the benefits and liabilities of self-esteem and self-serving bias.

11. Describe the impact of individualism and collectivism on self-identity and social relations.

12. Discuss the criticisms of the humanistic perspective.

The Social-Cognitive Perspective (pp. 522-528)

13.   Describe the social-cognitive perspective on personality, and explain reciprocal determinism.

14.   Discuss the important consequences of personal control, learned helplessness, and optimism.

15.   Describe how social-cognitive researchers assess behavior in realistic situations, and evaluate the social-cognitive perspective on personality.

Personality, p. 489
Medium, Factual/Definitional, Objective 1, Ans: a
1.   Personality is best defined as an individual's:
    a. characteristic pattern of thinking, feeling, and acting.
    b. most noticeable characteristics.
    c. biologically inherited temperament.
    d. hidden thoughts and emotions.

Personality, p. 489
Easy, Conceptual, Objective 1, Ans: e
2.   Mark typically responds to stress in a calm and thoughtful manner. Tom, on the other hand, usually becomes agitated. The reactions of Mark and Tom indicate that each has a distinctive:
    a. reaction formation.
    b. collective unconscious.
    c. Oedipus complex.
    d. self-serving bias.
    e. personality.

The psychoanalytic perspective, p. 490
Difficult, Factual/Definitional, Objective 1, Ans: b
3.   The belief that some distressing physical symptoms could not be readily explained in terms of neurological impairments contributed most directly to:
    a. Allport's interest in personality traits.
    b. Freud's interest in unconscious conflicts.
    c. Maslow's interest in self-actualization.
    d. Bandura's interest in personal control.
    e. Rogers's interest in unconditional positive regard.

Exploring the unconscious, p. 490
Easy, Factual/Definitional, Objective 1, Ans: a
4.   Prior to his use of free association, Freud had encouraged patients to retrieve their forgotten memories by means of:
    a. hypnosis.
    b. projective tests.
    c. psychoactive drugs.
    d. fixation.

Exploring the unconscious, p. 490
Easy, Conceptual, Objective 1, Ans: b

5. Which of the following techniques was Freud most likely to use in an attempt to discover the hidden conflicts underlying his patients' symptoms?
   a. factor analysis
   b. free association
   c. projective testing
   d. self-assessment techniques
   e. sublimation

Exploring the unconscious, p. 491
Easy, Factual/Definitional, Objective 1, Ans: d

6. In suggesting that the mind is like an iceberg, Freud was most clearly emphasizing the importance of the:
   a. ego.
   b. superego.
   c. instincts.
   d. unconscious.
   e. psychosexual stages.

Exploring the unconscious, p. 491
Easy, Factual/Definitional, Objective 1, Ans: e

7. According to Freud, our repressed impulses express themselves in:
   a. dreams.
   b. daily habits.
   c. our work.
   d. troubling symptoms.
   e. all the above.

Exploring the unconscious, p. 491
Easy, Factual/Definitional, Objective 1, Ans: b

8. Who emphasized that slips of the tongue often reveal the personality dynamics that contribute to psychological disorders?
   a. Allport
   b. Freud
   c. Bandura
   d. Maslow
   e. Rogers

The psychoanalytic perspective: personality structure, pp. 491-492
Medium, Factual/Definitional, Objective 2, Ans: d

9. According to Freud, understanding how the id, ego, and superego interact is essential to grasping the nature of:
   a. self-actualization.
   b. an external locus of control.
   c. reciprocal determinism.
   d. motivational conflict.
   e. an inferiority complex.

The psychoanalytic perspective: personality structure, p. 492
Medium, Factual/Definitional, Objective 2, Ans: d

10.   According to Freud's theory, the behavior of a newborn is controlled by:
      a. the collective unconscious.
      b. the ego.
      c. the superego.
      d. the id.
      e. all the above.

The psychoanalytic perspective: personality structure, pp. 492, 493
Medium, Conceptual, Objective 2, Ans: d

11.   Katrinka habitually makes nasty, hostile comments about her teachers. Freud would have suggested that her behavior illustrates the powerful influence of the:
      a. collective unconscious.
      b. superego.
      c. self-serving bias.
      d. id.
      e. Oedipus complex.

The psychoanalytic perspective: personality structure, p. 492
Medium, Conceptual, Objective 2, Ans: c

12.   The pleasure principle is to the _____ as the reality principle is to the _____.
      a. oral stage; anal stage
      b. id; superego
      c. id; ego
      d. life instinct; death instinct
      e. conscious; unconscious

The psychoanalytic perspective: personality structure, p. 492
Medium, Factual/Definitional, Objective 2, Ans: a

13.   According to Freud's theory, the ego:
      a. is the executive part of personality.
      b. develops before the id.
      c. operates on the pleasure principle.
      d. is the major source of guilt feelings.
      e. operates only on a conscious level.

The psychoanalytic perspective: personality structure, p. 492
Medium, Conceptual, Objective 2, Ans: d

14.   Georg often acts on impulse, without taking time to consider the consequences. A psychoanalyst would suggest that Georg shows signs of a:
      a. strong ego.
      b. strong superego.
      c. weak id.
      d. weak ego.

The psychoanalytic perspective: personality structure, p. 492
Medium, Factual/Definitional, Objective 2, Ans: c

15.   The superego is the part of personality that:
      a. mediates between the demands of biology and the external world.
      b. operates on the reality principle.
      c. generates feelings of guilt.
      d. does all the above.

The psychoanalytic perspective: personality structure, p. 492
Easy, Conceptual, Objective 2, Ans: b

16. Jordan feels ashamed that he hurt his younger brother. Freud would have attributed these feelings to Jordan's:
    a. id.
    b. superego.
    c. ego.
    d. collective unconscious.

The psychoanalytic perspective: personality structure, p. 492
Medium, Conceptual, Objective 2, Ans: e

17. While attending college, Saeb impulsively and carelessly spends all his time and money on "wine, women, and song." Freud would have suggested that Saeb shows signs of a(n):
    a. strong ego.
    b. inferiority complex.
    c. weak id.
    d. Electra complex.
    e. weak superego.

The psychoanalytic perspective: personality structure, p. 492
Difficult, Conceptual, Objective 2, Ans: a

18. Although Carl wants to interact sexually with his girlfriend, he also wants to avoid premarital sex. Freud would have suggested that both desires might be partially satisfied by Carl's:
    a. ego.
    b. collective unconscious.
    c. id.
    d. superego.
    e. Oedipus complex.

The psychoanalytic perspective: personality development, p. 492
Easy, Factual/Definitional, Objective 3, Ans: b

19. According to Freud, the most important erogenous zone during earliest infancy consists of the:
    a. eyes.
    b. mouth.
    c. bowels.
    d. breasts.
    e. urethra.

The psychoanalytic perspective: personality development, p. 493
Medium, Factual/Definitional, Objective 3, Ans: c

20. According to Freud, children develop unconscious sexual desires for the parent of the opposite sex during the _____ stage.
    a. oral
    b. genital
    c. phallic
    d. anal
    e. latency

The psychoanalytic perspective: personality development, p. 493
Easy, Factual/Definitional, Objective 3, Ans: b
21. A boy's sexual desires for his mother and feelings of hostility toward his father constitute what Freud called:
    a. reaction formation.
    b. the Oedipus complex.
    c. reciprocal determinism.
    d. an oral fixation.
    e. displacement.

The psychoanalytic perspective: personality development, p. 493
Medium, Conceptual, Objective 3, Ans: d
22. Boris does not like chemistry, but he has chosen it as his college major simply to prove that he is just as smart as his father, who is an outstanding chemist. A psychoanalyst would be most likely to suggest that Boris suffers from an unresolved:
    a. oral fixation.
    b. anal fixation.
    c. external locus of control.
    d. Oedipus complex.
    e. projection.

The psychoanalytic perspective: personality development, p. 493
Difficult, Conceptual, Objective 3, Ans: c
23. Freud's emphasis on the _____ stage of development may have led many psychoanalysts to discount the truth of patients' reports of sexual abuse.
    a. oral
    b. anal
    c. phallic
    d. latency
    e. genital

The psychoanalytic perspective: personality development, p. 493
Medium, Factual/Definitional, Objective 3, Ans: e
24. Freud suggested that the superego develops through the process of:
    a. self-actualization.
    b. fixation.
    c. free association.
    d. reciprocal determinism.
    e. identification.

The psychoanalytic perspective: personality development, p. 493
Difficult, Factual/Definitional, Objective 3, Ans: b
25. According to Freud, our gender identity develops most rapidly during the _____ stage.
    a. anal
    b. phallic
    c. genital
    d. oral

The psychoanalytic perspective: personality development, p. 493
Medium, Factual/Definitional, Objective 3, Ans: d
26. Freud suggested that in the process of development people pass through a _____ stage before they enter a(n) _____ stage.
   a. genital; latency
   b. latency; phallic
   c. genital; phallic
   d. latency; genital
   e. phallic; oral

The psychoanalytic perspective: personality development, p. 493
Easy, Factual/Definitional, Objective 3, Ans: e
27. Freud emphasized that unresolved childhood conflicts often lead to:
   a. reciprocal determinism.
   b. the collective unconscious.
   c. unconditional positive regard.
   d. an external locus of control.
   e. fixation.

The psychoanalytic perspective: personality development, p. 493
Difficult, Conceptual, Objective 3, Ans: c
28. Julie is a married woman who pursues sexual gratification by means of kissing rather than through sexual intercourse. According to Freud, this illustrates a(n):
   a. Oedipus complex.
   b. reaction formation.
   c. fixation.
   d. projection.
   e. rationalization.

The psychoanalytic perspective: personality development, p. 493
Difficult, Conceptual, Objective 3, Ans: e
29. Bill is always looking to others for advice, approval, and affection. According to the psychoanalytic perspective, Bill is most likely fixated at the _____ stage.
   a. phallic
   b. anal
   c. latency
   d. genital
   e. oral

The psychoanalytic perspective: personality development, p. 493
Medium, Factual/Definitional, Objective 3, Ans: c
30. Freud suggested that adults with an anal fixation often show signs of:
   a. passive dependence.
   b. overeating.
   c. compulsive neatness.
   d. learned helplessness.
   e. insomnia.

The psychoanalytic perspective: personality development, p. 493
Difficult, Conceptual, Objective 3, Ans: c

31.   Ms. Chavan is so concerned about keeping her house spotless that she daily rewashes her
       windows and picks up minute specks of lint from the furniture. A psychoanalyst would most
       likely suspect that Ms. Chavan is fixated at the _____ stage.
       a. oral
       b. phallic
       c. anal
       d. genital
       e. latency

Defense mechanisms, p. 494
Easy, Factual/Definitional, Objective 4, Ans: d

32.   Psychoanalytic theory suggests that the ego disguises threatening impulses and reduces anxiety
       by means of:
       a. free association.
       b. self-actualization.
       c. unconditional positive regard.
       d. defense mechanisms.
       e. learned helplessness.

Defense mechanisms, p. 494
Medium, Factual/Definitional, Objective 4, Ans: e

33.   The defense mechanism that underlies all others is:
       a. regression.
       b. reaction formation.
       c. projection.
       d. displacement.
       e. repression.

Defense mechanisms, p. 494
Easy, Factual/Definitional, Objective 4, Ans: c

34.   Freud suggested that a man's ability to remember his childhood Oedipus complex illustrates:
       a. sublimation.
       b. fixation.
       c. repression.
       d. displacement.
       e. projection.

Defense mechanisms, p. 494
Easy, Conceptual, Objective 4, Ans: c

35.   Although Gloria has detailed memories of her high school experiences, she can remember very
       little about the boyfriend who abruptly broke off their marriage engagement. According to
       psychoanalytic theory, it appears that Gloria is using the defense mechanism of:
       a. reaction formation.
       b. regression.
       c. repression.
       d. displacement.
       e. projection.

Defense mechanisms, p. 494
Easy, Factual/Definitional, Objective 4, Ans: d

36. Coping with anxiety by retreating to behavior patterns characteristic of an earlier, more infantile stage of development is called:
     a. repression.
     b. projection.
     c. reaction formation.
     d. regression.
     e. displacement.

Defense mechanisms, p. 494
Medium, Conceptual, Objective 4, Ans: d

37. For several months after he lost the job he had held for nearly 20 years, Mr. Ullomi frequently lost his temper and took excessively long afternoon naps. His behavior is most clearly an example of:
     a. repression.
     b. an Oedipus complex.
     c. reaction formation.
     d. regression.
     e. projection.

Defense mechanisms, p. 494
Medium, Factual/Definitional, Objective 4, Ans: d

38. Which defense mechanism involves the conscious expression of feelings that are the opposite of unconscious feelings?
     a. repression
     b. projection
     c. rationalization
     d. reaction formation
     e. displacement

Defense mechanisms, p. 494
Difficult, Conceptual, Objective 4, Ans: a

39. A religious leader who attempts to overcome his hidden doubts with intense expressions of spiritual certainty illustrates most clearly the defense mechanism of:
     a. reaction formation.
     b. projection.
     c. regression.
     d. displacement.
     e. fixation.

Defense mechanisms, p. 494
Difficult, Conceptual, Objective 4, Ans: e

40. As her parents became increasingly more abusive toward her, Winifred began, with apparent sincerity, to emphatically express her great admiration for her parents. Winifred's behavior illustrates most clearly the defense mechanism of:
     a. regression.
     b. projection.
     c. displacement.
     d. rationalization.
     e. reaction formation.

Defense mechanisms, p. 494
Medium, Factual/Definitional, Objective 4, Ans: c

41. Using the defense mechanism of projection, a person experiences an internal _____ as if it were an external _____.
    a. danger; virtue
    b. virtue; danger
    c. danger; danger
    d. virtue; virtue

Defense mechanisms, p. 494
Medium, Factual/Definitional, Objective 4, Ans: b

42. Projection refers to the process by which people:
    a. consciously express feelings that are the opposite of underlying unconscious impulses.
    b. disguise unacceptable, unconscious impulses by attributing them to others.
    c. retreat to behavior patterns characteristic of an earlier stage of development.
    d. offer self-justifying explanations in place of real, but unacceptable, unconscious reasons for action.

Defense mechanisms, p. 494
Difficult, Conceptual, Objective 4, Ans: c

43. Although Eduardo has repressed his own homosexual desires, he is distressed by a false suspicion that many men frequently stare lustfully at his body. According to psychoanalytic theory, Eduardo's thinking best illustrates:
    a. displacement.
    b. regression.
    c. projection.
    d. reaction formation.
    e. rationalization.

Defense mechanisms, p. 494
Medium, Conceptual, Objective 4, Ans: b

44. Unconsciously motivated by miserliness, Mr. Rioja refused to send his son money to buy the books he needs for his college courses. In defending his actions, Mr. Rioja explained that "parental financial aid prevents teenagers from developing into mature, independent adults." Mr. Rioja's explanation is an example of:
    a. repression.
    b. rationalization.
    c. projection.
    d. displacement.
    e. reaction formation.

Defense mechanisms, p. 494
Medium, Factual/Definitional, Objective 4, Ans: e

45. Displacement refers to the process by which people:
    a. offer self-justifying explanations in place of real, but unacceptable, unconscious reasons for action.
    b. consciously express feelings that are the opposite of unacceptable, unconscious impulses.
    c. disguise threatening impulses by attributing them to others.
    d. retreat to behavior patterns characteristic of an earlier stage of development.
    e. redirect aggressive or sexual impulses toward less threatening targets.

Defense mechanisms, p. 494
Difficult, Conceptual, Objective 4, Ans: d

46. Shortly after receiving a traffic ticket for speeding, Fred made numerous hostile comments to his wife about the incompetence of women drivers. Fred's comments illustrate most clearly the defense mechanism of:
    a. reaction formation.
    b. rationalization.
    c. identification.
    d. displacement.
    e. repression.

Defense mechanisms, p. 494
Difficult, Conceptual, Objective 4, Ans: c

47. Roberta thinks that her brother may have become a psychotherapist simply because this provided a socially acceptable way for him to satisfy his excessive curiosity about other people's private lives. Roberta most clearly suspects that her brother's therapeutic practice is a:
    a. rationalization.
    b. projection.
    c. sublimation.
    d. reaction formation.
    e. fixation.

Assessing the unconscious, p. 495
Easy, Factual/Definitional, Objective 5, Ans: b

48. Tests that present ambiguous stimuli designed to uncover hidden personality dynamics are called _____ tests.
    a. empirical
    b. projective
    c. multiphasic personality
    d. factor analytic
    e. aptitude

Assessing the unconscious, p. 495
Medium, Factual/Definitional, Objective 5, Ans: b

49. The Thematic Apperception Test requires people to respond to:
    a. incomplete sentences.
    b. ambiguous pictures.
    c. unfamiliar melodies.
    d. meaningless inkblots.
    e. all the above.

Assessing the unconscious, p. 495
Easy, Conceptual, Objective 5, Ans: a

50. Alice was asked by her psychotherapist to describe what she saw in 10 ambiguous inkblots. Alice was most likely responding to a(n) _____ test.
    a. projective
    b. Thematic Apperception
    c. multiphasic personality
    d. aptitude
    e. empirically derived

Assessing the unconscious, p. 495
Medium, Factual/Definitional, Objective 5, Ans: a
51.   The Rorschach test has been criticized because:
       a. it has not been very successful at predicting behavior.
       b. it can be used effectively only on individuals who are psychologically maladjusted.
       c. it inhibits individuals from communicating honestly in clinical interviews.
       d. there is only one accepted system for scoring the test.

Freud's descendants and dissenters, p. 496
Medium, Factual/Definitional, Objective 6, Ans: e
52.   Which neo-Freudian theorist emphasized that personality development is strongly influenced
       by feelings of inferiority?
       a. Jung
       b. Allport
       c. Horney
       d. Maslow
       e. Adler

Freud's descendants and dissenters, p. 496
Medium, Factual/Definitional, Objective 6, Ans: b
53.   Both Karen Horney and Alfred Adler placed greater emphasis than did Freud on the role of
       _____ in personality development.
       a. defense mechanisms
       b. social interactions
       c. the collective unconscious
       d. genetic predispositions

Freud's descendants and dissenters, pp. 496-497
Medium, Factual/Definitional, Objective 6, Ans: d
54.   Carl Jung emphasized the importance of _____ in personality functioning.
       a. social interest
       b. inferiority feelings
       c. psychosexual stages
       d. the collective unconscious
       e. unconditional positive regard

Freud's descendants and dissenters, pp. 496-497
Difficult, Conceptual, Objective 6, Ans: d
55.   Christie recently had a vivid dream that was strikingly similar to an ancient and unfamiliar
       religious myth. This coincidence would have been of particular interest to:
       a. Adler.
       b. Rogers.
       c. Allport.
       d. Jung.
       e. Horney.

Evaluating the psychoanalytic perspective, p. 497
Difficult, Conceptual, Objective 6, Ans: b

56. Twelve-year-old Adam demonstrates a strongly masculine sense of self-identity even though he was raised without a father or father substitute. This fact represents the most serious threat to _____ theory of personality.
    a. Maslow's
    b. Freud's
    c. Bandura's
    d. Rogers's
    e. Allport's

Evaluating the psychoanalytic perspective, p. 498
Medium, Factual/Definitional, Objective 6, Ans: b

57. Which of the following Freudian ideas is most clearly contradicted by contemporary psychological theory and research?
    a. Conscious awareness of what goes on in our minds is very limited.
    b. Painful experiences are commonly repressed.
    c. Memories are often distorted and incomplete.
    d. Individuals seek to defend themselves against anxiety.

Evaluating the psychoanalytic perspective, pp. 498-499
Easy, Factual/Definitional, Objective 6, Ans: d

58. Adults who were victims of sexual abuse as adolescents are often haunted by persistent and vivid memories of this experience. This most clearly serves to challenge Freud's concept of:
    a. free association.
    b. learned helplessness.
    c. motivational conflict.
    d. repression.
    e. fixation.

Evaluating the psychoanalytic perspective, p. 499
Difficult, Factual/Definitional, Objective 6, Ans: b

59. White research participants previously accused of racism give more money to a black panhandler than do their nonaccused counterparts. This generosity is most akin to Freud's concept of:
    a. sublimation.
    b. reaction formation.
    c. projection.
    d. displacement.
    e. fixation.

Evaluating the psychoanalytic perspective, p. 499
Medium, Factual/Definitional, Objective 6, Ans: d

60. Which of the following Freudian ideas is most consistent with contemporary psychological research findings?
    a. The conscience is largely formed in the process of resolving the Oedipus complex.
    b. People generally protect themselves by projecting their own undesirable traits onto others.
    c. Most memory loss results from unconsciously motivated repression.
    d. Conscious awareness of what goes on in our own minds is very limited.

Evaluating the psychoanalytic perspective, p. 499
Difficult, Factual/Definitional, Objective 6, Ans: b

61. Experimental tests of terror management theory indicate that anxiety about our own mortality can lead us to _____ our contempt for others and to _____ our self-esteem.
     a. decrease; decrease
     b. increase; increase
     c. decrease; increase
     d. increase; decrease

Evaluating the psychoanalytic perspective, p. 500
Medium, Factual/Definitional, Objective 6, Ans: c

62. Which theory has been most severely criticized for offering after-the-fact explanations without advancing testable predictions?
     a. humanistic theory
     b. trait theory
     c. psychoanalytic theory
     d. social-cognitive theory

The trait perspective, p. 502
Easy, Conceptual, Objective 7, Ans: d

63. Ellen is consistently optimistic, talkative, and impulsive. Each of these characteristics most clearly represents a:
     a. defense mechanism.
     b. personality type.
     c. fixation.
     d. trait.

The trait perspective, p. 502
Medium, Factual/Definitional, Objective 7, Ans: b

64. A concern with describing, classifying, and measuring the numerous ways in which individuals may differ from one another is most characteristic of the _____ perspective.
     a. social-cognitive
     b. trait
     c. humanistic
     d. psychoanalytic

The trait perspective, p. 502
Medium, Factual/Definitional, Objective 7, Ans: e

65. The ancient Greeks suggested that there was a strong relationship between four different personality types and:
     a. lunar cycles.
     b. brain structures.
     c. divine spirits.
     d. ocean tides.
     e. body fluids.

The trait perspective, p. 503
Medium, Factual/Definitional, Objective 7, Ans: b
66.   William Sheldon distinguished between the endomorph, mesomorph, and ectomorph:
a.   temperaments.
b.   body types.
c.   personality traits.
d.   habit patterns.
e.   defense mechanisms.

The trait perspective, p. 503
Difficult, Factual/Definitional, Objective 7, Ans: c
67.   Which of the following tests always describes personality in complimentary terms?
a.   Rorschach inkblot test
b.   Eysenck Personality Questionnaire
c.   Myers-Briggs Type Indicator
d.   MMPI
e.   TAT

Exploring traits, p. 503
Easy, Factual/Definitional, Objective 7, Ans: d
68.   In order to identify a relatively small number of the most basic personality traits, trait theorists
      have used:
a.   projective tests.
b.   free association.
c.   the MMPI-2.
d.   factor analysis.

Exploring traits, p. 504
Difficult, Conceptual, Objective 7, Ans: c
69.   Martin is optimistic, impulsive, excitable, and restless. In terms of the Eysencks' basic
      personality dimensions he would be classified as:
a.   external–dependent.
b.   manic–depressive.
c.   unstable–extraverted.
d.   passive–aggressive.
e.   internal–mesomorphic.

Exploring traits, p. 504
Medium, Factual/Definitional, Objective 7, Ans: c
70.   The "Big Five" is the term used to describe the basic:
a.   psychosexual stages.
b.   defense mechanisms.
c.   trait dimensions.
d.   sensory modalities.

Exploring traits, p. 504
Medium, Factual/Definitional, Objective 7, Ans: c

71. A person who is independent and imaginative most clearly ranks high on the Big Five trait
     dimension known as:
     a. emotional stability.
     b. extraversion.
     c. openness.
     d. agreeableness.
     e. conscientiousness.

Exploring traits, pp. 492, 504
Difficult, Conceptual, Objective 7, Ans: c

72. Which of the following Big Five trait dimensions is most closely related to whether or not an
     individual has a strong ego?
     a. extraversion
     b. agreeableness
     c. conscientiousness
     d. openness

Exploring traits, p. 505
Difficult, Factual/Definitional, Objective 7, Ans: d

73. In the decades after college, people's level of openness tends to _____ slightly and their
     level of agreeableness tends to _____ slightly.
     a. increase; increase
     b. decrease; decrease
     c. increase; decrease
     d. decrease; increase

Exploring traits, p. 505
Medium, Factual/Definitional, Objective 7, Ans: a

74. Extraverts experience _____ levels of brain arousal than introverts, and emotionally stable
     people experience _____ levels of autonomic nervous system arousal than those who are
     emotionally unstable.
     a. lower; lower
     b. higher; higher
     c. lower; higher
     d. higher; lower

How to be a "successful" astrologer or palm reader (Box), p. 507
Medium, Factual/Definitional, Objective 8, Ans: d

75. In convincing people that they can accurately assess their personalities, astrologers, palm
     readers, and graphologists take advantage of:
     a. factor analysis.
     b. the Electra complex.
     c. learned helplessness.
     d. the Barnum effect.
     e. free association.

How to be a "successful" astrologer or palm reader (Box), pp. 507, 515-516
Difficult, Conceptual, Objective 8, Ans: c

76.   As personality descriptions become more positive, the Barnum effect becomes stronger. This best illustrates:
a. reciprocal determinism.
b. unconditional positive regard.
c. self-serving bias.
d. an external locus of control.
e. attributional style.

Assessing traits, p. 508
Medium, Factual/Definitional, Objective 8, Ans: a

77.   Which of the following is true of the Minnesota Multiphasic Personality Inventory?
a. It is an empirically derived test.
b. It can be administered and scored only by a trained psychologist.
c. It is the most widely used projective test.
d. It was designed to assess the personality traits of normal, psychologically healthy individuals.

Assessing traits, p. 508
Medium, Conceptual, Objective 8, Ans: d

78.   Over the last few years, Mr. Helmus has been obsessed with bizarre thoughts and has become increasingly agitated and socially withdrawn. Which personality inventory would be most helpful for assessing the nature and severity of his symptoms?
a. Myers-Briggs Type Indicator
b. TAT
c. Rorschach inkblot test
d. MMPI-2

Assessing traits, p. 508
Difficult, Conceptual, Objective 8, Ans: e

79.   Which of the following questions would most likely appear on a lie scale?
a. Are you usually fairly happy?
b. Do your study habits affect your grades?
c. Do you constantly worry about your health?
d. Are most people willing to lie in order to get ahead?
e. Have you ever disliked anyone?

Evaluating the trait perspective, p. 509
Difficult, Factual/Definitional, Objective 8, Ans: c

80.   The temporal stability of personality traits is _____ among young children than among college students, and it is _____ among 30-year-olds than among 60-year-olds.
a. lower; higher
b. higher; lower
c. lower; lower
d. higher; higher

Evaluating the trait perspective, pp. 509-510
Medium, Factual/Definitional, Objective 8, Ans: c

81.   Trait theorists have been most criticized for:
      a.   underestimating the potential influence of biological factors on personality development.
      b.   underestimating the extent to which people differ from one another.
      c.   overestimating the consistency of behavior from one situation to another.
      d.   overestimating the importance of childhood experiences on adult personality traits.

Evaluating the trait perspective, pp. 509-510
Difficult, Conceptual, Objective 8, Ans: a

82.   Brenda has never cheated on a psychology test, but she often does so on chemistry tests. She recently stole some merchandise from a local store, but she also returned a lost billfold along with $28 to its rightful owner. Walter Mischel would suggest that this type of behavior should make psychologists more cautious about emphasizing:
      a.   personality traits.
      b.   personal control.
      c.   defense mechanisms.
      d.   reciprocal determinism.
      e.   unconditional positive regard.

Evaluating the trait perspective, pp. 509-510
Medium, Factual/Definitional, Objective 8, Ans: b

83.   People's scores on personality tests often fail to predict their behavior in a real-life situation. According to Walter Mischel, this should make us more cautious about emphasizing:
      a.   self-efficacy.
      b.   personality traits.
      c.   reciprocal determinism.
      d.   unconditional positive regard.
      e.   self-actualization.

Evaluating the trait perspective, p. 511
Medium, Factual/Definitional, Objective 8, Ans: d

84.   An individual's scores on a personality inventory would be most useful for predicting how that person would typically behave:
      a.   in a work setting.
      b.   in a recreational setting.
      c.   in a mental health setting.
      d.   across a wide variety of different settings.

Evaluating the trait perspective, p. 511
Medium, Factual/Definitional, Objective 8, Ans: a

85.   Observers' impressions of a mere 30 seconds of a teacher's expressive classroom behavior were very positively correlated with student ratings after an entire semester. This finding most directly supports the _____ perspective.
      a.   trait
      b.   humanistic
      c.   psychoanalytic
      d.   social-cognitive

The humanistic perspective, p. 512
Easy, Factual/Definitional, Objective 9, Ans: c
86. Which perspective on personality emphasizes the importance of our capacity for healthy growth and self-realization?
a. psychoanalytic
b. social-cognitive
c. humanistic
d. trait

Abraham Maslow's self-actualizing person, p. 512
Easy, Factual/Definitional, Objective 9, Ans: b
87. According to Maslow, the psychological need that arises after all other needs have been met is the need for:
a. personal control.
b. self-actualization.
c. self-esteem.
d. unconditional positive regard.

Abraham Maslow's self-actualizing person, p. 512
Difficult, Conceptual, Objective 9, Ans: b
88. Self-actualized people, as described by Maslow, are most likely to:
a. be self-centered.
b. have a strong ego.
c. experience an external locus of control.
d. lack a strong sense of gender identity.

Abraham Maslow's self-actualizing person, p. 512
Difficult, Conceptual, Objective 9, Ans: c
89. Self-actualized people, as described by Maslow, are least likely to:
a. have a strong ego.
b. have a well-developed superego.
c. experience an external locus of control.
d. have a strong sense of gender identity.

Carl Rogers's person-centered perspective, p. 513
Easy, Factual/Definitional, Objective 9, Ans: b
90. Carl Rogers emphasized the importance of:
a. the collective unconscious.
b. unconditional positive regard.
c. personality inventories.
d. reciprocal determinism.
e. free association.

Carl Rogers's person-centered perspective, p. 513
Difficult, Conceptual, Objective 9, Ans: c
91. Wesley has frequently been rebellious, inconsiderate, and self-centered, yet the pastor of his local church has always accepted and respected him. The pastor's attitude toward Wesley is most explicitly recommended by:
a. Freud.
b. Maslow.
c. Rogers.
d. Bandura.
e. Adler.

Carl Rogers's person-centered perspective, p. 513
Easy, Factual/Definitional, Objective 9, Ans: d

92.   The self-concept was first emphasized as a central feature of personality by the _____
       perspective.
       a. trait
       b. psychoanalytic
       c. social-cognitive
       d. humanistic

Assessing the self, p. 513
Medium, Factual/Definitional, Objective 10, Ans: b

93.   In order to assess a client's personal growth, Carl Rogers measured the correspondence
       between _____ and _____.
       a. locus of control; self-actualization
       b. ideal self; actual self
       c. the client's values; the therapist's values
       d. unconditional positive regard; self actualization
       e. self-esteem; locus of control

Research on the self, p. 514
Medium, Factual/Definitional, Objective 10, Ans: a

94.   Medical students earn higher grades if they have a clear vision of themselves as successful
       doctors. This best illustrates the motivational significance of:
       a. possible selves.
       b. unconditional positive regard.
       c. self-serving bias.
       d. an internal locus of control.
       e. identification.

Research on the self, p. 514
Medium, Factual/Definitional, Objective 10, Ans: b

95.   Our motivation to achieve success and avoid failure is most directly influenced by our:
       a. collective unconscious.
       b. possible selves.
       c. defense mechanisms.
       d. erogenous zones.

The benefits of self-esteem, p. 514
Medium, Factual/Definitional, Objective 10, Ans: c

96.   Self-esteem refers to:
       a. the sum total of all our thoughts about ourselves.
       b. our concept of what we would like to be.
       c. our feelings of high or low self-worth.
       d. all the above.

The benefits of self-esteem, p. 514
Easy, Factual/Definitional, Objective 10, Ans: d

97.   People with high self-esteem are less likely than those with low self-esteem to:
       a. experience an internal locus of control.
       b. overestimate the accuracy of their beliefs.
       c. manifest self-serving bias.
       d. succumb to conformity pressures.
       e. have a strong ego.

Culture and self-esteem, p. 515
Medium, Factual/Definitional, Objective 10, Ans: c

98. By comparing themselves to members of their own ethnic group, minorities are most likely to maintain their:
    a. individualism.
    b. collective unconscious.
    c. self-esteem.
    d. external locus of control.
    e. free association.

The pervasiveness of self-serving bias, p. 516
Easy, Factual/Definitional, Objective 10, Ans: c

99. The tendency to accept more personal responsibility for one's successes than for one's failures best illustrates:
    a. reaction formation.
    b. an external locus of control.
    c. self-serving bias.
    d. reciprocal determinism.
    e. the Barnum effect.

The pervasiveness of self-serving bias, p. 516
Easy, Factual/Definitional, Objective 10, Ans: c

100. The fact that most university students believe their Scholastic Assessment Test scores underestimate their actual academic ability best illustrates:
    a. the Barnum effect.
    b. displacement.
    c. self-serving bias.
    d. an external locus of control.
    e. projection.

The pervasiveness of self-serving bias, p. 516
Difficult, Conceptual, Objective 10, Ans: b

101. Which of the following statements is the least representative of self-serving bias?
    a. "I won the tennis match because of my athletic skill."
    b. "I lost the tennis match because I wasn't concentrating enough during the game."
    c. "I won the tennis match because I trained hard for the match during the last month."
    d. "I lost the tennis match because my opponent was a tennis professional."

The pervasiveness of self-serving bias, p. 516
Easy, Factual/Definitional, Objective 10, Ans: d

102. In national surveys, most business executives say they are more ethical than their average counterpart. This best illustrates:
    a. reaction formation.
    b. an external locus of control.
    c. the Barnum effect.
    d. self-serving bias.
    e. reciprocal determinism.

The pervasiveness of self-serving bias, p. 516
Difficult, Factual/Definitional, Objective 10, Ans: e
103. When people compare themselves with others, they are most likely to experience:
    a. reciprocal determinism.
    b. unconditional positive regard.
    c. an external locus of control.
    d. the Barnum effect.
    e. positive self-esteem.

The pervasiveness of self-serving bias, p. 516
Difficult, Factual/Definitional, Objective 10, Ans: c
104. Research on self-perception indicates that most people:
    a. are more critical of themselves than they are of other people.
    b. are unrealistically pessimistic about their personal future.
    c. more quickly believe flattering descriptions of themselves than unflattering feedback.
    d. feel more personally responsible for their failures than for their successes.

The pervasiveness of self-serving bias, p. 517
Medium, Factual/Definitional, Objective 10, Ans: d
105. People are most likely to react violently to an insult if they experience _____ self-esteem.
    a. unrealistically low
    b. moderately low
    c. moderately high
    d. unrealistically high

Culture and the individual self, p. 518
Medium, Conceptual, Objective 11, Ans: c
106. Social roles are especially likely to be central to people's self-identity in _____ cultures.
    a. individualist
    b. ethnically diverse
    c. collectivist
    d. racially diverse
    e. democratic

Culture and the individual self, p. 518
Medium, Conceptual, Objective 11, Ans: e
107. According to the humanistic therapist Fritz Perls, "I am not in this world to live up to your expectations." This sentiment would not be readily accepted in a culture that values:
    a. personal control.
    b. multiculturalism.
    c. self-actualization.
    d. racial diversity.
    e. collectivism.

Culture and the individual self, p. 518
Easy, Factual/Definitional, Objective 11, Ans: b
108. Collectivism is most likely to be emphasized in _____ cultures.
    a. North American
    b. Asian
    c. European
    d. industrialized

Culture and the individual self, p. 518
Difficult, Conceptual, Objective 11, Ans: e

109. Japanese university students are more likely than American university students to describe themselves in terms of:
    a. university affiliation.
    b. gender.
    c. family membership.
    d. nationality.
    e. any of the above.

Culture and the individual self, p. 518
Medium, Factual/Definitional, Objective 11, Ans: a

110. American students are more likely than Japanese students to describe themselves in terms of their:
    a. personal traits.
    b. gender.
    c. ethnic background.
    d. group memberships.
    e. social identities.

Culture and the individual self, pp. 518-519
Medium, Factual/Definitional, Objective 11, Ans: b

111. In a collectivist culture, individuals are likely to avoid:
    a. expressing personal humility.
    b. embarrassing other people.
    c. extended conversations.
    d. all the above.

Culture and the individual self, p. 519
Medium, Factual/Definitional, Objective 11, Ans: a

112. One would not expect high rates of divorce in a culture that promotes:
    a. collectivism.
    b. ethnic diversity.
    c. political pluralism.
    d. religious diversity.
    e. individual privacy.

Culture and the individual self, pp. 518-519
Difficult, Conceptual, Objective 11, Ans: d

113. Individualism is to collectivism as _____ is to _____.
    a. responsibility; freedom
    b. industrialization; democracy
    c. displacement; projection
    d. self-flattery; self-effacement
    e. pleasure principle; reality principle

Culture and the individual self, p. 518
Medium, Conceptual, Objective 11, Ans: d

114. Interdependence is to _____ as independence is to _____.
      a. learned helplessness; personal control
      b. reciprocal determinism; free association
      c. pleasure principle; reality principle
      d. collectivism; individualism

Culture and the individual self, p. 519
Medium, Factual/Definitional, Objective 11, Ans: d

115. Innovation and creativity are most likely to be appreciated in a culture that values:
      a. role models.
      b. collectivism.
      c. nationalism.
      d. individualism.
      e. free association.

Culture and the individual self, p. 519
Medium, Factual/Definitional, Objective 11, Ans: b

116. Compared with those living in individualist cultures, people in collectivist cultures are likely to experience _____ privacy and _____ loneliness.
      a. more; less
      b. less; less
      c. more; more
      d. less; more

Culture and the individual self, pp. 518-519
Medium, Conceptual, Objective 11, Ans: a

117. Parents in individualist cultures are more likely than parents in collectivist cultures to encourage children to value:
      a. nonconformity.
      b. cooperation.
      c. gender roles.
      d. cultural traditions.

Evaluating the humanistic perspective, p. 520
Difficult, Conceptual, Objective 12, Ans: e

118. Humanistic psychologists such as Carl Rogers would most likely be criticized for underestimating the value of:
      a. self-serving bias.
      b. the Barnum effect.
      c. unconditional positive regard.
      d. an internal locus of control.
      e. collectivism.

Evaluating the humanistic perspective, p. 520
Easy, Factual/Definitional, Objective 12, Ans: d

119. Which personality theorists have been criticized the most for encouraging individual selfishness and self-indulgence?
      a. trait theorists
      b. social-cognitive theorists
      c. psychoanalytic theorists
      d. humanistic theorists

Evaluating the humanistic perspective, p. 521
Easy, Factual/Definitional, Objective 12, Ans: b
120. Which theorists have been criticized for underestimating the human predisposition to engage in destructive and evil behaviors?
    a. trait theorists
    b. humanistic theorists
    c. psychoanalytic theorists
    d. social-cognitive theorists

Evaluating the humanistic perspective, p. 521
Difficult, Conceptual, Objective 12, Ans: b
121. Morris is hostile, aggressive, and socially destructive. According to Carl Rogers, this behavior pattern results from:
    a. reciprocal determinism.
    b. cultural influences.
    c. the collective unconscious.
    d. inborn personality traits.
    e. an internal locus of control.

The social-cognitive perspective, p. 522
Easy, Factual/Definitional, Objective 13, Ans: c
122. Which perspective most clearly emphasizes the interactive effects of internal personality dynamics and external environmental occurrences on human behavior?
    a. trait perspective
    b. psychoanalytic perspective
    c. social-cognitive perspective
    d. humanistic perspective

Reciprocal influences, p. 522
Easy, Factual/Definitional, Objective 13, Ans: b
123. Which perspective on human personality emphasizes reciprocal determinism?
    a. psychoanalytic
    b. social-cognitive
    c. trait
    d. humanistic

Reciprocal influences, p. 522
Easy, Conceptual, Objective 13, Ans: c
124. Connie's refusal to purchase fattening snacks at the grocery store is both a cause and a consequence of her superior dietary self-control. This best illustrates the importance of:
    a. reaction formation.
    b. self-serving bias.
    c. reciprocal determinism.
    d. an external locus of control.
    e. unconditional positive regard.

Reciprocal influences, pp. 522-523
Medium, Conceptual, Objective 13, Ans: e

125. Because she is often rejected by her parents, Sally mistrusts other people and treats them with hostility, which leads to their rejection of her. This cycle of rejection, mistrust, hostility, and further rejection illustrates what is meant by:
    a. an external locus of control.
    b. the Barnum effect.
    c. the self-serving bias.
    d. reaction formation.
    e. reciprocal determinism.

Reciprocal influences, pp. 522, 523
Difficult, Conceptual, Objective 13, Ans: d

126. Within the framework of Bandura's reciprocal determinism, an external locus of control refers to a(n):
    a. behavior.
    b. genetic predisposition.
    c. environmental factor.
    d. cognitive factor.
    e. defense mechanism.

Locus of control, p. 523
Medium, Conceptual, Objective 14, Ans: d

127. Julio believes that no matter how hard he works, the "system" is so biased against his ethnic group that he will be unable to achieve economic success. Julio's thinking most clearly demonstrates:
    a. displacement.
    b. reaction formation.
    c. self-serving bias.
    d. an external locus of control.
    e. the Barnum effect.

Locus of control, p. 523
Medium, Conceptual, Objective 14, Ans: c

128. George refuses to take reasonable precautions to protect his health because he believes good health is just a matter of luck anyway. George's attitude best illustrates:
    a. the Barnum effect
    b. reaction formation.
    c. an external locus of control.
    d. self-serving bias.
    e. reciprocal determinism.

Locus of control, p. 523
Easy, Factual/Definitional, Objective 14, Ans: d

129. The perception that one can strongly influence the outcome and destiny of one's own life exemplifies:
    a. the reality principle.
    b. the Barnum effect.
    c. the pleasure principle.
    d. an internal locus of control.
    e. reciprocal determinism.

Locus of control, p. 523
Medium, Conceptual, Objective 14, Ans: e

130. Paula expects that diligent study will enable her to earn good grades on her tests. Paula's belief best illustrates:
      a. self-serving bias.
      b. the Barnum effect.
      c. an Electra complex.
      d. unconditional positive regard.
      e. an internal locus of control.

Locus of control, p. 523
Medium, Factual/Definitional, Objective 14, Ans: c

131. Compared to those with an external locus of control, people who perceive an internal locus of control are:
      a. likely to experience low self-esteem.
      b. extremely introverted personalities.
      c. likely to be academically successful.
      d. not easily able to delay gratification of their personal desires.

Locus of control, p. 523
Medium, Factual/Definitional, Objective 14, Ans: c

132. Compared to those with an internal locus of control, individuals with an external locus of control are _____ likely to feel depressed and _____ likely to delay gratification.
      a. more; more
      b. less; less
      c. more; less
      d. less; more

Learned helplessness versus personal control, pp. 523-524
Easy, Factual/Definitional, Objective 14, Ans: c

133. Researchers have observed that the experience of repeated uncontrollable traumatic events contributes to:
      a. self-actualization.
      b. the Barnum effect.
      c. learned helplessness.
      d. reaction formation.
      e. an internal locus of control.

Learned helplessness versus personal control, pp. 523, 524
Easy, Conceptual, Objective 14, Ans: a

134. Veena gets poor grades no matter how hard she studies, so she has simply given up studying. Veena's behavior most clearly reflects:
      a. learned helplessness.
      b. an internal locus of control.
      c. an inferiority complex.
      d. the Barnum effect.
      e. an Electra complex.

Learned helplessness versus personal control, p. 524
Medium, Factual/Definitional, Objective 14, Ans: d

135. Differences in the body language of working-class men in East and West Berlin bars best illustrated the impact of:
    a. displacement.
    b. free association.
    c. reaction formation.
    d. personal control.
    e. reciprocal determinism.

Optimism, p. 524
Medium, Factual/Definitional, Objective 14, Ans: d

136. The trait of optimism is most closely related to a strong sense of:
    a. conditional positive regard.
    b. gender identity.
    c. ideal self.
    d. personal control.
    e. the pleasure principle.

Optimism, p. 524
Difficult, Conceptual, Objective 14, Ans: c

137. In order to assess how optimistic or pessimistic your college classmates are, you would be best advised to discover:
    a. how old they expect to be at the time of their death.
    b. what grades they anticipate receiving in future college courses.
    c. how they explain their academic failures, financial setbacks, and relationship difficulties.
    d. how much financial debt they are willing to incur in order to complete their education.
    e. how many people they consider to be their close friends.

Toward a more positive psychology (Close-up), p. 525
Easy, Factual/Definitional, Objective 14, Ans: a

138. Martin Seligman has advocated a positive psychology which focuses on topics such as:
    a. optimism.
    b. extraversion.
    c. the Barnum effect.
    d. external locus of control.
    e. free association.

Optimism, p. 526
Easy, Factual/Definitional, Objective 14, Ans: d

139. Most late adolescents perceive themselves as less at risk from the AIDS virus than are their peers. This best illustrates:
    a. repression.
    b. the Barnum effect.
    c. reaction formation.
    d. unrealistic optimism.
    e. an external locus of control.

Assessing behavior in situations, p. 527
Medium, Factual/Definitional, Objective 15, Ans: b

140. According to the social-cognitive perspective, one of the best ways to predict a person's future behavior is to:
    a. identify that person's most central traits by having him or her take a personality inventory.
    b. observe that person's behavior in various relevant situations.
    c. assess that person's general level of self-esteem.
    d. uncover that person's hidden motives, as revealed by projective tests.

Assessing behavior in situations, p. 527
Medium, Conceptual, Objective 15, Ans: b

141. According to the social-cognitive perspective, the best predictor of students' academic success in college would be their:
    a. college entrance test scores.
    b. high school grade point average.
    c. personal optimism about the future.
    d. performance on the MMPI-2.

Evaluating the social-cognitive perspective, p. 528
Medium, Factual/Definitional, Objective 15, Ans: c

142. A criticism of the social-cognitive perspective has been that it:
    a. overestimates the importance of unconscious factors in personality.
    b. is inconsistent with research demonstrating the pervasive nature of self-serving bias.
    c. underestimates the importance of enduring personality traits.
    d. is inconsistent with the results of contemporary research on learning processes.

CHAPTER **15**

Psychological Disorders

Learning Objectives

Perspectives on Psychological Disorders (pp. 532-538)

1. Identify the criteria for judging whether behavior is psychologically disordered.

2. Describe the medical model of psychological disorders, and discuss the bio-psycho-social perspective offered by critics of this model.

3. Describe the aims of DSM-IV, and discuss the potential dangers associated with the use of diagnostic labels.

Anxiety Disorders (pp. 539-544)

4. Describe the symptoms of generalized anxiety disorders, phobias, and obsessive-compulsive disorders.

5. Explain the development of anxiety disorders from both a learning and a biological perspective.

Mood Disorders (pp. 545-553)

6. Describe major depressive disorder and bipolar disorder.

7. Explain the development of mood disorders, paying special attention to the biological and social-cognitive perspectives.

Thinking Critically About Dissociation and Multiple Personalities (pp. 554-555)

8. Describe the characteristics and possible causes of dissociative identity disorder.

Schizophrenia (pp. 556-562)

9. Describe the various symptoms and types of schizophrenia, and discuss research on its causes.

Personality Disorders (pp. 562-564)

10. Describe the nature of personality disorders, focusing on the characteristics of the antisocial personality disorder.

Rates of Psychological Disorders (pp. 564-565)

11.   Describe the prevalence of various disorders and the timing of their onset.

Defining psychological disorders, p. 532
Medium, Factual/Definitional, Objective 1, Ans: d
1.   Psychologists are most likely to define maladaptive behavior as disordered if it is:
      a. unloving and prejudicial.
      b. biologically based and habitual.
      c. unconsciously motivated.
      d. unusual and socially unacceptable.

Defining psychological disorders, p. 533
Medium, Factual/Definitional, Objective 1, Ans: b
2.   Tobacco dependence has been classified as a behavioral disorder largely because it is:
      a. statistically infrequent.
      b. personally maladaptive.
      c. socially unacceptable.
      d. ethically unjustifiable.
      e. biologically motivated.

Understanding psychological disorders, p. 533
Easy, Factual/Definitional, Objective 2, Ans: c
3.   The conception of psychological disorders as biologically based sicknesses is known as the
      _____ model.
      a. psychoanalytic
      b. humanistic
      c. medical
      d. bio-psycho-social
      e. trait

Understanding psychological disorders, p. 533
Easy, Conceptual, Objective 2, Ans: c
4.   Mira claims that alcoholism is a disease that, like pneumonia or meningitis, can be cured or
      prevented with proper treatment. Her belief is most clearly consistent with:
      a. the humanistic perspective.
      b. psychoanalytic theory.
      c. the medical model.
      d. the social-cognitive perspective.

Understanding psychological disorders, p. 533
Medium, Conceptual, Objective 2, Ans: c
5.   If research indicated that phobias result from a chemical imbalance in the central nervous
      system, this would most clearly give added credibility to:
      a. trait theory.
      b. psychoanalytic theory.
      c. the medical model.
      d. the humanistic perspective.
      e. the DSM-IV.

Understanding psychological disorders, p. 534
Medium, Factual/Definitional, Objective 2, Ans: b

6. The medical model of psychologically disordered behavior is most likely to be criticized for neglecting the importance of:
   a. anxiety and depression.
   b. social circumstances.
   c. personality disorders.
   d. the DSM-IV.
   e. genetic abnormalities.

Understanding psychological disorders, p. 534
Easy, Factual/Definitional, Objective 2, Ans: d

7. Most mental health workers assume that disordered behavior is influenced by:
   a. social circumstances.
   b. inner psychological dynamics.
   c. genetic predispositions and physiological states.
   d. all the above.

Classifying psychological disorders, p. 535
Medium, Factual/Definitional, Objective 3, Ans: e

8. A psychotherapist is most likely to use the DSM-IV in order to _____ various psychological disorders.
   a. cure
   b. prevent
   c. excuse
   d. explain
   e. identify

Classifying psychological disorders, p. 535
Medium, Conceptual, Objective 3, Ans: d

9. The DSM-IV would be most useful for deciding whether:
   a. Paula is chronically unfriendly.
   b. Robert is excessively introverted.
   c. Christie is insane.
   d. Ronald is obsessive-compulsive.
   e. Stacey is overly altruistic.

Classifying psychological disorders, p. 535
Easy, Factual/Definitional, Objective 3, Ans: b

10. Neurotic disorders are most often contrasted with the more debilitating:
    a. phobias.
    b. psychotic disorders.
    c. personality disorders.
    d. panic disorder.
    e. post-traumatic stress disorder.

Classifying psychological disorders, p. 535
Difficult, Conceptual, Objective 3, Ans: b

11.   Which of the following disorders would Freud have been most likely to describe as a manifestation of neurosis?
      a. antisocial personality disorder
      b. obsessive-compulsive disorder
      c. bipolar disorder
      d. schizophrenia

Classifying psychological disorders, p. 535
Easy, Factual/Definitional, Objective 3, Ans: c

12.   Psychological disorders in which people lose contact with reality and experience irrational ideas and distorted perceptions are known as _____ disorders.
      a. panic
      b. generalized anxiety
      c. psychotic
      d. obsessive-compulsive
      e. dissociative

Classifying psychological disorders, p. 535
Difficult, Factual/Definitional, Objective 3, Ans: c

13.   In order to facilitate diagnostic reliability, the DSM-IV typically bases diagnoses on:
      a. chemical analyses of blood and urine samples.
      b. physiological measures of blood pressure, perspiration, and muscle tension.
      c. observable patterns of behavior.
      d. all the above.

Labeling psychological disorders, p. 536
Medium, Factual/Definitional, Objective 3, Ans: e

14.   In a study by David Rosenhan (1973), researchers were admitted as patients into various mental hospitals after they falsely claimed to be "hearing voices." This study best illustrated the negative effects of:
      a. the medical model.
      b. schizophrenia.
      c. hallucinations.
      d. linkage analysis.
      e. diagnostic labels.

Labeling psychological disorders, p. 536
Medium, Conceptual, Objective 3, Ans: d

15.   After Anika learned that her history professor had suffered an anxiety disorder, she concluded that the professor's tendency to talk loudly was simply a way of disguising feelings of personal insecurity. This best illustrates the:
      a. value of the psychoanalytic perspective.
      b. shortcomings of the medical model.
      c. unreliability of DSM-IV.
      d. biasing power of diagnostic labels.
      e. impact of student expectations on professors' behavior.

Labeling psychological disorders, p. 536
Medium, Factual/Definitional, Objective 3, Ans: a
16.   If people form their impressions of psychological disorder from television, they are most likely to overestimate the percentage of people suffering psychological disorders who are:
a.   violent.
b.   depressed.
c.   shy.
d.   anxious.

Insanity and responsibility (Box), p. 538
Medium, Factual/Definitional, Objective 3, Ans: d
17.   Insanity is most clearly characterized by:
a.   a selective loss of memory.
b.   hallucinations and delusions.
c.   a hyperactive, wildly optimistic state of emotion.
d.   an inability to appreciate the wrongfulness of one's own destructive actions.
e.   a persistent, irrational fear of people that causes one to commit crimes against society.

Insanity and responsibility (Box), p. 538
Medium, Conceptual, Objective 3, Ans: e
18.   When Mr. Greenbaum set his house on fire, he was unable to control himself or appreciate that he was doing something wrong. Mr. Greenbaum's case most clearly provides an example of:
a.   an antisocial personality disorder.
b.   an obsessive-compulsive disorder.
c.   a dissociative disorder.
d.   schizophrenia.
e.   insanity.

Generalized anxiety disorder, p. 539
Easy, Factual/Definitional, Objective 4, Ans: a
19.   In which of the following disorders is a person continually tense, apprehensive, and in a state of autonomic arousal?
a.   generalized anxiety disorder
b.   antisocial personality disorder
c.   dysthymic disorder
d.   dissociative identity disorder
e.   bipolar disorder

Generalized anxiety disorder, p. 539
Medium, Conceptual, Objective 4, Ans: d
20.   Indira, a third-grade teacher, frequently suffers from dizziness, headaches, muscle tremors, fatigue, and irritability in the classroom. She is also continually agitated and unable to relax outside the classroom, but she cannot pinpoint a reason for her problems. Her behavior is most indicative of a(n):
a.   dysthymic disorder.
b.   phobia.
c.   obsessive-compulsive disorder.
d.   generalized anxiety disorder.
e.   dissociative disorder.

Generalized anxiety disorder, p. 539
Medium, Factual/Definitional, Objective 4, Ans: b
21.   Episodes of intense dread that last for several minutes and are accompanied by shortness of
       breath, trembling, dizziness, choking, or heart palpitations are most characteristic of a(n):
       a. manic episode.
       b. panic disorder.
       c. obsessive-compulsive disorder.
       d. dysthymic disorder.
       e. dissociative disorder.

Generalized anxiety disorder, p. 539
Difficult, Factual/Definitional, Objective 4, Ans: b
22.   Panic attacks are most closely associated with:
       a. schizophrenia.
       b. anxiety disorders.
       c. dissociative disorders.
       d. mood disorders.
       e. personality disorders.

Generalized anxiety disorder, p. 540
Difficult, Conceptual, Objective 4, Ans: d
23.   A person who has agoraphobia is most likely to:
       a. avoid dust and dirt.
       b. stay away from fire.
       c. avoid household pets.
       d. stay close to home.

Phobias, p. 540
Easy, Factual/Definitional, Objective 4, Ans: a
24.   Phobias are most likely to be characterized by:
       a. a persistent, irrational fear of a specific object or situation.
       b. offensive and unwanted thoughts that persistently preoccupy the person.
       c. the misinterpretation of normal physical sensations as signs of a disease.
       d. a continuous state of tension, apprehension, and autonomic nervous system arousal.
       e. alternations between extreme hopelessness and unrealistic optimism.

Phobias, p. 540
Medium, Conceptual, Objective 4, Ans: d
25.   Mark is extremely shy and is so easily embarrassed in front of other people that he often misses
       his college classes just to avoid social interactions. Mark appears to suffer from a(n):
       a. dissociative disorder.
       b. dysthymic disorder.
       c. antisocial personality disorder.
       d. phobia.
       e. generalized anxiety disorder.

Obsessive-compulsive disorder, pp. 540-541
Easy, Factual/Definitional, Objective 4, Ans: b

26. An anxiety disorder characterized by unwanted repetitive thoughts and actions is called a(n)
    _____ disorder.
    a. bipolar
    b. obsessive-compulsive
    c. dissociative
    d. panic
    e. post-traumatic stress

Obsessive-compulsive disorder, pp. 540-541
Medium, Conceptual, Objective 4, Ans: b

27. Ravi brushes his teeth 18 times a day. Each time, he uses exactly 83 strokes up and 83 strokes
    down. After he eats, he must brush twice with two different brands of toothpaste. Ravi suffers
    from a(n):
    a. dysthymic disorder.
    b. obsessive-compulsive disorder.
    c. phobia.
    d. generalized anxiety disorder.
    e. bipolar disorder.

Obsessive-compulsive disorder, pp. 540-541
Medium, Conceptual, Objective 4, Ans: c

28. While driving to work, Pedro hears a radio advertisement for a new restaurant. Throughout the
    day, the tune associated with the advertisement keeps running through his head. Pedro's
    inability to forget the tune best illustrates the nature of a(n):
    a. delusion.
    b. hallucination.
    c. obsession.
    d. compulsion.
    e. phobia.

Obsessive-compulsive disorder, pp. 540-541
Easy, Factual/Definitional, Objective 4, Ans: b

29. Compulsions are best described as:
    a. persistent fears.
    b. repetitive behaviors.
    c. illusory sensations.
    d. suicidal thoughts.
    e. false beliefs.

Obsessive-compulsive disorder, pp. 540-541
Difficult, Conceptual, Objective 4, Ans: b

30. Repeatedly checking to see if your stove is turned off is to _____ as repeatedly thinking
    you might kill your own children is to _____.
    a. depression; mania
    b. compulsion; obsession
    c. hallucination; delusion
    d. neurotic; psychotic

Explaining anxiety disorders, pp. 541-542
Easy, Conceptual, Objective 5, Ans: c

31.   A rape victim may experience a panic attack when she sees anyone wearing a ski mask like the
       one worn by her attacker. This reaction is best explained from a _____ perspective.
       a. trait
       b. psychoanalytic
       c. learning
       d. biological
       e. humanistic

Explaining anxiety disorders, pp. 541-542
Difficult, Conceptual, Objective 5, Ans: d

32.   Predictable aversive stimulation is to _____ as unpredictable aversive stimulation is to

       _____.
       a. obsessive-compulsive disorder; a dissociative disorder
       b. a mood disorder; schizophrenia
       c. a depressive disorder; bipolar disorder
       d. a phobia; generalized anxiety disorder

Explaining anxiety disorders, p. 542
Medium, Conceptual, Objective 5, Ans: a

33.   A therapist suggests that Mr. Ozawa's fear of darkness can probably be traced back to his early
       childhood when he was occasionally beaten and locked up in a small, dark closet by an older
       brother. The therapist's suggestion most clearly reflects a _____ perspective.
       a. learning
       b. psychoanalytic
       c. humanistic
       d. biological
       e. trait

Explaining anxiety disorders, p. 542
Medium, Factual/Definitional, Objective 5, Ans: b

34.   Learning theorists have suggested that obsessive-compulsive disorders are:
       a. habitual defenses against unconscious impulses.
       b. reinforced by anxiety reduction.
       c. classically conditioned habits.
       d. conditioned reactions to childhood sexual abuse.

Explaining anxiety disorders, p. 542
Medium, Conceptual, Objective 5, Ans: d

35.   A therapist suggests that Mr. Broshi continues to bite his fingernails because this behavior
       often reduced his feelings of anxiety in the past. The therapist's suggestion most clearly reflects
       a _____ perspective.
       a. biological
       b. humanistic
       c. psychoanalytic
       d. learning
       e. trait

Post-traumatic stress disorder (Close-up), p. 543
Easy, Conceptual, Objective 4, Ans: b
36. Two years after being brutally beaten and raped, Susan still experiences anxiety and has trouble sleeping and vivid flashbacks of her assault. Susan is most clearly showing signs of:
a. a dissociative disorder.
b. post-traumatic stress disorder.
c. dysthymic disorder.
d. obsessive-compulsive disorder.
e. bipolar disorder.

Post-traumatic stress disorder (Close-up), p. 543
Medium Conceptual, Objective 4, Ans: e
37. A post-traumatic stress disorder could best be described as a(n) _____ disorder.
a. psychotic
b. dissociative
c. dysthymic
d. personality
e. anxiety

Explaining anxiety disorders, p. 542
Medium, Factual/Definitional, Objective 5, Ans: c
38. Although World War II air raids were extremely traumatic for those who experienced them, few of these people developed lasting phobic reactions to overhead planes. This fact is best explained from a(n) _____ perspective.
a. learning
b. psychoanalytic
c. biological
d. humanistic

Explaining anxiety disorders, p. 542
Medium, Factual/Definitional, Objective 5, Ans: a
39. Research on anxiety disorders indicates that:
a. some people are genetically predisposed to develop anxiety disorders.
b. obsessive-compulsive disorders are more common than phobias.
c. people, but not animals, may acquire fear through observational learning.
d. phobic reactions to cats are much more common than to dogs.

Explaining anxiety disorders, p. 544
Difficult, Factual/Definitional, Objective 5, Ans: b
40. An overarousal of brain areas involved in impulse control and habitual behaviors is most characteristic of:
a. dissociative identity disorder.
b. generalized anxiety disorder.
c. schizophrenia.
d. major depressive disorder.
e. antisocial personality disorder.

Major depressive disorder, p. 545
Medium, Factual/Definitional, Objective 6, Ans: c

41.   Because it is so pervasive, _____ is often considered "the common cold" of psychological disorders.
      a. agoraphobia
      b. schizophrenia
      c. depression
      d. dissociation
      e. low self-esteem

Major depressive disorder, p. 545
Easy, Conceptual, Objective 6, Ans: a

42.   Norby, an 18-year-old college freshman, has missed almost all his classes during the past month. He spends most of his time in his bedroom, frequently not even bothering to get dressed or eat meals. He thinks his whole life has been a failure and blames himself for being a social misfit. Norby is most likely suffering from:
      a. major depression disorder.
      b. an antisocial personality disorder.
      c. a dissociative disorder.
      d. agoraphobia.
      e. panic disorder.

Major depressive disorder, p. 545
Medium, Factual/Definitional, Objective 6, Ans: b

43.   Low self-esteem is most likely to be characterized by:
      a. specific phobias.
      b. dysthymic disorder.
      c. manic episodes.
      d. antisocial personality disorder.

Bipolar disorder, p. 546
Medium, Factual/Definitional, Objective 6, Ans: d

44.   Bipolar disorder is most likely to be characterized by:
      a. a massive dissociation of self from ordinary consciousness.
      b. the simultaneous experience of delusions of persecution and delusions of grandeur.
      c. offensive and unwanted thoughts that persistently intrude into conscious awareness.
      d. alternations between extreme hopelessness and unrealistic optimism.
      e. a chronic lack of guilt feelings.

Bipolar disorder, p. 546
Medium, Factual/Definitional, Objective 6, Ans: b

45.   Which of the following disorders is classified as a mood disorder?
      a. catatonia
      b. bipolar disorder
      c. generalized anxiety disorder
      d. antisocial personality disorder
      e. phobia

Bipolar disorder, p. 546
Easy, Factual/Definitional, Objective 6, Ans: c

46. Manic episodes are most likely to be associated with a(n):
    a. panic attack.
    b. phobia.
    c. bipolar disorder.
    d. generalized anxiety disorder.
    e. antisocial personality disorder.

Bipolar disorder, p. 546
Medium, Factual/Definitional, Objective 6, Ans: d

47. Mania is most likely to be characterized by feelings of:
    a. guilt.
    b. fear.
    c. ambivalence.
    d. optimism.
    e. indifference.

Bipolar disorder, p. 546
Medium, Conceptual, Objective 6, Ans: c

48. After several weeks of feeling very apathetic and dissatisfied with his life, Mark has suddenly become extremely cheerful and so talkative he can't be interrupted. He seems to need less sleep and becomes irritated when his friends tell him to slow down. Mark's behavior is indicative of:
    a. an obsessive-compulsive disorder.
    b. schizophrenia.
    c. bipolar disorder.
    d. dissociative disorder.
    e. dysthymic disorder.

Explaining mood disorders, p. 546
Medium, Factual/Definitional, Objective 7, Ans: d

49. Compared to men, women are much more likely to be diagnosed as suffering from:
    a. an antisocial personality disorder.
    b. a bipolar disorder.
    c. alcoholism.
    d. depression.
    e. any of the above.

Explaining mood disorders, p. 547
Medium, Factual/Definitional, Objective 7, Ans: a

50. According to the psychoanalytic perspective, depression results from:
    a. the internalization of anger.
    b. learned helplessness.
    c. self-defeating attributions.
    d. an unconscious fear of death.
    e. a weak conscience.

Explaining mood disorders, p. 547
Medium, Conceptual, Objective 7, Ans: d
51. Although it has been 2 years since his girlfriend left him, Joaquin still suffers from depression. His therapist believes that Joaquin remains depressed because the girlfriend reminded him of his mother, who died when he was a child. The therapist's interpretation most clearly reflects the _____ perspective.
    a. humanistic
    b. social-cognitive
    c. trait
    d. psychoanalytic
    e. biological

Explaining mood disorders, pp. 547-548
Easy, Factual/Definitional, Objective 7, Ans: c
52. The incidence of major depressive disorder is _____ among those with an identical twin who suffers from depression than among those with a fraternal twin who suffers from depression. The incidence of bipolar disorder is _____ among those with an identical twin who experiences a bipolar disorder than among those with a fraternal twin who experiences a bipolar disorder.
    a. higher; lower
    b. lower; higher
    c. higher; higher
    d. lower; lower

Suicide (Close-up), p. 548
Difficult, Factual/Definitional, Objective 7, Ans: a
53. In the United States, _____ are much more likely to attempt suicide than _____.
    a. women; men
    b. the poor; the rich
    c. adolescents; adults
    d. blacks; whites

Suicide (Close-up), p. 548
Difficult, Factual/Definitional, Objective 7, Ans: c
54. Suicide rates are _____ among the rich than the poor, and they are _____ among younger men than older men.
    a. higher; higher
    b. lower; lower
    c. higher; lower
    d. lower; higher

Suicide (Close-up), p. 548
Easy, Factual/Definitional, Objective 7, Ans: b
55. Suicidal thoughts are most likely to be associated with:
    a. generalized anxiety disorder.
    b. a mood disorder.
    c. schizophrenia.
    d. dissociative identity disorder
    e. antisocial personality disorder

Explaining mood disorders, p. 549
Medium, Factual/Definitional, Objective 7, Ans: d
56. Depression is associated with _____ norepinephrine levels and _____ serotonin levels.
    a. high; low
    b. low; high
    c. high; high
    d. low; low

Explaining mood disorders, p. 550
Difficult, Factual/Definitional, Objective 7, Ans: b
57. Severely depressed individuals are especially likely to show reduced brain activity in the:
    a. right frontal lobe.
    b. left frontal lobe.
    c. right occipital lobe.
    d. left occipital lobe.

Explaining mood disorders, p. 550
Medium, Factual/Definitional, Objective 7, Ans: b
58. Learned helplessness is most closely associated with:
    a. dissociative disorders.
    b. depression.
    c. schizophrenia.
    d. phobias.
    e. compulsions.

Explaining mood disorders, p. 550
Medium, Factual/Definitional, Objective 7, Ans: d
59. Self-blaming attributions are most likely to be associated with:
    a. schizophrenia.
    b. obsessive-compulsive disorders.
    c. phobias.
    d. mood disorders.

Explaining mood disorders, pp. 550-551
Difficult, Factual/Definitional, Objective 7, Ans: c
60. Failures are most likely to lead to depression if they are explained in terms that are:
    a. internal, unstable, and specific.
    b. external, unstable, and global.
    c. internal, stable, and global.
    d. external, stable, and specific.

Explaining mood disorders, p. 550
Difficult, Conceptual, Objective 7, Ans: b
61. A therapist believes that Chet is chronically depressed because he takes too little credit for his many achievements and assumes too much responsibility for his few failures. The therapist's interpretation reflects a _____ perspective.
    a. psychoanalytic
    b. social-cognitive
    c. trait
    d. humanistic
    e. biological

Explaining mood disorders, p. 550
Difficult, Factual/Definitional, Objective 7, Ans: a
62.   The rise of Western individualism appears most clearly responsible for an increase in:
   a. depression.
   b. schizophrenia.
   c. personality disorders.
   d. obsessive-compulsive disorder.
   e. phobias.

Explaining mood disorders, p. 551
Easy, Factual/Definitional, Objective 7, Ans: d
63.   It has been suggested that women are more vulnerable to depression than men because women are more likely to respond to negative life events with self-focused rumination. This suggestion best illustrates a _____ perspective.
   a. trait
   b. biological
   c. psychoanalytic
   d. social-cognitive

Explaining mood disorders, pp. 551-552
Medium, Factual/Definitional, Objective 7, Ans: d
64.   The vicious cycle of depression is often initiated by:
   a. a breakdown in selective attention.
   b. unrealistic optimism about the future.
   c. excessive levels of norepinephrine.
   d. stressful life experiences.
   e. external attributions of blame.

Explaining mood disorders, pp. 552-553
Difficult, Factual/Definitional, Objective 7, Ans: d
65.   One way for people to break the vicious cycle of depression is to:
   a. accept more personal responsibility for their own bad moods.
   b. spend more time in quiet rest, seclusion, and personal meditation.
   c. frequently talk to their friends about their negative thoughts and depressive feelings.
   d. participate more often in activities they consider pleasant and rewarding.
   e. do all the above.

Loneliness (Close-Up), p. 553
Medium, Factual/Definitional, Objective 7, Ans: c
66.   Which of the following is thought to contribute most to feelings of loneliness?
   a. people's tendency to generalize their feelings of inadequacy
   b. reinforcement for avoidance of social contacts
   c. the emphasis on self-fulfillment
   d. lack of personal control

Dissociation and multiple personalities (Box), p. 554
Easy, Factual/Definitional, Objective 8, Ans: a

67.   Dissociative disorders are most likely to be characterized by:
   a. disruptions in conscious awareness and sense of identity.
   b. offensive and unwanted thoughts that persistently preoccupy a person.
   c. a hyperactive, wildly optimistic state of emotion.
   d. alternations between extreme hopelessness and unrealistic optimism.

Dissociation and multiple personalities (Box), p. 554
Medium, Factual/Definitional, Objective 8, Ans: d

68. The major characteristic of dissociative disorders is a disturbance of:
    a. sleep.
    b. mood.
    c. appetite.
    d. memory.
    e. perception.

Dissociation and multiple personalities (Box), p. 554
Medium, Conceptual, Objective 8, Ans: a

69. Several weeks after being fired from a job he had held for over 20 years, Harold awoke one morning in a state of bewildered confusion. He had little sense of who he was and even failed to recognize his wife. Harold's experience is most indicative of:
    a. dissociative disorder.
    b. phobia.
    c. generalized anxiety disorder.
    d. panic disorder.
    e. dysthymic disorder.

Dissociation and multiple personalities (Box), p. 554
Medium, Factual/Definitional, Objective 8, Ans: c

70. Individuals with a dissociative identity disorder are usually:
    a. males.
    b. victims of schizophrenia.
    c. nonviolent.
    d. children of permissive and overindulgent parents.

Dissociation and multiple personalities (Box), p. 555
Difficult, Conceptual, Objective 8, Ans: b

71. Sharon demonstrates seven different personalities that appear to take turns controlling her behavior. Evidence that all the alternate personalities actually share the same common life memories would most clearly rule out the contribution of _____ to her disorder.
    a. childhood sexual trauma
    b. dissociation
    c. motivational conflict
    d. role playing

Dissociation and multiple personalities (Box), p. 555
Medium, Factual/Definitional, Objective 8, Ans: e

72. The dramatic increase in reported cases of dissociative identity disorder during the past 30 or so years most strongly suggests that symptoms of this disorder involve:
    a. low self-esteem.
    b. illicit drug usage.
    c. promiscuous sexual behavior.
    d. internal attribution of blame.
    e. role playing.

Dissociation and multiple personalities (Box), p. 555
Difficult, Factual/Definitional, Objective 8, Ans: b

73. Evidence that dissociative identity disorder is not simply a product of conscious role playing is most clearly provided by the:
    a. periodic intervals during which patients become uncontrollably violent.
    b. distinct brain and body states associated with differing personalities.
    c. inability of psychiatric experts to hypnotize these patients.
    d. dramatic increase in reported cases of this disorder during the past 30 or so years.
    e. persistent autonomic nervous system arousal experienced by patients.

Dissociation and multiple personalities (Box), p. 555
Medium, Conceptual, Objective 8, Ans: e

74. Midori's therapist suggests that she developed a dissociative identity disorder as a way of protecting herself from an awareness of her own hatred for her abusive mother. The therapist's suggestion most directly reflects a _____ perspective.
    a. trait
    b. social-cognitive
    c. humanistic
    d. biological
    e. psychoanalytic

Symptoms of schizophrenia, p. 556
Easy, Factual/Definitional, Objective 9, Ans: b

75. Schizophrenia is most likely to be characterized by:
    a. suicidal thoughts.
    b. disorganized and fragmented thinking.
    c. a lack of guilt feelings.
    d. alternations between extreme hopelessness and unrealistic optimism.
    e. periodic intervals of uncontrollable violence.

Symptoms of schizophrenia, p. 556
Easy, Conceptual, Objective 9, Ans: c

 76. Mr. Kalish, a long-term government employee, falsely believed that his supervisor was a communist agent who was putting poison in the employees' coffee. When Mr. Kalish was referred to a psychiatrist, he claimed to be the grandson of Abraham Lincoln. Mr. Kalish is most likely suffering from:
    a. dissociative identity disorder.
    b. a phobia.
    c. schizophrenia.
    d. panic disorder.

Symptoms of schizophrenia, p. 556
Easy, Factual/Definitional, Objective 9, Ans: c

77. False beliefs of persecution that may accompany psychotic disorders are called:
    a. obsessions.
    b. compulsions.
    c. delusions.
    d. phobias.
    e. hallucinations.

Symptoms of schizophrenia, p. 556
Easy, Factual/Definitional, Objective 9, Ans: b
78.   Hallucinations and delusions are most likely to be experienced by those who suffer from:
    a. dissociative identity disorder.
    b. schizophrenia.
    c. major depressive disorder.
    d. agoraphobia.
    e. borderline personality disorder.

Symptoms of schizophrenia, p. 556
Medium, Conceptual, Objective 9, Ans: e
79.   Seeing one-eyed monsters would be a(n) _____. Believing that you are Abraham Lincoln
    would be a _____.
    a. delusion; compulsion
    b. obsession; delusion
    c. hallucination; compulsion
    d. obsession; compulsion
    e. hallucination; delusion

Symptoms of schizophrenia, p. 556
Difficult, Factual/Definitional, Objective 9, Ans: c
80.   The hallucinations experienced by those who suffer from schizophrenia are most likely to
    involve _____ things that are not there.
    a. seeing
    b. feeling
    c. hearing
    d. tasting
    e. smelling

Symptoms of schizophrenia, p. 557
Easy, Factual/Definitional, Objective 9, Ans: d
81.   Which of the following disorders is most resistant to cure?
    a. generalized anxiety disorder
    b. dysthymic disorder
    c. phobia
    d. schizophrenia
    e. dissociative identity disorder

Types of schizophrenia, p. 557
Difficult, Factual/Definitional, Objective 9, Ans: c
82.   One of the positive symptoms of schizophrenia includes:
    a. an expressionless face.
    b. a lack of guilt feelings.
    c. delusions of persecution.
    d. flat affect.

Types of schizophrenia (Table 15.2), p. 557
Medium, Factual/Definitional, Objective 9, Ans: a
83.   A tendency to remain motionless for long periods of time is most common among those with
_____ schizophrenia.
   a. catatonic
   b. disorganized
   c. undifferentiated
   d. paranoid

Types of schizophrenia, p. 557
Difficult, Conceptual, Objective 9, Ans: b
84.   "Gradually developing" is to "suddenly developing" as _____ schizophrenia is to _____
schizophrenia.
   a. reactive; process
   b. chronic; acute
   c. process; chronic
   d. acute; reactive

Types of schizophrenia, p. 557
Medium, Factual/Definitional, Objective 9, Ans: a
85.   The chances for recovery from schizophrenia are considered to be greatest when the disorder
develops:
   a. rapidly in response to a stressful life situation.
   b. slowly over a period of years.
   c. in reaction to abnormalities in brain chemistry.
   d. during adolescence or early adulthood.

Types of schizophrenia, p. 557
Difficult, Factual/Definitional, Objective 9, Ans: d
86.   People are more likely to recover from _____ schizophrenia than from _____
schizophrenia.
   a. acute; reactive
   b. process; chronic
   c. chronic; acute
   d. reactive; process

Understanding schizophrenia, p. 558
Medium, Factual/Definitional, Objective 9, Ans: c
87.   Cocaine may _____ symptoms of schizophrenia by _____ dopamine levels.
   a. increase; decreasing
   b. decrease; increasing
   c. increase; increasing
   d. decrease; decreasing

Understanding schizophrenia, p. 558
Easy, Factual/Definitional, Objective 9, Ans: e
88.   A shrinkage of cerebral tissue is most likely to be associated with:
   a. dissociative disorders.
   b. obsessive-compulsive disorder.
   c. post-traumatic stress disorder.
   d. dysthymic disorder.
   e. schizophrenia.

Understanding schizophrenia, p. 559
Difficult, Factual/Definitional, Objective 9, Ans: a
89. Schizophrenia victims' difficulty with focusing attention is most likely to be related to a shrinkage of the:
    a. thalamus.
    b. cerebellum.
    c. hypothalamus.
    d. pituitary gland

Understanding schizophrenia, p. 559
Medium, Factual/Definitional, Objective 9, Ans: e
90. Evidence suggests that _____ contribute(s) to schizophrenia.
    a. the internalization of anger
    b. depressed serotonin levels
    c. a pessimistic explanatory style
    d. conscious role playing
    e. prenatal viral infections

Understanding schizophrenia, p. 559
Medium, Factual/Definitional, Objective 9, Ans: d
91. North Americans born during the winter and spring months are at a slightly increased risk for:
    a. depression.
    b. bipolar disorder.
    c. generalized anxiety disorder.
    d. schizophrenia.
    e. antisocial personality disorder.

Understanding schizophrenia, p. 559
Difficult, Factual/Definitional, Objective 9, Ans: c
92. People born in _____ during the month of _____ are at an increased risk for schizophrenia.
    a. the United States; September
    b. Argentina; February
    c. Australia; September
    d. South Africa; February

Understanding schizophrenia, pp. 559-560
Difficult, Factual/Definitional, Objective 9, Ans: c
93. If one identical twin is diagnosed as having schizophrenia, the probability that the other twin will at some point be similarly diagnosed is approximately _____ percent.
    a. 10
    b. 25
    c. 50
    d. 75
    e. 90

Understanding schizophrenia, p. 561
Difficult, Factual/Definitional, Objective 9, Ans: d
94.   A short attention span is an early warning sign of:
       a. dysthymic disorder.
       b. a phobia.
       c. obsessive-compulsive disorder.
       d. schizophrenia.
       e. antisocial personality disorder.

Personality disorders, p. 562
Easy, Factual/Definitional, Objective 10, Ans: d
95.   Psychological disorders characterized by inflexible, enduring, and socially maladaptive
       behavior patterns are called _____ disorders.
       a. psychotic
       b. dissociative
       c. schizophrenia
       d. personality

Personality disorders, p. 562
Medium, Factual/Definitional, Objective 10, Ans: a
96.   A schizoid personality disorder is most likely to be characterized by:
       a. a detachment from social relationships.
       b. shallow, attention-getting emotional displays.
       c. a sense of self-importance.
       d. an insatiable desire for attention.
       e. a fear of social rejection.

Personality disorders, p. 562
Medium, Factual/Definitional, Objective 10, Ans: d
97.   Those with a histrionic personality disorder are most likely to display:
       a. a lack of guilt feelings.
       b. delusions of persecution.
       c. apathy and lack of energy.
       d. shallow, attention-getting emotions.

Personality disorders, p. 562
Medium, Factual/Definitional, Objective 10, Ans: d
98.   A borderline personality disorder is most clearly characterized by a(n):
       a. insatiable desire for attention.
       b. irrational fear of people.
       c. lack of guilt feelings.
       d. unstable sense of self.

Personality disorders, p. 562
Easy, Factual/Definitional, Objective 10, Ans: b
99.   A lack of conscience is most characteristic of those who have a(n) _____ disorder.
       a. dissociative
       b. antisocial personality
       c. dysthymic
       d. panic
       e. obsessive-compulsive

Personality disorders, p. 562
Medium, Conceptual, Objective 10, Ans: a

100. Within the last year, Mr. Shangkun has been fired by three different employers because they each discovered that he was stealing money or materials from their companies. Although he feels no remorse for his misdeeds, his outward signs of repentance have dissuaded his former employers from taking him to court. Mr. Shangkun's behavior is most indicative of:

  a. a personality disorder.
  b. a phobia.
  c. schizophrenia.
  d. a dissociative disorder.
  e. obsessive-compulsive disorder.

Personality disorders, p. 563
Easy, Factual/Definitional, Objective 10, Ans: c

101. The surging rates of violent crime in Western nations during the past 40 years are best explained from a(n) _____ perspective.

  a. medical
  b. psychoanalytic
  c. bio-psycho-social
  d. evolutionary
  e. trait

Rates of psychological disorders (Table 15.3), p. 565
Easy, Factual/Definitional, Objective 11, Ans: b

102. Compared to women, men are _____ vulnerable to depression and _____ vulnerable to alcohol abuse.

  a. more; more
  b. less; more
  c. more; less
  d. less; less

CHAPTER **16**

Therapy

Learning Objectives

The Psychological Therapies (pp. 568-581)

1. Discuss the aims and methods of psychoanalysis and explain the critics' concerns with this form of therapy.

2. Identify the basic characteristics of the humanistic therapies as well as the specific goals and techniques of client-centered therapy.

3. Identify the basic assumptions of behavior therapy and discuss the classical conditioning techniques of systematic desensitization, flooding, and aversive conditioning.

4. Describe therapeutic applications of operant conditioning principles and explain the critics' concerns with this behavior modification process.

5. Describe the assumptions and goals of the cognitive therapies and their application to the treatment of depression.

6. Discuss the rationale and benefits of group therapy, including family therapy.

Evaluating Psychotherapies (pp. 581-592)

7. Discuss the findings regarding the effectiveness of the psychotherapies, and explain why ineffective therapies are often mistakenly perceived to be of value.

8. Describe the commonalities among the psychotherapies, and discuss the role of values and cultural differences in the therapeutic process.

The Biomedical Therapies (pp. 592-598)

9. Identify the common forms of drug therapy.

10. Describe the use of electroconvulsive therapy and psychosurgery in the treatment of psychological disorders.

Preventing Psychological Disorders (pp. 598-599)

11. Explain the rationale of preventive mental health programs.

The psychological therapies, p. 568
Easy, Factual/Definitional, Objective 1, Ans: b

1. A therapist who uses a variety of psychological theories and therapeutic methods is said to be:
    a. client-centered.
    b. eclectic.
    c. humanistic.
    d. psychoanalytic.
    e. meta-analytic.

The psychological therapies, p. 568
Medium, Conceptual, Objective 1, Ans: d

2. As a therapist, Dr. Quist often uses systematic desensitization. She also considers active listening to be an invaluable therapeutic tool, and she frequently makes use of free association. Dr. Quist's therapeutic approach would best be described as:
    a. psychoanalytic.
    b. client-centered.
    c. behavioral.
    d. eclectic.
    e. meta-analytic.

Psychoanalysis, p. 568
Medium, Factual/Definitional, Objective 1, Ans: c

3. Psychoanalytic techniques are designed primarily to help clients:
    a. focus on their immediate conscious feelings.
    b. feel more trusting toward others.
    c. become aware of their repressed conflicts and impulses.
    d. develop greater self-esteem.

Psychoanalysis, p. 569
Easy, Factual/Definitional, Objective 1, Ans: b

4. Which of the following therapists introduced the use of free association?
    a. Carl Rogers
    b. Sigmund Freud
    c. Aaron Beck
    d. Joseph Wolpe
    e. Mary Carver Jones

Psychoanalysis, p. 569
Easy, Factual/Definitional, Objective 1, Ans: d

5. Free association involves the:
    a. expression toward a therapist of feelings linked with earlier relationships.
    b. therapeutic interpretation of a client's unconscious conflicts.
    c. repeated association of a relaxed state with anxiety-arousing stimuli.
    d. uncensored reporting of any thoughts that come to mind.
    e. replacement of a negative response to a harmless stimulus with a positive response.

Psychoanalysis, p. 569
Medium, Conceptual, Objective 1, Ans: b

6. Sheena's therapist tells her to relax, close her eyes, and state aloud whatever comes to mind no matter how trivial or absurd. The therapist is using a technique that is central to:
    a. client-centered therapy.
    b. psychoanalysis.
    c. cognitive therapy.
    d. EMDR.
    e. systematic desensitization.

Psychoanalysis, p. 569
Medium, Factual/Definitional, Objective 1, Ans: c

7. According to Freud, a patient's hesitation to free associate is most likely a sign of:
    a. transference.
    b. the placebo effect.
    c. resistance.
    d. spontaneous recovery.
    e. meta-analysis.

Psychoanalysis, p. 569
Medium, Factual/Definitional, Objective 1, Ans: e

8. Psychoanalysts would suggest that resistance during therapy supports and maintains the process of:
    a. sublimation.
    b. transference.
    c. free association.
    d. dream interpretation.
    e. repression.

Psychoanalysis, p. 569
Medium, Conceptual, Objective 1, Ans: b

9. Just as Jerome began telling his therapist about a painful childhood experience, he complained of a headache and abruptly ended the session. A psychoanalyst would most likely suggest that Jerome's behavior is an example of:
    a. fixation.
    b. resistance.
    c. transference.
    d. counterconditioning.
    e. free association.

Psychoanalysis, p. 569
Easy, Factual/Definitional, Objective 1, Ans: e

10. The interpretation of dreams is most closely associated with:
    a. cognitive therapy.
    b. virtual reality exposure therapy.
    c. client-centered therapy.
    d. systematic desensitization.
    e. psychoanalysis.

Psychoanalysis, p. 569
Easy, Factual/Definitional, Objective 1, Ans: b

11. The expression toward a therapist of feelings linked with earlier relationships is known as:
    a. free association.
    b. transference.
    c. fixation.
    d. projection.
    e. eclectic therapy.

Psychoanalysis, p. 569
Difficult, Conceptual, Objective 1, Ans: a

12. Mr. Phillips has recently begun to express feelings of hostility and resentment toward his therapist, who is consistently friendly, caring, and helpful. A psychoanalyst would most likely consider Mr. Phillips's hostility to be an example of:
    a. transference.
    b. flooding.
    c. the placebo effect.
    d. counterconditioning.
    e. regression toward the mean.

Psychoanalysis, p. 569
Difficult, Factual/Definitional, Objective 1, Ans: a

13. Psychoanalysts are most likely to:
    a. attend to patients' positive and negative feelings toward their therapists.
    b. associate a client's undesirable behavior with unpleasant experiences.
    c. repeat or rephrase what a client says during the course of therapy.
    d. help clients identify a hierarchy of anxiety-arousing experiences.
    e. vigorously challenge clients' illogical ways of thinking.

Psychoanalysis, p. 570
Medium, Factual/Definitional, Objective 1, Ans: d

14. Which form of therapy is most likely to be criticized for being too lengthy and time-consuming?
    a. systematic desensitization
    b. family therapy
    c. client-centered therapy
    d. psychoanalysis
    e. cognitive therapy

Psychoanalysis, p. 571
Medium, Factual/Definitional, Objective 1, Ans: e

15. Which of the following provides a brief alternative to psychodynamic therapy and is effective with depressed patients?
    a. flooding
    b. systematic desensitization
    c. EMDR
    d. therapeutic touch
    e. interpersonal psychotherapy

Humanistic therapies, p. 571
Difficult, Factual/Definitional, Objective 2, Ans: c
16. Humanistic therapists are most likely to:
    a. encourage clients to carefully observe the consequences of their maladaptive behaviors.
    b. focus special attention on clients' positive and negative feelings toward their therapists.
    c. emphasize the importance of self-awareness for psychological adjustment.
    d. use a wide variety of psychological theories and therapeutic methods.
    e. help clients identify a hierarchy of anxiety-arousing experiences.

Client-centered therapy, p. 571
Easy, Factual/Definitional, Objective 2, Ans: d
17. Carl Rogers is known for the development of:
    a. therapeutic touch.
    b. the token economy.
    c. cognitive therapy.
    d. client-centered therapy.
    e. systematic desensitization.

Client-centered therapy, p. 571
Easy, Factual/Definitional, Objective 2, Ans: a
18. Which of the following is considered to be the most nondirective form of therapy?
    a. client-centered therapy
    b. cognitive therapy
    c. psychoanalysis
    d. systematic desensitization
    e. light-exposure therapy

Client-centered therapy, p. 571
Difficult, Conceptual, Objective 2, Ans: d
19. Dr. Buist does not analyze people's motives or diagnose the nature of their difficulties because he believes that they are in the best position to diagnose and solve their own problems. Dr. Buist's position is most characteristic of _____ therapy.
    a. cognitive
    b. psychoanalytic
    c. operant conditioning
    d. client-centered
    e. biomedical

Client-centered therapy, p. 572
Medium, Factual/Definitional, Objective 2, Ans: d
20. Client-centered therapists are most likely to:
    a. encourage clients to stop blaming themselves for their failures.
    b. help clients associate anxiety-arousing stimuli with a pleasant state of relaxation.
    c. encourage clients to carefully observe the consequences of their maladaptive behaviors.
    d. restate and seek further clarification of what clients say during the course of therapy.
    e. vigorously challenge clients' self-defeating thoughts.

Client-centered therapy, p. 572
Medium, Factual/Definitional, Objective 2, Ans: d

21. Which approach emphasizes the importance of providing patients with feelings of unconditional acceptance?
    a. cognitive therapy
    b. psychoanalysis
    c. biomedical therapy
    d. client-centered therapy
    e. systematic desensitization

Psychoanalysis and client-centered therapy, pp. 569, 572
Medium, Conceptual, Objectives 1 & 2, Ans: b

22. Freud is to _____ as Rogers is to _____.
    a. psychoanalysis; counterconditioning
    b. free association; active listening
    c. dream analysis; systematic desensitization
    d. active listening; empathy

Behavior therapies, p. 573
Easy, Factual/Definitional, Objective 3, Ans: c

23. Which of the following therapies is more concerned with removing specific troubling symptoms than with providing special insights into the personality of the client?
    a. eclectic therapy
    b. psychoanalysis
    c. behavior therapy
    d. client-centered therapy
    e. cognitive therapy

Behavior therapies, p. 573
Difficult, Conceptual, Objective 3, Ans: a

24. Geraldine suggested that her nail biting might be a symptom of unconscious resentment toward her parents. Her therapist chuckled and said, "No, Geraldine, your problem isn't unconscious hostility; your problem is nail biting." Geraldine's therapist sounds most like a _____ therapist.
    a. behavior
    b. humanistic
    c. cognitive
    d. psychoanalytic
    e. biomedical

Classical conditioning techniques, p. 573
Medium, Factual/Definitional, Objective 3, Ans: b

25. Counterconditioning techniques were derived from principles first developed by:
    a. Aaron Beck.
    b. Ivan Pavlov.
    c. Carl Rogers.
    d. B. F. Skinner.
    e. Sigmund Freud.

Classical conditioning techniques, p. 573
Difficult, Conceptual, Objective 3, Ans: e

26. In an effort to reduce his daughter's fear of the dark, Mr. Chew would hug and gently rock her immediately after turning off the lights at bedtime. Mr. Chew's strategy best illustrates the technique of:
    a. relaxation training.
    b. transference.
    c. unconditioned positive regard.
    d. aversive conditioning.
    e. counterconditioning.

Classical conditioning techniques, p. 573
Medium, Factual/Definitional, Objective 3, Ans: e

27. Mowrer trained children to discontinue bed-wetting by arranging for an alarm to sound each time they wet their beds. This technique best illustrates a therapeutic application of:
    a. systematic desensitization.
    b. observational learning.
    c. cognitive-behavior therapy.
    d. the placebo effect.
    e. classical conditioning.

Systematic desensitization, p. 573
Medium, Factual/Definitional, Objective 3, Ans: c

28. Which of the following techniques is derived from classical conditioning principles?
    a. the token economy
    b. light-exposure therapy
    c. systematic desensitization
    d. stress inoculation training
    e. transference

Systematic desensitization, p. 573
Difficult, Factual/Definitional, Objective 3, Ans: b

29. The technique of systematic desensitization was refined by:
    a. Sigmund Freud.
    b. Joseph Wolpe.
    c. Aaron Beck.
    d. Egas Moniz.
    e. Carl Rogers.

Systematic desensitization, p. 574
Medium, Factual/Definitional, Objective 3, Ans: b

30. The repeated association of pleasant relaxing states with stimuli that arouse fear is a central feature of:
    a. humanistic therapy.
    b. systematic desensitization.
    c. cognitive therapy.
    d. aversive conditioning.
    e. stress inoculation training.

Systematic desensitization, p. 574
Easy, Factual/Definitional, Objective 3, Ans: c
31.   The construction of an anxiety hierarchy and training in relaxation are important aspects of:
    a. biomedical therapy.
    b. aversive conditioning.
    c. systematic desensitization.
    d. client-centered therapy.
    e. stress inoculation training.

Systematic desensitization, p. 574
Medium, Conceptual, Objective 3, Ans: d
32.   To help Michael overcome his fear of taking tests, his therapist instructs him to relax and then to imagine taking a quiz. The therapist is using:
    a. psychoanalysis.
    b. client-centered therapy.
    c. cognitive therapy.
    d. systematic desensitization.
    e. aversive conditioning.

Systematic desensitization, p. 574
Medium, Conceptual, Objective 3, Ans: b
33.   Mr. Vogt is terribly fearful of being alone in his own house at night. In order to reduce this fear, a behavior therapist would most likely use:
    a. the double-blind technique.
    b. systematic desensitization.
    c. a token economy.
    d. aversive conditioning.
    e. ECT.

Systematic desensitization, p. 574
Difficult, Conceptual, Objective 3, Ans: a
34.   With aversive conditioning, the therapist replaces a positive response with a negative response. With _____, the therapist replaces a negative response with a positive response.
    a. systematic desensitization
    b. free association
    c. client-centered therapy
    d. transference
    e. meta-analysis

Systematic desensitization, p. 574
Difficult, Factual/Definitional, Objective 3, Ans: d
35.   When people are forced to face situations that make them extremely fearful, their fear often begins to extinguish. This fact underlies the use of a procedure known as:
    a. aversive conditioning.
    b. transference.
    c. the double-blind technique.
    d. flooding.
    e. ECT.

Systematic desensitization, p. 574
Medium, Factual/Definitional, Objective 3, Ans: e

36. Virtual reality exposure therapy is most likely to prove effective in the treatment of:
    a. personality disorders.
    b. hallucinations.
    c. obsessions.
    d. depression.
    e. phobias.

Aversive conditioning, p. 575
Medium, Factual/Definitional, Objective 3, Ans: d

37. Aversive conditioning involves:
    a. replacing a negative response to a harmless stimulus with a positive response.
    b. identifying a hierarchy of anxiety-arousing experiences.
    c. depriving a client of access to an addictive drug.
    d. associating unwanted behaviors with unpleasant experiences.
    e. systematically controlling the consequences of patients' maladaptive behaviors.

Aversive conditioning, pp. 575, 597
Easy, Conceptual, Objective 3, Ans: c

38. A lobotomy is to psychosurgery as aversive conditioning is to:
    a. systematic desensitization.
    b. flooding.
    c. behavior therapy.
    d. EMDR.
    e. electroconvulsive therapy.

Aversive conditioning, p. 575
Easy, Factual/Definitional, Objective 3, Ans: d

39. A therapeutic technique in which child molesters receive electric shocks as they view photos of nude children best illustrates the use of:
    a. systematic desensitization.
    b. EMDR.
    c. stress inoculation training.
    d. aversive conditioning.
    e. electroconvulsive therapy.

Aversive conditioning, p. 575
Medium, Conceptual, Objective 3, Ans: c

40. Whenever 2-year-old Calista runs into the street in front of her house, her mother immediately spanks her. The mother's technique most closely resembles the procedure known as:
    a. systematic desensitization.
    b. electroconvulsive therapy.
    c. aversive conditioning.
    d. stress inoculation training.
    e. transference.

Aversive conditioning, p. 575
Difficult, Conceptual, Objective 3, Ans: e

41. Mrs. Laiti is a compulsive gambler. In order to reduce her attraction to this self-defeating activity, a behavior therapist would most likely use:
     a. EMDR
     b. systematic desensitization.
     c. a token economy.
     d. the double-blind technique.
     e. aversive conditioning.

Operant conditioning, p. 576
Medium, Factual/Definitional, Objective 4, Ans: d

42. Influencing psychotherapeutic clients by controlling the consequences of their actions illustrates an application of:
     a. humanistic therapy.
     b. classical conditioning.
     c. systematic desensitization.
     d. operant conditioning.

Operant conditioning, p. 576
Difficult, Conceptual, Objective 4, Ans: d

43. What would be most helpful for encouraging mentally retarded adults to make their beds every morning?
     a. cognitive therapy
     b. aversive conditioning
     c. client-centered therapy
     d. a token economy
     e. systematic desensitization

Operant conditioning, p. 576
Medium, Conceptual, Objective 4, Ans: b

44. In which operant conditioning procedure are positive reinforcers given for desired behaviors?
     a. flooding
     b. a token economy
     c. systematic desensitization
     d. aversive conditioning
     e. free association

Operant conditioning, p. 576
Medium, Conceptual, Objective 4, Ans: c

45. Mr. Thompson, a fifth-grade teacher, gives five blue stars to each student who achieves a perfect score on a math or spelling test. At the end of the semester, students can exchange their stars for prizes. Mr. Thompson's classroom strategy illustrates an application of:
     a. the placebo effect.
     b. transference.
     c. operant conditioning.
     d. systematic desensitization.
     e. counterconditioning.

Operant conditioning, p. 577
Medium, Factual/Definitional, Objective 4, Ans: d
46.   Which of the following is most often criticized for violating clients' rights to personal freedom and self-determination?
    a. psychoanalysis
    b. cognitive therapy
    c. client-centered therapy
    d. behavior modification
    e. EMDR

Cognitive therapies, p. 577
Medium, Factual/Definitional, Objective 5, Ans: a
47.   Cognitive therapists are most likely to emphasize that emotional disturbances result from:
    a. irrational beliefs.
    b. chemical abnormalities within the brain.
    c. overly permissive child-rearing practices.
    d. poverty, unemployment, racism, and sexism.

Cognitive therapy for depression, p. 578
Medium, Conceptual, Objective 5, Ans: a
48.   Natasha claimed that her failure to get straight "A's" in college meant she was incompetent. Her therapist calmly challenged this assertion, commenting, "By your strange calculations, well over 90 percent of all college students are incompetent!" The therapist's response was most typical of a(n) _____ therapist.
    a. cognitive
    b. behavior
    c. eclectic
    d. client-centered
    e. psychoanalytic

Cognitive therapy for depression, p. 578
Easy, Factual/Definitional, Objective 5, Ans: b
49.   Training people to stop blaming themselves for failures and negative circumstances beyond their control is of most direct concern to _____ therapists.
    a. psychoanalytic
    b. cognitive
    c. eclectic
    d. client-centered
    e. behavior

Cognitive therapy for depression, p. 578
Medium, Conceptual, Objective 5, Ans: d
50.   Cognitive therapists are most likely to encourage depressed clients to accept _____ personal responsibility for their failures and _____ personal responsibility for their successes.
    a. more; more
    b. less; less
    c. more; less
    d. less; more

Cognitive therapy for depression, p. 578
Difficult, Conceptual, Objective 5, Ans: a

51.   Mark, who suffers from chronic depression, is particularly upset about the low grade he
       received on his chemistry midterm exam. A cognitive therapist would be most likely to
       encourage Mark to attribute his failure to his:
       a. lack of adequate study time.
       b. lack of effective study skills.
       c. chronic test anxiety.
       d. lack of ability.

Cognitive therapy for depression, p. 579
Medium, Conceptual, Objective 5, Ans: b

52.   Although Mel is actually doing very well in college, he continues to feel academically
       incompetent. His therapist has instructed him to explain in writing how his own hard work and
       personal abilities contributed to each of the good grades he received during the previous
       semester. This therapeutic procedure is most characteristic of _____ therapy.
       a. behavior
       b. cognitive
       c. psychoanalytic
       d. humanistic
       e. biomedical

Cognitive therapy for depression, p. 579
Difficulty, Conceptual, Objective 5, Ans: d

53.   Cynthia is afraid of speaking to a large audience. Her therapist suggests that prior to a speaking
       she should reassure herself with comments like, "Cheer up, Cynthia. You know what you're
       talking about and your topic is really interesting!" This approach to reducing Cynthia's fear
       most clearly illustrates:
       a. aversion conditioning.
       b. client-centered therapy.
       c. systematic desensitization.
       d. stress inoculation training.
       e. psychoanalysis.

Group and family therapies, p. 580
Difficult, Conceptual, Objective 6, Ans: c

54.   A useful feature of group therapy is that it:
       a. ensures that therapists will become more emotionally involved in clients' real-life problems.
       b. eliminates the possibility that clients will experience anxiety during therapy.
       c. encourages clients to develop active listening skills.
       d. enables severely disturbed individuals to quickly regain normal social functioning.

Group and family therapies, p. 580
Easy, Factual/Definitional, Objective 6, Ans: b

55.   The belief that no person is an island is the fundamental assumption of:
       a. psychoanalysis.
       b. family therapy.
       c. client-centered therapy.
       d. cognitive therapy.
       e. systematic desensitization.

Group and family therapies, p. 580
Medium, Conceptual, Objective 6, Ans: d

56. In order to help Mrs. Otsuki lose weight, Dr. Watson first attempted to assess whether her weight loss might be personally threatening to her husband. The therapist's concern is most characteristic of a:
  a. eclectic therapist.
  b. biomedical therapist.
  c. client-centered therapist.
  d. family therapist.
  e. psychoanalyst.

Is psychotherapy effective?, p. 582
Easy, Factual/Definitional, Objective 7, Ans: a

57. Research on the effectiveness of psychotherapy indicates that:
  a. clients are generally satisfied with the effectiveness of therapy.
  b. clients' perceptions are the best evidence available for the effectiveness of therapy.
  c. clients tend to underestimate how much they have improved as a result of therapy.
  d. it is no more effective than having a friend to talk to.

Is psychotherapy effective?, p. 583
Difficult, Factual/Definitional, Objective 7, Ans: b

58. Therapists' perceptions of the effectiveness of psychotherapy are likely to be misleading because:
  a. therapists typically minimize the seriousness of their clients' symptoms when therapy begins.
  b. clients typically emphasize their problems at the start of therapy and their well-being at the end of therapy.
  c. therapists typically blame their own therapeutic ineffectiveness on clients' resistance.
  d. clients tend to focus on their observable behavioral problems rather than on their mental and emotional difficulties.
  e. therapists typically overestimate their clients' potential levels of adjustment.

"Regressing" from unusual to usual (Box), p. 584
Medium, Factual/Definitional, Objective 7, Ans: c

59. Which phenomenon refers to the tendency for extraordinary or unusual events to be followed by more ordinary events?
  a. the placebo effect
  b. systematic desensitization
  c. regression toward the mean
  d. free association
  e. flooding

"Regressing" from unusual to usual (Box), p. 584
Easy, Factual/Definitional, Objective 7, Ans: d

60. Which of the following is most likely to contribute to inflated perceptions of the effectiveness of psychotherapy?
  a. meta-analysis
  b. flooding
  c. free association
  d. regression toward the mean
  e. the double-blind technique

"Regressing" from unusual to usual (Box), p. 584
Medium, Conceptual, Objective 7, Ans: c

61. Students who receive unusually low scores on their first psychology test can reasonably anticipate _____ scores on their second psychology test.
    a. even lower
    b. equally low
    c. somewhat higher
    d. very high

"Regressing" from unusual to usual (Box), p. 584
Medium, Factual/Definitional, Objective 7, Ans: a

62. Unusual ESP subjects who defy chance when first tested nearly always lose their "psychic powers" when retested. This best illustrates:
    a. regression toward the mean.
    b. stress inoculation training.
    c. systematic desensitization.
    d. the double-blind technique.
    e. the placebo effect.

"Regressing" from unusual to usual (Box), p. 584
Medium, Conceptual, Objective 7, Ans: b

63. Although Shien once scored 37 points during a single high school basketball game, he was subsequently unable to beat or match this record no matter how hard he tried. His experience may be at least partially explained in terms of:
    a. the placebo effect.
    b. regression toward the mean.
    c. flooding.
    d. systematic desensitization.
    e. stress inoculation training.

Is psychotherapy effective?, p. 585
Easy, Factual/Definitional, Objective 7, Ans: d

64. Which of the following is a procedure for statistically combining the results of many different studies?
    a. factor analysis
    b. correlational analysis
    c. regression toward the mean
    d. meta-analysis
    e. rTMS

Is psychotherapy effective?, p. 585
Medium, Conceptual, Objective 7, Ans: e

65. Klaus is a psychology graduate student who wants to determine whether electroconvulsive therapy is an effective treatment for schizophrenia. In assessing the results of numerous published studies on this issue, Klaus should use a technique called:
    a. eclectic therapy.
    b. the double-blind procedure.
    c. factor analysis.
    d. counterconditioning.
    e. meta-analysis.

Is psychotherapy effective?, pp. 585-586
Medium, Factual/Definitional, Objective 7, Ans: c
66. The most convincing evidence for the effectiveness of psychotherapy comes from:
    a. studies of client satisfaction with the treatment received.
    b. reports from therapists concerning their perceptions of client improvement.
    c. meta-analyses of psychotherapeutic outcome studies.
    d. the reactions of family and friends to those who had recently undergone psychotherapeutic treatment.

Is psychotherapy effective?, pp. 586-587
Medium, Conceptual, Objective 7, Ans: c
67. Psychotherapy is most likely to be effective in freeing:
    a. Sharon from the feeling that her life is meaningless and worthless.
    b. Portia from her delusions of persecution and auditory hallucinations.
    c. Jim from an excessive fear of giving speeches in public.
    d. Luther from his antisocial personality disorder.

The relative effectiveness of different therapies, p. 586
Medium, Factual/Definitional, Objective 7, Ans: b
68. On the basis of a statistical analysis of some 475 psychotherapy outcome studies, Smith and her colleagues noted that:
    a. psychotherapy is no more effective than talking to a friend.
    b. no single form of therapy proves consistently superior to the others.
    c. psychotherapy actually harms just as many people as it helps.
    d. it is impossible to measure the effectiveness of psychotherapy.

The relative effectiveness of different therapies, p. 587
Difficult, Conceptual, Objective 7, Ans: d
69. Gretchen compulsively avoids shaking people's hands or touching doorknobs, because she is afraid of contracting infectious diseases. Research suggests that an especially effective treatment for her difficulty would involve:
    a. client-centered therapy.
    b. psychoanalysis.
    c. interpersonal therapy.
    d. counterconditioning.
    e. electroconvulsive therapy.

Therapeutic touch, p. 587
Medium, Factual/Definitional, Objective 7, Ans: e
70. In which procedure do practitioners claim to detect and manipulate human energy fields?
    a. electroconvulsive therapy
    b. eye movement desensitization and reprocessing
    c. light-exposure therapy
    d. therapeutic touch

Therapeutic touch, p. 588
Medium, Factual/Definitional, Objective 7, Ans: d
71. Which of the following has not been shown to be a beneficial treatment?
    a. stress inoculation training
    b. exposure therapy
    c. electroconvulsive therapy
    d. therapeutic touch

Eye movement desensitization and reprocessing, p. 588
Difficult, Factual/Definitional, Objective 7, Ans: d

72. EMDR was originally developed for the treatment of:
     a. alcoholism.
     b. bulimia.
     c. depression.
     d. anxiety.
     e. schizophrenia.

Eye movement desensitization and reprocessing, pp. 588-589
Easy, Factual/Definitional, Objective 7, Ans: e

73. Which of the following is most likely to contribute to inflated estimates of the value of eye movement desensitization and reprocessing?
     a. meta-analysis
     b. stress inoculation training
     c. therapeutic touch
     d. the double-blind technique
     e. the placebo effect

Eye movement desensitization and reprocessing, p. 589
Difficult, Conceptual, Objective 7, Ans: c

74. EMDR is most similar to a technique known as:
     a. stress inoculation training.
     b. therapeutic touch.
     c. systematic desensitization
     d. electroconvulsive therapy

Light-exposure therapy, p. 589
Easy, Factual/Definitional, Objective 7, Ans: d

75. Which of the following has been demonstrated to provide relief for those who suffer from SAD?
     a. flooding
     b. EMDR
     c. systematic desensitization
     d. light-exposure therapy
     e. therapeutic touch

Light-exposure therapy, p. 589
Medium, Factual/Definitional, Objective 7, Ans: b

76. The value of light-exposure therapy appears to result from its influence on people's:
     a. unconscious conflicts.
     b. circadian rhythm.
     c. self-blaming explanations for failure.
     d. social relationships.
     e. visual acuity.

Commonalities among psychotherapies, pp. 589-590
Easy, Factual/Definitional, Objective 8, Ans: b
77. The beneficial consequence of a person's expecting that a treatment will be therapeutic is known as:
a. systematic desensitization.
b. the placebo effect.
c. meta-analysis.
d. transference.
e. behavior modification.

Commonalities among psychotherapies, p. 590
Medium, Conceptual, Objective 8, Ans: c
78. Because she mistakenly thought that completing a diagnostic test was a therapeutic treatment for her anxiety disorder, Mrs. Shyam felt considerable relief for several weeks following the test. Mrs. Shyam's reaction best illustrates:
a. transference.
b. the double-blind technique.
c. the placebo effect.
d. meta-analysis.
e. systematic desensitization.

Commonalities among psychotherapies, p. 590
Difficult, Factual/Definitional, Objective 8, Ans: b
79. The psychotherapeutic value of hope is best illustrated by:
a. meta-analysis.
b. the placebo effect.
c. systematic desensitization.
d. transference.
e. active listening.

Commonalities among psychotherapies, p. 590
Medium, Factual/Definitional, Objective 8, Ans: d
80. The most effective psychotherapists are those who:
a. employ personality tests to accurately diagnose their clients' difficulties.
b. utilize a wide variety of therapeutic techniques.
c. have had many years of experience practicing psychotherapy.
d. establish an empathic, caring relationship with their clients.
e. discourage clients from using antianxiety or antidepressant drugs.

A consumer's guide to psychotherapists (Close-up and Table 16.2), p. 591
Medium, Factual/Definitional, Objective 8, Ans: a
81. Which therapeutic specialists are most likely to have received a Ph.D. degree in psychology?
a. clinical psychologists
b. clinical social workers
c. psychiatrists
d. pastoral counselors

A consumer's guide to psychotherapists (Close-up and Table 16.2), p. 591
Easy, Factual/Definitional, Objective 8, Ans: e

82. A physician who specializes in the treatment of psychological disorders is called a:
    a. psychoanalyst.
    b. clinical psychologist.
    c. behavioral neuroscientist.
    d. cognitive therapist.
    e. psychiatrist.

A consumer's guide to psychotherapists (Close-up and Table 16.2), p. 591
Medium, Conceptual, Objective 8, Ans: d

83. Although Dr. Anderson utilizes systematic desensitization for the treatment of phobias, he prescribes antianxiety drugs as well. It is most likely that Dr. Anderson is a:
    a. psychoanalyst.
    b. client-centered therapist.
    c. cognitive therapist.
    d. psychiatrist.

Culture and values in psychotherapy, p. 591
Medium, Factual/Definitional, Objective 8, Ans: b

84. Immigrants from Asia would most likely experience difficulty as clients of American psychotherapists who emphasized the value of:
    a. marital fidelity.
    b. individualism.
    c. forgiveness.
    d. humility.

Drug therapies, p. 592
Medium, Factual/Definitional, Objective 9, Ans: e

85. The biomedical treatment most widely used today is:
    a. psychoanalysis.
    b. electroconvulsive therapy.
    c. psychosurgery.
    d. systematic desensitization.
    e. drug therapy.

Drug therapies, pp. 592-593
Easy, Factual/Definitional, Objective 9, Ans: d

86. The study of the effect of drugs on mind and behavior is called:
    a. psychosurgery.
    b. psychobiology.
    c. ECT.
    d. psychopharmacology.

Drug therapies, p. 593
Medium, Factual/Definitional, Objective 9, Ans: b
87.   The double-blind technique involves:
a.   the avoidance of eye contact between patient and therapist during free association.
b.   a procedure in which neither patients nor health care staff know whether a given patient is receiving a drug or a placebo.
c.   blocking anxiety-arousing material from consciousness during therapy.
d.   the simultaneous use of two or more therapeutic treatments in the hope that at least one will be effective.
e.   replacing a positive response to a harmful stimulus with a negative response.

Drug therapies, p. 593
Difficult, Conceptual, Objective 9, Ans: a
88.   Dr. Abdul is a researcher who wants to distinguish between the direct effects of a new antianxiety medication and effects arising simply from expectations of the drug's effectiveness. Dr. Abdul is most likely to use a procedure known as:
a.   the double-blind technique.
b.   meta-analysis.
c.   transference.
d.   counterconditioning.
e.   systematic desensitization.

Antipsychotic drugs, p. 593
Easy, Factual/Definitional, Objective 9, Ans: b
89.   Antipsychotic drugs have proved helpful in the treatment of:
a.   dissociative disorders.
b.   schizophrenia.
c.   depression.
d.   anxiety disorders.
e.   all the above.

Antipsychotic drugs, p. 593
Difficult, Factual/Definitional, Objective 9, Ans: b
90.   Thorazine and Clozaril are _____ drugs.
a.   antidepressant
b.   antipsychotic
c.   antimanic
d.   antianxiety

Antipsychotic drugs, pp. 593-594
Difficult, Conceptual, Objective 9, Ans: c
91.   Of the following individuals, who is most likely to benefit from therapeutic drugs that block receptor sites for dopamine?
a.   Amr, who complains about feeling tense and fearful most of the time but doesn't know why
b.   Matthew, who has lost his sense of identity and wandered from his home to a distant city
c.   Betsy, who hears imaginary voices telling her she will soon be killed
d.   Marcella, who is so obsessed with fear of a heart attack that she frequently counts her heartbeats aloud

Antipsychotic drugs, p. 594
Difficult, Factual/Definitional, Objective 9, Ans: a

92.   Which of the following drugs is most likely to produce extremely unpleasant physical side effects?
       a. Thorazine
       b. Prozac
       c. Valium
       d. Librium

Antianxiety drugs, p. 594
Medium, Conceptual, Objective 9, Ans: c

93.   Prozac is to depression as _____ is to anxiety.
       a. Thorazine
       b. lithium
       c. Valium
       d. Clozaril

Antianxiety drugs, p. 594
Difficult, Conceptual, Objective 9, Ans: c

94.   In order to help an adult client overcome fears of venturing out of his own home, Dr. Jansen plans to use behavior therapy in combination with drug therapy. Which of the following drugs would Dr. Jansen be most likely to prescribe?
       a. lithium
       b. Clozaril
       c. Valium
       d. Thorazine

Antidepressant drugs, p. 594
Medium, Factual/Definitional, Objective 9, Ans: b

95.   An increase in the availability of neurotransmitters such as norepinephrine and serotonin is most likely to result from the administration of _____ drugs.
       a. antipsychotic
       b. antidepressant
       c. antianxiety
       d. antimanic

Antidepressant drugs, p. 594
Difficult, Factual/Definitional, Objective 9, Ans: c

96.   Most antidepressants _____ the availability of norepinephrine and _____ the availability of serotonin.
       a. increase; decrease
       b. decrease; increase
       c. increase; increase
       d. decrease; decrease

Antidepressant drugs, p. 594
Medium, Conceptual, Objective 9, Ans: b

97.   Alex feels so hopeless and depressed that he has recently thought about taking his own life. The drug most likely to prove beneficial to him is:
       a. Valium.
       b. Prozac.
       c. Librium.
       d. Thorazine.

Antidepressant drugs, p. 595
Easy, Factual/Definitional, Objective 9, Ans: c
98. Inflated estimates of the value of antidepressant drugs are in large part due to:
   a. therapeutic touch.
   b. the double-blind technique.
   c. the placebo effect.
   d. meta-analysis.
   e. stress inoculation training.

Antidepressant drugs, p. 596
Easy, Factual/Definitional, Objective 9, Ans: d
99. Lithium has been found to be especially effective in the treatment of:
   a. anxiety disorders.
   b. schizophrenia.
   c. dissociative disorders.
   d. bipolar disorder.

Antidepressant drugs, p. 596
Difficult, Conceptual, Objective 9, Ans: d
100. Mr. Thorndyke's excessive feelings of helplessness and despondency are periodically interrupted by episodes in which he experiences extreme feelings of personal power and a grandiose optimism about his future. Which drug would most likely be prescribed to alleviate his symptoms?
   a. Valium
   b. Thorazine
   c. Librium
   d. lithium

Electroconvulsive therapy, p. 596
Easy, Factual/Definitional, Objective 10, Ans: b
101. Which of the following procedures is used only when drug therapy is ineffective?
   a. aversive conditioning
   b. electroconvulsive therapy
   c. systematic desensitization
   d. flooding
   e. stress inoculation training

Electroconvulsive therapy, p. 596
Difficult, Factual/Definitional, Objective 10, Ans: d
102. Which of the following treatments is most likely to be used only with severely depressed patients?
   a. flooding
   b. drug therapy
   c. systematic desensitization
   d. electroconvulsive therapy
   e. stress inoculation training

Electroconvulsive therapy, p. 596
Medium, Conceptual, Objective 10, Ans: a

103. Which of the following individuals is most likely to benefit from electroconvulsive therapy?
    a. Mark, who feels so dejected and discouraged that he contemplates killing himself
    b. Mary, who suffers from amnesia and has lost her sense of identity
    c. Jim, who experiences visual hallucinations and suffers from a delusion that communist spies are following him
    d. Luke, who suffers from a compulsion to wash his hands at least once every 15 minutes

Electroconvulsive therapy, p. 597
Medium, Factual/Definitional, Objective 10, Ans: c

104. Depressed moods are most likely to improve in response to:
    a. therapeutic touch.
    b. eye movement desensitizational and reprocessing.
    c. repetitive transcranial magnetic stimulation.
    d. virtual reality exposure therapy.

Psychosurgery, p. 597
Easy, Factual/Definitional, Objective 10, Ans: d

105. Surgically cutting the nerves connecting the frontal lobes to the emotion-controlling centers of the inner brain is called:
    a. psychopharmacology.
    b. a split-brain operation.
    c. rTMS.
    d. a lobotomy.
    e. ECT.

Psychosurgery, p. 597
Easy, Factual/Definitional, Objective 10, Ans: d

106. Which psychosurgical procedure was designed to calm uncontrollably emotional or violent patients?
    a. electroconvulsive therapy
    b. aversive conditioning
    c. the double-blind technique
    d. lobotomy
    e. systematic desensitization

Psychosurgery, pp. 575, 597
Medium, Conceptual, Objective 10, Ans: c

107. Aversive conditioning is to behavior therapy as a lobotomy is to:
    a. systematic desensitization.
    b. electroconvulsive therapy.
    c. psychosurgery.
    d. the placebo effect.
    e. drug therapy.

Preventing psychological disorders, p. 598
Medium, Factual/Definitional, Objective 11, Ans: b

108. Preventive mental health is based on the assumption that psychological disorders result from:
    a. repressed impulses and conflicts.
    b. stressful social situations.
    c. abnormal personality traits.
    d. regression toward the mean.

Preventing psychological disorders, pp. 598-599
Easy, Conceptual, Objective 11, Ans: d

109. Which approach would attempt to minimize psychological disorders by working to reduce the incidence of child abuse and illiteracy in society?
    a. biomedical therapy
    b. counterconditioning
    c. psychoanalysis
    d. preventive mental health
    e. token economy

CHAPTER 17

Stress and Health

Learning Objectives

1. Identify the major concerns of health psychology.

Stress and Illness (pp. 602-615)

2. Describe the biology of the "fight or flight" response to stress and the physical characteristics and phases of the general adaptation syndrome.

3. Discuss the health consequences of catastrophes, significant life changes, and daily hassles.

4. Describe the effects of a perceived lack of control, economic inequality, and a pessimistic outlook on health.

5. Discuss the role of stress in causing coronary heart disease, and contrast Type A and Type B personalities.

6. Describe how stress increases the risk of disease by inhibiting the activities of the body's immune system.

7. Describe the impact of learning on immune system functioning.

Promoting Health (pp. 616-640)

8. Identify and discuss different strategies for coping with stress, and explain why people should be skeptical about the value of complementary and alternative medicine.

9. Explain why people smoke, and discuss ways of preventing and reducing this health hazard.

10. Discuss the relationship between nutrition and physical well-being, and describe the research findings on obesity and weight control.

Behavioral medicine and health psychology, p. 601
Easy, Factual/Definitional, Objective 1, Ans: d

1. The interdisciplinary field that integrates and applies behavioral and medical knowledge to
    health and disease is:
    a. medical psychology.
    b. psychopharmacology.
    c. neuropsychology.
    d. behavioral medicine.
    e. holistic medicine.

Behavioral medicine and health psychology, p. 601
Medium, Conceptual, Objective 1, Ans: e

2. As a psychologist employed by a medical school, Dr. Konwicki specializes in research on the
    causes of stress and on the effectiveness of various techniques for coping with stress. Dr.
    Konwicki is most likely a(n) _____ psychologist.
    a. educational
    b. behavioral
    c. consumer
    d. forensic
    e. health

Behavioral medicine and health psychology, p. 601
Medium, Factual/Definitional, Objective 1, Ans: c

3. Health psychologists are *least* likely to focus attention on:
    a. the effective control of stress.
    b. how emotions influence our risk of disease.
    c. the role of bacteria in producing illness.
    d. understanding why people seek medical help.

Stress and stressors, p. 602
Easy, Factual/Definitional, Objective 2, Ans: a

4. The process by which we perceive and respond to events that threaten or challenge us is called:
    a. stress.
    b. psychophysiological illness.
    c. frustration.
    d. biofeedback.
    e. burnout.

Stress and stressors, p. 602
Medium, Factual/Definitional, Objective 2, Ans: c

5. A stressor is a(n):
    a. lower back muscle that frequently produces a feeling of physical tension.
    b. competitive, hard-driving, impatient person.
    c. environmental event that threatens or challenges us.
    d. exercise program designed to increase our ability to handle normal stress.
    e. hormone released by the adrenal glands during periods of stress.

Stress and stressors, p. 603
Medium, Conceptual, Objective 2, Ans: c
6.   Estée's legs are paralyzed, but she is able to minimize the stress that the inability to walk might have caused by viewing this handicap as a challenge rather than a threat. This illustrates the importance of:
a.   biofeedback.
b.   relaxation training.
c.   stress appraisal.
d.   the general adaptation syndrome.
e.   the Type A personality.

The stress response system, p. 603
Medium, Conceptual, Objective 2, Ans: d
7.   After being told that his parents have just been involved in a serious automobile accident, Bill is likely to experience an outpouring of:
a.   lymphocytes.
b.   serotonin.
c.   dopamine.
d.   epinephrine.
e.   leptin.

The stress response system, p. 603
Medium, Factual/Definitional, Objective 2, Ans: d
8.   Walter Cannon perceived the stress response to be highly adaptive because it prepared the organism for:
a.   spontaneous remission.
b.   the production of lymphocytes.
c.   the avoidance of burnout.
d.   fight or flight.

The stress response system, p. 603
Difficult, Conceptual, Objective 2, Ans: e
9.   When Milly is told that a tornado has destroyed her house, her body is likely to react by:
a.   releasing testosterone.
b.   producing more androgens.
c.   increasing production of lymphocytes.
d.   producing teratogens.
e.   secreting cortisol.

The stress response system, p. 604
Difficult, Factual/Definitional, Objective 2, Ans: d
10. Hans Selye found that in response to a variety of stressors, animals exhibit:
a.   bleeding ulcers.
b.   enlargement of the adrenal cortex.
c.   shrinkage of the thymus gland.
d.   all the above.

The stress response system, pp. 603-604
Difficult, Conceptual, Objective 2, Ans: d
11. The "fight-or-flight" response is to _____ as the general adaptation syndrome is to

_____.
    a. Cannon; Friedman
    b. Friedman; Selye
    c. Selye; Cannon
    d. Cannon; Selye

The stress response system, p. 604
Easy, Factual/Definitional, Objective 2, Ans: b
12. Hans Selye referred to the body's response to stress as:
    a. the fight-or-flight response.
    b. the general adaptation syndrome.
    c. Type B behavior.
    d. psychophysiological illness.
    e. burnout.

The stress response system, p. 604
Medium, Factual/Definitional, Objective 2, Ans: c
13. The first phase of the general adaptation syndrome is:
    a. stress appraisal.
    b. resistance.
    c. alarm.
    d. exhaustion.
    e. adjustment.

The stress response system, p. 604
Medium, Factual/Definitional, Objective 2, Ans: a
14. During which phase of the general adaptation syndrome are organisms best able to physically cope with stress?
    a. resistance
    b. appraisal
    c. adjustment
    d. fight or flight

The stress response system, p. 604
Difficult, Conceptual, Objective 2, Ans: a
15. After overcoming the initial shock of having her car stolen, Marlys calls the police for help and begins to question possible witnesses. At this point, Marlys is most likely in the _____ stage of the general adaptation syndrome.
    a. resistance
    b. exhaustion
    c. fight-or-flight
    d. adjustment
    e. stress appraisal

The stress response system, p. 605
Difficult, Factual/Definitional, Objective 2, Ans: d
16. Prolonged stress due to sustained child abuse is associated with reductions in the size of the:
    a. adrenal cortex.
    b. temporal lobe.
    c. cerebellum.
    d. hippocampus.

Stressful life events, pp. 605-606
Easy, Factual/Definitional, Objective 3, Ans: b
17. Natural disasters and nuclear accidents trigger _____ rates of heart attacks and _____ rates of depression.
    a. decreased; decreased
    b. increased; increased
    c. decreased; increased
    d. increased; decreased

Stressful life events, p. 607
Easy, Factual/Definitional, Objective 3, Ans: e
18. The state of physical, mental, and emotional exhaustion brought on by persistent job-related stress is known as:
    a. post-traumatic stress disorder.
    b. the general adaptation syndrome.
    c. the alarm reaction.
    d. hypochondriasis.
    e. burnout.

Stress and perceived control, p. 607
Easy, Factual/Definitional, Objective 4, Ans: b
19. Research has indicated that rats become more vulnerable to ulcers when exposed to _____ shock.
    a. predictable
    b. uncontrollable
    c. low intensity
    d. repeated

Stress and perceived control, p. 607
Medium, Factual/Definitional, Objective 4, Ans: a
20. When "executive" and "subordinate" rats received simultaneous electric shocks, the _____ rat was subsequently more likely to develop _____.
    a. "subordinate"; ulcers
    b. "executive"; heart disease
    c. "executive"; hypertension
    d. "subordinate"; immunity to disease

Stress and perceived control, p. 608
Medium, Factual/Definitional, Objective 4, Ans: d
21. Monkeys at the top of the social pecking order are less likely to contract viral infections than those with lower social status. This best illustrates the value of:
    a. the general adaptation syndrome.
    b. spontaneous remission.
    c. the fight-or-flight response.
    d. perceived control.

Stress and perceived control, p. 608
Medium, Factual/Definitional, Objective 4, Ans: a

22.   Students are least likely to suffer fatigue and other stress-related symptoms at the end of a
       semester if they are:
       a. optimistic.
       b. extraverted.
       c. creative.
       d. Type A personalities.

Stress and perceived control, p. 609
Medium, Factual/Definitional, Objective 4, Ans: a

23.   When animals or humans lose control of their environments, cortisol levels _____ and
       immune responses _____.
       a. rise; drop
       b. drop; rise
       c. rise; rise
       d. drop; drop

Stress and perceived control, p. 609
Difficult, Conceptual, Objective 4, Ans: e

24.   After being crowded into a small dormitory room with two other freshman roommates,
       18-year-old Rolf feels he has little control over his environment. His body is most likely to
       respond with a(n):
       a. reduction of blood cholesterol levels.
       b. elevation of blood glucose levels.
       c. reduction in the release of epinephrine.
       d. proliferation of lymphocytes.
       e. elevation in cortisol levels.

Stress and heart disease, p. 609
Medium, Factual/Definitional, Objective 5, Ans: b

25.   The closing of the vessels that nourish the heart muscle is known as:
       a. myocarditis.
       b. coronary heart disease.
       c. coronary aneurysm.
       d. thrombophlebitis.

Stress and heart disease, p. 609
Medium, Factual/Definitional, Objective 5, Ans: d

26.   The greatest number of deaths in North America today result from:
       a. AIDS.
       b. strokes.
       c. cancer.
       d. heart disease.
       e. accidents.

Stress and heart disease, pp. 609-610
Medium, Conceptual, Objective 5, Ans: a

27.   Who is the best example of a Type A personality?
       a. Mara, a highly ambitious, time-conscious secretary
       b. Joan, a highly intelligent, introverted librarian
       c. Wilma, a friendly, altruistic social worker
       d. Charisse, a fun-loving, self-indulgent college student

Stress and heart disease, p. 609
Easy, Factual/Definitional, Objective 5, Ans: e
28. Friedman and Rosenman referred to noncompetitive, relaxed, and easygoing individuals as
_____ personalities.
     a. passive-aggressive
     b. extraverted
     c. health-prone
     d. Type A
     e. Type B

Stress and heart disease, p. 609
Medium, Conceptual, Objective 5, Ans: d
29. Type A is to _____ as Type B is to _____.
     a. realistic; idealistic
     b. introverted; extraverted
     c. bright; dull
     d. hard-driving; easy-going
     e. optimistic; pessimistic

Stress and heart disease, p. 609
Medium, Conceptual, Objective 5, Ans: b
30. Who is the best example of a Type B personality?
     a. Tammy, an ambitious, self-confident waitress
     b. Mauriucca, a relaxed, understanding social worker
     c. Tena, a time-conscious, competitive lawyer
     d. Juanita, an impatient, pessimistic librarian

Stress and heart disease, p. 609
Medium, Factual/Definitional, Objective 5, Ans: c
31. In their classic 9-year study, Friedman and Rosenman found that Type A men are especially
susceptible to:
     a. stomach ulcers.
     b. cancer.
     c. heart attacks.
     d. obesity.

Stress and heart disease, p. 609
Medium, Factual/Definitional, Objective 5, Ans: b
32. Compared to Type A people, Type B individuals are _____ likely to smoke and _____
likely to consume caffeinated drinks.
     a. more; more
     b. less; less
     c. more; less
     d. less; more

Stress and heart disease, p. 609
Medium, Factual/Definitional, Objective 5, Ans: d
33. The major characteristic that contributes to the disease vulnerability of Type A personalities is
their feelings of:
     a. urgency.
     b. competitiveness.
     c. ambition.
     d. anger.

Stress and heart disease, p. 610
Difficult, Conceptual, Objective 5, Ans: a

34. Who would be most susceptible to heart disease?
     a. Marvin, an impatient lawyer who often becomes irritated with family and friends over insignificant matters
     b. Oswald, a purchasing agent who is very competitive and always wants to be a winner
     c. Michael, a time-conscious banking executive who is always 5 minutes early for appointments because of his sense of urgency
     d. Jozsef, a highly ambitious salesperson who is determined to become the manager of his company

Stress and susceptibility to disease, p. 611
Easy, Factual/Definitional, Objective 6, Ans: a

35. Physical illnesses, such as hypertension and some headaches, that are not caused by an organic disorder but instead seem linked to stress are referred to as _____ illnesses.
     a. psychophysiological
     b. psychopharmacological
     c. hypochondriacal
     d. neuropsychological
     e. neurotic

Stress and susceptibility to disease, p. 611
Medium, Conceptual, Objective 6, Ans: b

36. Joshi has been experiencing severe headaches and his physician strongly recommends that he enroll in a stress-management class. The physician has probably diagnosed Joshi's headaches as a(n) _____ disorder.
     a. hereditary
     b. psychophysiological
     c. immune system
     d. hypochondriacal

Stress and the immune system, p. 611
Easy, Factual/Definitional, Objective 6, Ans: a

37. The white blood cells that fight bacterial infections and attack cancer cells and viruses are called:
     a. lymphocytes.
     b. glial cells.
     c. teratogens.
     d. stress hormones.
     e. steroids.

Stress and the immune system, p. 611
Medium, Conceptual, Objective 6, Ans: c

38. Viral infections are to _____ as bacterial infections are to _____.
     a. B lymphocytes; T lymphocytes
     b. Type B personalities; Type A personalities
     c. T lymphocytes; B lymphocytes
     d. Type A personalities; Type B personalities

Stress and the immune system, p. 611
Difficult, Factual/Definitional, Objective 6, Ans: d
39. Compared to men, women are _____ susceptible to infections and _____ susceptible to lupus and multiple sclerosis.
   a. more; more
   b. less; less
   c. more; less
   d. less; more

Stress and the immune system, p. 611
Difficult, Conceptual, Objective 6, Ans: d
40. The release of large amounts of epinephrine, norepinephrine, and cortisol:
   a. decreases chronic hypertension.
   b. diverts blood flow from muscle tissue to the body's internal organs.
   c. inhibits the buildup of plaques on artery walls.
   d. suppresses the production of lymphocytes.

Stress and the immune system, pp. 611-612
Difficult, Conceptual, Objective 6, Ans: c
41. After breaking up with his girlfriend, Mark came down with a severe respiratory infection. His illness may have been caused to a large extent by a(n) _____ in his body's production of _____.
   a. decrease; cortisol
   b. increase; androgens
   c. decrease; lymphocytes
   d. increase; teratogens
   e. decrease; steroids

Stress and AIDS, p. 613
Easy, Factual/Definitional, Objective 6, Ans: d
42. A rapid progression from HIV infection to AIDS is _____ by the death of a loved one and _____ by participation in bereavement support groups.
   a. inhibited; inhibited
   b. facilitated; facilitated
   c. inhibited; facilitated
   d. facilitated; inhibited

Stress and cancer, p. 613
Easy, Factual/Definitional, Objective 6, Ans: d
43. Cancer rates are _____ than normal among the widowed and _____ than normal among the divorced.
   a. higher; lower
   b. lower; lower
   c. lower; higher
   d. higher; higher

Stress and cancer, p. 613
Medium, Conceptual, Objective 6, Ans: c

44.   Margaret's physician has recently informed her that she has breast cancer. In order to increase her chances of survival, the doctor should encourage her to:
       a. take an extended vacation.
       b. ignore her fears and negative feelings about cancer.
       c. continue to hope for a restoration of health.
       d. work on repairing any painful social relationships in her life.

Conditioning the immune system, p. 614
Medium, Factual/Definitional, Objective 7, Ans: a

45.   In researching taste aversion in rats, Ader and Cohen discovered that saccharin-sweetened water was a conditioned stimulus for:
       a. the suppression of the immune system.
       b. the release of pain-killing endorphins.
       c. an overproduction of acetylcholine.
       d. a proliferation of lymphocytes.
       e. overeating.

Conditioning the immune system, p. 614
Medium, Factual/Definitional, Objective 7, Ans: b

46.   Ader and Cohen discovered that the suppression of rats' immune systems was a conditioned response to:
       a. electric shocks.
       b. sweetened water.
       c. hormone injections.
       d. bacterial infections.

Coping with stress, p. 616
Medium, Conceptual, Objective 8, Ans: a

47.   Sharon, a college sophomore, is experiencing stress and feels mildly depressed. She would be best advised to:
       a. start a program of regular aerobic exercise.
       b. receive training in meditation.
       c. make use of biofeedback.
       d. discontinue her relationship with her steady boyfriend.

Coping with stress, pp. 616-617
Easy, Factual/Definitional, Objective 8, Ans: d

48.   Regular aerobic exercise has been found to reduce the incidence of:
       a. heart attacks.
       b. high blood pressure.
       c. depression.
       d. all the above.

Coping with stress, pp. 616-617
Medium, Conceptual, Objective 8, Ans: d

49.   Yeugeny, a high school teacher, experiences a great deal of stress, considerable anxiety, and occasional bouts of depression. Research findings suggest that regular aerobic exercise would:
       a. reduce his stress and anxiety but increase his feelings of depression.
       b. reduce his stress and anxiety but have no effect on his feelings of depression.
       c. reduce his stress but have no effect on his feelings of anxiety or depression.
       d. reduce his stress, anxiety, and depression.

Coping with stress, p. 617
Difficult, Factual/Definitional, Objective 8, Ans: c
50. The growth of new brain cells in mice has been found to be promoted by:
    a. acupuncture.
    b. biofeedback.
    c. aerobic exercise.
    d. the placebo effect.
    e. the fight-or-flight response.

Coping with stress, p. 617
Medium, Factual/Definitional, Objective 8, Ans: b
51. Neal Miller observed that rats decrease their heartbeat if they receive pleasurable brain stimulation whenever their heartbeat slows. This best illustrated that:
    a. suppression of the immune system can be classically conditioned.
    b. biofeedback can facilitate autonomic nervous system control.
    c. loss of personal control heightens reactions to stressful situations.
    d. positive as well as negative stimulation can trigger the general adaptation syndrome.

Coping with stress, p. 617
Easy, Factual/Definitional, Objective 8, Ans: b
52. Electronically recording, amplifying, and displaying information regarding subtle physiological responses is called:
    a. stress management.
    b. biofeedback.
    c. relaxation training.
    d. behavioral medicine.

Coping with stress, pp. 617-618
Easy, Conceptual, Objective 8, Ans: b
53. Lewis has suffered from acute stress for years. He is presently learning to relax with a device that provides him with information about changes in tension in his forehead muscle. Lewis's case illustrates the use of:
    a. cognitive therapy.
    b. biofeedback.
    c. desensitization.
    d. physiological scanning.

Coping with stress, p. 618
Medium, Factual/Definitional, Objective 8, Ans: c
54. Biofeedback would most likely be used to provide someone with information about his or her:
    a. blood type.
    b. cholesterol level.
    c. finger temperature.
    d. pain tolerance.
    e. life expectancy.

Coping with stress, p. 619
Difficult, Factual/Definitional, Objective 8, Ans: c

55.   In a study of Type A heart-attack survivors, Friedman and his colleagues found that the most effective technique for preventing recurrent heart attacks was:
      a. laughter.
      b. nutrition education.
      c. relaxation training.
      d. biofeedback.

Coping with stress, pp. 620-621
Medium, Factual/Definitional, Objective 8, Ans: b

56.   People have been found to suffer fewer health problems following the death of their spouse if they:
      a. stay busy and avoid thinking about their loss.
      b. communicate their painful feelings of loss to close friends.
      c. spend time thinking about all the experiences they shared with their loved one.
      d. quickly make plans for developing a new romantic relationship.

Coping with stress, p. 621
Medium, Factual/Definitional, Objective 8, Ans: b

57.   Which of the following has *not* been proposed as a possible reason for the link between social support and health?
      a. Family members help patients to receive medical treatment more quickly.
      b. After marriage, people adopt many behaviors of their spouse, such as overeating.
      c. A loving spouse boosts one's self-esteem.
      d. Support for one's need to belong fosters immune functioning.
      e. Supportive spouses encourage adherence to an exercise program.

Coping with stress, pp. 616-622
Easy, Conceptual, Objective 8, Ans: d

58.   Yuri is a real estate agent who is under great stress because he has not sold any houses over the last few months. Research suggests that he may effectively alleviate his stress by:
      a. confiding his fears and frustrations to his close friends.
      b. beginning an exercise program.
      c. practicing meditation.
      d. doing any of the above.

Coping with stress, p. 623
Easy, Factual/Definitional, Objective 8, Ans: d

59.   Weekly participation in religious services is associated with a(n) _____ risk of death from suicide and a(n) _____ risk of death from coronary heart disease.
      a. heightened; reduced
      b. reduced; heightened
      c. heightened; heightened
      d. reduced; reduced

Coping with stress, pp. 623-626
Easy, Factual/Definitional, Objective 8, Ans: d

60. Intervening variables that mediate the relationship between religious involvement and physical health are likely to include:
    a. healthy eating practices.
    b. the stability of marriages.
    c. coherent world views
    d. all of the above.

Alternative medicine (Box), p. 625
Difficult, Factual/Definitional, Objective 8, Ans: c

61. People are most likely to give inflated assessments of the value of alternative medicine for the treatment of:
    a. coronary heart disease.
    b. lung cancer.
    c. arthritis.
    d. Parkinson's disease.
    e. schizophrenia.

Alternative medicine (Box), p. 625
Medium, Conceptual, Objective 8, Ans: d

62. Judy suffers from a number of different allergies, which she treats with herbal remedies. The placebo effect is likely to lead her to _____ the value of these remedies, and the spontaneous remission of her allergy reactions is likely to lead her to _____ the value of those remedies.
    a. underestimate; overestimate
    b. overestimate; underestimate
    c. underestimate; underestimate
    d. overestimate; overestimate

Smoking, p. 627
Medium, Conceptual, Objective 9, Ans: e

63. Which of the following would do the most to increase life expectancy in the United States?
    a. automobiles designed to run only if drivers and passengers were wearing seat belts
    b. marriage counseling that eliminated divorce
    c. a diet program that eliminated obesity
    d. an educational program that eliminated consumption of alcoholic beverages
    e. new federal laws that eliminated cigarette usage

Smoking, p. 627
Easy, Factual/Definitional, Objective 9, Ans: d

64. Compared with nonsmokers, smokers experience _____ rates of depression and _____ rates of divorce.
    a. lower; higher
    b. higher; lower
    c. lower; lower
    d. higher; higher

Smoking, p. 628
Easy, Factual/Definitional, Objective 9, Ans: a
65. Young adolescents are especially likely to begin smoking if they:
    a. have friends and relatives who smoke.
    b. are Type A personalities.
    c. are optimistic about their future.
    d. suffer hypertension.

Smoking, p. 628
Easy, Factual/Definitional, Objective 9, Ans: d
66. According to the National Center for Health Statistics, smoking tobacco is _____ correlated with alcohol use and is _____ correlated with marijuana use.
    a. negatively; positively
    b. negatively; negatively
    c. positively; negatively
    d. positively; positively

Smoking, p. 628
Easy, Factual/Definitional, Objective 9, Ans: a
67. Which of the following is a common symptom of nicotine withdrawal?
    a. anxiety
    b. drowsiness
    c. diminished appetite
    d. insensitivity to pain

Smoking, p. 628
Medium, Conceptual, Objective 9, Ans: a
68. Smokers with _____ levels of nicotine tolerance are likely to suffer the most severe withdrawal symptoms when they discontinue smoking.
    a. high
    b. moderate
    c. low
    d. high or low

Smoking, p. 628
Difficult, Factual/Definitional, Objective 9, Ans: a
69. Nicotine triggers a(n) _____ in blood pressure and a(n) _____ in pain sensitivity.
    a. increase; decrease
    b. increase; increase
    c. decrease; decrease
    d. decrease; increase

Smoking, p. 629
Difficult, Factual/Definitional, Objective 9, Ans: b
70. Smokers and nonsmokers have been found to differ in a gene that influences responses to:
    a. serotonin.
    b. dopamine.
    c. acetylcholine.
    d. norepinephrine.

Smoking, p. 629
Difficult, Factual/Definitional, Objective 9, Ans: d
71.   Research on the smoking habits of North Americans indicates that:
    a.   men are nearly twice as likely as women to smoke.
    b.   the percentage of teenage smokers has decreased during the past decade.
    c.   smoking rates have declined more rapidly among women than among men.
    d.   smoking is more common among the poor than among the rich.

For those of you who want to quit smoking (Close-up), p. 630
Easy, Factual/Definitional, Objective 9, Ans: b
72.   Which of the following is most likely to interfere with one's efforts to successfully quit smoking?
    a.   use of nicotine gum
    b.   consumption of alcohol
    c.   striving for total smoking abstinence
    d.   informing others of one's intentions to quit
    e.   beginning an aerobic exercise program

Smoking, p. 630
Easy, Factual/Definitional, Objective 9, Ans: b
73.   Effective smoking prevention programs are most likely to provide information about:
    a.   burnout.
    b.   peer pressure.
    c.   psychophysiological illness.
    d.   Type A personality dynamics.

Nutrition, p. 631
Medium, Factual/Definitional, Objective 10, Ans: c
74.   High-carbohydrate foods increase:
    a.   mental alertness.
    b.   pain sensitivity.
    c.   relaxation.
    d.   anxiety.

Nutrition, p. 631
Difficult, Factual/Definitional, Objective 10, Ans: a
75.   The consumption of high-carbohydrate foods _____ the amount of tryptophan reaching the brain and _____ the brain's level of serotonin.
    a.   increases; increases
    b.   decreases; increases
    c.   increases; decreases
    d.   decreases; decreases

Nutrition, pp. 631-632
Difficult, Conceptual, Objective 10, Ans: b
76.   College students who want to improve their mental concentration and alertness for study would be wise to follow a _____-carbohydrate, _____-protein diet.
    a.   high; low
    b.   low; high
    c.   high; high
    d.   low; low

Nutrition, p. 632
Medium, Factual/Definitional, Objective 10, Ans: e

77. Hypertension has been linked to a diet that is:
    a. high in calcium.
    b. low in fat.
    c. high in carbohydrates.
    d. low in protein.
    e. high in salt.

Nutrition, p. 632
Difficult, Factual/Definitional, Objective 10, Ans: d

78. The consumption of fish rich in omega-3 fatty acid is most likely to account for Japan's low rate of:
    a. diabetes.
    b. stomach ulcers.
    c. arthritis.
    d. depression.

Obesity and weight control, p. 633
Medium, Factual/Definitional, Objective 10, Ans: e

79. Obesity increases the risk of:
    a. gallstones.
    b. arthritis.
    c. diabetes.
    d. heart disease.
    e. all the above.

Obesity and weight control, p. 634
Medium, Factual/Definitional, Objective 10, Ans: c

80. Research studies suggest that workplace discrimination against those who are overweight is _____ common than gender discrimination and _____ common than race discrimination.
    a. more; less
    b. less; more
    c. more; more
    d. less; less

The physiology of obesity, p. 634
Difficult, Factual/Definitional, Objective 10, Ans: c

81. Research on fat cells indicates that:
    a. they are destroyed by sustained dieting.
    b. their number is genetically determined and is not influenced by eating patterns.
    c. they increase in number as a result of overeating.
    d. their number is determined by childhood eating patterns and remains fixed after adolescence.

The physiology of obesity, p. 634
Medium, Conceptual, Objective 10, Ans: c

82. Compared with those who are not obese, obese individuals are relatively:
    a. less likely to suffer from stress-related diseases.
    b. less likely to become hungry at the sight of tempting food.
    c. more likely to feel hungry when they are on a restricted diet.
    d. more likely to have a high rate of body metabolism.

The physiology of obesity, p. 634
Medium, Conceptual, Objective 10, Ans: a

83. Although Cara has been obese for as long as she can remember, she is determined to lose excess body weight with a low-calorie diet. Cara is most likely to have difficulty becoming and staying thin because:
    a. she may have a higher-than-average set point for body weight.
    b. fat cells can be lost only with vigorous exercise.
    c. the number of calories a person consumes daily has no effect on body weight.
    d. lean tissue is maintained by fewer calories than is fat tissue.
    e. her resting metabolic rate will increase and prompt her to overeat.

The physiology of obesity, p. 634
Difficult, Conceptual, Objective 10, Ans: b

84. Rudy has been on a strict diet of 1000 calories per day for the last 6 weeks. He lost considerably more weight in the first 3 weeks of his diet than in the last 3 because:
    a. his insulin level has decreased.
    b. his metabolic rate has decreased.
    c. his set point has increased.
    d. lean tissue is maintained by fewer calories than is fat tissue.
    e. his fat cells are no longer decreasing in number.

The physiology of obesity, p. 635
Medium, Factual/Definitional, Objective 10, Ans: d

85. Research on obesity and weight control indicates that:
    a. obesity is often the result of guilt or very low self-esteem.
    b. one pound is always lost for every 3500-calorie reduction in diet.
    c. fat cells are lost when sustained dieting is combined with exercise.
    d. once we become fat, we require less food to maintain our weight than we did to attain it.
    e. it is easier for people to lose weight on the second or third attempt at dieting than on the first try.

The physiology of obesity, p. 635
Medium, Factual/Definitional, Objective 10, Ans: a

86. Research on the genetic and environmental influences on body weight has revealed that:
    a. the weight of adopted people correlates with that of their biological parents, not with that of their adoptive parents.
    b. the weight of fraternal twins reared together is more highly correlated than the weight of identical twins reared apart.
    c. obesity is somewhat more common among American upper-class women than among American lower-class women.
    d. weight resemblance is somewhat greater among identical twin women than among identical twin men.

The physiology of obesity, p. 635
Difficult, Factual/Definitional, Objective 10, Ans: d

87.   Levels of the hormone leptin have been related to _____ in mice.
       a. stomach ulcers
       b. respiratory infections
       c. cancer
       d. obesity

The physiology of obesity, p. 636
Medium, Factual/Definitional, Objective 10, Ans: d

88.   Obesity is _____ common among Americans today than it was in 1900 and _____
       common among upper-class than among lower-class American women.
       a. less; less
       b. more; more
       c. less; more
       d. more; less

Helpful hints for dieters (Close-up), p. 638
Medium, Conceptual, Objective 10, Ans: c

89.   Which of the following statements would be the *best* advice for people who plan to lose weight
       by going on a restricted diet?
       a. "Don't worry if you fail to lose weight on your first diet; the second diet is always easier
           than the first."
       b. "Between meals, help yourself to soft drinks high in sugar in order to reduce your hunger at
           meal-times."
       c. "Don't violate your diet by occasionally treating yourself to forbidden foods."
       d. "Avoid eating during the day so you can enjoy a big meal in the evening."

The physiology of obesity, p. 639
Medium, Factual/Definitional, Objective 10, Ans: c

90.   The greatest hurdle health psychologists face in persuading people to adopt healthier life-styles
       is to get them to realize that:
       a. they exert some control over their own future health.
       b. they are personally vulnerable to health problems that might arise from their own behaviors.
       c. physical health contributes to psychological well-being.
       d. the high costs of medical care today make a healthy lifestyle particularly important.

CHAPTER 18

Social Psychology

Learning Objectives

Social Thinking (pp. 643-649)

1. Describe the importance of attribution in social behavior and the dangers of the fundamental attribution error.

2. Identify the conditions under which attitudes have a strong impact on actions.

3. Explain the foot-in-the-door phenomenon and the effect of role playing on attitudes in terms of cognitive dissonance theory.

Social Influence (pp. 649-661)

4. Discuss the results of experiments on conformity, and distinguish between normative and informational social influence.

5. Describe Milgram's controversial experiments on obedience, and discuss their implications for understanding our susceptibility to social influence.

6. Describe conditions in which the presence of others is likely to result in social facilitation, social loafing, or deindividuation.

7. Discuss how group interaction can facilitate group polarization and groupthink, and describe how self-fulfilling prophecies and minority influence illustrate the power of individuals.

Social Relations (pp. 661-688)

8. Describe the social, emotional, and cognitive factors that contribute to the persistence of cultural, ethnic, and gender prejudice and discrimination.

9. Describe the impact of biological factors, aversive events, and learning experiences on aggressive behavior.

10. Discuss the effects of observing filmed violence and pornography on social attitudes and relationships.

11. Explain how social traps and mirror-image perceptions fuel social conflict.

12. Describe the influence of proximity, physical attractiveness, and similarity on interpersonal attraction.

13. Explain the impact of physical arousal on passionate love, and discuss how companionate love is nurtured by equity and self-disclosure.

14. Describe and explain the bystander effect, and explain altruistic behavior in terms of social exchange theory and social norms.

15. Discuss effective ways of encouraging peaceful cooperation and reducing social conflict.

Social psychology, p. 643
Easy, Factual/Definitional, Objective 1, Ans: b
1. The text defines social psychology as the scientific study of how people _____ one another.
   a. understand, feel about, and behave toward
   b. think about, influence, and relate to
   c. observe, understand, and communicate with
   d. understand, predict, and control
   e. perceive, think about, and talk about

Attributing behavior to persons or to situations, p. 643
Easy, Factual/Definitional, Objective 1, Ans: d
2. In order to analyze how people explain others' behavior, Fritz Heider developed:
   a. cognitive dissonance theory.
   b. impression management theory.
   c. social exchange theory.
   d. attribution theory.
   e. self-disclosure theory.

Attributing behavior to persons or to situations, p. 643
Easy, Conceptual, Objective 1, Ans: e
3. Victor explains that his brother's aggressive behavior results from his brother's insecurity. Victor's explanation of his brother's behavior is an example of:
   a. the reciprocity norm.
   b. deindividuation.
   c. the bystander effect.
   d. the foot-in-the-door phenomenon.
   e. an attribution.

Attributing behavior to persons or to situations, p. 643
Easy, Factual/Definitional, Objective 1, Ans: b
4. The tendency for observers to underestimate the impact of the situation and to overestimate the impact of personal dispositions upon another's behavior is called:
   a. the bystander effect.
   b. the fundamental attribution error.
   c. deindividuation.
   d. ingroup bias.
   e. the mere exposure effect.

Attributing behavior to persons or to situations, pp. 643-644
Difficult, Conceptual, Objective 1, Ans: c

5.   A dispositional attribution is to _____ as a situational attribution is to _____.
      a. normative influence; informational influence
      b. high ability; low motivation
      c. personality traits; social roles
      d. politically liberal; politically conservative
      e. introversion; extraversion

Attributing behavior to persons or to situations, pp. 643-644
Difficult, Conceptual, Objective 1, Ans: c

6.   Rhonda has just learned that her neighbor Patricia was involved in an automobile accident at a
      nearby intersection. The tendency to make the fundamental attribution error may lead Rhonda
      to conclude:
      a. "They need to improve the visibility at that corner."
      b. "Patricia's brakes must have failed."
      c. "Patricia's recklessness has finally gotten her into trouble."
      d. "Patricia's children probably distracted her."
      e. "The road must have been wet and slippery."

Attributing behavior to persons or to situations, pp. 643-644
Medium, Factual/Definitional, Objective 1, Ans: a

7.   Students who were told that a young woman had been instructed to act in a very unfriendly way
      for the purposes of the experiment concluded that her behavior:
      a. reflected her personal disposition.
      b. was situationally determined.
      c. demonstrated role playing.
      d. illustrated normative social influence.
      e. was the product of deindividuation.

Attributing behavior to persons or to situations, p. 644
Difficult, Conceptual, Objective 1, Ans: a

8.   You would probably be *least* likely to commit the fundamental attribution error in explaining
      why:
      a. you failed a college test.
      b. a fellow classmate was late for class.
      c. your professor gave a boring lecture.
      d. the college administration decided to raise next year's tuition costs.

Attributing behavior to persons or to situations, p. 644
Difficult, Factual/Definitional, Objective 1, Ans: c

9.   One explanation for the fundamental attribution error involves:
      a. deindividuation.
      b. group polarization.
      c. attentional focus.
      d. the mere exposure effect.
      e. social loafing.

The effects of attribution, pp. 644-645
Difficult, Conceptual, Objective 1, Ans: b

10.   The fundamental attribution error is most likely to lead observers to conclude that unemployed people:
      a.   are victims of discrimination.
      b.   are irresponsible and unmotivated.
      c.   have parents who provided poor models of social responsibility.
      d.   attended schools that provided an inferior education.
      e.   are victims of bad luck.

The effects of attribution, pp. 644-645
Difficult, Factual/Definitional, Objective 1, Ans: c

11.   Poverty and unemployment are likely to be explained in terms of _____ by political liberals and in terms of _____ by political conservatives.
      a.   personal dispositions; situational constraints
      b.   normative influence; informational influence
      c.   situational constraints; personal dispositions
      d.   informational influence; normative influence

The effects of attribution, p. 645
Difficult, Conceptual, Objective 1, Ans: c

12.   Compared to the Japanese, Americans are likely to underestimate the extent to which another's behavior is influenced by:
      a.   genetic predispositions.
      b.   level of motivation.
      c.   social roles.
      d.   intellectual abilities.
      e.   psychological traits.

Attitudes and actions, p. 645
Easy, Factual/Definitional, Objective 2, Ans: c

13.   Beliefs and feelings that predispose us to respond in particular ways to objects, people, and events are called:
      a.   roles.
      b.   norms.
      c.   attitudes.
      d.   attributions.

Do our attitudes guide our actions?, p. 645
Easy, Factual/Definitional, Objective 2, Ans: b

14.   During the 1960s, dozens of research studies challenged the common assumption that attitudes:
      a.   can be measured.
      b.   guide our actions.
      c.   are shaped through social influence.
      d.   remain stable throughout our life.
      e.   are correlated with personality traits.

Do our attitudes guide our actions?, pp. 645-646
Easy, Conceptual, Objective 2, Ans: c

15. Which of the following individuals is *least* likely to cheat on his income tax returns?
    a. Jake, who loves his country
    b. Joe, who admires personal honesty
    c. Al, who values paying his full income tax
    d. Andy, who cares little about personal wealth

Do our attitudes guide our actions?, p. 646
Difficult, Factual/Definitional, Objective 2, Ans: c

16. Our attitudes are more likely to guide our actions when we:
    a. experience a sense of deindividuation.
    b. feel incompetent or insecure.
    c. are self-conscious.
    d. are made aware of social norms.

Do our actions affect our attitudes?, p. 646
Easy, Factual/Definitional, Objective 3, Ans: d

17. The tendency for initial compliance with a small request to facilitate subsequent compliance with a larger request is known as the:
    a. mere exposure effect.
    b. fundamental attribution error.
    c. reciprocity norm.
    d. foot-in-the-door phenomenon.
    e. bystander effect.

Do our actions affect our attitudes?, p. 646
Medium, Factual/Definitional, Objective 3, Ans: e

18. In order to "brainwash" captured American soldiers during the Korean War, Chinese communists made effective use of:
    a. the just-world phenomenon.
    b. the bystander effect.
    c. the frustration-aggression principle.
    d. the fundamental attribution error.
    e. the foot-in-the-door phenomenon.

Do our actions affect our attitudes?, p. 646
Medium, Conceptual, Objective 3, Ans: c

19. After giving in to her friends' request that she drink alcohol with them, 16-year-old Jessica found that she couldn't resist the pressure they exerted on her to snort cocaine. Her experience best illustrates:
    a. ingroup bias.
    b. the mere exposure effect.
    c. the foot-in-the-door phenomenon.
    d. the fundamental attribution error.
    e. the bystander effect.

Do our actions affect our attitudes?, p. 647
Difficult, Conceptual, Objective 3, Ans: c
20. A life insurance salesperson who takes advantage of the foot-in-the-door phenomenon would be most likely to:
     a. emphasize that his company is one of the largest in the insurance industry.
     b. promise a free gift to those who agree to purchase any insurance policy.
     c. ask customers to respond to a brief survey on their life insurance needs and attitudes.
     d. address customers by their first names.
     e. meet potential customers by paying them an unexpected visit at their homes.

Do our actions affect our attitudes?, p. 647
Easy, Conceptual, Objective 3, Ans: c
21. Italo has voluntarily done a number of favors for his new neighbor. As a result, Italo is likely to show:
     a. increased feelings of deindividuation.
     b. decreased feelings of deindividuation.
     c. increased liking for his neighbor.
     d. decreased liking for his neighbor.
     e. a lowered sense of self-esteem.

Do our actions affect our attitudes?, p. 647
Medium, Factual/Definitional, Objective 3, Ans: d
22. Studies of role playing most directly highlight the effects of:
     a. group size on social loafing.
     b. personal anonymity on deindividuation.
     c. an audience on social facilitation.
     d. actions on attitudes.
     e. bystanders on altruism.

Do our actions affect our attitudes?, p. 648
Medium, Factual/Definitional, Objective 3, Ans: c
23. The participants in Philip Zimbardo's simulated prison study:
     a. were assigned the roles of prisoner or guard on the basis of their personality test scores.
     b. found it very difficult to play the role of prison guard.
     c. were so endangered by their role-playing experience that the study was discontinued.
     d. became a cohesive unit when they pursued superordinate goals.

Why do our actions affect our attitudes?, p. 648
Easy, Factual/Definitional, Objective 3, Ans: b
24. Which theory assumes that we adopt certain attitudes in order to justify our past actions?
     a. social exchange theory
     b. cognitive dissonance theory
     c. scapegoat theory
     d. attribution theory
     e. equity theory

Why do our actions affect our attitudes?, p. 648
Medium, Conceptual, Objective 3, Ans: b
25.   Feeling responsible for behavior that violates our conscience is most likely to contribute to:
      a. the bystander effect.
      b. cognitive dissonance.
      c. the fundamental attribution error.
      d. group polarization.
      e. social loafing.

Why do our actions affect our attitudes?, p. 648
Medium, Conceptual, Objective 3, Ans: d
26.   Cognitive dissonance theory is most helpful for understanding:
      a. the mere exposure effect.
      b. group polarization.
      c. the fundamental attribution error.
      d. the foot-in-the-door phenomenon.
      e. the bystander effect.

Why do our actions affect our attitudes?, p. 648
Difficult, Conceptual, Objective 3, Ans: d
27.   During a test, Abe impulsively copied several answers from a nearby student's paper. He felt
      very uncomfortable about having done this until he convinced himself that copying answers is
      not wrong if classmates are careless enough to expose their test sheets. Which theory best
      explains why Abe adopted this new attitude?
      a. frustration-aggression theory
      b. attribution theory
      c. social exchange theory
      d. cognitive dissonance theory
      e. the two-factor theory

Conformity and obedience, p. 650
Medium, Conceptual, Objective 4, Ans: e
28.   If one student in a classroom begins to cough, others are likely to do the same. This best
      illustrates:
      a. deindividuation.
      b. ingroup bias.
      c. the mere exposure effect.
      d. the bystander effect.
      e. the chameleon effect.

Conformity and obedience, p. 650
Medium, Factual/Definitional, Objective 4, Ans: a
29.   The text indicates that the clusters of teenage suicides that occasionally occur in some
      communities may be the result of:
      a. suggestibility.
      b. the bystander effect.
      c. groupthink.
      d. deindividuation.
      e. social facilitation.

Group pressure and conformity, p. 651
Easy, Factual/Definitional, Objective 4, Ans: e

30. Solomon Asch asked people to identify which of three comparison lines was identical to a standard line. His research was designed to study:
   a. the mere exposure effect.
   b. the fundamental attribution error.
   c. social facilitation.
   d. deindividuation.
   e. conformity.

Conditions that strengthen conformity, p. 652
Difficult, Conceptual, Objective 4, Ans: c

31. Naseeb opposes all his classmates in his opinion on an issue. During a class discussion of the issue, Naseeb is most likely to conform to his classmates' opinion if he:
   a. has a high level of self-esteem.
   b. does not have to reveal his personal opinion at the close of the class discussion.
   c. has a lot of good friends in the class.
   d. verbally expresses his own unique opinion early in the class discussion.

Reasons for conforming, p. 652
Easy, Factual/Definitional, Objective 4, Ans: c

32. Conformity resulting from a person's desire to gain approval or avoid disapproval is said to be a response to:
   a. the reciprocity norm.
   b. social facilitation.
   c. normative social influence.
   d. informational social influence.
   e. deindividuation.

Reasons for conforming, p. 652
Easy, Conceptual, Objective 4, Ans: d

33. Professor Maslova attends faculty meetings simply to avoid the disapproval of the college dean. Professor Maslova's behavior exemplifies the importance of:
   a. ingroup bias.
   b. informational social influence.
   c. social facilitation.
   d. normative social influence.
   e. deindividuation.

Reasons for conforming, p. 652
Difficult, Conceptual, Objective 4, Ans: d

34. Toby publicly agrees with his fraternity brothers that Ron, a senior, would make the best Student Senate President. On the secret ballot, however, he actually votes for Yoram. Toby's public conformity to his fraternity brothers' opinion best illustrates the power of:
   a. social facilitation.
   b. informational social influence.
   c. deindividuation.
   d. normative social influence.
   e. the mere exposure effect.

Reasons for conforming, p. 652
Easy, Factual/Definitional, Objective 4, Ans: c

35.   Conformity resulting from the acceptance of others' opinions about reality is said to be a response to:
    a. group polarization.
    b. social facilitation.
    c. informational social influence.
    d. normative social influence.
    e. deindividuation.

Reasons for conforming, p. 652
Easy, Conceptual, Objective 4, Ans: b

36.   Tom recently read that prolonged stress may produce illness. His subsequent decision to enroll in a stress-management class illustrates the effect of:
    a. normative social influence.
    b. informational social influence.
    c. deindividuation.
    d. social loafing.
    e. social facilitation.

Reasons for conforming, p. 652
Difficult, Factual/Definitional, Objective 4, Ans: c

37.   Participants in an experiment were asked to judge which individual in a slide of a four-person lineup had been presented alone in a slide they had just seen. They were most likely to conform to the wrong answers of two confederates when the task was:
    a. easy and important.
    b. easy and unimportant.
    c. difficult and important.
    d. difficult and unimportant.

Reasons for conforming, p. 653
Difficult, Conceptual, Objective 4, Ans: c

38.   The value of social conformity is most likely to be emphasized in:
    a. England.
    b. France.
    c. Japan.
    d. North America.

Obedience, p. 653
Medium, Factual/Definitional, Objective 5, Ans: d

39.   In Milgram's first study of obedience, the majority of "teachers" who were ordered to shock a "learner":
    a. refused to deliver even slight levels of shock.
    b. initially complied but refused to deliver more than slight levels of shock.
    c. complied until ordered to deliver intense levels of shock.
    d. complied fully and delivered the highest level of shock.

Obedience, p. 654
Medium, Factual/Definitional, Objective 5, Ans: c

40. When the subjects in Milgram's study were later surveyed concerning their participation in the research, most reported that they:
     a. did not believe they were actually delivering shock to the "learner."
     b. had actually enjoyed shocking the "learner."
     c. did not regret their participation in the experiment.
     d. did not believe the study should be repeated.

Obedience, pp. 653-654
Medium, Factual/Definitional, Objective 5, Ans: d

41. In Milgram's obedience experiments, subjects were temporarily deceived about:
     a. the purpose of the research.
     b. the experimental role of the other subject with whom they participated.
     c. the amount of shock the "learner" actually received.
     d. all the above.

Obedience, p. 654
Difficult, Factual/Definitional, Objective 5, Ans: c

42. In Milgram's obedience experiments, "teachers" were *least* likely to deliver the highest levels of shock when:
     a. the experiment was conducted at a prestigious institution such as Yale University.
     b. the experimenter became too pushy and told hesitant subjects, "You have no choice, you must go on."
     c. the "teachers" observed other subjects refuse to obey the experimenter's orders.
     d. the "learner" said he had a heart condition.

Lessons from the conformity and obedience studies, p. 655
Easy, Factual/Definitional, Objective 5, Ans: d

43. Conformity and compliance studies have suggested that social influences are:
     a. less powerful than personality traits in shaping behavior.
     b. powerful in shaping behavior, except when they conflict with people's moral standards.
     c. powerful in shaping judgments only when people are unsure about the correct course of action.
     d. powerful enough to lead ordinary people to conform to falsehoods and act cruelly.

Lessons from the conformity and obedience studies, p. 655
Medium, Factual/Definitional, Objective 5, Ans: e

44. The gradually escalating levels of destructive obedience in the Milgram experiments best illustrate one of the potential dangers of:
     a. deindividuation.
     b. social facilitation.
     c. the bystander effect.
     d. the fundamental attribution error.
     e. the foot-in-the-door phenomenon.

Thinking critically about social influence (Box), p. 656
Medium, Factual/Definitional, Objective 5, Ans: e
45.   Advocates of "facilitated communication" suggested that this technique was a useful way to deal with the problem of:
   a. group polarization.
   b. social loafing.
   c. deindividuation.
   d. aggression.
   e. autism.

Social facilitation, p. 657
Easy, Factual/Definitional, Objective 6, Ans: c
46.   Norman Triplett observed that adolescents wound a fishing reel faster in the presence of someone working simultaneously on the same task. This best illustrates:
   a. the mere exposure effect.
   b. the bystander effect.
   c. social facilitation.
   d. group polarization.
   e. deindividuation.

Social facilitation, p. 657
Medium, Factual/Definitional, Objective 6, Ans: d
47.   Social facilitation is most likely to occur in the performance of _____ tasks.
   a. challenging
   b. unenjoyable
   c. novel
   d. simple

Social facilitation, p. 657
Medium, Factual/Definitional, Objective 6, Ans: e
48.   The presence of observers improves a person's performance on _____ tasks and hinders a person's performance on _____ tasks.
   a. unenjoyable; enjoyable
   b. poorly learned; well-learned
   c. physical; mental
   d. verbal; mathematical
   e. easy; difficult

Social facilitation, p. 657
Difficult, Conceptual, Objective 6, Ans: e
49.   On which of the following tasks would the presence of observers be *least* likely to lead to better and faster performance?
   a. raking leaves
   b. washing dishes
   c. bicycle racing
   d. reciting the alphabet
   e. solving a crossword puzzle

Social facilitation, p. 657
Difficult, Conceptual, Objective 6, Ans: b

50. Job applicants are interviewed by either friendly or unfriendly employers who sit either very close to or at a normal distance from the applicants. Research suggests that applicants will like best the friendly employers who sit at a _____ distance and will like least the unfriendly employers who sit at a _____ distance.
     a. very close; normal
     b. very close; very close
     c. normal; normal
     d. normal; very close

Social loafing, p. 657
Medium, Factual/Definitional, Objective 6, Ans: b

51. Social loafing refers to the tendency for people to:
     a. perform a complex task more poorly when others are present.
     b. exert less effort when they are pooling their efforts toward a common goal.
     c. exert less effort when they are paid by the hour, not by the amount of work completed.
     d. become more distracted from their tasks when working with friends than when working with strangers.
     e. stop working once they have reached their goal.

Social loafing, p. 657
Easy, Factual/Definitional, Objective 6, Ans: c

52. Blindfolded subjects were observed to clap louder when they thought they were clapping alone than when they thought they were clapping with others. This best illustrates:
     a. the bystander effect.
     b. the mere exposure effect.
     c. social loafing.
     d. group polarization.
     e. the foot-in-the-door phenomenon.

Social loafing, p. 657
Medium, Conceptual, Objective 6, Ans: a

53. Class members are asked to work cooperatively in groups on major course papers. Every member of a group is to receive exactly the same grade based on the quality of the group's paper. This situation is most likely to lead to:
     a. social loafing.
     b. social facilitation.
     c. deindividuation.
     d. the bystander effect.
     e. the fundamental attribution error.

Social loafing, p. 657
Difficult, Conceptual, Objective 6, Ans: c

54. In which of the following groups is social loafing *least* likely?
     a. a highway crew responsible for filling potholes in streets and expressways
     b. girl scouts who must gather wood for a campfire
     c. factory workers who are each paid on the basis of the number of bicycles each assembles individually
     d. a game show audience instructed to applaud when the host appears on stage
     e. high school students working on a group project for which they will all receive the same grade

Deindividuation, p. 658
Medium, Factual/Definitional, Objective 6, Ans: c
55.   Circumstances that increase _____ are likely to decrease _____.
   a. self-awareness; cognitive dissonance
   b. anonymity; social loafing
   c. self-awareness; deindividuation
   d. anonymity; groupthink
   e. self-awareness; social facilitation

Deindividuation, p. 658
Medium, Conceptual, Objective 6, Ans: d
56.   Individuals who are normally law-abiding may vandalize and loot when they become part of a mob. This change in behavior is best understood in terms of:
   a. social facilitation.
   b. the bystander effect.
   c. the mere exposure effect.
   d. deindividuation.
   e. ingroup bias.

Deindividuation, p. 658
Medium, Conceptual, Objective 6, Ans: a
57.   Masked bandits might be more likely than unmasked bandits to physically injure their victims due to:
   a. deindividuation.
   b. group polarization.
   c. the mere exposure effect.
   d. social facilitation.
   e. social loafing.

Group polarization, p. 658
Medium, Factual/Definitional, Objective 7, Ans: d
58.   Group polarization refers to:
   a. the lack of critical thinking that results from a strong desire for harmony within a group.
   b. a split within a group produced by striking differences of opinion among group members.
   c. the tendency of individuals to exert more effort when working as part of a group.
   d. the enhancement of a group's prevailing attitudes through group discussion.
   e. the failure to give aid in an emergency situation observed by many onlookers.

Group polarization, p. 658
Medium, Conceptual, Objective 7, Ans: c
59.   Professors Maksoud, Struthers, and Vasic each tend to think that obtaining a college degree is easier today than it was when they were college students. After discussing the matter over coffee, they are even more convinced that obtaining a college degree is easier today. This episode provides an example of:
   a. the fundamental attribution error.
   b. social facilitation.
   c. group polarization.
   d. deindividuation.
   e. the foot-in-the-door phenomenon.

Group polarization, p. 658
Difficult, Conceptual, Objective 7, Ans: c

60. An unlikable person is likely to be perceived more _____ a group discussion of that person's qualities, and a likable person is likely to be perceived more _____ a group discussion of that person's qualities.
    a. negatively before; positively after
    b. positively after; negatively after
    c. negatively after; positively after
    d. positively after; negatively before

Group polarization, p. 659
Medium, Conceptual, Objective 7, Ans: c

61. By providing racially prejudiced people with electronic "chat rooms" for interfacing online with others who share their attitudes, the Internet most likely serves as a medium for:
    a. social facilitation.
    b. the bystander effect.
    c. group polarization.
    d. cognitive dissonance.
    e. GRIT

Groupthink, p. 659
Medium, Factual/Definitional, Objective 7, Ans: d

62. An overwhelming desire for harmony in a decision-making group increases the probability of:
    a. social facilitation.
    b. the mere exposure effect.
    c. the bystander effect.
    d. groupthink.
    e. the foot-in-the-door phenomenon.

Groupthink, p. 659
Medium, Factual/Definitional, Objective 7, Ans: d

63. The NASA executive who made the final decision to launch the space shuttle *Challenger* was shielded from information and dissenting views that might have led to a delay of the tragic launch. This best illustrates the dangers of:
    a. social facilitation.
    b. deindividuation.
    c. the mere exposure effect.
    d. groupthink.
    e. the bystander effect.

Groupthink, p. 659
Easy, Conceptual, Objective 7, Ans: a

64. Which of the following comments is most likely to be made by the leader of a group characterized by groupthink?
    a. "We have been united on matters in the past and I hope that will continue."
    b. "We will need some outside experts to critique our decisions."
    c. "It's important for each of us to think critically about this issue."
    d. "We should probably divide into subgroups and arrive at independent decisions."

Groupthink, p. 659
Difficult, Factual/Definitional, Objective 7, Ans: b
65. Groupthink can be prevented by a leader who:
    a. is directive and makes his or her own position clear from the start.
    b. invites outside experts to critique a group's developing plans.
    c. tries to maintain high morale among group members.
    d. emphasizes the importance of the issue under discussion.

Self-fulfilling prophecies, p. 660
Difficult, Factual/Definitional, Objective 7, Ans: b
66. Those who idealize their dating partners as having many virtues and few faults actually tend to develop more satisfying relationships than do those who are more realistic. This best illustrates the social significance of:
    a. the mere exposure effect.
    b. self-fulfilling prophecies.
    c. the fundamental attribution error.
    d. the foot-in-the-door phenomenon.
    e. mirror-image perceptions.

Self-fulfilling prophecies, p. 660
Medium, Conceptual, Objective 7, Ans: e
67. Because he mistakenly expects substandard work from his minority employees, Mr. Johnson treats them in a patronizing manner that causes them to become demoralized and unproductive. This best illustrates the importance of:
    a. the chameleon effect.
    b. social facilitation.
    c. the fundamental attribution error.
    d. mirror-image perceptions.
    e. self-fulfilling prophecies.

Minority influence, p. 660
Medium, Factual/Definitional, Objective 7, Ans: d
68. Research indicates that minorities are most influential when they:
    a. argue positions widely divergent from those of the majority.
    b. make use of emotional rather than logical appeals.
    c. acknowledge the wisdom of the majority position.
    d. unswervingly hold to their own position.

Prejudice, p. 662
Easy, Factual/Definitional, Objective 8, Ans: e
69. An unjustifiable and usually negative attitude toward a group and its members is called:
    a. scapegoating.
    b. deindividuation.
    c. groupthink.
    d. discrimination.
    e. prejudice.

Prejudice, p. 662
Medium, Conceptual, Objective 9, Ans: a

70. Bernard believes that most young women from California are extremely good looking and that extremely good-looking women are usually selfish and egotistical. His beliefs are examples of:
     a. stereotypes.
     b. mirror-image perceptions.
     c. sexual discrimination.
     d. ingroup bias.
     e. deindividuation.

Prejudice (Figure 18.10), p. 662
Easy, Factual/Definitional, Objective 9, Ans: c

71. Over the last 55 years, Americans have expressed:
     a. decreasing readiness to support laws guaranteeing a pregnant woman's right to a leave of absence from the workplace.
     b. increasing approval of women marrying at earlier ages.
     c. increasing readiness to vote for a female presidential candidate.
     d. decreasing support for a woman's right to abortion.

Prejudice, p. 663
Medium, Factual/Definitional, Objective 8, Ans: c

72. Cross-cultural research on gender relations indicates that:
     a. the majority of the world's children without basic schooling are boys.
     b. in most countries men and women share equally in the duties of child-rearing.
     c. people perceive their fathers as more intelligent than their mothers despite gender equality in intelligence scores.
     d. there is little evidence that females are more likely to be aborted than males.

Social inequalities, p. 664
Medium, Conceptual, Objective 8, Ans: d

73. Government officials who emphasize that African-Americans are personally responsible for the economically disadvantaged position of their ethnic group are most likely to promote:
     a. deindividuation.
     b. social loafing.
     c. the social responsibility norm.
     d. prejudice.
     e. conciliation.

Social inequalities, p. 664
Medium, Conceptual, Objective 8, Ans: c

74. Mr. and Mrs. Wang never encouraged their daughter to excel in mathematics because they believe that women have inferior mathematical aptitude. Their daughter's poor performance on her recent college entrance mathematics exam best illustrates the impact of:
     a. the mere exposure effect.
     b. mirror-image perceptions.
     c. a self-fulfilling prophecy.
     d. social facilitation.
     e. ingroup bias.

Us and them: ingroup and outgroup, p. 664
Medium, Conceptual, Objective 8, Ans: c
75. A sense of social identity is most likely to be enhanced by:
    a. social facilitation.
    b. group polarization.
    c. ingroup bias.
    d. deindividuation.
    e. cognitive dissonance.

Us and them: ingroup and outgroup, p. 664
Medium, Conceptual, Objective 8, Ans: c
76. Six-year-old Ezra believes that boys are better than girls, while 5-year-old Arlette believes that girls are better than boys. Their beliefs most clearly illustrate:
    a. the reciprocity norm.
    b. deindividuation.
    c. ingroup bias.
    d. the mere exposure effect.
    e. the fundamental attribution error.

Us and them: ingroup and outgroup, p. 664
Medium, Conceptual, Objective 8, Ans: e
77. During a Girl Scout picnic, Lavinia was randomly selected to be on one baseball team and Carla on the opposing team. Before the game started, both Lavinia and Carla were convinced that their own team was the better one. The girls' reactions best illustrate:
    a. the fundamental attribution error.
    b. deindividuation.
    c. the reciprocity norm.
    d. the mere exposure effect.
    e. ingroup bias.

Scapegoating, pp. 664-665
Medium, Factual/Definitional, Objective 8, Ans: d
78. Evidence that people exhibit heightened levels of prejudice when they are economically frustrated offers support for:
    a. cognitive dissonance theory.
    b. the just-world phenomenon.
    c. social exchange theory.
    d. the scapegoat theory.
    e. attribution theory.

Scapegoating, pp. 664-665
Medium, Conceptual, Objective 8, Ans: e
79. Ever since he lost his job, Richard has become increasingly hostile toward the "socialist bankers who are leading the country toward bankruptcy." Richard's increasing prejudice toward bankers can best be explained in terms of:
    a. the just-world phenomenon.
    b. the fundamental attribution error.
    c. ingroup bias.
    d. social facilitation.
    e. the scapegoat theory.

Cognitive roots of prejudice: categorization, p. 665
Medium, Factual/Definitional, Objective 8, Ans: e

80. In one experiment, university students were asked to evaluate the performance of a student basketball player. Those who saw a photo of a black player evaluated him more favorably than did those who saw a photo of a white player. This best illustrates the impact of:
    a. ingroup bias.
    b. the mere exposure effect.
    c. social facilitation.
    d. the fundamental attribution error.
    e. stereotypes.

Cognitive roots of prejudice: categorization, p. 665
Medium, Factual/Definitional, Objective 8, Ans: b

81. We are most likely to _____ the diversity among members of an _____.
    a. overestimate; outgroup
    b. underestimate; outgroup
    c. correctly estimate; outgroup
    d. underestimate; ingroup

Cognitive roots of prejudice: categorization, p. 665
Difficult, Conceptual, Objective 8, Ans: a

82. Joie, age 19, is a black female college sophomore. Research on how we categorize social information suggests that Joie is most likely to believe that most:
    a. elderly people tend to look pretty much alike.
    b. black people tend to dress pretty much alike.
    c. teenagers tend to prefer the same kinds of music.
    d. women tend to share similar attitudes about sex.

Cognitive roots of prejudice: vivid cases, p. 665
Medium, Factual/Definitional, Objective 8, Ans: c

83. A vivid example of an individual's behavior has an unusually strong influence on people's judgments of a whole social group primarily because people:
    a. are motivated to confirm their current stereotypes of specific groups.
    b. typically categorize other individuals on the basis of barely noticeable characteristics.
    c. estimate the frequency of group characteristics in terms of the memorability of these characteristics.
    d. strongly resent those who draw a lot of attention to themselves.

The just-world phenomenon, pp. 665-666
Medium, Factual/Definitional, Objective 8, Ans: b

84. The just-world phenomenon often leads people to:
    a. dislike and distrust those who are wealthy.
    b. believe that victims of misfortune deserve to suffer.
    c. express higher levels of prejudice after suffering frustration.
    d. respond with kindness to those who mistreat them.

The just-world phenomenon, p. 666
Difficult, Conceptual, Objective 8, Ans: e

85.   Mr. Ignatenko thinks that most unemployed people are to blame for their own misfortune. His belief best illustrates a potential consequence of:
    a.   ingroup bias.
    b.   deindividuation.
    c.   the social responsibility norm.
    d.   the mere exposure effect.
    e.   the just-world phenomenon.

Aggression, p. 666
Easy, Factual/Definitional, Objective 9, Ans: e

86.   The risk of being murdered is the highest for residents of:
    a.   Europe.
    b.   Canada.
    c.   Australia.
    d.   New Zealand.
    e.   the United States.

The biology of aggression, p. 666
Easy, Factual/Definitional, Objective 9, Ans: c

87.   Who argued that human aggression is instinctive?
    a.   Stanley Milgram
    b.   Fritz Heider
    c.   Sigmund Freud
    d.   Albert Bandura
    e.   B. F. Skinner

The biology of aggression, p. 666
Difficult, Factual/Definitional, Objective 9, Ans: b

88.   An explanation of aggression in terms of instinct would have the most difficulty accounting for:
    a.   unexpected and unprovoked outbursts of aggression.
    b.   wide cultural variations in aggressiveness.
    c.   aggression that arises out of anger and hostility.
    d.   the use of nuclear weapons to kill millions of unseen victims.

The biology of aggression, p. 667
Easy, Factual/Definitional, Objective 9, Ans: c

89.   Research on the biology of aggression has clearly demonstrated that:
    a.   human aggression is an unlearned instinct.
    b.   there is no physiological basis for aggression in humans.
    c.   animals can be bred for aggressiveness.
    d.   neural influences contribute to aggressive behavior by males but not by females.

The biology of aggression, p. 667
Medium, Factual/Definitional, Objective 9, Ans: a

90.   Violent male criminals tend to have relatively _____ levels of serotonin and _____ levels of testosterone.
       a. low; high
       b. high; low
       c. low; low
       d. high; high

The psychology of aggression: aversive events, p. 668
Medium, Conceptual, Objective 9, Ans: d

91.   After Jim lost the student election for president of his high school class, he spread false rumors intended to spoil the newly chosen president's reputation. Jim's behavior is best explained in terms of the:
       a. ingroup bias.
       b. foot-in-the-door phenomenon.
       c. mere exposure effect.
       d. frustration-aggression principle.
       e. fundamental attribution error.

The psychology of aggression: aversive events, p. 669
Medium, Factual/Definitional, Objective 9, Ans: a

92.   Research on the relationship between aversive events and aggression indicates that:
       a. hot temperatures often lead people to react to provocations with greater hostility.
       b. aversive events often distract people from acting on their hostile intentions.
       c. frustration inevitably leads people to act aggressively.
       d. aversive events lead to hostility in males but not in females.

Learning to express and inhibit aggression, p. 669
Medium, Conceptual, Objective 9, Ans: c

93.   Helmer has become increasingly involved in violent fights at school because this gains him the attention and respect of many of his classmates. This most clearly suggests that his aggression is a(n):
       a. reaction to frustration.
       b. instinctive behavior.
       c. learned response.
       d. product of deindividuation.
       e. result of group polarization.

Learning to express and inhibit aggression, p. 669
Easy, Factual/Definitional, Objective 9, Ans: d

94.   High rates of violence are most common among those who experience minimal levels of:
       a. cognitive dissonance.
       b. deindividuation.
       c. social facilitation.
       d. father care.
       e. group polarization.

Television watching and aggression, pp. 671-672
Medium, Factual/Definitional, Objective 9, Ans: c

95. Prolonged exposure to TV crime shows leads viewers to perceive the world as _____ dangerous and to experience _____ sympathy for victims of violence.
     a. more; more
     b. less; less
     c. more; less
     d. less; more

Do video games teach or release violence? (Box), p. 672
Medium, Factual/Definitional, Objective 9, Ans: d

96. Research on the effects of playing violent video games most clearly provides disconfirming evidence for the:
     a. mere exposure effect.
     b. frustration-aggression principle.
     c. cognitive dissonance theory.
     d. catharsis hypothesis.
     e. just-world phenomenon.

Television watching and aggression, p. 672
Difficult, Conceptual, Objective 10, Ans: b

97. Ten-year-old Karen frequently watches violent movies on television. This is most likely to lead her to:
     a. underestimate the actual frequency of violent crimes in the real world.
     b. experience less distress at the sight of other children fighting on the school playground.
     c. become more hesitant about personally starting a fight with another child.
     d. become less fearful about being criminally assaulted.

Sexual aggression and the media, p. 673
Medium, Factual/Definitional, Objective 10, Ans: d

98. Surveys of the incidence of sexual harassment in the United States indicate that:
     a. the majority of women report that they have never experienced any form of sexual harassment.
     b. women tend to define many sexual advances as rape attempts when legally they are not.
     c. victims of acquaintance rape are more likely to report the crime to police than are victims of stranger rape.
     d. the majority of rapes are never reported to the police.
     e. women are more likely to be victimized by stranger rape than by acquaintance rape.

Sexual aggression and the media, p. 673
Medium, Conceptual, Objective 10, Ans: c

99. After a month of watching violent pornographic movies on late-night cable TV, Myron will probably be:
     a. less likely to believe that women enjoy aggressive sexual treatment.
     b. more likely to believe that rape is a serious crime.
     c. more likely to favor shorter prison sentences for convicted rapists.
     d. less likely to believe that rape occurs quite frequently in society.

Sexual aggression and the media, p. 674
Medium, Factual/Definitional, Objective 10, Ans: d

100. Extensive exposure to violent pornographic films contributes to a(n) _____ willingness to hurt women and that is due primarily to the _____.
    a. increasing; eroticism
    b. decreasing; eroticism
    c. decreasing; depiction of sexual violence
    d. increasing; depiction of sexual violence

TV violence, pornography, and society, p. 674
Medium, Factual/Definitional, Objective 10, Ans: a

101. Several factors other than the media can create a predisposition to sexual violence. These include all of the following *except*:
    a. a tendency toward criminal behavior.
    b. dominance motives.
    c. disinhibition by alcohol.
    d. a history of child abuse.

Social traps, p. 675
Medium, Factual/Definitional, Objective 11, Ans: a

102. A situation in which the individual pursuit of self-interest leads to collective destruction is known as:
    a. a social trap.
    b. the self-serving bias.
    c. deindividuation.
    d. groupthink.
    e. ingroup bias.

Social traps, p. 675
Medium, Factual/Definitional, Objective 11, Ans: c

103. Simple "non-zero-sum games" have been used in laboratory settings in order to study:
    a. the just-world phenomenon.
    b. the mere exposure effect.
    c. social traps.
    d. the bystander effect.
    e. the foot-in-the-door phenomenon.

Social traps, p. 675
Medium, Conceptual, Objective 11, Ans: b

104. After a year-long drought, the city of Pine Bluffs has banned all lawn sprinkling. Many residents believe, however, that continued watering of their own lawn will have little effect on total water reserves. Consequently, there is a disastrous drain on city water reserves caused by widespread illegal sprinkling. This incident best illustrates the dynamics of:
    a. ingroup bias.
    b. social traps.
    c. the fundamental attribution error.
    d. the bystander effect.
    e. the just-world phenomenon.

Enemy perceptions, p. 676
Difficult, Conceptual, Objective 11, Ans: e

105. Mrs. Crane frequently thinks she has to shout at her husband in order to get his attention, but he thinks she yells because she's angry. Mr. Crane typically feels he has to shout back at his wife in order to defend himself, but she thinks his screaming proves that he's hostile. This couple's experience best illustrates:
    a. scapegoating.
    b. deindividuation.
    c. the reciprocity norm.
    d. superordinate goals.
    e. mirror-image perceptions.

Enemy perceptions, p. 676
Medium, Conceptual, Objective 11, Ans: c

106. The country of Danasia increased the size of its military force because its leaders expected their rival, the country of Wallonia, to do the same. The Wallonians felt it was necessary to respond to the Danasian military buildup with a military expansion of their own. The Wallonian response best illustrates the danger of:
    a. social facilitation.
    b. the mere exposure effect.
    c. the fundamental attribution error.
    d. self-fulfilling prophecies.
    e. the foot-in-the-door phenomenon.

The psychology of attraction: proximity, p. 677
Easy, Factual/Definitional, Objective 12, Ans: e

107. The mere exposure effect most directly contributes to the positive relationship between _____ and liking.
    a. similarity
    b. physical arousal
    c. physical attractiveness
    d. self-disclosure
    e. proximity

The psychology of attraction: proximity, p. 677
Medium, Conceptual, Objective 12, Ans: e

108. When Harold first heard the hit song "Back to Basics," he wasn't at all sure he liked it. The more often he heard it played, however, the more he enjoyed it. Harold's reaction illustrates:
    a. the bystander effect.
    b. social facilitation.
    c. companionate love.
    d. the foot-in-the-door phenomenon.
    e. the mere exposure effect.

The psychology of attraction: proximity, p. 677
Difficult, Factual/Definitional, Objective 12, Ans: a

109. People tend to prefer a(n) _____ photograph of themselves and a(n) _____ photograph of a close friend.
    a. mirror-image; actual
    b. actual; mirror-image
    c. actual; actual
    d. mirror-image; mirror-image

The psychology of attraction: physical attractiveness, p. 678
Easy, Factual/Definitional, Objective 12, Ans: c

110. Our first impressions of those we meet are most likely to be determined by their:
     a. attitudes.
     b. intelligence.
     c. physical appearance.
     d. superordinate goals.

The psychology of attraction: physical attractiveness, p. 678
Medium, Factual/Definitional, Objective 12, Ans: c

111. The physical attractiveness of high school and college students is a good predictor of their:
     a. happiness.
     b. academic competence.
     c. frequency of dating.
     d. altruism.

The psychology of attraction: physical attractiveness, p. 678
Medium, Conceptual, Objective 12, Ans: b

112. Mark, a 21-year-old college junior, is physically unattractive. Compared to good-looking students, Mark is more likely to:
     a. be physically coordinated and athletic.
     b. have difficulty making a favorable impression on potential employers.
     c. become a very loving and dependable parent.
     d. earn low grades in his college courses.
     e. be well liked by other male college students.

The psychology of attraction: physical attractiveness, p. 679
Difficult, Factual/Definitional, Objective 12, Ans: c

113. Research on physical attractiveness indicates that men are more likely than women to:
     a. express dissatisfaction with their own physical appearance.
     b. deny that their liking for physically attractive dates is influenced by good looks.
     c. judge members of the opposite sex as more attractive if they have a youthful appearance.
     d. marry someone who is less physically attractive than they themselves are.
     e. be attracted to dating partners whose hips are narrower than their waists.

The psychology of attraction: similarity, p. 680
Medium, Factual/Definitional, Objective 12, Ans: e

114. We are likely to become friends with others who are similar to us in:
     a. attitudes.
     b. intelligence.
     c. age.
     d. economic status.
     e. any of the above areas.

The psychology of attraction: similarity, p. 680
Medium, Conceptual, Objective 12, Ans: c

115. Olive, a 21-year-old college junior, is outgoing, intelligent, domineering, and politically liberal. Research suggests that she would most likely become a good friend of:
     a. Abe, who is intelligent and shy.
     b. Thorwald, who is politically liberal and submissive.
     c. Philip, who is domineering and outgoing.
     d. Padrig, who is shy and submissive.

Passionate love, p. 681
Easy, Factual/Definitional, Objective 13, Ans: e

116. The two-factor theory of emotion specifically suggests that passionate love can be facilitated by:
a. the mere exposure effect.
b. self-disclosure.
c. equity.
d. group polarization.
e. physical arousal.

Passionate love, p. 681
Medium, Conceptual, Objective 13, Ans: b

117. While driving his girlfriend to work, Nate narrowly avoided a collision with another vehicle. Moments later, he experienced an unusually warm glow of affection for his girlfriend. His romantic reaction is best explained in terms of:
a. social exchange theory.
b. the two-factor theory of emotion.
c. social facilitation.
d. the mere exposure effect.
e. the bystander effect.

Passionate love, p. 681
Difficult, Factual/Definitional, Objective 13, Ans: b

118. In investigating the impact of physical arousal on passionate love, Dutton and Aron arranged for an attractive woman to briefly interact with men who had recently:
a. consumed an alcoholic beverage.
b. crossed a swaying footbridge.
c. listened to romantic music.
d. intervened in an emergency.
e. failed a midterm test.

Companionate love, pp. 681-682
Easy, Factual/Definitional, Objective 13, Ans: c

119. Equity and self-disclosure are important to the development of:
a. groupthink.
b. deindividuation.
c. companionate love.
d. social facilitation.
e. all the above.

Companionate love, p. 682
Medium, Conceptual, Objective 13, Ans: c

120. Jerry thinks his girlfriend derives more benefits from their relationship than he does, even though he contributes more to the relationship. Jerry most clearly believes that their relationship lacks:
a. self-disclosure.
b. romantic love.
c. equity.
d. superordinate goals.

Companionate love, p. 682
Easy, Factual/Definitional, Objective 13, Ans: d
121. A gradual escalation of intimacy is most positively related to a gradual escalation of:
    a. cognitive dissonance.
    b. social facilitation.
    c. groupthink.
    d. self disclosure.
    e. normative social influence.

Bystander intervention, p. 683
Difficult, Conceptual, Objective 14, Ans: d
122. As Arlette walks through a shopping mall, she happens to pass by an elderly woman who is sitting on a bench, clutching her arm, and moaning in pain. The presence of many other shoppers in the mall will most likely increase the probability that Arlette will:
    a. experience contempt for the elderly woman.
    b. help the woman by calling an ambulance.
    c. experience a sense of empathy for the elderly woman.
    d. fail to notice the elderly woman's problem.

Bystander intervention, p. 683
Medium, Factual/Definitional, Objective 14, Ans: c
123. The presence of many bystanders at the scene of an emergency increases the likelihood that any individual bystander will:
    a. notice the emergency.
    b. report the emergency to the police.
    c. fail to interpret the incident as an emergency.
    d. assume responsibility for personally intervening in the emergency.

Bystander intervention, pp. 683-684
Easy, Conceptual, Objective 14, Ans: d
124. Mrs. Pinheiro fell on a busy city sidewalk and broke her leg. Although hundreds of pedestrians saw her lying on the ground, most failed to recognize that she was in need of medical assistance. Their oversight best illustrates one of the dynamics involved in:
    a. the fundamental attribution error.
    b. social loafing.
    c. the foot-in-the-door phenomenon.
    d. the bystander effect.
    e. the mere exposure effect.

Bystander intervention, p. 684
Difficult, Factual/Definitional, Objective 14, Ans: e
125. Social psychologists have arranged for people to drop coins or pencils in elevators in order to study:
    a. the foot-in-the-door phenomenon.
    b. the mere exposure effect.
    c. social facilitation.
    d. social loafing.
    e. the bystander effect.

Bystander intervention, p. 684
Easy, Factual/Definitional, Objective 14, Ans: c
126. The fact that people are less likely to give aid if an emergency occurs in the presence of many observers is called:
    a. group polarization.
    b. social loafing.
    c. the bystander effect.
    d. the mere exposure effect.
    e. social facilitation.

Bystander intervention, p. 684
Medium, Conceptual, Objective 14, Ans: d
127. When 68-year-old Mrs. Blake had a flat tire on a fairly isolated highway, she received help from a passerby in less than 10 minutes. One year later, she had a flat tire on a busy freeway and an hour elapsed before someone finally stopped to offer assistance. Mrs. Blake's experience best illustrates:
    a. the fundamental attribution error.
    b. the mere exposure effect.
    c. group polarization.
    d. the bystander effect.
    e. social loafing.

Bystander intervention, p. 684
Medium, Conceptual, Objective 14, Ans: a
128. The Plattsville blood bank is desperately in need of blood donors. Which of the following college students would most likely contribute to the blood bank, if asked?
    a. Ardyce, who has just fallen head-over-heels in love
    b. Grigory, who is busy studying for a history midterm
    c. Sigrid, who unexpectedly lost her part-time job and has time on her hands
    d. Fred, who is depressed because he just learned he got a D on a chemistry exam

The psychology of helping, pp. 684-685
Easy, Factual/Definitional, Objective 14, Ans: b
129. Which theory suggests that altruistic behavior is governed by calculations of rewards and costs?
    a. attribution theory
    b. social exchange theory
    c. cognitive dissonance theory
    d. the two-factor theory of emotion

The psychology of helping, pp. 684-685
Difficult, Conceptual, Objective 14, Ans: c
130. Katya donated money to a religious charity in order to boost her own feelings of self-esteem. Jennifer failed to contribute to the same charity because she was fearful of running out of money. Differences in their altruistic behavior are best explained in terms of:
    a. the two-factor theory of emotion.
    b. the reciprocity norm.
    c. social exchange theory.
    d. attribution theory.
    e. the social responsibility norm.

The psychology of helping, p. 685
Medium, Factual/Definitional, Objective 14, Ans: a
131. Two social norms that influence altruistic behavior are:
    a. reciprocity and social responsibility.
    b. social responsibility and social exchange.
    c. reciprocity and kin selection.
    d. kin selection and social exchange.

The psychology of helping, p. 685
Medium, Conceptual, Objective 14, Ans: c
132. After the Greenway family accepted their neighbor's invitation to Thanksgiving dinner, Mrs. Greenway felt obligated to invite the neighbors to dinner on Christmas. Mrs. Greenway's sense of obligation most likely resulted from:
    a. the ingroup bias.
    b. the foot-in-the-door phenomenon.
    c. the reciprocity norm.
    d. the fundamental attribution error.
    e. the mere exposure effect.

Peacemaking, p. 685
Easy, Conceptual, Objective 15, Ans: d
133. After their country was ravaged by a series of earthquakes, two bitterly antagonistic political groups set aside their differences and worked cooperatively on effective disaster relief. This cooperation best illustrates the importance of:
    a. groupthink.
    b. mirror-image perceptions.
    c. the just-world phenomenon.
    d. superordinate goals.
    e. the mere exposure effect.

Peacemaking, p. 685
Medium, Conceptual, Objective 15, Ans: b
134. The concept of a superordinate goal is best illustrated by:
    a. the intent of a college freshman to enter medical school and eventually become a physician.
    b. the efforts of management and labor to produce a fuel-efficient automobile that will outsell any car on the market.
    c. the desire of a social worker to do volunteer work in the inner city in order to improve race relations.
    d. a college president's desire to give both faculty and students two extra days of spring vacation.

Peacemaking, p. 686
Medium, Factual/Definitional, Objective 15, Ans: d
135. The success of interracial cooperative learning in classroom settings best illustrates the value of _____ for reducing racial conflict.
    a. the mere exposure effect
    b. social facilitation
    c. the just-world phenomenon
    d. superordinate goals
    e. deindividuation

Peacemaking, p. 686
Medium, Factual/Definitional, Objective 15, Ans: b

136. Two friends quarreled over possession of a single orange without realizing that one of them simply wanted orange juice and the other simply wanted the orange peel to make a cake. This classic episode best illustrates the pitfalls of:
    a. the mere exposure effect.
    b. a win-lose orientation.
    c. the fundamental attribution error.
    d. the foot-in-the-door phenomenon.
    e. a self-fulfilling prophecy.

Peacemaking, p. 687
Medium, Conceptual, Objective 15, Ans: e

137. Adherence to the reciprocity norm is most relevant to the utility of:
    a. social facilitation.
    b. superordinate goals.
    c. the just-world phenomenon.
    d. the mere exposure effect.
    e. GRIT.

Peacemaking, p. 687
Difficult, Factual/Definitional, Objective 15, Ans: d

138. In 1963, President John F. Kennedy announced to the then Soviet Union that the United States would discontinue all atmospheric nuclear tests. The Soviet's positive response to this conciliatory gesture illustrated the potential value of:
    a. mirror-image perceptions.
    b. superordinate goals.
    c. the mere exposure effect.
    d. GRIT.
    e. the just-world phenomenon.

Supplement A

PsychSim

This test bank supplement includes five multiple-choice questions on each of the PsychSim programs.

PsychSim: neural messages
Medium, Factual/Definitional, Ans: a

1.   (PsychSim: Neural Messages) Anions are _____ charged molecules located _____ the axon.
     a. negatively; inside
     b. negatively; outside
     c. positively; inside
     d. positively; outside

PsychSim: neural messages
Medium, Factual/Definitional, Ans: a

2.   (PsychSim: Neural Messages) An axon is polarized when:
     a. the inside of the axon is electrically negative with respect to the outside.
     b. positively charged sodium molecules rush into the axon through special sodium gates.
     c. the outside of the axon contains more negatively charged chlorine molecules than the inside.
     d. the inside of the axon contains more positively charged sodium molecules than the outside.

PsychSim: neural messages
Difficult, Factual/Definitional, Ans: c

3.   (PsychSim: Neural Messages) During depolarization, _____ molecules rush into the axon; during repolarization, _____ molecules rush out of the axon.
     a. potassium; chloride
     b. chloride; sodium
     c. sodium; potassium
     d. potassium; chloride
     e. sodium; chloride

PsychSim: neural messages
Easy, Factual/Definitional, Ans: e

4.   (PsychSim: Neural Messages) The process by which a single neuron relays messages to other neurons is called:
     a. networking.
     b. polarization.
     c. depolarization.
     d. axonal transmission.
     e. synaptic transmission.

PsychSim: neural messages
Medium, Factual/Definitional, Ans: d

5.   (PsychSim: Neural Messages) In the process of communication between neurons, neurotransmitter molecules are released into the gap between neurons by the:
     a. soma.
     b. dendrites.
     c. cell nucleus.
     d. synaptic vesicles.

PsychSim: hemispheric specialization
Medium, Factual/Definitional, Ans: e

6.   (PsychSim: Hemispheric Specialization) The left hemisphere of a split-brain patient receives visual input only from the _____ visual field of _____.
     a.   right; only the left eye
     b.   left; only the right eye
     c.   right; only the right eye
     d.   left; both right and left eyes
     e.   right; both right and left eyes

PsychSim: hemispheric specialization
Easy, Factual/Definitional, Ans: a

7.   (PsychSim: Hemispheric Specialization) Right-handed split-brain patients are able to:
     a.   name unseen objects placed in their right hands but not objects placed in their left hands.
     b.   name unseen objects placed in their left hands but not objects placed in their right hands.
     c.   name unseen objects placed in either their right or left hands.
     d.   hardly ever name unseen objects placed in either their right or left hands.

PsychSim: hemispheric specialization
Easy, Factual/Definitional, Ans: c

8.   (PsychSim: Hemispheric Specialization) Evidence that the left hemisphere is especially effective at processing language is provided by the fact that split-brain patients are able to:
     a.   repeat words more quickly when they are whispered into their left rather than their right ear.
     b.   name an unseen object more rapidly when it is placed in their left rather than their right hand.
     c.   read words more easily when they are flashed briefly in their right rather than their left visual field.
     d.   do all the above.

PsychSim: hemispheric specialization
Medium, Factual/Definitional, Ans: b

9.   (PsychSim: Hemispheric Specialization) Normal people who have been blindfolded can name an object placed in their left hand because:
     a.   the absence of visual cues facilitates spatial imagery in the right hemisphere of the brain.
     b.   information about the object is transferred across the corpus callosum to the left hemisphere of the brain.
     c.   information about the object is transferred directly and simultaneously to both hemispheres of the brain.
     d.   the right hemisphere of normal people can process language without the aid of the left hemisphere.

PsychSim: hemispheric specialization
Easy, Factual/Definitional, Ans: c

10. (PsychSim: Hemispheric Specialization) A right-handed split-brain patient can most effectively assemble a puzzle with the _____ hand because the _____ hemisphere of the brain excels at spatial tasks.
     a.   left; left
     b.   right; left
     c.   left; right
     d.   right; right

PsychSim: cognitive development
Medium, Factual/Definitional, Ans: e

11. (PsychSim: Cognitive Development) A young child who sees a cow for the first time calls it a "doggie." This illustrates the process of:
   a. accommodation.
   b. object permanence.
   c. conservation.
   d. reversible thinking.
   e. assimilation.

PsychSim: cognitive development
Medium, Factual/Definitional, Ans: d

12. (PsychSim: Cognitive Development) A child's mental framework for interpreting reality becomes increasingly complex through the process of:
   a. conservation.
   b. assimilation.
   c. reversible thinking.
   d. accommodation.
   e. egocentrism.

PsychSim: cognitive development
Easy, Factual/Definitional, Ans: b

13. (PsychSim: Cognitive Development) A young child is shown two identical balls of clay. When one is rolled into a long rope, the child perceives it to contain more clay. This child is unable to understand:
   a. object permanence.
   b. conservation.
   c. assimilation.
   d. accommodation.

PsychSim: cognitive development
Easy, Factual/Definitional, Ans: b

14. (PsychSim: Cognitive Development) Lisa's incorrect responses to the checkers problem indicate that she is still in the _____ stage of cognitive development.
   a. formal operational
   b. preoperational
   c. concrete operational
   d. sensorimotor

PsychSim: cognitive development
Medium, Factual/Definitional, Ans: c

15. (PsychSim: Cognitive Development) Both Mike and Leah respond correctly to the water-jar problem. This illustrates that they have developed what Piaget calls:
   a. formal operations.
   b. object permanence.
   c. reversible thinking.
   d. accommodation.

PsychSim: the auditory system
Difficult, Factual/Definitional, Ans: d

16. (PsychSim: The Auditory System) The stimulus energy underlying your experience of sound involves continuous changes in:
a. wave frequency.
b. wave amplitude.
c. waveform.
d. air pressure.
e. timbre.

PsychSim: the auditory system
Easy, Factual/Definitional, Ans: c

17. (PsychSim: The Auditory System) The conversion of the mechanical energy produced by sound waves into neural impulses occurs in the:
a. eardrum.
b. middle ear.
c. cochlea.
d. ear canal.
e. vestibulary system.

PsychSim: the auditory system
Easy, Factual/Definitional, Ans: d

18. (PsychSim: The Auditory System) As compared to long objects, short objects vibrate
_____ and produce sound waves of _____ frequency.
a. slower; lower
b. slower; higher
c. faster; lower
d. faster; higher

PsychSim: the auditory system
Medium, Factual/Definitional, Ans: c

19. (PsychSim: The Auditory System) The frequency of a sound wave is measured in:
a. amps.
b. sines.
c. Hertz.
d. decibels.
e. millimeters.

PsychSim: the auditory system
Medium, Factual/Definitional, Ans: c

20. (PsychSim: The Auditory System) The waveform of a sound determines our experience of:
a. loudness.
b. pitch.
c. timbre.
d. kinesthesis.
e. amplitude.

PsychSim: visual illusions
Easy, Factual/Definitional, Ans: c
21. (PsychSim: Visual Illusions) In the Müller-Lyer illusion, the arrowheads at the ends of the lines lead people to misjudge the _____ of the two horizontal lines.
   a. continuity
   b. relative height
   c. length
   d. convergence
   e. thickness

PsychSim: visual illusions
Easy, Factual/Definitional, Ans: c
22. (PsychSim: Visual Illusions) The Ponzo Illusion illustrates that people judge the size of an object in terms of its perceived:
   a. shape.
   b. height.
   c. distance.
   d. continuity.
   e. convergence.

PsychSim: visual illusions
Medium, Factual/Definitional, Ans: b
23. (PsychSim: Visual Illusions) In the Ponzo Illusion, most people _____ the length of the bar that appears to be more _____.
   a. underestimate; distant
   b. overestimate; distant
   c. underestimate; horizontal
   d. overestimate; horizontal

PsychSim: visual illusions
Difficult, Factual/Definitional, Ans: d
24. (PsychSim: Visual Illusions) In the horizontal/vertical illusion, most people perceive a _____ line as _____.
   a. horizontal; longer than an equally long vertical line
   b. vertical; less distant than an equally distant horizontal line
   c. horizontal; straighter than an equally straight vertical line
   d. vertical; longer than an equally long horizontal line
   e. horizontal; more distant than an equally distant vertical line

PsychSim: visual illusions
Medium, Factual/Definitional, Ans: a
25. (PsychSim: Visual Illusions) In the Poggendorf illusion involving a rectangular post with a line segment protruding from each side, most people fail to correctly align the two line segments because they:
   a. underestimate the width of the rectangular post.
   b. overestimate the width of the rectangular post.
   c. underestimate the length of the two line segments.
   d. overestimate the length of the two line segments.

PsychSim: EEG and sleep stages
Easy, Factual/Definitional, Ans: c

26. (PsychSim: EEG and Sleep Stages) The distinctive brain waves that accompany various stages of sleep are detected by:
    a. ultrasound recordings.
    b. magnetic resonance imaging.
    c. an electroencephalogram.
    d. a CT scan.
    e. all the above.

PsychSim: EEG and sleep stages
Medium, Factual/Definitional, Ans: c

27. (PsychSim: EEG and Sleep Stages) As a person gradually shifts from Stage 1 to Stage 4 sleep, brain waves become progressively _____ in frequency and _____ in amplitude.
    a. lower; lower
    b. higher; higher
    c. lower; higher
    d. higher; lower

PsychSim: EEG and sleep stages
Easy, Factual/Definitional, Ans: d

28. (PsychSim: EEG and Sleep Stages) Sleep spindles are characteristic of _____ sleep.
    a. REM
    b. Stage 4
    c. Stage 3
    d. Stage 2
    e. Stage 1

PsychSim: EEG and sleep stages
Medium, Factual/Definitional, Ans: d

29. (PsychSim: EEG and Sleep Stages) REM sleep is characterized by _____ frequency and _____ amplitude brain waves.
    a. low; low
    b. high; high
    c. low; high
    d. high; low

PsychSim: EEG and sleep stages
Medium, Factual/Definitional, Ans: a

30. (PsychSim: EEG and Sleep Stages) Getting only half of a normal night of sleep is likely to cut most deeply into your _____ sleep time.
    a. REM
    b. Stage 4
    c. Stage 3
    d. Stage 2

PsychSim: classical conditioning
Easy, Factual/Definitional, Ans: d
31.   (PsychSim: Classical Conditioning) In the example of classical conditioning in which the child feared the doctor, the CS was:
       a. fear.
       b. a painful injection.
       c. a severe illness.
       d. the presence of the doctor.

PsychSim: classical conditioning
Easy, Factual/Definitional, Ans: d
32.   (PsychSim: Classical Conditioning) In the example of the child fearing the doctor, the child's fear of a scientist in a white lab coat illustrates the process of:
       a. shaping.
       b. spontaneous recovery.
       c. latent learning.
       d. generalization.
       e. secondary reinforcement.

PsychSim: classical conditioning
Medium, Factual/Definitional, Ans: c
33.   (PsychSim: Classical Conditioning) A single acquisition trial may be sufficient for classical conditioning when the:
       a. CS is a neutral stimulus.
       b. UCS is presented before the CS.
       c. UCS is a very powerful stimulus.
       d. UCR quickly follows the UCS.

PsychSim: classical conditioning
Easy, Factual/Definitional, Ans: d
34.   (PsychSim: Classical Conditioning) In the experiment in which you were to condition a subject to blink her eye whenever she heard a certain tone, the UCS was a(n):
       a. bright light.
       b. eye blink.
       c. tone.
       d. puff of air.

PsychSim: classical conditioning
Medium, Factual/Definitional, Ans: a
35.   (PsychSim: Classical Conditioning) In the experiment in which you were to condition a subject to blink her eye whenever she heard a certain tone, an eye blink was most likely to be scored as a _____ when it preceded the _____.
       a. CR; UCS
       b. CR; CS
       c. UCR; UCS
       d. UCR; CS

PsychSim: operant conditioning
Medium, Factual/Definitional, Ans: b

36. (PsychSim: Operant Conditioning) If we stop nagging a young boy as soon as he makes his bed, we are giving him _____ reinforcement for making his bed.
    a. intermittent
    b. negative
    c. spontaneous
    d. unconditional
    e. variable

PsychSim: operant conditioning
Easy, Factual/Definitional, Ans: c

37. (PsychSim: Operant Conditioning) Continuous reinforcement produces _____ learning and _____ extinction.
    a. fast; slow
    b. slow; fast
    c. fast; fast
    d. slow; slow

PsychSim: operant conditioning
Easy, Factual/Definitional, Ans: d

38. (PsychSim: Operant Conditioning) In the experiment in which you reinforced various rats for pressing a bar, the reinforcement was:
    a. negative.
    b. secondary.
    c. delayed.
    d. intermittent.
    e. spontaneous.

PsychSim: operant conditioning
Difficult, Factual/Definitional, Ans: a

39. (PsychSim: Operant Conditioning) The highest rates of responding occurred when rats reinforced for pressing a bar were placed on _____ and _____ schedules of reinforcement.
    a. fixed-ratio; variable-ratio
    b. fixed-ratio; fixed-interval
    c. variable-ratio; variable-interval
    d. variable-interval; fixed-interval

PsychSim: operant conditioning
Difficult, Factual/Definitional, Ans: d

40. (PsychSim: Operant Conditioning) Which schedule of reinforcement produces the greatest resistance to extinction?
    a. fixed ratio
    b. fixed interval
    c. variable ratio
    d. variable interval

PsychSim: maze learning
Medium, Factual/Definitional, Ans: c

41.   (PsychSim: Maze Learning) This program invited you to consider whether finding your way
       from one location to another is facilitated by _____ or by _____.
       a. classical conditioning; operant conditioning
       b. generalization; discrimination
       c. chained associations; cognitive maps
       d. continuous reinforcement; partial reinforcement
       e. reinforcement; punishment

PsychSim: maze learning
Medium, Factual/Definitional, Ans: d

42.   (PsychSim: Maze Learning) If you learn the way from home to school as a specific sequence
       of right and left turns, you have learned by means of:
       a. classical conditioning.
       b. a cognitive map.
       c. generalization.
       d. chained associations.
       e. continuous reinforcement.

PsychSim: maze learning
Easy, Factual/Definitional, Ans: b

43.   (PsychSim: Maze Learning) Travelers whose familiar route to a destination is blocked are
       often able to reach their destination quickly and easily by taking an unusual sequence of turns
       down other streets. This suggests that people often find their way by means of:
       a. generalization.
       b. cognitive maps.
       c. partial reinforcement.
       d. chained associations.
       e. negative reinforcement.

PsychSim: maze learning
Easy, Factual/Definitional, Ans: a

44.   (PsychSim: Maze Learning) In this program, you were asked to find your way through
       different mazes. The reinforcer for reaching the goal box in each case was:
       a. cheese.
       b. bread.
       c. cake.
       d. water.
       e. meat.

PsychSim: maze learning
Easy, Factual/Definitional, Ans: c

45.   (PsychSim: Maze Learning) In the maze-learning task, most people make _____ turns on
       their _____ run.
       a. more left-hand; second
       b. more right-hand; second
       c. fewer wrong; second
       d. fewer wrong; first

PsychSim: iconic memory
Medium, Factual/Definitional, Ans: c

46. (PsychSim: Iconic Memory) This program partially recreates an experiment conducted by:
    a. B. F. Skinner.
    b. Karl Lashley.
    c. George Sperling.
    d. Herman Ebbinghaus.
    e. Elizabeth Loftus.

PsychSim: iconic memory
Easy, Factual/Definitional, Ans: c

47. (PsychSim: Iconic Memory) In this program, you were asked to observe a random group of six letters flashed briefly on the screen. In a free recall memory task, an average college student is most likely to recall _____ of the letters.
    a. none
    b. only one
    c. three
    d. five
    e. all

PsychSim: iconic memory
Medium, Factual/Definitional, Ans: a

48. (PsychSim: Iconic Memory) The technique used by the program to demonstrate the full extent of your iconic memory is called:
    a. partial report.
    b. priming.
    c. chunking.
    d. free recall.
    e. retroactive interference.

PsychSim: iconic memory
Medium, Factual/Definitional, Ans: e

49. (PsychSim: Iconic Memory) Most people recall a higher percentage of briefly flashed letters in a _____ task than in a _____ task.
    a. partial report; cued recall
    b. cued recall; partial report
    c. free recall; partial report
    d. free recall; cued recall
    e. cued recall; free recall

PsychSim: iconic memory
Medium, Factual/Definitional, Ans: d

50. (PsychSim: Iconic Memory) Iconic memory typically lasts about _____ milliseconds.
    a. 5
    b. 10
    c. 100
    d. 250
    e. 500

PsychSim: forgetting
Easy, Factual/Definitional, Ans: b
51. (PsychSim: Forgetting) The decay or fading of memory with time is considered to be a failure in:
a. encoding.
b. storage.
c. retrieval.
d. all the above.

PsychSim: forgetting
Medium, Factual/Definitional, Ans: d
52. (PsychSim: Forgetting) The process of interference can lead to a failure in:
a. encoding.
b. storage.
c. retrieval.
d. any of the above.

PsychSim: forgetting
Easy, Factual/Definitional, Ans: a
53. (PsychSim: Forgetting) In the "memory for letters" task, you probably found it difficult to identify the uppercase letter briefly presented along with a random assortment of lowercase letters. This difficulty was said to illustrate a failure in:
a. encoding.
b. storage.
c. retrieval.
d. all the above.

PsychSim: forgetting
Easy, Factual/Definitional, Ans: d
54. (PsychSim: Forgetting) The paired associates task was included in this program in order to demonstrate:
a. chunking.
b. memory decay.
c. the spacing effect.
d. proactive interference.
e. the serial position effect.

PsychSim: forgetting
Medium, Factual/Definitional, Ans: e
55. (PsychSim: Forgetting) The greatest interference occurs when old and new material are:
a. emotionally significant.
b. learned through distributed practice.
c. automatically processed.
d. each learned on separate days.
e. similar to each other.

PsychSim: rational thinking
Easy, Factual/Definitional, Ans: d
56. (PsychSim: Rational Thinking) This program highlights the use of base rates and conditional probabilities to formulate:
    a. prototypes.
    b. algorithms.
    c. percentile ranks.
    d. likelihood estimates.
    e. correlation coefficients.

PsychSim: rational thinking
Medium, Factual/Definitional, Ans: c
57. (PsychSim: Rational Thinking) In calculating risks, conditional probabilities are _____ simple probabilities.
    a. added to
    b. subtracted from
    c. multiplied by
    d. divided by

PsychSim: rational thinking
Medium, Conceptual, Ans: b
58. (PsychSim: Rational Thinking) Suppose that 40 percent of Americans are smokers and that 50 percent of American smokers die prematurely from smoking. The likelihood that a particular American will die prematurely from smoking is _____ percent.
    a. 10
    b. 20
    c. 30
    d. 40
    e. 50

PsychSim: rational thinking
Medium, Conceptual, Ans: b
59. (PsychSim: Rational Thinking) About 50 million Americans (1/5th of the American population) jog during a typical year. Each year, about 1,000,000 Americans seek emergency-room treatment for injuries received while jogging. The likelihood that any given American will seek emergency-room treatment for a jogging injury this year is _____ percent.
    a. .1
    b. .4
    c. 1
    d. 4
    e. 10

PsychSim: rational thinking
Difficult, Conceptual, Ans: a
60.   (PsychSim: Rational Thinking) Mark would like to become a college sociology professor. He
knows that his college grades and his GRE scores give him about a 25 percent chance of being
accepted into a sociology graduate school program. He also knows that, of all the students
admitted into sociology graduate school programs, 40 percent drop out before completing a
Ph.D., and only 20 percent of those who earn a Ph.D. ever become college sociology
professors. Mark's best estimate of his chances of becoming a college sociology professor is
_____ percent.
a. 2
b. 10
c. 20
d. 25
e. 40

PsychSim: hunger and the fat rat
Easy, Factual/Definitional, Ans: d
61.   (PsychSim: Hunger and the Fat Rat) In this program, you had an opportunity to simulate:
a. the stimulation of a rat's reticular system.
b. the destruction of a rat's corpus callosum.
c. the stimulation of a rat's cerebral cortex.
d. the destruction of a rat's lateral hypothalamus.
e. all the above.

PsychSim: hunger and the fat rat
Medium, Factual/Definitional, Ans: b
62.   (PsychSim: Hunger and the Fat Rat) Overeating and weight gain in rats result from either
_____ or _____.
a. destruction of the LH; stimulation of the VMH
b. destruction of the VMH; stimulation of the LH
c. stimulation of the LH; stimulation of the VMH
d. destruction of the VMH; destruction of the LH

PsychSim: hunger and the fat rat
Medium, Factual/Definitional, Ans: e
63.   (PsychSim: Hunger and the Fat Rat) Destruction of a rat's lateral hypothalamus does not:
a. endanger life.
b. influence long-term eating habits.
c. affect overall body weight.
d. change the set-point for body weight.
e. destroy the ability to feel hungry.

PsychSim: hunger and the fat rat
Medium, Factual/Definitional, Ans: c
64.   (PsychSim: Hunger and the Fat Rat) In order to permanently raise a rat's set point, you would:
a. destroy its LH.
b. stimulate its LH.
c. destroy its VMH.
d. stimulate its VMH.

PsychSim: hunger and the fat rat
Medium, Factual/Definitional, Ans: a
65. (PsychSim: Hunger and the Fat Rat) In order to permanently lower a rat's set point, you would:
    a. destroy its LH.
    b. stimulate its LH.
    c. destroy its VMH.
    d. stimulate its VMH.

PsychSim: culture and gestures
Medium, Factual/Definitional, Ans: e
66. (PsychSim: Culture and Gestures) Which of the following is an incidental gesture?
    a. pretending to spit
    b. sticking out the tongue
    c. pointing the thumb upward
    d. tapping a finger against the temple
    e. crossing the legs while sitting in a chair

PsychSim: culture and gestures
Medium, Factual/Definitional, Ans: d
67. (PsychSim: Culture and Gestures) Gestures that highlight one or two important features of an object are _____ gestures.
    a. incidental
    b. mimic
    c. relic
    d. schematic

PsychSim: culture and gestures
Difficult, Factual/Definitional, Ans: d
68. (PsychSim: Culture and Gestures) In the Middle East, stupidity is often signalled by:
    a. tapping one's finger against the temple.
    b. rubbing one's hand against the forehead.
    c. rotating one's finger close to the temple.
    d. placing one's fingertip just below the eye.

PsychSim: culture and gestures
Easy, Factual/Definitional, Ans: c
69. (PsychSim: Culture and Gestures) Sticking out the tongue to signal disgust is a(n) _____ gesture.
    a. incidental
    b. mimic
    c. relic
    d. schematic

PsychSim: culture and gestures
Medium, Factual/Definitional, Ans: b
70. (PsychSim: Culture and Gestures) In rural Greece, pushing out an open palm toward a person's face is a sign of:
    a. fear.
    b. ridicule.
    c. welcome.
    d. surprise.
    e. happiness.

PsychSim: expressing emotion
Easy, Factual/Definitional, Ans: c

71.   (PsychSim: Expressing Emotion) This program enabled you to simulate the nonverbal expression of emotion by manipulating:
      a. body posture.
      b. hand gestures.
      c. the shape of eyes.
      d. the tone of voice.
      e. the positioning of arms.

PsychSim: expressing emotion
Medium, Factual/Definitional, Ans: c

72.   (PsychSim: Expressing Emotion) The facial expression of fear includes a(n) _____ mouth and _____ eyebrows.
      a. open; lowered
      b. closed; lowered
      c. open; raised
      d. closed; raised

PsychSim: expressing emotion
Easy, Factual/Definitional, Ans: d

73.   (PsychSim: Expressing Emotion) The facial expression of disgust includes _____ lips and _____ eyebrows.
      a. raised; raised
      b. lowered; lowered
      c. lowered; raised
      d. raised; lowered

PsychSim: expressing emotion
Difficult, Conceptual, Ans: a

74.   (PsychSim: Expressing Emotion) Raised eyebrows are to lowered eyebrows as _____ is to

      _____.
      a. surprise; disgust
      b. happiness; fear
      c. anger; sadness
      d. disgust; anger
      e. fear; surprise

PsychSim: expressing emotion
Medium, Factual/Definitional, Ans: b

75.   (PsychSim: Expressing Emotion) The inner corners of the eyebrows are most likely to be lowered when experiencing:
      a. fear.
      b. anger.
      c. sadness.
      d. surprise.

PsychSim: mystery client
Easy, Factual/Definitional, Ans: c

76. (PsychSim: Mystery Client) In this program, you are asked to diagnose various clients on the basis of:
    a. your observation of their day-to-day behavior.
    b. your in-depth interviews with them.
    c. information contained in their files.
    d. all the above.

PsychSim: mystery client
Medium, Factual/Definitional, Ans: a

77. (PsychSim: Mystery Client) This program most clearly revealed that different psychological disorders:
    a. can involve similar symptoms.
    b. are often indistinguishable from one another.
    c. are all equally disturbing to the clients who experience them.
    d. can be diagnosed accurately only by professional psychologists and psychiatrists.

PsychSim: mystery client
Medium, Factual/Definitional, Ans: d

78. (PsychSim: Mystery Client) After the interviewer observes that H. G. weeps frequently and shows evidence of guilt and remorse, which of the following informational categories is likely to be most relevant for making an accurate diagnosis of this case?
    a. gender
    b. occupation
    c. marital status
    d. self-description of adult personality
    e. information from police or military records

PsychSim: mystery client
Medium, Conceptual, Ans: e

79. (PsychSim: Mystery Client) J. S. had received a dishonorable discharge from the military and had been fired from several jobs. The interviewer observed, however, that J. S. appeared calm and alert. Which of the following informational categories is now likely to be most relevant for making an accurate diagnosis of this case?
    a. ethnic origin
    b. occupation
    c. medical history
    d. self-description of adult personality
    e. information from spouse, parents, or other relatives

PsychSim: mystery client
Medium, Conceptual, Ans: c

80. (PsychSim: Mystery Client) After the interviewer observes that C. F. talked very fast, swallowed pills at frequent intervals, and seemed highly compulsive and agitated, which of the following informational categories is likely to be most relevant for making an accurate diagnosis of this case?
    a. family background
    b. occupation
    c. medical history
    d. information from police or military records
    e. gender

PsychSim: computer therapist
Easy, Factual/Definitional, Ans: a

81.   (PsychSim: Computer Therapist) In this program, you are asked to play the role of a:
      a. client.
      b. psychotherapist.
      c. psychoanalyst.
      d. diagnostic consultant.

PsychSim: computer therapist
Easy, Factual/Definitional, Ans: d

82.   (PsychSim: Computer Therapist) This program is a simulation of:
      a. psychoanalysis.
      b. systematic desensitization.
      c. cognitive therapy.
      d. person-centered therapy.
      e. rational-emotive therapy.

PsychSim: computer therapist
Easy, Factual/Definitional, Ans: c

83.   (PsychSim: Computer Therapist) In this program, the therapist is programmed to:
      a. identify a hierarchy of anxiety-arousing situations experienced by a client.
      b. challenge a client's self-defeating beliefs.
      c. help a client clarify his or her own feelings.
      d. diagnose a client's problem or disorder.
      e. use whatever therapeutic approach is most effective for dealing with a client's specific
          problem.

PsychSim: computer therapist
Medium, Conceptual, Ans: c

84.   (PsychSim: Computer Therapist) Imagine that you have just told the "Computer Therapist"
      that you are feeling like you're a failure in life. The therapist's response is most likely to be:
      a. "Many people feel that way at times."
      b. "You shouldn't be so hard on yourself."
      c. "Tell me more about your feeling like a failure."
      d. "It must feel terrible to feel like a failure."
      e. "How long have you been suffering from depression?"

PsychSim: computer therapist
Medium, Factual/Definitional, Ans: b

85.   (PsychSim: Computer Therapist) A major lesson of this program is that the act of expressing
      feelings to a computer sometimes helps people:
      a. feel less lonely.
      b. understand themselves better.
      c. reduce their negative emotions.
      d. learn to express their feelings to other people.

PsychSim: social decision making
Medium, Factual/Definitional, Ans: a

86.   (PsychSim: Social Decision Making) Which of the following is true of zero-sum situations?
      a. They discourage trust and cooperation.
      b. They are very common in real life.
      c. They involve the allocation of virtually unlimited resources.
      d. They ensure that no participants can lose.

PsychSim: social decision making
Medium, Factual/Definitional, Ans: d

87.   (PsychSim: Social Decision Making) In a non-zero-sum game involving two players:
a. both can win.
b. both can lose.
c. one can win and the other can lose.
d. any of the above can occur.

PsychSim: social decision making
Easy, Factual/Definitional, Ans: b

88.   (PsychSim: Social Decision Making) In this program, you had an opportunity to play a prisoner's dilemma game with a non-zero-sum payoff matrix. Cooperation in this game was most likely when participants were willing to:
a. take turns using the same road.
b. settle for small gains on each round of the game.
c. take time to think about their game strategy before each round of the game.
d. use a gate to block the other player's road.

PsychSim: social decision making
Medium, Factual/Definitional, Ans: b

89.   (PsychSim: Social Decision Making) The trucking game that you played in this program illustrates:
a. a zero-sum environment.
b. a non-zero-sum environment.
c. both a zero-sum and a non-zero-sum environment.
d. neither a zero-sum nor a non-zero-sum environment.

PsychSim: social decision making
Easy, Factual/Definitional, Ans: c

90.   (PsychSim: Social Decision Making) Player mistrust is most likely to be increased in the trucking game when:
a. the game is played in a non-zero-sum environment.
b. both players can avoid using the same road.
c. both players can set up a roadblock.
d. both players can choose to wait at the shortcut if it's already in use.

PsychSim: descriptive statistics
Easy, Factual/Definitional, Ans: c

91.   (PsychSim: Descriptive Statistics) When most scores in a data set are toward the low end of the range of scores, the distribution is said to be:
a. subnormal.
b. symmetrical.
c. skewed.
d. normal.
e. weak.

PsychSim: descriptive statistics
Medium, Factual/Definitional, Ans: b

92.   (PsychSim: Descriptive Statistics) If a distribution is badly skewed, researchers are more
      likely than usual to prefer the _____ as a measure of central tendency.
      a. mode
      b. median
      c. mean
      d. standard deviation

PsychSim: descriptive statistics
Difficult, Factual/Definitional, Ans: d

93.   (PsychSim: Descriptive Statistics) The median of a skewed distribution is likely to be
      _____ the mean.
      a. equal to
      b. equal to or less than
      c. equal to or greater than
      d. less than or greater than

PsychSim: descriptive statistics
Easy, Factual/Definitional, Ans: c

94.   (PsychSim: Descriptive Statistics) The standard deviation is the average distance of each score
      in a distribution from the:
      a. range.
      b. median.
      c. mean.
      d. mode.

PsychSim: descriptive statistics
Medium, Conceptual, Ans: a

95.   (PsychSim: Descriptive Statistics) Imagine that you have entered the following distribution of
      scores into the program: 7, 9, 6, 3, 7, 8, 4, 10, 7, 9. The mean of this distribution of scores
      would be changed the most if a score of _____ was removed from the data set.
      a. 3
      b. 6
      c. 7
      d. 8
      e. 10

PsychSim: correlation
Easy, Factual/Definitional, Ans: c

96.   (PsychSim: Correlation) A correlation between variables can be detected by visual inspection
      of a:
      a. frequency polygon.
      b. normal curve.
      c. scatterplot.
      d. bar graph.

PsychSim: correlation
Easy, Factual/Definitional, Ans: a
97. (PsychSim: Correlation) If persons with low scores on one variable also have low scores on another variable, the two variables are:
a. positively correlated.
b. negatively correlated.
c. perfectly correlated.
d. not correlated.
e. normally distributed.

PsychSim: correlation
Medium, Factual/Definitional, Ans: d
98. (PsychSim: Correlation) If persons with high scores on one variable are equally likely to have either high or low scores on a second variable, the two variables are:
a. positively correlated.
b. negatively correlated.
c. perfectly correlated.
d. not correlated.
e. normally distributed.

PsychSim: correlation
Easy, Factual/Definitional, Ans: d
99. (PsychSim: Correlation) The correlation coefficient enables researchers to specify the _____ and _____ of the relationship between two variables.
a. central tendency; variability
b. range; standard deviation
c. degree; stability
d. direction; strength
e. cause; importance

PsychSim: correlation
Difficult, Conceptual, Ans: b
100. (PsychSim: Correlation) Imagine that the program has provided the following pairs of test scores received by five different children.

	Score on Test A	Score on Test B
Tino	3	7
Jordan	4	9
Joshua	6	10
Jill	2	6
Yvette	7	11

The correlation coefficient between these two sets of test scores would increase the most if you did not include the scores received by:
a. Tino.
b. Jordan.
c. Joshua.
d. Jill.
e. Yvette.

Supplement B

PsychQuest

This test bank supplement includes five multiple-choice questions on each of the PsychQuest Modules.

PsychQuest: How do athletes use perceptual cues?
Easy, Factual/Definitional, Ans: b

1. (PsychQuest: How Do Athletes Use Perceptual Cues?) The process by which the eyeballs turn inward to focus on an object and provide a cue to the distance of objects is called:
    a. retinal disparity.
    b. convergence.
    c. interposition.
    d. accommodation.

PsychQuest: How do athletes use perceptual cues?
Medium, Conceptual, Ans: c

2. (PsychQuest: How Do Athletes Use Perceptual Cues?) Debbie throws a stick for her dog to fetch. As she watches her dog run away from her, she experiences a decrease in:
    a. retinal disparity and interposition.
    b. convergence and linear perspective.
    c. retinal disparity and convergence.
    d. accommodation and relative size.

PsychQuest: How do athletes use perceptual cues?
Easy, Factual/Definitional, Ans: a

3. (PsychQuest: How Do Athletes Use Perceptual Cues?) Interposition, linear perspective, and texture gradients are classified as _____ depth cues.
    a. monocular
    b. binocular
    c. kinesthetic
    d. a. and c.

PsychQuest: How do athletes use perceptual cues?
Medium, Conceptual, Ans: c

4. (PsychQuest: How Do Athletes Use Perceptual Cues?) By filming a movie with two cameras, the director is able to simulate the depth cue of:
    a. convergence.
    b. interposition.
    c. retinal disparity.
    d. accommodation.

PsychQuest: How do athletes use perceptual cues?
Medium, Conceptual, Ans: a

5. (PsychQuest: How Do Athletes Use Perceptual Cues?) Standing at the starting line of the hurdle race, Jackie notices that the width of the hurdles seems to narrow the nearer they are to the finish line. Jackie is using the monocular cue of _____ to determine distance.
    a. linear perspective
    b. texture gradient
    c. relative size
    d. shading

PsychQuest: How do psychoactive drugs affect us?
Easy, Factual/Definitional, Ans: d
6. (PsychQuest: How Do Psychoactive Drugs Affect Us?) Nicotine, caffeine, heroin, and other chemicals that alter activity in the central nervous system are called:
    a. depressants.
    b. stimulants.
    c. hallucinogens.
    d. psychoactive drugs.

PsychQuest: How do psychoactive drugs affect us?
Medium, Factual/Definitional, Ans: c
7. (PsychQuest: How Do Psychoactive Drugs Affect Us?) Which drug produces its effects by facilitating the action of dopamine, norepinephrine, and serotonin?
    a. amphetamine
    b. alcohol
    c. cocaine
    d. nicotine

PsychQuest: How do psychoactive drugs affect us?
Difficult, Factual/Definitional, Ans: b
8. (PsychQuest: How Do Psychoactive Drugs Affect Us?) Which of the following is *not* one of the ways neurons adapt to the presence of drugs?
    a. by increasing the number of receptors
    b. by altering the rate at which nerve impulses are generated
    c. by increasing sensitivity to the drug
    d. by increasing the production of enzymes that metabolize the drug

PsychQuest: How do psychoactive drugs affect us?
Medium, Conceptual, Ans: c
9. (PsychQuest: How Do Psychoactive Drugs Affect Us?) After having used heroin for several months, Clarence finds that he needs a larger dose to feel "high," and feels withdrawal symptoms when he tries to go without any heroin for a few days. Clarence evidently has developed:
    a. physical dependence.
    b. psychological dependence.
    c. tolerance.
    d. a., b., and c.

PsychQuest: How do psychoactive drugs affect us?
Medium, Factual/Definitional, Ans: a
10. (PsychQuest: How Do Psychoactive Drugs Affect Us?) Human and animal research reveals that the major brain area of the "drug system" is called the _____, which is especially responsive to the neurotransmitter _____.
    a. nucleus accumbens; dopamine
    b. hippocampus; serotonin
    c. thalamus; acetylcholine
    d. corpus callosum; endorphin

PsychQuest: Can we rely on our memory?
Medium, Conceptual, Ans: b

11. (PsychQuest: Can We Rely on our Memory?) Implicit memory is to explicit memory as remembering _____ is to remembering _____ .
   a. your telephone number; the date
   b. how to ride a bicycle; the combination of your locker
   c. your fifth birthday; your mother's maiden name
   d. what you had for dinner last night; how to use a knife and fork

PsychQuest: Can we rely on our memory?
Easy, Conceptual, Ans: a

12. (PsychQuest: Can We Rely on our Memory?) Essay questions are an example of a(n) _____ test of memory.
   a. recall
   b. recognition
   c. implicit
   d. episodic

PsychQuest: Can we rely on our memory?
Medium, Conceptual, Ans: b

13. (PsychQuest: Can We Rely on our Memory?) Brendan recently suffered damage to the hippocampus in his brain. It is likely that Brendan now has difficulty:
   a. remembering his past.
   b. forming new long-term memories.
   c. with speech.
   d. in all of these areas.

PsychQuest: Can we rely on our memory?
Medium, Factual/Definitional, Ans: b

14. (PsychQuest: Can We Rely on our Memory?) What type of memory is typically lost in cases of amnesia?
   a. procedural
   b. explicit
   c. implicit
   d. None of the above types of memory is lost.

PsychQuest: Can we rely on our memory?
Difficult, Factual/Definitional, Ans: b

15. (PsychQuest: Can We Rely on our Memory?) When a subject falsely recognizes a word during a recognition test of memory, the parietal and temporal areas of the brain are not activated because:
   a. the memory has no emotional component.
   b. there are no sensory details to remember.
   c. the word was automatically encoded.
   d. memory for the word was not transferred to long-term memory.

PsychQuest: How do we control how much we eat?
Medium, Factual/Definitional, Ans: c

16. (PsychQuest: How Do We Control How Much We Eat?) According to set-point theory, when our weight exceeds our body's internal set point, we:
    a. feel hungry, especially if we are motivated by external factors.
    b. feel satisfied.
    c. are motivated to behave in ways that will restore our weight to its set point.
    d. are at risk for developing an eating disorder.

PsychQuest: How do we control how much we eat?
Medium, Conceptual, Ans: b

17. (PsychQuest: How Do We Control How Much We Eat?) Carl has just eaten a large meal. It is likely that the level of glucose in his bloodstream is _____; as a result, the brain signals the _____ to release insulin.
    a. falling; pancreas
    b. rising; pancreas
    c. falling; stomach
    d. rising; kidneys

PsychQuest: How do we control how much we eat?
Easy, Factual/Definitional, Ans: a

18. (PsychQuest: How Do We Control How Much We Eat?) Researchers at first thought that glucose set-point theory explained _____ regulation of eating behavior, whereas body fat set-point theory explained _____ regulation of eating behavior.
    a. short-term; long-term
    b. long-term; short-term
    c. metabolic; caloric
    d. caloric; metabolic

PsychQuest: How do we control how much we eat?
Medium, Conceptual, Ans: d

19. (PsychQuest: How Do We Control How Much We Eat?) After dieting for several weeks, Ben has lost 10 pounds but just can't seem to lose any more. What is the most likely explanation for Ben's difficulty?
    a. He is probably "cheating" on his diet.
    b. His body set point is too low.
    c. He inherited a genetic predisposition toward obesity.
    d. His metabolic rate has slowed as a result of sustained dieting.

PsychQuest: How do we control how much we eat?
Medium, Factual/Definitional, Ans: d

20. (PsychQuest: How Do We Control How Much We Eat?) Recent research into the cause(s) of obesity has revealed that:
    a. some people have a genetic tendency to store more fat than other people.
    b. in obese mice, the gene for producing leptin, the protein that "turns off" eating, is defective.
    c. obese people have higher levels of leptin than non-obese people.
    d. all of the above are true.

PsychQuest: Why do we feel depressed?
Easy, Factual/Definitional, Ans: d

21.   (PsychQuest: Why Do We Feel Depressed?) Which of the following is the most important factor in a diagnosis of clinical depression?
      a. loss of appetite
      b. lack of energy
      c. sleeplessness
      d. the frequency and severity of symptoms, and whether they can be traced to external events.

PsychQuest: Why do we feel depressed?
Medium, Factual/Definitional, Ans: c

22.   (PsychQuest: Why Do We Feel Depressed?) Research indicates that most cases of clinical depression are:
      a. genetic in origin.
      b. triggered by unrelenting stress or other aversive life events.
      c. the result of an interaction between genetic predisposition and a particular set of environmental experiences.
      d. unpredictable because people generally do not show signs of developing symptoms.

PsychQuest: Why do we feel depressed?
Medium, Conceptual, Ans: c

23.   (PsychQuest: Why Do We Feel Depressed?) Dr. Gerhard believes that Jay is depressed because he feels the same sense of loss after his divorce that he felt when his father died years earlier. Dr. Gerhard evidently subscribes to the theory of depression suggested by:
      a. Martin Seligman.
      b. Renée Spitz.
      c. Sigmund Freud.
      d. Lenore Ratliff.

PsychQuest: Why do we feel depressed?
Easy, Factual/Definitional, Ans: a

24.   (PsychQuest: Why Do We Feel Depressed?) In his research with dogs, Martin Seligman discovered that learned helplessness resulted from:
      a. the delivery of repeated, uncontrollable electric shocks.
      b. training in which the dogs learned to avoid the shocks.
      c. training in which the dogs learned to escape the shocks.
      d. negative reinforcement.

PsychQuest: Why do we feel depressed?
Difficult, Factual/Definitional, Ans: b

25.   (PsychQuest: Why Do We Feel Depressed?) The brains of people who are clinically depressed typically have:
      a. smaller frontal lobes.
      b. abnormally low levels of serotonin and norepinephrine.
      c. an unusually low rate of metabolism.
      d. a more active hippocampus.

PsychQuest: How does chronic stress affect us?
Easy, Factual/Definitional, Ans: a

26.   (PsychQuest: How Does Chronic Stress Affect Us?) Which of the following is *not* a stage in the general adaptation syndrome?
       a. adjustment
       b. alarm
       c. exhaustion
       d. resistance

PsychQuest: How does chronic stress affect us?
Difficult, Factual/Definitional, Ans: d

27.   (PsychQuest: How Does Chronic Stress Affect Us?) Which of the following is *not* true of the catecholamine system's response to an external stressor?
       a. It has been described as the "fight-or-flight" reaction.
       b. It involves the release of epinephrine and norepinephrine from the adrenal medulla.
       c. It produces a state of physiological arousal.
       d. It responds more slowly than the glucocorticoid system.

PsychQuest: How does chronic stress affect us?
Medium, Factual/Definitional, Ans: a

28.   (PsychQuest: How Does Chronic Stress Affect Us?) The glucocorticoid system's response to stress:
       a. provides the energy for a sustained effort to battle against the stressor.
       b. involves the release of the hormone cortisol from the adrenal medulla.
       c. helps preserve energy in the form of stored fat.
       d. includes all of the above.

PsychQuest: How does chronic stress affect us?
Medium, Factual/Definitional, Ans: c

29.   (PsychQuest: How Does Chronic Stress Affect Us?) Research has demonstrated that laboratory animals become more vulnerable to stress-related health problems when they experience aversive events that are:
       a. predictable.
       b. under their control.
       c. uncontrollable.
       d. infrequent but very intense.

PsychQuest: How does chronic stress affect us?
Medium, Factual/Definitional, Ans: d

30.   (PsychQuest: How Does Chronic Stress Affect Us?) Chronically high levels of stress hormones:
       a. suppress the functioning of the body's immune system.
       b. cause the hippocampus to shrink.
       c. damage brain neurons involved in memory.
       d. have all of the above effects.

PsychQuest: How do we form social stereotypes?
Medium, Factual/Definitional, Ans: b

31. (PsychQuest: How Do We Form Social Stereotypes?) The process by which people infer personality characteristics from the behaviors they observe is called:
    a. stereotyping.
    b. attribution.
    c. social facilitation.
    d. illusory correlation.

PsychQuest: How do we form social stereotypes?
Easy, Factual/Definitional, Ans: a

32. (PsychQuest: How Do We Form Social Stereotypes?) The fundamental attribution error refers to the tendency of people to overestimate:
    a. dispositional influences on the behavior of others.
    b. situational influences on the behavior of others.
    c. both dispositional and situational influences on the behavior of others.
    d. dispositional influences on their own behavior.

PsychQuest: How do we form social stereotypes?
Medium, Conceptual, Ans: a

33. (PsychQuest: How Do We Form Social Stereotypes?) Later in the evening, when she tripped stepping of a curb, she knew that she was simply not paying attention to where she was placing her foot. The difference in Sheila's interpretation of her own behavior and that of her date illustrates:
    a. the actor-observer bias.
    b. illusory correlation.
    c. the fundamental attribution error.
    d. social facilitation.

PsychQuest: How do we form social stereotypes?
Medium, Conceptual, Ans: b

34. (PsychQuest: How Do We Form Social Stereotypes?) Believing that the harder he presses the selection button on the soft-drink machine, the more likely it is to work, Raymond is illustrating:
    a. actor-observer bias.
    b. illusory correlation.
    c. the fundamental attribution error.
    d. social facilitation.

PsychQuest: How do we form social stereotypes?
Medium, Factual/Definitional, Ans: b

35. (PsychQuest: How Do We Form Social Stereotypes?) Research by Hamilton and Rose demonstrates that racial stereotypes may persist because:
    a. people tend to ignore memorable but unexpected behaviors of minorities.
    b. once stereotypes are formed, people are more likely to remember new information if it fits those stereotypes than if it contradicts them.
    c. people overestimate the accuracy of their judgments of others.
    d. of all the above reasons.

PsychQuest: How do we pick our mates?
Easy, Factual/Definitional, Ans: d

36.   (PsychQuest: How Do We Pick Our Mates?) Which of the following is true regarding the phrase "opposites attract"?
a. It does not describe mate selection anywhere in the world.
b. It is primarily a characteristic of individualistic societies such as the United States.
c. It is primarily a characteristic of communal societies such as Japan.
d. It applies to both individualistic and communal societies.

PsychQuest: How do we pick our mates?
Easy, Factual/Definitional, Ans: d

37.   (PsychQuest: How Do We Pick Our Mates?) Which of the following have social psychologists found to be important factor(s) in romantic attraction?
a. physical attractiveness
b. similarity
c. proximity
d. All of the above are important factors in romantic attraction.

PsychQuest: How do we pick our mates?
Medium, Factual/Definitional, Ans: d

38.   (PsychQuest: How Do We Pick Our Mates?) Charles Darwin proposed that specific traits in the animal kingdom evolved because they:
a. increased the likelihood that an animal found a mate.
b. increased the likelihood that an animal's offspring would survive and reproduce themselves.
c. increased the animal's chances for survival.
d. did both a. and b.
e. did a., b., and c.

PsychQuest: How do we pick our mates?
Easy, Factual/Definitional, Ans: c

39.   (PsychQuest: How Do We Pick Our Mates?) In selecting a potential mate, women are more likely than men to prefer a partner who is:
a. young.
b. healthy.
c. of high social status.
d. physically attractive.

PsychQuest: How do we pick our mates?
Medium, Conceptual, Ans: d

40.   (PsychQuest: How Do We Pick Our Mates?) Dr. Owens believes that gender differences in mate selection developed in response to the different reproductive challenges faced by women and men. Dr. Owens is evidently a(n):
a. sociobiologist.
b. psychobiologist.
c. biopsychologist.
d. evolutionary psychologist.

Supplement C

The Brain Series, 2nd Edition

This test bank supplement includes one multiple-choice question on each of *The Brain* video modules.

The brain: organization and evaluation of brain function
Medium, Factual/Definitional, Ans: d

1. ("The Brain" video: Organization and Evaluation of Brain Function) A race car driver participates in a highly competitive race. The part of his brain that enables him to plan a strategy to win the race is said to be the:
    a. sensory cortex.
    b. limbic system.
    c. cerebellum.
    d. frontal lobe.
    e. reticular system.

The brain: the effects of hormones and the environment on brain development
Difficult, Factual/Definitional, Ans: a

2. ("The Brain" video: Hormones and Sexual Development) Marion Diamond, who is seen freezing and slicing sections of rat brain cortex, has observed that removing the _____ of newly born rats facilitates the development of _____ hemisphere(s) of their brains.
    a. ovaries; the right
    b. testes; the right
    c. ovaries; both
    d. testes; both

The brain—gender development: social influences
Medium, Factual/Definitional, Ans: d

3. ("The Brain" video—Gender Development: Social Influences) In this module, mothers are observed playing with babies they have never met before. In comparing the mothers' reactions to girls and boys, it was noted that mothers were:
    a. equally likely to talk to boys and to girls.
    b. more likely to talk to boys than to girls.
    c. equally likely to encourage boys and girls to explore their environment.
    d. more likely to encourage boys rather than girls to explore their environment.
    e. equally likely to tell boys and girls they are pretty

The brain: intelligence and culture
Easy, Factual/Definitional, Ans: b

4. ("The Brain" video: Intelligence and Culture) Judy Kearins' research shows that, compared with white Australian children, Aborigine children are better able to remember:
    a. random sequences of digits.
    b. the location of natural objects.
    c. the lyrics of familiar songs.
    d. the melody and rhythm of unfamiliar musical selections.
    e. the physical movements involved in a novel dance.

The brain: the divided brain
Medium, Factual/Definitional, Ans: a

5. ("The Brain" video: The Divided Brain) A picture of a woman on the telephone was briefly flashed in the left visual field of Vicki, a split-brain patient. In order to indicate that she had actually seen the telephone, Vicki used her _____ hand to _____.
    a. left; write the word "telephone"
    b. right; write the word "telephone"
    c. left; draw a picture of a telephone
    d. right; draw a picture of a telephone

The brain—language and speech: Broca and Wernicke's areas
Medium, Factual/Definitional, Ans: a

6.   ("The Brain" video: Language and Speech) When spoken language is processed in the brain, sound first travels as nerve impulses to:
a. Wernicke's area.
b. the angular gyrus.
c. Broca's area.
d. the cerebellum.

The brain—brain anomaly and plasticity: hydrocephalus
Medium, Factual/Definitional, Ans: d

7.   ("The Brain" video—Brain Anomaly and Plasticity: Hydrocephalus) In the case studies of Sharon and Nicole, who suffered brain damage from hydrocephalus, CT scans reveal an expansion in the size of the brain's:
a. hypothalamus.
b. brainstem.
c. cerebellum.
d. ventricles.
e. occipital lobe.

The brain—visual information processing: elementary concepts
Easy, Factual/Definitional, Ans: c

8.   ("The Brain" video—Visual Information Processing: Elementary Concepts) In this module, David Hubel describes how he and Torsten Wiesel discovered individual feature detector cells in a cat's primary visual cortex that responded to:
a. a black dot.
b. concentric circles.
c. the straight edge of a glass slide.
d. patterns of lightwaves changing in frequency.

The brain—visual information processing: perception
Easy, Factual/Definitional, Ans: e

9.   ("The Brain" video—Visual Information Processing: Perception) In describing a visual pathway that moves down to the inferior temporal lobe, Mortimer Mishkin notes that single cumulative cells in this region of monkey brains have been found to be selectively activated by:
a. lightwaves of a specific frequency.
b. patterns of changing light intensity.
c. straight lines of a specific length.
d. the intersection of two different lines.
e. monkey faces.

The brain—perception: inverted vision
Easy, Factual/Definitional, Ans: d

10.   ("The Brain" video—Perception: Inverted Vision) In this module, Susannah Fiennes wears inverting lenses for a week. With the inverting spectacles still on at the end of the week she demonstrates that she can:
a. ski down a mountain slope.
b. play tennis.
c. drive a car.
d. write her name so it appears right side up to others.

The brain: sensory-motor integration
Medium, Factual/Definitional, Ans: b

11. ("The Brain" video: Sensory-Motor Integration) After Olympic Gold Medalist Greg Louganis performs three spectacular dives, the narrator indicates that underlying Greg's elegant body movements are the coordinated activities of the basal ganglia, motor cortex, and:

a. hypothalamus.
b. cerebellum.
c. angular gyrus.
d. amygdala.

The brain—Huntington's disease
Medium, Factual/Definitional, Ans: d

12. ("The Brain" video: Huntington's Disease) The best way to predict whether a person will be afflicted by Huntington's disease is to make use of:

a. standardized intelligence tests.
b. measures of visual acuity.
c. an electroencephalograph.
d. DNA testing.

The brain: sleep and circadian rhythms
Easy, Factual/Definitional, Ans: e

13. ("The Brain" video: Sleep and Circadian Rhythms) In this module, Michael Siffre describes his experience of living underground in a Texas cave for 7 months. His research confirmed the findings that most humans arc biologically programmcd to follow a:

a. 50-minute sleep cycle.
b. 7-hour sleep cycle.
c. 8-hour sleep cycle.
d. 24-hour circadian rhythm.
e. 25-hour circadian rhythm.

The brain—sleep: brain functions
Medium, Factual/Definitional, Ans: d

14. ("The Brain" video—Sleep: Brain Functions) As a night of sleep progresses, the percentage of time spent in deep sleep _____ and the percentage of time spent in REM sleep _____.

a. increases; increases
b. decreases; decreases
c. increases; decreases
d. decreases; increases

The brain: REM sleep and dreaming
Medium, Factual/Definitional, Ans: a

15. ("The Brain" video: REM Sleep and Dreaming) J. Allan Hobson's theory is that dreams result from bursts of neural activity originating from the:

a. brainstem.
b. sensory cortex.
c. frontal lobe.
d. occipital lobe.

The brain: the locus of learning and memory
Medium, Factual/Definitional, Ans: e
16. ("The Brain" video: The Locus of Learning and Memory) After attempting to identify the area of a rat's brain where memories are stored, Karl Lashley concluded that memories:
a. are localized in the amygdala.
b. are localized in the hippocampus.
c. are localized in the frontal lobe.
d. are localized in the temporal lobe.
e. cannot be discretely localized.

The brain: learning as synaptic change
Medium, Factual/Definitional, Ans: a
17. ("The Brain" video: Learning as Synaptic Change) This module suggests that learning involves physical changes in brain circuitry. Gary Lynch describes his research on the formation of new synaptic connections in which sections of rat brains were monitored before and after:
a. electrical stimulation.
b. serotonin injections.
c. classical conditioning.
d. maze learning.

The brain—living with amnesia: the hippocampus and memory
Medium, Factual/Definitional, Ans: d
18. ("The Brain" video—Living with Amnesia: The Hippocampus and Memory) Drugs that interfere with the ability of rats to remember the location of a platform in a water maze provide evidence that memory consolidation is mediated by:
a. ACh.
b. chunking.
c. dopamine.
d. LTP.
e. GABA.

The brain: Alzheimer's disease
Difficult, Factual/Definitional, Ans: a
19. ("The Brain" video: Alzheimer's Disease) Alzheimer's disease results from a deterioration of the nucleus basalis and the loss of:
a. acetylcholine.
b. dopamine.
c. norepinephrine.
d. endorphins.

The brain—a super-memorist advises on study strategies
Easy, Factual/Definitional, Ans: c
20. ("The Brain" video—A Super-Memorist Advises on Study Strategies) In this module, Rajam Mahadevan demonstrates his extraordinary memory for:
a. names.
b. faces.
c. numbers.
d. letters.
e. all the above.

The brain: emotions, stress, and health
Medium, Factual/Definitional, Ans: d

21. ("The Brain" video: Emotions, Stress, and Health) An air traffic controller in Montreal survived the stress of a radar shutdown thanks to the inhibitory effects of the neurotransmitter:
a. serotonin.
b. dopamine.
c. ACh.
d. GABA.
e. norepinephrine.

The brain—stress: locus of control and predictability
Medium, Factual/Definitional, Ans: e

22. ("The Brain" video—Stress: Locus of Control and Predictability) Two rats receive identical electric shocks but only one of them is able to stop the shocks by turning a wheel. Dr. Weiss indicates that the helpless rat is more likely to suffer:
a. increased lymphocyte production.
b. shrinkage of the adrenal cortex.
c. elevation of blood glucose levels.
d. enlargement of the thymus gland.
e. stomach lesions.

The brain: multiple personality
Medium, Factual/Definitional, Ans: a

23. ("The Brain" video: Multiple Personality) Frank Putnam shows that three of the personalities exhibited by Tony, a patient with 53 different personalities, display distinctly different:
a. evoked potentials.
b. levels of intelligence.
c. eye-muscle coordination patterns.
d. blood glucose levels.

The brain: aggression, violence, and the brain
Medium, Factual/Definitional, Ans: e

24. ("The Brain" video: Aggression, Violence, and the Brain) This module highlights the case of Mark Larribus, who was accused of almost killing his girlfriend's 2-year-old daughter. Mark's aggressiveness was dramatically reduced after removal of a brain tumor that exerted pressure on his:
a. motor cortex.
b. cerebellum.
c. reticular system.
d. angular gyrus.
e. hypothalamus.

The brain: the frontal lobe and behavior: the story of Phineas Gage
Easy, Factual/Definitional, Ans: b

25. ("The Brain" video: The Frontal Lobe and Behavior: The Story of Phineas Gage) The tamping rod severed connections between Phineas Gage's frontal cortex and his:
a. brainstem.
b. limbic system.
c. parietal lobe.
d. sympathetic nervous system.
e. cerebellum.

The brain—schizophrenia: symptoms
Easy, Factual/Definitional, Ans: e
26. ("The Brain" video—Schizophrenia: Symptoms) Jerry, a schizophrenia patient, is described as having a(n) _____ disorder rather than a(n) _____ disorder.
  a. acute; chronic
  b. cognitive; emotional
  c. sensory; motor
  d. cognitive; behavioral
  e. global; specific

The brain—schizophrenia: etiology
Medium, Factual/Definitional, Ans: c
27. ("The Brain" video—Schizophrenia: Etiology) In describing the organic nature of schizophrenia, Dr. Arnold Scheibel identifies and diagrams the abnormal orientation and organization of nerve cells located within the:
  a. cerebellum.
  b. brainstem.
  c. hippocampus.
  d. thalamus.
  e. amygdala.

The brain—schizophrenia: pharmacological treatment
Easy, Factual/Definitional, Ans: a
28. ("The Brain" video—Schizophrenia: Pharmacological Treatment) Drugs that are effective in the treatment of schizophrenia seem to reduce the activity of the neurotransmitter:
  a. dopamine.
  b. serotonin.
  c. norepinephrine.
  d. GABA.
  e. ACh.

The brain: autism
Medium, Factual/Definitional, Ans: b
29. ("The Brain" video: Autism) By studying brain sections at autopsy, Dr. Margaret Bauman and her colleagues discovered that autism is related to structural abnormalities in:
  a. frontal association areas.
  b. limbic and cerebellar circuits.
  c. the visual and auditory cortex.
  d. the angular gyrus and Wernicke's area.

The brain: understanding the brain through epilepsy
Medium, Factual/Definitional, Ans: b
30. ("The Brain" video: Understanding the Brain Through Epilepsy) Dr. Dreifuss suspects that valproic acid controls the frequency of Jeremy's seizures by increasing the presence of the inhibitory neurotransmitter:
  a. ACh.
  b. GABA.
  c. dopamine.
  d. serotonin.
  e. norepinephrine.

The brain: brain transplants in Parkinson's patients
Medium, Factual/Definitional, Ans: c

31. ("The Brain" video: Brain Transplants in Parkinson's Patients) Surgeons have implanted fetal tissue into the basal ganglia of Parkinson's patients in order to increase the availability of the neurotransmitter:
     a. serotonin.
     b. ACh.
     c. dopamine.
     d. norepinephrine.
     e. GABA.

The brain: neurorehabilitation
Medium, Factual/Definitional, Ans: c

32. ("The Brain" video: Neurorehabilitation) Dr. Michael Thaut explains his use of _____ in rehabilitating brain-injured patients who experience difficulty walking normally.
     a. ACh injections
     b. brain tissue implants
     c. music and rhythmic stimulation
     d. electrical stimulation of the brain
     e. the electroencephalograph

Supplement D

The Mind Series, 2nd Edition

This test bank supplement includes one multiple-choice question on each of *The Mind* modules.

The mind: unraveling the mysteries of the mind
Easy, Factual/Definitional, Ans: e

1.   ("The Mind" video: Unraveling the Mysteries of the Mind) Who suggested that the bumps and contours of one's skull are indicative of an individual's unique personality traits?
      a. Aristotle
      b. Descartes
      c. Darwin
      d. Freud
      e. Gall

The mind: hypnotic dissociation and pain relief
Medium, Factual/Definitional, Ans: d

2.   ("The Mind" video: Hypnotic Dissociation and Pain Relief) An arthritic patient reports a lack of pain in her right hand while under hypnosis. This module suggests that hypnosis reduces her pain by affecting the:
      a. activation of specific neural fibers in the spinal cord.
      b. release of pain-killing endorphins in the brain.
      c. deactivation of the pain receptors in the hand.
      d. information-processing mechanisms of the cortex.

The mind: the placebo effect: mind-body relationship
Easy, Factual/Definitional, Ans: b

3.   ("The Mind" video: The Placebo Effect: Mind-Body Relationship) In Jon Levine's research with patients who have just had their wisdom teeth extracted, the placebo effect most clearly occurred when patients received a post-operative:
      a. computer-administered injection of a saline solution.
      b. physician-administered injection of a saline solution.
      c. computer-administered injection of a pain-killing medication.
      d. physician-administered injection of a pain-killing medication.

The mind: cognition and the immune system: mind/body interaction
Medium, Factual/Definitional, Ans: c

4.   ("The Mind" video: Cognition and the Immune System: Mind/Body Interaction) In this module, Rachele Beales, a victim of breast cancer, attributes the longevity of her survival to the fact that she:
      a. has been able to maintain her sense of humor.
      b. inherited her genes from parents who lived very long lives.
      c. actively participates with the doctor in her own treatment.
      d. experiences a profound sense of spiritual tranquility and peace of mind.

The mind: endorphins: the brain's natural morphine
Medium, Factual/Definitional, Ans: d

5.   ("The Mind" video: Endorphins: The Brain's Natural Morphine) Hans Kosterlitz found that endorphin receptor sites are identical to neural receptor sites for:
      a. LSD.
      b. cocaine.
      c. marijuana.
      d. heroin.
      e. alcohol.

The mind: brain mechanisms of pleasure and addiction
Medium, Factual/Definitional, Ans: e

6. ("The Mind" video: Brain Mechanisms of Pleasure and Addiction) The nucleus accumbens is the center of a(n) _____ circuit that is active in both hunger for food and pleasurable stimulation from addictive drugs.
    a. serotonin
    b. endocrine
    c. acetylcholine
    d. frontal lobe
    e. dopamine

The mind: the frontal lobes: cognition and awareness
Easy, Factual/Definitional, Ans: e

7. ("The Mind" video: The Frontal Lobes: Cognition and Awareness) As a result of an aneurism that damaged his frontal lobe, Bill, a law school graduate, experiences the greatest difficulty in:
    a. speaking fluently.
    b. understanding other people speak.
    c. recognizing familiar faces.
    d. remembering the past.
    e. planning for the future.

The mind: language processing in the brain
Medium, Factual/Definitional, Ans: d

8. ("The Mind" video: Language Processing in the Brain) A PET scan records brain activity while a subject, Patty, responds to single nouns. Patty's left frontal lobe was most extensively activated when she:
    a. read each noun aloud.
    b. wrote each noun.
    c. defined each noun.
    d. generated a verb for each noun.
    e. formed a vivid mental image of each noun.

The mind: studying the effects of subliminal stimulation on the mind
Medium, Factual/Definitional, Ans: d

9. ("The Mind" video: Studying Effects of Subliminal Stimulation on the Mind) The words "wild" and "disrespectful" are presented to a subject both subliminally and supraliminally. The Freudian concept of repression is said to be illustrated by the subject's:
    a. incorrect recall of the subliminally presented words.
    b. denial that he has ever seen the supraliminally presented words.
    c. diminished brain response to the subliminally presented words.
    d. delayed brain response to the supraliminally presented words.

The mind: life without memory: the case of Clive Wearing
Medium, Factual/Definitional, Ans: d

10. ("The Mind" video: Life Without Memory: The Case of Clive Wearing) This module highlights the tragic experience of a renowned musician, Clive Wearing. The destruction of Clive's _____ is primarily responsible for his severe memory impairment.
    a. occipital lobe
    b. hypothalamus
    c. brainstem
    d. hippocampus
    e. thalamus

The mind: Clive Wearing, part 2: living without memory
Medium, Factual/Definitional, Ans: d

11.   ("The Mind" video: Clive Wearing, Part 2, Living Without Memory) Brain scans indicate that Clive Wearing suffered the greatest loss of brain tissue in his _____ lobe.
       a. right frontal
       b. left parietal
       c. right occipital
       d. left temporal

The mind: teratogens and their effects on the developing brain and mind
Medium, Factual/Definitional, Ans: d

12.   ("The Mind" video: Teratogens and Their Effects on the Developing Brain and Mind) The physical consequences of fetal alcohol syndrome include:
       a. a larger-than-normal size brain.
       b. abnormally small brain ventricles.
       c. a higher-than-normal number of brain convolutions.
       d. abnormal brain cell migrations.

The mind: capabilities of the newborn
Easy, Factual/Definitional, Ans: d

13.   ("The Mind" video: Capabilities of the Newborn) An infant indicates its preference for its mother's voice by:
       a. smiling.
       b. crying.
       c. babbling.
       d. sucking.
       e. head turning.

The mind: infant cognitive development
Medium, Factual/Definitional, Ans: c

14.   ("The Mind" video: Infant Cognitive Development) Jerome Kagan notes that at 2 to 3 months of age, infants begin to react with surprise to changing circumstances and smile at people. He calls this the smile of:
       a. habituation.
       b. attachment.
       c. assimilation.
       d. accommodation.
       e. reorientation.

The mind: social development in infancy
Medium, Factual/Definitional, Ans: c

15.   ("The Mind" video: Social Development in Infancy) A young child is bothered by the fact that a doll is missing a head. The child's reaction is said to illustrate the emergence of:
       a. object permanence.
       b. conservation.
       c. a moral sense.
       d. egocentrism.
       e. stranger anxiety.

The mind: the effect of aging on cognitive function: nature/nurture
Difficult, Factual/Definitional, Ans: c

16.   ("The Mind" video: the effect of aging on cognitive function: nature/nurture) In accounting for individual differences in cognitive abilities among elderly identical twins, Dr. Gerald McClearn found that nonshared environmental influences are _____ than shared environmental influences and _____ important than genetic influences.
       a. more; more
       b. less; less
       c. more; less
       d. less; more

The mind: aging and memory
Medium, Factual/Definitional, Ans: a

17.   ("The Mind" video: Aging and Memory) Drs. Mark McDaniel and Gilles Einstein observed that age-related differences in _____ memory are greatest for _____ tasks.
       a. prospective; time-based.
       b. retrospective; time-based
       c. prospective; event-based
       d. retrospective; event-based

The mind: effects of mental and physical activity on brain/mind
Medium, Factual/Definitional, Ans: d

18.   ("The Mind" video: Effects of Mental and Physical Activity on Brain/Mind) Research has shown that old rats placed in an enriched environment develop:
       a. an increase in the size of the brain ventricles.
       b. an increase in the number of brain neurons.
       c. a decrease in the number of glial cells in the brain.
       d. new connections between neurons in the brain.
       e. a reduction in the size of the limbic system.

The mind: understanding Alzheimer's disease
Medium, Factual/Definitional, Ans: a

19.   ("The Mind" video: Understanding Alzheimer's Disease) Brain tissue infected with Alzheimer's disease is distinguished by:
       a. a proliferation of plaques and tangles.
       b. excess levels of acetylcholine.
       c. abnormal brain cell migrations.
       d. ventricular constriction.
       e. deterioration of glial cells.

The mind: phantom limb pain: fooling the mind
Easy, Factual/Definitional, Ans: a

20.   ("The Mind" video: Phantom Limb Pain: Fooling the Mind) A peripheral interpretation of phantom limb pain suggests that false pain signals are generated by:
       a. cut nerves in what remains of the severed limb.
       b. spinal chord cells that increase their normal level of excitability.
       c. the sympathetic branch of the autonomic nervous system.
       d. the sensory cortex of the brain.

The mind: treating chronic pain
Medium, Factual/Definitional, Ans: d

21.   ("The Mind" video: Treating Chronic Pain) After describing the case of Fran Brooks, who
       suffers incapacitating shoulder, back, and leg pain, a pain expert suggests that pain from an
       injury often becomes chronic because pain victims:
       a. frequently engage in strenuous activities before completely healing.
       b. fail to carefully monitor the exact physical sensations involved in their pain.
       c. suffer from an increased excitability of cells in their sensory cortex.
       d. are overprotected by others who observe signs of their suffering.

The mind: depressants and their addictive effect on the brain
Difficult, Factual/Definitional, Ans: b

22.   ("The Mind" video: Depressants and Their Addictive Effect on the Brain) This module
       indicates that the painful symptoms that occur when alcohol use is discontinued result from:
       a. a loss of the brain's pain-killing endorphins.
       b. excessive calcium channel activity in the brain's synapses.
       c. the destruction of the brain's nutritive glial cells.
       d. the brain's compensatory overproduction of acetylcholine.

The mind: infant speech sound discrimination
Easy, Factual/Definitional, Ans: e

23.   ("The Mind" video: Infant Speech Sound Discrimination) An infant indicates its ability to
       discriminate between subtle sound differences by:
       a. babbling.
       b. sucking.
       c. smiling.
       d. crying.
       e. head turning.

The mind: language predisposition
Medium, Factual/Definitional, Ans: d

24.   ("The Mind" video: Language Predisposition) A 6-month-old is exposed to two vowel sounds:
       "ah" and "e." This research shows that the infant does not confuse a change in _____ with
       a change in vowel sound.
       a. consonant sound
       b. language
       c. facial expression
       d. human voice

The mind: human language: signed and spoken
Easy, Factual/Definitional, Ans: c

25.   ("The Mind" video: Human Language: Signed and Spoken) This module indicates that spoken
       language is generally processed by the _____ cerebral hemisphere and that sign language is
       generally processed by the hearing impaired in the _____ hemisphere.
       a. left; right
       b. right; left
       c. left; left
       d. right; right

The mind: the bilingual brain
Medium, Factual/Definitional, Ans: d

26. ("The Mind" video: The Bilingual Brain) If you learn a second language in adolescence or later, the brain processes that language in a separate region of Broca's area than the one where your original language is processed. This is demonstrated by Dr. Joy Hirsch using:
    a. computed tomography scans.
    b. position emission tomography scans.
    c. an electroencephalogram.
    d. functional magnetic resonance imaging.

The Mind: animal language
Medium, Factual/Definitional, Ans: b

27. (The "Mind" video: Animal Language) Using video recording techniques, Roger and Debbie Fouts have discovered that chimpanzees:
    a. demonstrate grammatical competence equal to that of most 3-year-old humans.
    b. spontaneously use sign language to communicate with other members of their own species.
    c. mentally associate their own sign language with spoken words.
    d. acquire language vocabulary as rapidly as most 3-year-old humans.

The mind: language and culture
Easy, Factual/Definitional, Ans: d

28. ("The Mind" video: Language and Culture) The _____ of Surinam slaves created a new Creole language by introducing _____ to the slaves' pidgin speech.
    a. owners; new words
    b. owners; grammar
    c. children; new morphemes
    d. children; grammar

The mind: alcohol addiction: hereditary factors
Easy, Factual/Definitional, Ans: d

29. ("The Mind" video: Alcohol Addiction: Hereditary Factors) This module strongly suggests that an inherited susceptibility to alcoholism is associated with:
    a. abnormal brain cell migrations.
    b. excessive levels of acetylcholine in the brain.
    c. an autonomic nervous system that is overly reactive to stress.
    d. the absence of P3 brain waves.
    e. excessive calcium channel activity in the brain's synapses.

The mind: treating drug addiction: a behavioral approach
Easy, Factual/Definitional, Ans: d

30. ("The Mind" video: Treating Drug Addiction: A Behavioral Approach) Therapists help Jim Sloan overcome his craving for drugs by:
    a. gradually reducing his drug intake over a period of several weeks.
    b. providing him with a substitute drug that is physically nonaddictive.
    c. delivering an electric shock to his arm while he vividly imagines that he is taking drugs.
    d. repeatedly exposing him to stimuli that trigger drug use.
    e. isolating him from contact with friends who use drugs.

The mind: mood disorders: mania and depression
Easy, Factual/Definitional, Ans: d

31.   ("The Mind" video: Mood Disorders: Mania and Depression) Mania is most likely to be characterized by:
      a. suicidal thoughts.
      b. a persistent, irrational fear of people.
      c. a preoccupation with offensive and unwanted thoughts.
      d. excessive and rapid talking.
      e. delusions of persecution.

The mind: mood disorders: hereditary factors
Easy, Factual/Definitional, Ans: c

32.   ("The Mind" video: Mood Disorders: Hereditary Factors) Janice Egeland describes research suggesting that genetic factors contribute to manic-depressive disorders among the:
      a. Navajo Indians in New Mexico.
      b. Cuban community in Florida.
      c. Amish people in Pennsylvania.
      d. Chinese Americans in California.
      e. Mexican migrant workers in Michigan.

The mind: mood disorders: medication and talk therapy
Medium, Factual/Definitional, Ans: c

33.   ("The Mind" video: Mood Disorders: Medication and Talk Therapy) Anti-depressant drugs increase the availability of _____ and _____ in the synapses of depressed people.
      a. sodium; chlorine
      b. lithium; dopamine
      c. serotonin; norepinephrine
      d. acetylcholine; dopamine
      e. lithium; endorphins

The mind: treating depression: electroconvulsive therapy (ECT)
Easy, Factual/Definitional, Ans: c

34.   ("The Mind" video: Treating Depression: Electroconvulsive Therapy [ECT]) While being treated with electroconvulsive therapy, Mary, a suicidal patient:
      a. stays wide awake and alert.
      b. experiences a momentary panic attack.
      c. displays a grand mal convulsion.
      d. does all the above.

The mind: the mind of the psychopath
Easy, Factual/Definitional, Ans: c

35.   ("The Mind" video: The Mind of the Psychopath) Studies using Single Photon Emission Computerized Tomography (SPECT) indicate that psychopaths are unusually likely to process briefly flashed words primarily in their _____ lobes.
      a. fontal
      b. parietal
      c. occipital
      d. temporal